W9-DFU-802

Guide to
AMERICAN POETRY EXPLICATION
Volume 2

Modern and Contemporary

A
Reference
Publication
in
Literature

Nancy Martinez
Editor

Guide to
AMERICAN POETRY EXPLICATION
Volume 2

Modern and Contemporary

JOHN R. LEO

G.K. HALL &CO.
70 LINCOLN STREET, BOSTON, MASS.

Library of Congress Cataloging-in-Publication Data

Leo, John R.
      Modern and contemporary / John R. Leo.
          p. cm. -- (Guide to American poetry explication: v. 2)
    (A Reference publication in literature)
      ISBN 0-8161-8918-8
      1. American poetry--20th century--History and criticism-
-Bibliography. 2. American poetry--Explication--Bibliography.
I. Title. II. Series. III. Series: A Reference publication in literature.
Z1231.P7L46 1989
[PS221]
016.811'509--dc20   89-2195
                                       CIP

4/24/90

Contents

The Author

John R. Leo is associate professor of English and Comparative Literature Studies at The University of Rhode Island, where he also teaches media and critical theory. He holds degrees from Yale and Northwestern Universities, and has also studied at Indiana University, the University of California at Irvine, and at UCLA. His many articles have appeared in such journals as *Philosophy and Literature, Journal of American Culture, Centennial Review, Poetry*, and *South Atlantic Quarterly*, and for ten years he was a bibliographer for *The Explicator*. Currently he is finishing a book on American media and cultural studies.

Preface

This bibliography of modern and contemporary American poetry is the companion volume to that on colonial and nineteenth-century American poetry and part of an extensive new series of guides to poetry explication published by G. K. Hall. This ambitious project is similar to--and draws from--Joseph M. Kuntz and Nancy C. Martinez's monumental third edition of *Poetry Explication: A Checklist of Interpretation since 1925* (Boston: G. K. Hall, 1980), yet the individual volumes differ from their predecessor in major ways. Like the *Checklist*, this new *Guide to American Poetry Explication* offers a comprehensive index of poetry explication since 1925. It incorporates all appropriate entries from the *Checklist* editions of 1950, 1962, and 1980; updates the list through 1987; and includes some citations from 1988. Entries continue to be ordered alphabetically, but the current *Guide* puts them in an easier-to-read format. Users of this volume, like users of the *Checklist*, will first look up a poet's name, then the title of a poem or collection (also arranged alphabetically), and finally check through the gloss of explications for that poem, which are listed alphabetically by critic. Under Main Sources consulted at the back of the volume, users will continue to find full citations for any journals, books, and authors' names that are shortened in the explications themselves. A separate table at the front gives full titles for all abbreviations of names of journals and periodicals.

The biggest change to be noted is the expansion into a five-volume series. While the *Checklist* housed explications of both "British and American Poems Past and Present," from Old English lyrics to those of Zukofsky, explications of American and British poetry now appear separately; and, with the exception of the modern and contemporary periods, each volume consolidates several historical phases and movements (Anglo-Saxon through Renaissance and Restoration through Victorian for British, Colonial through the nineteenth century for American poetry). Other changes I discuss in more detail below.

The current volume has modified some of the aims, scope, and limitations of *Poetry Explication: A Checklist*. The *Guide to American Poetry Explication*, Volume 2, *Modern and Contemporary*, now contains explications from books devoted solely to one author, although it retains earlier citations of reprints that have appeared in various collections or periodicals. We have also included for the first time citations for longer works (i.e., poems of more than five hundred lines, a limitation of the *Checklist* dictated by space requirements). Thus the *Guide* includes explication for H. D.'s *Helen in Egypt*, William Carlos Williams's *Paterson*, Charles Olson's *Maximus Poems*, John Ashbery's *Self-Portrait in a Convex Mirror*, and other works whose importance for American poetry is registered by the commentaries they have generated in the last decade. Also new is the inclusion of significant interviews with poets and occasional correspondence, especially where poets self-explicate either untitled works, their conditions of composition, or their poetic tactics and aesthetics. Another difference from editions of the *Checklist* is the significant increase in the number and variety of journals and periodicals consulted.

Most noticeable in the new volumes, however, is their specialization. Separating American and British poetry and focusing, in this volume, on the modern and contemporary periods allowed for both an intensification and extension of entries. On the one hand, a large number of new citations from approximately 1977 through 1987 were added to the already substantial 1925-1977 compilation for major or canonical authors (traditionally defined). On the other hand, and in keeping with the intent of the compilers of the *Checklist*, the number of citations for Canadian, noncanonical, or lesser-known poets has increased dramatically in order to make this volume more fully representative of the richly textured and varied poetic practices of North America. Indeed, *American* also means *North American*, and the new *Guide* includes a measurably greater number of Canadian poets and citations from Canadian journals in order to reflect this large fact.

Poetry's own inclusiveness and openness led me to seek consciously for poetry and explication wherever they occur--including at the margins of dominant institutional recognition and practice in the United States. I am not claiming, of course, that poetic and critical activity is necessarily *better* among the supposedly minor leagues or in Montréal or Vancouver, but I am agreeing with William Carlos Williams that American poetry spins into numerous heterologous traditions and dialogues with its ambient cultures. In an age of information and its transmission, it is not surprising to find the many regions and poetry-producing subcultures of the United States, Mexico, the Caribbean, and Canada, all impinging. Thus I have not been as much concerned to validate a strict notion of the canon as to make available a tool for discovering the plurality of poetic traditions, voices, and dialogues occurring in the modern and postmodern North American scene.

It has been stimulating for me to examine old and new poetics and perspectives, to read old and new journals dedicated to their interpretation, and to rediscover the utter vitality and historicity of written and spoken language in the service of a people's pleasure, distraction, or desire. I have tried to incorporate that excitement in the following pages. As a consequence Cajun poetry, ballads, songs, lyrics, and Asian-American poetry (emerging mostly on the West Coast since the 1960s and a prognostication of even greater cultural exchanges with the Pacific rim) are represented here. So too are Hispanic-American poets with their differing Mexican-American or Chicano traditions and their singular intermixtures of Mexican, Indian, and Anglo forms or their complex reworkings of Puerto Rican, Cuban-American, and Caribbean materials. Afro-American artists are also compiled more abundantly and thoroughly than before, a situation reflecting the growth over the past two decades in Afro-American studies curricula and research, and of ethnic self-consciousness and celebration. For example, explication now reflects the scholarly and cultural rediscovery of the Harlem Renaissance and its place in American Modernism, and the many traditions and historical modes of expression of Afro-American literature, including the lyrics of Caribbean music, jazz, and popular songs, especially the blues. By the late 1980s the evidence is in for a distinct women's poetry (i.e., one that draws from women's ethnic, regional, and biological histories and whose explications attempt to clarify women's constructions across a range of cultural contradictions and discourses).

Explications of other kinds of poetry continue to clarify the astonishing array of poetic voices and practices and their established or emergent traditions. Gays and lesbians from Whitman to O'Hara, Merrill, and Ginsberg and from Millay to Stein and Rich have created a special set of conditions for explication in ways that shed light on the sociosexual politics of cultural meaning and interpretation. Commentaries tend to focus on a poem's "coded" languages and subtexts, for example, or on the complex reception dynamics of what Stanley Fish has called "interpretive communities." Native Americans comprise yet another interpretive community that produces an oral and written literature, one whose poetic traditions are a palimpsest of modern forms over the debris of sacred words. Explication frequently stresses how Amerindian poetics offers utopian glimpses of a usable past through native rituals and landscape and through the recognition, not the repression, of the brutality of colonization. At another extreme, punk poetry may be taken as a poetics and palimpsest of the debris of secular words: the possibility and the outcome of both rock music and lyrics and of an urban expressionism taken to certain limits of representation. Criticism that to some degree exemplifies this cultural diversity is found in the following pages.

Other sorts of extraordinary poetic practices come out of bilingual ethnic traditions, where the palimpsest is formally rendered by the attempt to integrate different languages, cultures, and positions of address (e.g. québécois, Hispanic). In this regard a special bibliographical problem is presented by non-English poetic practices. North American poetry and explication are being produced in languages other than English. French--to take the most obvious example--is also one of the "official" (by legislative fiat) languages of Canada, a situation reflecting that country's unique history of settlement, political recognition of provincial differences within federal consolidation, and subsequent cultural diversification. In short, linguistic difference in Canada has produced historically distinct cultural institutions. Consequently I have included a few French-language explications for some Canadian poets and listed some commentaries under Main Sources, on the grounds that the explications and commentaries were exceptional and useful for studying both specific poems and ethnocentric constraints on meaning. In the case of Bill Bissett, searches turned up almost no English-language explication comparable to the French, although he is rightly regarded as an important contemporary Canadian poet. In short, to privilege exclusively Anglo-Canadian poetry and its explication at the expense of French-Canadian would be a falsification of Canadian political experience and expression.

The situation with Spanish-language poetry and explication in the United States is somewhat different and no less complex. While québécois poetry tends to occur exclusively in French, most nonfolk Hispanic-American (and particularly Chicano) poetry that generates explication tends to appear in English or in a mixture of English and Spanish (e.g., Alurista, Luís Salinas). In recognition of this state of affairs, I have supplemented the Main Sources with useful and mainly English-language commentary on the history, current state of, and future directions of this Hispanic-American poetic production. (See, for example, José David Saldívar, "Towards a Chicano Poetics: The Making of the Chicano Subject, 1969-1982," *Confluencia* 1 [1986]: 10-17.) I note in passing the increasingly important body of Spanish-language criticism on this indigenous literature being published in Spain and in Central and South America. Future editions of the *Guide* will no doubt reflect the growing poetic significance of Hispanic America and the linguistic fact that Spanish, next to English, is the most widely spoken language in the United States.

To round off this inventory of sites for poetic production let me add one yielding explications now and just mention others to which I suspect a future edition of the *Guide* will have to tend. Oral or performance poetry (not too distant, after all, from verse drama, song, and ritual) has recently generated an increased amount of scholarship and commentary. Some of these explications I have indexed. Video texts of all sorts offer poetry in yet another form. Examples of these include mixed media performance productions or a critical series such as the United States's Public Broadcasting System series "Voices and Visions" (1988). In the case of the PBS series, explication and interpretation were both built into the program content and filming technique. Certainly these media conditions themselves are altering our conceptions of poetry and its genres, just as they are surely altering our notions of what constitutes explication.

North American poetry, in short, is not in danger of disappearing in a post-Gutenberg era, nor do we seem to be faced with any falling off of literary criticism. This is not to say that reputations remain enshrined forever, or that some poets will continue to command intensive amounts of critical attention. T. S. Eliot is not quite the giant at the close of the twentieth century that he was at its middle, when he spoke for an *anomie* that ultimately savaged itself in Vietnam and for philosophical traditions exhausted by Sartre even as they were displaced by structuralism and poststructuralism. Other more contemporary poets, such as the "L=A=N=G=U=A=G=E" group, or older poets such as Charles Olson and Marianne Moore, long neglected by academic preoccupations and hidebound tradition, seem to be appearing in more journals or as dissertation topics. The extraordinary growth of women's studies alone in the past ten years suggests that women poets, both historical and contemporary, will receive considerable critical attention. Similarly, poststructuralist criticism clearly sees the Modernist writers as the inhabitants of a canonizing "period" now open to revision. The current *Guide* offers much evidence of the impact of these changes on the *hows*, the *whys*, and the *whats*--the *critical objects*--for explication.

Several people and institutions have been of invaluable help during this project. Jim Ruppert, compiler of of the colonial and nineteenth-century volume of *Guide to American Poetry Explication*, and my colleague Alice Parker, both steered me off Anglo reservations into the immensely complex, dense, and rewarding territory of Native American literature. They were helpful and committed guides through the rapidly growing body of poetry and explication in this field. Jean Sheridan, of the University of Rhode Island Library and its director at the university's College of Continuing Education, and Elizabeth Futas and Leena Siitonen, both professors of library and information studies at the University of Rhode Island, were generously available for innumerable searches through the *MLA International Bibliography* (using DIALOG Information Retrieval Service) and always helpful in finding computer time. For two years Professor Sheridan also helped me draw up a master list of poets, conducted the preliminary searches with DIALOG, and gave me first-rate technical assistance, including training with bibliography-intensive software such as Pro-Cite. Her willingness to help was further characterized by a friendly promptness that went beyond professional courtesy. Her staff, especially Lorraine Bliss, Caroline Gifford, Bernice Mellen, and Pauline Moulson, could help locate troublesome citations in a blackout. Michele Hussey, our faculty secretary, found ways to make life and work easier in the face of dozens of claims on her time (and some crises). In addition to my colleagues at URI, I thank happily the serials and periodicals, reference, and circulation staffs of the Rockefeller Library and of the Hay Library's Harris Collection, both at Brown University. It is impossible to imagine researching as thoroughly as we have managed without the combined resources of the University of Rhode Island and Brown University libraries.

A special acknowledgment goes to my editors. Nancy Martinez, series editor for all the projected volumes, originated and designed the project. She promptly came up with information and contacts in response to dozens of inquiries. Her hard work and resourcefulness made the third edition of *Poetry Explication* the invaluable bibliographical tool it is, and this volume of the *Guide to American Poetry Explication* much easier to assemble. Both Risa Sorkin and Henriette Campagne at G. K. Hall were helpful in innumerable ways, whether tracking down technical materials, relaying information back and forth among editorial, production, and marketing departments, or keeping up morale. I thank them also for their superb humor and drollery under pressure. Ara Salibian and his copy editors are among the very best in the business. Their proofmarks and editorial queries were simultaneous testimony to foible and its ruthless (but good-humored) detection and correction. I also thank John Amburg for his thoroughness and patience in production.

For two years I had the luck (and mind-saving grace) to have four graduate students from the University of Rhode Island's English department assist me with the gathering of citations, the indexing of thousands of cards, and the inputting of data into PC's. Stephanie Almagno, Walter Best, Louisa Campos, and (for one year) Susan Pagac spent more hours in the stacks or before the monitors than any of us care to remember, resisting better than I did the inevitable despair and late-night hunger attacks attending seemingly endless tasks of purest detail. They are truly collaborators in the production of this volume. Stephanie in this regard is the first among equals. During the long winter and spring of 1988, when we were winding up, she put in many extra hours with me and saved me several months of solo labor. She is the compleat companionable manager of information flow, one who could turn just about any task into a moment of delight and friendship.

Lastly a small word of thanks to two friends who are also writers and editors. Without the good prodding of David Ricketts and Richard Sax, a lot of things in my life would be airy nothing.

Abbreviations

AI	American Imago
AIQ	American Indian Quarterly
AL	American Literature
ALR	American Literary Realism 1870-1910
AmerP	American Poetry
AmRev	Americas Review
AmerS	American Studies
AN&Q	American Notes and Queries

APR   American Poetry Review

AQ   American Quarterly

ArielE   Ariel: A Review of International English Literature

ArQ   Arizona Quarterly

ASch   American Scholar

BALF   Black American Literature Forum

Boundary   Boundary 2

BSUF   Ball State University Forum

BuR   Bucknell Review

CanL   Canadian Literature

CanPo   Canadian Poetry

CE   College English

CEA   CEA Critic

CentR   Centennial Review

ChiR   Chicago Review

CimR   Cimarron Review

CL   Comparative Literature

CLAJ   College Language Association Journal

CLQ   Colby Library Quarterly

CLS   Comparative Literature Studies

CollL   College Literature

CompD   Comparative Drama

ConL   Contemporary Literature

ContempR   Contemporary Review

CP   Concerning Poetry

CQ   Cambridge Quarterly

CR   Critical Review

CrevAS   Canadian Review of American Studies

CritI   Critical Inquiry

CritQ   Critical Quarterly

ABBREVIATIONS

DAI	Dissertation Abstracts International
DicS	Dickinson Studies
DQ	Denver Quarterly
DR	Dalhousie Review
EA	Études Anglaises
EAL	Early American Literature
E&S	Essays and Studies by Members of the English Association
ECW	Essays on Canadian Writing
EIC	Essays in Criticism
EJ	English Journal
ELH	English Literary History
ELit	Études Littéraires
ELN	English Language Notes
ELT	English Literature in Transition (1880-1920)
ELWIU	Essays in Literature

EngR	English Record
ES	English Studies
ESC	English Studies in Canada
ESQ	ESQ: Journal of the American Renaissance
Expl	Explicator
FMLS	Forum for Modern Language Studies
GaR	Georgia Review
GPQ	Great Plains Quarterly
HC	Hollins Critic
HLQ	Huntington Library Quarterly
HudR	Hudson Review
IEY	Iowa English Bulletin: Yearbook
IndL	Indian Literature (Calcutta)
IowaR	Iowa Review
JAAC	Journal of Aesthetics and Art Criticism

MELUS   MELUS: The Journal of the Society for the Study of the

Multi-Ethnic Literature of the United States

MHLS   Mid-Hudson Language Studies

MinnR   Minnesota Review

MissQ   Mississippi Quarterly

MissR   Missouri Review

MLN   Modern Language Notes

MLQ   Modern Language Quarterly

MLR   Modern Language Review

MLS   Modern Language Studies

ModA   Modern Age

MP   Modern Philology

MPS   Modern Poetry Studies

MQ   Midwest Quarterly

MQR   Michigan Quarterly Review

MR   Massachusetts Review

MSE   Massachusetts Studies in English

N&Q   Notes and Queries

NConL   Notes on Contemporary Literature

NEQ   New England Quarterly

NER   New England Review and Breadloaf Quarterly

NewL   New Letters

NLH   New Literary History

NWR   Northwest Review

OhR   Ohio Review

OJES   The Old Northwest: A Journal of Regional Life and Letters

ON   Osmania Journal of English Studies

PAPA   Publications of the Arkansas Philological Association

PLL   Papers on Language and Literature

PMLA   Publications of the Modern Language Association of America

PoT	Poetics Today
PQ	Philological Quarterly
PR	Partisan Review
PrS	Prairie Schooner
QJS	Quarterly Journal of Speech
QQ	Queen's Quarterly
RALS	Resources for American Literary Study
RES	Review of English Studies
RJN	Robinson Jeffers Newsletter
RLet	Revista Letras (Parná, Brazil)
RMR	Rocky Mountain Review of Language and Literature
SAQ	South Atlantic Quarterly
SatR	Saturday Review
SBL	Studies in Black Literature
SCL	Studies in Canadian Literature

ABBREVIATIONS

SCR	South Carolina Review
SHR	Southern Humanities Review
SIR	Studies in Romanticism
SJS	San Jose Studies
SLitI	Studies in the Literary Imagination
SLRev	Stanford Literature Review
SoQ	The Southern Quarterly
SoR	Southern Review
SoRA	Southern Review (Adelaide, Australia)
SP	Studies in Philology
SR	Sewanee Review
SSF	Studies in Short Fiction
SWR	Southwest Review
TCL	Twentieth Century Literature
ThirdR	Third Rail

TLS	Times Literary Supplement (London)
TriQ	TriQuarterly
TSE	TSE: Tulane Studies In English
TSL	Tennesse Studies in Literature
TSLL	Texas Studies in Literature and Language
UDR	University of Dayton Review
UMSE	University of Mississippi Studies in English
UTQ	University of Toronto Quarterly
UWR	University of Windsor Review
VCom	Visionary Company
VP	Victorian Poetry
VQR	Virginia Quarterly Review
WAL	Western American Literature
W&L	Women and Literature
WF	Western Folklore

Checklist of Interpretation

ABSHER, TOM

Forms of Praise

Kathy Callaway, "Apple Genii," *Parnassus* 10 (Spring/Summer 1982): 185-208.

"Heloise and Abelard"

Kathy Callaway, "Apple Genii," *Parnassus* 10 (Spring/Summer 1982): 185-208.

ADAMS, ROBERT SIMSON

"I Am No Prince of Darkness, Lord of Sorrow"

Adams, *The Context of Poetry*, 8-12.

AGEE, JAMES

"Pygmalion"

V. A. Kramer, "Agee's Early Poem 'Pygmalion' and His Aesthetic," *MissR* 29 (Spring 1976): 191-96.

"Sunday: Outskirts of Knoxville, Tenn."

Drew, *Poetry: A Modern Guide*, 211-14.

Drew and Sweeney, *Directions in Modern Poetry*, 243-47.

James A. Freeman, "Agee's 'Sunday Meditation,'" *CP* 3 (Fall 1970): 37-39.

AIKEN, CONRAD

"Antennae of the Race"

Helen Hagenbüchle, "Antennae of the Race: Conrad Aiken's Poetry and the Evolution of Consciousness," *HLQ* 45 (Summer 1982): 215-26.

"The Crystal"

E. P. Bollier, "Conrad Aiken's Ancestral Voices: A Reading of Four Poems," *SLitI* 13 (Fall 1980): 63-76.

James Dickey, "A Gold-Mine of Consciousness," *Poetry* 94 (Apr. 1959): 42-43.

"Dead Leaf in May"

James Zigerell, *Expl* 25 (Sept. 1966): 5.

"Hallowe'en"

E. P. Bollier, "Conrad Aiken's Ancestral Voices: A Reading of Four Poems," *SLitI* 13 (Fall 1980): 63-76.

Harry Marten, "The Unconquerable Ancestors: 'Mayflower,' 'The Kid,' 'Hallowe'en,'" *SLitI* 13 (Fall 1980): 51-62.

"The Kid"

Harry Marten, "The Unconquerable Ancestors: 'Mayflower,' 'The Kid,' 'Hallowe'en,'" *SLitI* 13 (Fall 1980): 51-62.

"Mayflower"

E. P. Bollier, "Conrad Aiken's Ancestral Voices: A Reading of Four Poems," *SLitI* 13 (Fall 1980): 63-76.

Harry Marten, "The Unconquerable Ancestors: 'Mayflower,' 'The Kid,' 'Hallowe'en,'" *SLitI* 13 (Fall 1980): 51-62.

"Morning Song from 'Senlin'"

Perrine and Reid, *100 American Poems*, 143-44.

"Poem 13" (from Preludes for Memnon)

Helen Hagenbuechle, "Epistemology and Musical Form in Conrad Aiken's Poetry," *SLitI* 13 (Fall 1980): 7-26.

Silent Snow, Secret Snow

L. A. Slap, "Conrad Aiken's *Silent Snow, Secret Snow*: Defenses Against the Primal Scene," *AI* 37 (Spring 1980): 1-11.

"South End"

Perrine and Reid, *100 American Poems*, 145.

"Sursum Corda"

Donald A. Stauffer, "Genesis, or the Poet as Maker," *Poets at Work*, 72-76. Reprinted in Engle and Carrier, *Reading Modern Poetry*, 240-41.

ALGARIN, MIGUEL

[Interview]

Miguel Algarin, "Volume and Value of the Breath in Poetry," in Waldman and Webb, *Talking Poetics from Naropa Institute* 2:325-45.

ALLEN, PAULA GUNN

[Interview]

Joseph Bruchac III, "I Climb the Mesas in My Dreams: An Interview with Paula Gunn Allen," in *Survival This Way: Interviews with American Indian Poets* (Tucson: University of Arizona Press, 1987), 1-21.

The Coyote's Daylight Trip

Elaine Jahner, "A Laddered, Rain-Bearing Rug: Paula Gunn Allen's Poetry," in *Women and Western American Literature*, ed. Helen Winter Stauffer and Susan J. Rosowski (Troy, N.Y.: Whitson, 1982), 311-26.

Kenneth Lincoln, "Native American Literature: 'old like hills, like stars,'" in Baker, *Three American Literatures*, 139-40.

Lincoln, *Native American Renaissance*, passim.

"Relations"

Kenneth Lincoln, "Native American Literatures: 'old like hills, like stars,'" in Baker, *Three American Literatures*, 138-39.

Shadow Country

Kenneth Lincoln, "Native American Literatures: 'old like hills, like stars,'" in Baker, *Three American Literatures*, 137-40.

Lincoln, *Native American Renaissance*, passim.

ALURISTA (ALBERTO URISTA)

"Mis ojos hinchados"

Tatum, *Chicano Literature*, 143-44.

AMMONS, A. R.

[Interview]

Cynthia Haythe, "An Interview with A. R. Ammons," *ConL* 21 (1980): 173-90.

"Corsons Inlet"

Elder, *Imagining the Earth*, passim.

Guy Rotella, "Ghostlier Demarcations, Keener Sounds: A. R. Ammons' 'Corsons Inlet,'" *CP* 10 (Fall 1977): 25-33.

"Easter Morning"

Cynthia Haythe, "An Interview with A. R. Ammons," *ConL* 21 (1980): 173-90.

"Essay on Poetics"

Elder, *Imagining the Earth*, passim.

"Hibernaculum"

Richard Pevear, "Poetry Chronicle," *HudR* 26 (Spring 1973): 217-18.

"Identity"

Elder, *Imagining the Earth*, passim.

AMMONS, A.R.

"I Went to the Summit"

Bloom, *A Map of Misreading*, 200-203.

"Loss"

Wyatt Prunty, "Emaciated Poetry," *SR* 93 (Winter 1985): 78-94.

"Periphery"

Harold Bloom, "Dark and Radiant Peripheries: Mark Strand and A. R. Ammons," *SoR*, n.s. 8 (Winter 1972): 145.

"Play"

Lawrence Kramer, "The Wodwo Watches the Water Clock: Language in Postmodern British and American Poetry," *ConL* 18 (Summer 1977): 329-31.

"The Snow Poems"

Michael McFee, "A. R. Ammons and "The Snow Poems" Reconsidered," *ChiR* 33 (Summer 1981): 32-38.

"Sphere"

Elder, *Imagining the Earth*, passim.

John W. Erwin, "The Reader Is the Medium: Ashbery and Ammons Ensphered," *ConL* 21 (1980): 588-610.

James E. Miller, "Whitman's Leaves and the American 'Lyric-Epic,'" in Fraistat, *Poems in Their Place*, 289-307.

"Tape for the Turn of the Year"

Cynthia Haythe, "An Interview with A. R. Ammons," *ConL* 21 (1980): 173-90.

"Utensil"

Cynthia Haythe, "An Interview with A. R. Ammons," *ConL* 21 (1980): 173-90.

ANDREWS, BRUCE

A Cappella

McCaffery, *North of Intention*, 23-24.

"Bananas Are an Example"

Pinsky, *The Situation of Poetry*, 87-89.

Praxis

Joan Retallack, "The Meta-Physick of Play: $L=A=N=G=U=A=G=E$ USA," *Parnassus* 12 (Fall/Winter 1984): 213-44.

"The Red Hallelujah"

McCaffery, *North of Intention*, 24-25.

ANONYMOUS

"The Black and Tan Gun"

D. K. Wilgus, "American Ballads in Ireland: Two Examples," in *Essays in Honor of Peter Crossley-Holland on His Sixty-Fifth Birthday* (Los Angeles: UCLA Music Department, 1983), 269-84.

"Deer and Coyote" (Chinook coyote/trickster narrative poem)

Dell Hymes, "Bungling Host, Benevolent Host: Louis Simpson's 'Deer and Coyote,'" *AIQ* 8 (Summer 1984): 171-98.

"Frankie and Johnny"

Brooks, Purser, and Warren, *An Approach to Literature*, 431-32; 3d ed., 285-86; 4th ed., 287-88.

"Hohoyaw'u" [Stinkbug]

Kathleen M. Sands and Emory Sekaquaptewa, "Four Hopi Lullabies: A Study in Method and Meaning," *AIQ* 4 (1978): 197-210.

"Koskalaka Wan Wanagi Wan Kici Kiciza"
[A Young Man Fights With a Ghost]

Julian Rice, "How Lakota Stories Keep the Spirit and Feed the Ghost," *AIQ* 8 (Fall 1984): 331-47.

La Delgadina

Maria Herrera-Sobek, "*La Delgadina*: Incest and Patriarchal Structure in a Spanish/Chicano Romance-Corrido," *Studies in Latin American Popular Culture* 5 (1986): 90-107.

"The Lovers"

Julian Rice, "How Lakota Stories Keep the Spirit and Feed the Ghost," *AIQ* 8 (Fall 1984): 331-47.

"El Renegado" [The Renegade]

Raymund A. Paredes, "The Evolution of Chicano Literature," in Baker, *Three American Literatures*, 42-44.

"Song of the Deer Dancing" (Ojibwa oral narrative)

Karl Kroeber, "Poem, Dream, and the Consuming of Culture," *GaR* 32 (Summer 1978): 266-80.

"So'yok Manawya" [Little Girl]

Kathleen M. Sands and Emory Sekaquaptewa, "Four Hopi Lullabies: A Study in Method and Meaning," *AIQ* 4 (1978): 197-210.

"Tutakyawyamu" [Prairie Dogs]

Kathleen M. Sands and Emory Sekaquaptewa, "Four Hopi Lullabies: A Study in Method and Meaning," *AIQ* 4 (1978): 197-210.

"Twenty-One Years"

D. K. Wilgus, "American Ballads in Ireland: Two Examples," in *Essays in Honor of Peter Crossley-Holland on His Sixty-Fifth Birthday* (Los Angeles: UCLA Music Department, 1983), 269-84.

[Untitled narratives]

Franchot Ballinger, "The Responsible Center: Man and Nature in Pueblo and Navajo Ritual Songs and Prayers," *AQ* 30 (1978): 90-107.

J. C. Scott, "Horses of Different Colors: The Plains Indians in Stories for Children," *AIQ* 8 (Spring 1984): 117-25.

"Wanagi Gli Wan Woyaka" [A Returned Ghost Talks]

Julian Rice, "How Lakota Stories Keep the Spirit and Feed the Ghost," *AIQ* 8 (Fall 1984): 331-47.

"Wanagi Tackanku Kin" [The Ghost Road]

Julian Rice, "How Lakota Stories Keep the Spirit and Feed the Ghost," *AIQ* 8 (Fall 1984): 331-47.

ANTIN, DAVID

"Radical Coherency" (oral performance poetry)

Henry M. Sayre, "David Antin and the Oral Poetics Movement," *ConL* 23 (1982): 428-50.

Talking at the Boundaries

Paul, *In Search of the Primitive*, passim.

Tuning

Charles Altieri, "The Postmodernism of David Antin's *Tuning*," *CE* 48 (Jan. 1986): 9-26.

Paul, *In Search of the Primitive*, passim.

ASHBERY, JOHN

[Interview]

John Ashbery, "Interview," *APR* (1984): 29-33.

A. Poulin, Jr., "The Experience of Experience: A Conversation with John Ashbery," *MQR* (1981): 242-55.

"The Absence of a Noble Presence"

John Gery, "En Route to Annihilation: John Ashbery's *Shadow Train*," *CP* 20 (1987): 99-116.

"As You Came from the Holy Land"

Bloom, *A Map of Misreading*, 204-6.

"Breezy Stories"

John Gery, "En Route to Annihilation: John Ashbery's *Shadow Train*," *CP* 20 (1987): 99-116.

"The Chateau Hardware"

Charles Molesworth, "'This Leaving-Out Business': The Poetry of John Ashbery," *Salmagundi* 38-39 (Summer/Fall 1977): 28-29.

"Clouds"

John Bensko, "Reflexive Narration in Contemporary American Poetry: Some Examples from Mark Strand, John Ashbery, Norman Dubie, and Louis Simpson," *JNT* 16 (Spring 1986): 81-96.

Dream of Spring

L. Keller, "'Thinkers without Final Thoughts': John Ashbery's Evolving Debt to Wallace Stevens," *ELH* 49 (Spring 1982): 235-61.

"Europe"

Edward Haworth Hoeppner, "Visual Gestalt and John Ashbery's 'Europe,'" *CP* 20 (1987): 87-97.

Marjorie G. Perloff, "The Poetry of John Ashbery and Frank O'Hara," *YES* 8 (1978): 171-96.

"Everyman's Library"

John Bensko, "Reflexive Narration in Contemporary American Poetry: Some Examples from Mark Strand, John Ashbery, Norman Dubie, and Louis Simpson," *JNT* 16 (Spring 1986): 81-96.

John Gery, "En Route to Annihilation: John Ashbery's *Shadow Train*," *CP* 20 (1987): 99-116.

"Frontispiece"

John Gery, "En Route to Annihilation: John Ashbery's *Shadow Train*," *CP* 20 (1987): 99-116.

"Houseboat Days"

Thomas A. Fink, "The Comic Thrust in Ashbery's Poetry," *TCL* 30 (Spring 1984): 6-10.

Mary Kinzie, "'Irreference': The Poetic Diction of John Ashbery, Part I: Styles of Avoidance," *MP* 84 (Feb. 1987): 267-81.

Mary Kinzie, "'Irreference': The Poetic Diction of John Ashbery, Part II: Prose, Prosody, and Dissembled Time," *MP* 84 (Feb. 1987): 382-400.

R. Miklitsch, "John Ashbery," *ConL* 21 (Winter 1980): 118-35.

"Indelible, Indelible"

John Bensko, "Reflexive Narration in Contemporary American Poetry: Some Examples from Mark Strand, John Ashbery, Norman Dubie, and Louis Simpson," *JNT* 16 (Spring 1986): 81-96.

"Leaving the Atocha Station"

Carroll, *The Poem in Its Skin*, 6-23.

Fred Moramarco, "John Ashbery and Frank O'Hara: The Painterly Poets," *JML* 5 (Sept. 1976): 452-53.

"Litany"

Altieri, *Self and Sensibility in Contemporary American Poetry*, passim.

Blasing, *American Poetry: The Rhetoric of Its Forms*, 200-201, 208-10, 212.

James E. Miller, "Whitman's Leaves and the American 'Lyric-Epic,'" in Fraistat, *Poems in Their Place*, 289-307.

"Metamorphosis"

Charles Altieri, "Sensibility, Rhetoric, and Will: Some Tension in Contemporary Poetry," *ConL* 23 (Fall 1982): 451-79.

"The Painter"

Fred Moramarco, "John Ashbery and Frank O'Hara: The Painterly Poets," *JML* 5 (Sept. 1976): 449-50.

"Self-Portrait in a Convex Mirror"

Charles Altieri, "Motives in Metaphor: John Ashbery and the Modernist Long Poem," *Genre* 11 (1978): 653-87.

Altieri, *Self and Sensibility in Contemporary American Poetry*, passim.

John Ashbery, "Interview," *APR* (1984): 29-33.

Harold Bloom, "Breaking of Form," in Lehman, *Beyond Amazement*, 115-26.

Harold Bloom, "The Internalization of Quest Romance," in *The Ringers in the Tower*, 13-35.

Merle Brown, "Poetic Listening," *NLH* 10 (Autumn 1978) 125-39.

Joan Dayan, "Finding What Will Suffice: John Ashbery's *A Wave*," *MLN* 100, no. 5 (1985): 1045-79.

M. Davidson, "Ekphrasis and the Postmodern Painter Poem," *JAAC* 42 (Fall 1983): 69-79.

Lee Edelman, "The Prose of Imposture: Ashbery's Self-Portrait in a Convex Mirror," *TCL* 32 (Spring 1986): 95-114.

John W. Erwin, "The Reader Is the Medium: Ashbery and Ammons Ensphered," *ConL* 21 (1980): 588-610.

D. Kalstone, *Five Temperaments* (New York: Oxford University Press, 1977), 170-99.

R. Miklitsch, "John Ashbery," *ConL* 21 (Winter 1980): 118-35.

S. P. Mohanty and Jonathan Monroe, "John Ashbery and the Articulation of the Social," *Diacritics* 17 (Summer 1987): 37-63.

Charles Molesworth, "'This Leasing-Out Business': The Poetry of John Ashbery," *Salmagundi* 38-39 (Summer/Fall 1977): 20-41.

A. Poulin, "The Experience of Experience: A Conversation with John Ashbery," *MQR* (1981): 242-55.

Herman Rapaport, "Deconstructing Apocalyptic Rhetoric: Ashbery, Derrida, Blanchot," *Criticism* 27 (1985): 387-400.

Andrew Ross, "Doubting John Thomas," in *Failures of Modernism*, 159-208.

Richard Stamelman, "Critical Reflections: Poetry and Art Criticism in Ashbery's 'Self-Portrait in a Convex Mirror,'" *NLH* 15 (Spring 1984): 605-30.

Alan Williamson, "The Diffracting Diamond: Ashbery, Romanticism, and Anti-Art," in *Introspection and Contemporary Poetry*, 116-48.

"The Skaters"

S. P. Mohanty and Jonathan Monroe, "John Ashbery and the Articulation of the Social," *Diacritics* 17 (Summer 1987): 37-63.

Fred Moramarco, "John Ashbery and Frank O'Hara: The Painterly Poets," *JML* 5 (Sept. 1976): 453-55.

Marjorie G. Perloff, "The Poetry of John Ashbery and Frank O'Hara," *YES* 8 (1978): 171-96.

Perloff, *Frank O'Hara: Poet Among the Painters*, 193-96.

"The Songs We Know Best"

James Applewhite, "Painting, Poetry, Abstraction, and Ashbery," *SoR* 24 (Spring 1988): 272-90.

"The Tennis Court Oath"

Fred Moramarco, "John Ashbery and Frank O'Hara: The Painterly Poets," *JML* 5 (Sept. 1976): 451-52.

"They Dream Only of America"

Marjorie G. Perloff, "The Poetry of John Ashbery and Frank O'Hara," *YES* 8 (1978): 171-96.

"Two Scenes"

Marjorie G. Perloff, "The Poetry of John Ashbery and Frank O'Hara," *YES* 8 (1978): 171-96.

"A Wave"

Charles Altieri, "Motives in Metaphor: John Ashbery and the Modernist Long Poem," *Genre* 11 (1978): 653-87.

Altieri, *Self and Sensibility in Contemporary American Poetry*, passim.

James Applewhite, "Painting, Poetry, Abstraction, and Ashbery," *SoR* 24 (Spring 1988): 272-290.

John Ashbery, "Interview," *APR* (1984): 29-33.

Joan Dayan, "Finding What Will Suffice: John Ashbery's 'A Wave,'" *MLN* 100, no. 5 (1985): 1045-79.

S. P. Mohanty and Jonathan Monroe, "John Ashbery and the Articulation of the Social," *Diacritics* 17 (Summer 1987): 37-63.

A. Poulin, Jr., "The Experience of Experience: A Conversation with John Ashbery," *MQR* (1981): 242-255.

ASHLEY, LEONARD R. N.

"The Game"

Leonard R. N. Ashley, "The Rules of the Games," *CP* 1 (Spring 1968): 38-44.

ATWOOD, MARGARET

[Interview]

"A Conversation with Margaret Atwood," in *Margaret Atwood: Reflection and Reality*, ed. Beatrice Mendez-Egle (Edinburg: Pan American University, 1987), 172-80.

Karla Hammond, "Margaret Atwood," *CP* 12 (Fall 1979): 73-81.

"At First I Was Given Centuries"

Ostriker, *Stealing the Language*, 152-53.

Bodily Harm

S. R. Wilson, "Turning Life into Popular Art: *Bodily Harm*'s Life-Tourist," *SCL* 10 (1985): 136-45.

"Circe/Mud Poems"

Gordon Johnston, "The Ruthless Story and the Future Tense in Margaret Atwood's 'Circe/Mud Poems,'" *SCL* 5 (1980): 167-76.

Estella Lauter, *Women as Mythmakers*, 62-78.

"He Reappears"

George Johnson, "Diction in Poetry," *CanL* 97 (Summer 1983): 39-44.

"More and More"

Suzanne Juhasz, "Subjective Formalism; or, The Lady and the Text, A Demonstration," *CLAJ* 24 (June 1981): 465-80.

Selected Poems

Barbara Blakely, "The Pronunciation of Flesh: A Feminist Reading of Margaret Atwood's Poetry," in *Margaret Atwood: Language, Text, and System*, ed. Sherrill E. Grace and Lorraine Weir (Vancouver: University of British Columbia Press, 1983), 33-51.

Linda W. Wagner, "The Making of Selected Poems: The Process of Surfacing," in *The Art of Margaret Atwood: Essays in Criticism*, ed. Arnold E. Davidson and Cathy N. Davidson (Toronto: Anansi, 1981), 81-94.

Cheryl Walker, "Turning to Margaret Atwood: From Anguish to Language," in *Margaret Atwood: Reflection and Reality*, ed. Beatrice Mendez-Egle (Edinburg: Pan American University, 1987), 154-71.

Gayle Wood, "On Margaret Atwood's *Selected Poems*," *APR* 8 (1979): 30-32.

Brenda Wineapple, "Margaret Atwood's Poetry: Against Still Life," *DR* 62 (Summer 1982): 212-22.

"This Is a Photograph of Me"

Ostriker, *Stealing the Language*, 63-65.

"Tricks with Mirrors"

Thomas A. Fink, *Expl* 43 (Winter 1985): 60-61.

"Two-Headed Poems"

George Bowering, "Margaret Atwood's Hands," *SCL* 6 (1981): 39-52.

Shannon Hengen, "Your Father the Thunder, Your Mother the Rain: Lacan and Atwood," *L&P* 32 (1986): 36-42.

Lorna Irvine, "One Woman Leads to Another," in *The Art of Margaret Atwood: Essays in Criticism*, ed. Arnold E. Davidson and Cathy N. Davidson (Toronto: Anansi, 1981), 95-106.

Lorraine Weir, "Atwood in a Landscape," in *Margaret Atwood: Language, Text, and System*, ed. Sherrill E. Grace and Lorraine Weir (Vancouver: University of British Columbia Press, 1983), 143-53.

You are Happy

Maureen Dilliot, "Emerging from the Cold: Margaret Atwood's *You are Happy*," *MPS* 8 (Spring 1977): 73-90.

AUBERT, ALVIN

South Louisiana

Herbert Woodward Martin, untitled review, *BALF* 21 (Fall 1987): 343-48.

AUSTIN, MARY

California

Norwood and Monk, *The Desert Is No Lady*, 16-19.

The Land of Little Rain

Norwood and Monk, *The Desert Is No Lady*, 16-19.

AVISON, MARGARET

"The Agnes Cleves Papers"

J. M. Kertzer, "Margaret Avison's Portrait of a Lady: 'The Agnes Cleves Papers,'" *CP* 12 (Fall 1979): 17-24.

"Butterfly Bones; or Sonnet against Sonnets"

William H. New, "The Mind's Eyes (I's) (Ice): The Poetry of Margaret Avison," *TCL* 16 (July 1970): 191.

"Dispersed Titles"

J. M. Zezulka, "Refusing the Sweet Surrender: Margaret Avison's 'Dispersed Titles,'" *CanPo* 1 (1977): 44-53.

"Natural/Unnatural"

William H. New, "The Mind's Eyes (I's) (Ice): The Poetry of Margaret Avison," *TCL* 16 (July 1970): 199-200.

"Neverness, or The One Ship Beached on One Far Distant Shore"

D. G. Jones, "The Sleeping Giant," *CanL* 26 (1965). Reprinted in Woodcock, *A Choice of Critics*, 3-24.

Milton Wilson, "The Poetry of Margaret Avison," *CanL* 2 (1959). Reprinted in Woodcock, *A Choice of Critics*, 221-32.

"Prelude"

William H. New, "The Mind's Eyes (I's) (Ice): The Poetry of Margaret Avison," *TCL* 16 (July 1970): 188-89.

Sunblue

Prabhu S. Guptara, "A Dark Reservoir of Gladness: Margaret Avison's Third Volume of Verse," *Literary Criticism* 16 (1981): 42-45.

Ernest H. Redekop, "Sun/Son Light/Light: Avison's Elemental *Sunblue*," *CanPo* 7 (Fall/Winter 1980): 21-37.

BAKER, KARLE W.

"Courage"

Sanders, *The Discovery of Poetry*, 180-81.

BARAKA, IMAMU AMIRI (LeROI JONES)

"All in the Street"

James A. Miller, "'I Investigate the Sun': Amiri Baraka in the 1980s," *Callaloo* 9 (Winter 1986): 184-92.

"The Alternative"

Klinkowitz, *Literary Disruptions*, 107-9.

"AM/TRAK"

Henry C. Lacey, "Baraka's 'AM/TRAK': Everybody's Coltrane Poem," *Obsidian II: Black Literature in Review* 1 (Spring/Summer 1986): 12-21.

James A. Miller, "'I Investigate the Sun': Amiri Baraka in the 1980s," *Callaloo* 9 (Winter 1986): 184-92.

"Black Art"

Kathleen Gallagher, "The Art(s) of Poetry: Jones and MacLeish," *MQ* 12 (Summer 1971): 383-92.

"Black Dada Nihilismus"

William C. Fischer, "The Pre-Revolutionary Writings of Imamu Amiri Baraka," *MR* 14 (Spring 1973): 290-92.

Lacey, *To Raise, Destroy, and Create: The Poetry, Drama, and Fiction of Imamu Amiri Baraka*, passim.

Black Music

Klinkowitz, *Literary Disruptions*, 103-4, passim.

"A Chase (Alghieri's Dream)"

Klinkowitz, *Literary Disruptions*, 106-7.

"For the Revolutionary Outburst by Black People"

James A. Miller, "'I Investigate the Sun': Amiri Baraka in the 1980s," *Callaloo* 9 (Winter 1986): 184-92.

"Hymn for Lanie Poo"

William C. Fischer, "The Pre-Revolutionary Writings of Imamu Amiri Baraka," *MR* 14 (Spring 1973): 266-67.

"In Memory of Radio"

John Hakac, "Baraka's 'In Memory of Radio,'" *CP* 10 (Spring 1977): 85.

"Like, This Is What I Mean"

James A. Miller, "'I Investigate the Sun': Amiri Baraka in the 1980s," *Callaloo* 9 (Winter 1986): 184-267.

The System of Dante's Hell

Klinkowitz, *Literary Disruptions*, 104-6, 110.

Jerry W. Ward, Jr., *"The System of Dante's Hell*: Underworlds of Art and Liberation," *Griot: Journal of the Southern Conference on Afro-American Studies* 6 (1987): 58-64.

BARNES, DICK

"A Lake on the Earth"

David E. James, "Poetry/Punk/Production: Some Recent Writing in L.A.," *MinnR*, n.s. 23 (Fall 1984): 127-48.

BELITT, BEN

"Double Poem"

Robert Weisberg, "Ben Belitt: Speaking Words against the Word," *MPS* 7 (Spring 1976): 52-55.

"Full Moon: The Gorge"

Robert Weisberg, "Ben Belitt: Speaking Words against the Word," *MPS* 7 (Spring 1976): 57-59.

"Xerox"

Robert Weisberg, "Ben Belitt: Speaking Words against the Word," *MPS* 7 (Spring 1976): 48-49.

BELL

"Manicure"

Philip Hobsbaum, *Theory of Criticism* (Bloomington and London: Indiana University Press, 1970), 172-76.

BELL, MARVIN

[Interview]

"Interview with Marvin Bell," *IowaR* 12 (Winter 1981): 2-36.

BENET, STEPHEN VINCENT

"Ode to Walt Whitman"

Morton D. Zabel, "The American Grain," *Poetry* 48 (Aug. 1936): 279-81.

BERNSTEIN, CHARLES

Disfrutes

McCaffery, *North of Intention*, 149-50.

Resistance

Joan Retallack, "The Meta-Physick of Play: $L=A=N=G=U=A=G=E$ USA," *Parnassus* 12 (Fall/Winter 1984): 213-44.

BERRIGAN, TED

[Interview]

Barry Alpert, "Ted Berrigan: An Interview," *Vort* 2 (1972): 21-44.

Ted Berrigan, "The Business of Writing Poetry," in Waldman and Webb, *Talking Poetics from Naropa Institute* 1:39-61.

"American Express"

Neil Baldwin, review of *So Going Around Cities*, *Credences*, n.s. 1 (Fall/Winter 1981/1982): 167-71.

So Going Around Cities

Neil Baldwin, untitled review, *Credences*, n.s. 1 (Fall/Winter 1981/1982): 167-71.

BERRY, WENDELL

"The Apple Tree"

John Ditsky, "Wendell Berry: Homage to the Apple Tree," *MPS* 2 (Spring 1971): 9.

"Enriching the Earth"

Elder, *Imagining the Earth*, passim.

"The Morning's News"

Elder, *Imagining the Earth*, passim.

"The Return"

Robert Hass, "Wendell Berry: Finding the Land," *MPS* 2 (Spring 1971): 18-25.

"The Slip"

Elder, *Imagining the Earth*, passim.

"The White and Waking of the House"

Robert Hass, "Wendell Berry: Finding the Land," *MPS* 2 (Spring 1971): 31-34.

BERRYMAN, JOHN

"The Desires of Men and Women"

Richard Wilbur, "Poetry's Debt to Poetry," *HudR* 26 (Summer 1973): 290-93.

"The Disciple"

Robert Fitzgerald, "Poetry and Perfection," *SR* 56 (Autumn 1948): 690-91.

"The Dispossessed"

J. F. Nims, *Poetry: A Critical Supplement*, Apr. 1948, 1-5.

The Dream Songs

G. Q. Arpin, *The Poetry of John Berryman* (Port Washington: Kennikat Press, 1978), passim.

Jack Vincent Barbera, *Expl* 38 (1980): 29.

Jack Vincent Barbera, "Shape and Flow in *The Dream Songs*," *TCL* 22 (May 1976): 146-62.

Kathe Davis, "Honey Dusk Do Sprawl: Does Black Minstrel Dialect Obscure *The Dream Songs*?" *Lang&S* 18 (Winter 1985): 30-45.

Donald H. Hedrick, "Berryman Text Dreams," *NLH* 12 (Winter 1981): 289-301.

Dona Hickey, "John Berryman and the Art of *The Dream Songs*," *ChiR* 32 (Spring 1981): 34-43.

Steven K. Hoffman, "Lowell, Berryman, Roethke, and Ginsberg: The Communal Function of Confessional Poetry," *LitR* 22 (Spring 1979): 329-41.

A. Oberg, *The Modern American Lyric: Lowell, Berryman, Creeley, and Plath* (New Brunswick: Rutgers University Press, 1978), passim.

R. Pooley, "Berryman's Last Poems: Plain Style and Christian Style," *MLR* 76 (April 1981): 291-97.

Thurley, *The American Moment--American Poetry in the Mid-Century*, 51-69.

Linda W. Wagner, *American Modern: Essays in Fiction and Poetry* (Port Washington: Kennikat, 1980), passim.

R. Wallace, *God Be with the Clown*, passim.

Paul D. Wardzinski, *Expl* 34 (1976): 70.

"Dream Song 97"

David K. Weiser, *Expl* 41 (Fall 1982): 56-58.

"Dream Song 110"

Jack V. Barbera, *Expl* 38 (Spring 1980): 29-31.

"Dream Song 255"

Kathe Davis Finney, *Expl* 39 (Summer 1981): 44-45.

"Elegy, for Alun Lewis"

J. Pikoulis, "John Berryman's 'Elegy, for Alun Lewis,'" *AL* 56 (Mar. 1984): 100-101.

"Eleven Addresses"

Mariani, *A Usable Past*, passim.

"Formal Elegy"

Ann Stanford, "The Elegy of Mourning in Modern American and English Poetry," *SoR* 11 (Apr. 1975): 370-72.

"His Toy, His Dream, His Rest"

Kathleen Kelly, "Berryman's 'His Toy, His Dream, His Rest,'" *Expl* 42 (Spring 1984): 56.

"Homage to Mistress Bradstreet"

Sarah Provost, "Erato's Fool and Bitter Sister: Two Aspects of John Berryman," *TCL* 30 (Spring 1984): 69-79.

"Love and Fame"

Steven K. Hoffman, "Lowell, Berryman, Roethke, and Ginsberg: The Communal Function of Confessional Poetry," *LitR* 22 (Spring 1979): 329-41.

"Sonnets"

David K. Weiser, "Berryman's Sonnets: In and Out of the Tradition," *AL* 55 (Oct. 1983): 388-404.

"A Strut for Roethke"

Mariani, *A Usable Past: Essays on Modern and Contemporary Poetry*, 214-25.

Jo Porterfield, *Expl* 32 (Dec. 1973): 25.

"Winter Landscape"

David M. Wyatt, "Completing the Picture: Williams, Berryman, and 'Spatial Form,'" *CLQ* 13 (Dec. 1977): 257-61.

"World's Fair"

Margaret M. McBride, *Expl* 34 (Nov. 1975): 22.

Nims, *Poetry: A Critical Supplement*, 6.

BIRNEY, EARLE

Ice Cod Bell Or Stone

Paul West, "Earle Birney and the Compound Ghost," *CanL* 13 (1962). Reprinted in Woodcock, *A Choice of Critics*, 131-41.

BISHOP, ELIZABETH

[Correspondence]

L. Keller, "Words Worth a Thousand Postcards: The Bishop/Moore Correspondence," *AL* 55 (Oct. 1983): 405-29.

"Arrival at Santos"

Von Hallberg, *American Poetry and Culture, 1945-1980*, passim.

"At the Fishhouses"

Sybil Estess, "'Shelters for What is Within': Meditation and Epiphany in the Poetry of Elizabeth Bishop," *MPS* 8 (Spring 1977): 53-59.

Crale D. Hopkins, "Inspiration as Theme: Art and Nature in the Poetry of Elizabeth Bishop," *ArQ* 32 (Autumn 1976): 204-5.

Nancy L. McNally, "Elizabeth Bishop: The Discipline of Description," *TCL* 11 (Jan. 1966): 197-200.

Willard Spiegelman, "Landscape and Knowledge: The Poetry of Elizabeth Bishop," *MPS* 6 (Winter 1975): 204-8.

Patricia B. Wallace, "The Wildness of Elizabeth Bishop," *SR* 93 (Winter 1985): 95-115.

"The Bight"

Sybil P. Estess, "Elizabeth Bishop: The Delicate Art of Map Making," *SoR* 13 (Oct. 1977): 717-18.

Willard Spiegelman, "Landscape and Knowledge: The Poetry of Elizabeth Bishop," *MPS* 6 (Winter 1975): 209-11.

"Brazil, January 1, 1502"

Bonnie Costello, "Vision and Mastery in Elizabeth Bishop," *TCL* 28 (Winter 1982): 351-70.

Alicia Ostriker, "Dancing at the Devil's Party: Some Notes on Politics and Poetry," *CritI* 13 (Spring 1987): 584-85.

"Cape Breton"

Sybil P. Estess, "Toward the Interior: Epiphany in 'Cape Breton' as Representative Poem," *WLT* 51 (Winter 1977): 49-52.

Marjorie Perloff, "Elizabeth Bishop: The Course of a Particular," *MPS* 8 (Winter 1977): 188-90.

Willard Spiegelman, "Elizabeth Bishop's 'Natural Heroism,'" *CentR* 22 (Winter 1978): 28-44.

"The Colder the Air"

Karl F. Thompson, *Expl* 12 (Mar. 1954): 33. Reprinted in *The Explicator Cyclopedia* 1:18.

Complete Poems

Helen Vendler, "The Poems of Elizabeth Bishop," *CritI* 13 (Summer 1987): 825-38.

"Crusoe in England"

Patricia B. Wallace, "The Wildness of Elizabeth Bishop," *SR* 93 (Winter 1985): 95-115.

"The End of March"

Patricia B. Wallace, "The Wildness of Elizabeth Bishop," *SR* 93 (Winter 1985): 95-115.

"Faustina, or Rock Roses"

Willard Spiegelman, "Elizabeth Bishop's 'Natural Heroism,'" *CentR* 22 (Winter 1978): 28-44.

"First Death in Nova Scotia"

Martha Carlson-Bradley, "Lowell's 'My Last Afternoon with Uncle Devereux Winslow': The Model for Bishop's 'First Death in Nova Scotia,'" *CP* 19 (1986): 117-31.

"The Fish"

Sybil P. Estess, "Elizabeth Bishop: The Delicate Art of Map Making," *SoR* 13 (Oct. 1977): 713-17.

Crale D. Hopkins, "Inspiration as Theme: Art and Nature in the Poetry of Elizabeth Bishop," *ArQ* 32 (Autumn 1976): 200-202.

R. E. McFarland, "Some Observations on Elizabeth Bishop's 'The Fish,'" *ArQ* 38 (Winter 1982): 364-76.

Nancy L. McNally, "Elizabeth Bishop: The Discipline of Description," *TCL* 11 (Jan. 1966): 192-94.

Richard Moore, "Elizabeth Bishop: 'The Fish,'" *Boston University Studies in English* 2 (Winter 1956-57): 251-59.

Perrine and Reid, *100 American Poems*, 212-13.

Willard Spiegelman, "Elizabeth Bishop's 'Natural Heroism,'" *CentR* 22 (Winter 1978): 28-44.

"Florida"

Charles Sanders, *Expl* 39 (Fall 1980): 16-17.

"Gentleman of Shalott"

Mutlu Konuk Blasing, "'Mont d'Espoir or Mount Despair,' The Re-verses of Elizabeth Bishop," *ConL* 25 (1984): 341-53.

Blasing, *American Poetry: The Rhetoric of Its Forms*, 102-5.

Charles Sanders, *Expl* 42 (Fall 1983): 55-56.

"Geography III"

Lorrie Goldensohn, "Elizabeth Bishop's Originality," *APR* 7 (Mar./Apr. 1978): 18-22.

Leonard S. Marcos, "Elizabeth Bishop: The Poet as Mapmaker," *MQR* 17 (1978): 108-18.

"The Imaginary Iceberg"

Willard Spiegelman, "Landscape and Knowledge: The Poetry of Elizabeth Bishop," *MPS* 6 (Winter 1975): 215-16.

"In the Waiting Room"

Lee Edelman, "The Geography of Gender: Elizabeth Bishop's 'In the Waiting Room,'" *ConL* 26 (1985): 179-96.

Ostriker, *Stealing the Language*, 70-72.

Lorna Jean Silver, "Waiting to Wait," *Susquehanna University Studies* 11 (1980): 90-96.

Willard Spiegelman, "Elizabeth Bishop's 'Natural Heroism,'" *CentR* 22 (Winter 1978): 28-44.

Patricia B. Wallace, "The Wildness of Elizabeth Bishop," *SR* 93 (Winter 1985): 95-115.

"The Man-Moth"

Mills, *Contemporary American Poetry*, 78-82.

"Manuelzinho"

Von Hallberg, *American Poetry and Culture, 1945-1980*, passim.

Willard Spiegelman, "Elizabeth Bishop's 'Natural Heroism,'" *CentR* 22 (Winter 1978): 28-44.

"The Map"

Blasing, *American Poetry: The Rhetoric of Its Forms*, 106-8.

Sybil P. Estess, "Elizabeth Bishop: The Delicate Art of Map Making," *SoR* 13 (Oct. 1977): 708-13.

Frankenberg, *Pleasure Dome*, 331-33. Reprinted in Engle and Carrier, *Reading Modern Poetry*, 228-29.

"A Miracle for Breakfast"

Charles Sanders, "A Hol[e]y Communion: Elizabeth Bishop's 'A Miracle for Breakfast,'" *Notes on Modern American Literature* 5 (Spring 1981): item 14.

"Monument"

Nancy L. McNally, "Elizabeth Bishop: The Discipline of Description," *TCL* 11 (Jan. 1966): 194-97.

Richard Mullen, "Elizabeth Bishop's Surrealistic Inheritance," *AL* 54 (Mar. 1982): 63-80.

Marjorie Perloff, "Elizabeth Bishop: The Course of a Particular," *MPS* 8 (Winter 1977): 185-87.

Charles Sanders, *Expl* 40 (Summer 1982): 54-55.

"The Moose"

Willard Spiegelman, "Elizabeth Bishop's 'Natural Heroism,'" *CentR* 22 (Winter 1978): 28-44.

Patricia B. Wallace, "The Wildness of Elizabeth Bishop," *SR* 93 (Winter 1985): 95-115.

North and South

Lloyd Schwartz, "The Mechanical Horse and The Indian Princess: Two Poems from *North and South*," *WLT* 51 (Winter 1977): 41-44.

"One Art"

Blasing, *American Poetry: The Rhetoric of Its Forms*, 106-7.

David Shapiro, "On a Villanelle by Elizabeth Bishop," *IowaR* 10 (Winter 1979): 77-81.

"Over 2000 Illustrations and a Complete Concordance"

Jennifer Krauss, *Expl* 42 (Summer 1984): 47-48.

Von Hallberg, *American Poetry and Culture, 1945-1980*, passim.

"Poem"

Sybil P. Estess, "Elizabeth Bishop: The Delicate Art of Map Making," *SoR* 13 (Oct. 1977): 721-26.

"Quai d'Orleans"

Mills, *Contemporary American Poetry*, 75-77.

"Questions of Travel"

Crale D. Hopkins, "Inspiration as Theme: Art and Nature in the Poetry of Elizabeth Bishop," *MPS* 8 (Spring 1977): 208-12.

Willard Spiegelman, "Landscape and Knowledge: The Poetry of Elizabeth Bishop," *MPS* 6 (Winter 1975): 218-20.

"Roosters"

Charles Sanders, *Expl* 38 (Spring 1980): 28-29.

Charles Sanders, *Expl* 40 (Summer 1982): 55-57.

Willard Spiegelman, "Elizabeth Bishop's 'Natural Heroism,'" *CentR* 22 (Winter 1978): 28-44.

"The Sandpiper"

Sybil P. Estess, "Elizabeth Bishop: The Delicate Art of Map Making," *SoR* 13 (Oct. 1977): 719-21.

"Sonnet"

Sanders, "Bishop's 'Sonnets,'" *Expl* 40 (Spring 1983): 63-64.

"Visits to St. Elizabeth's"

Joyce M. Wegs, "Poets in Bedlam: Sexton's Use of Bishop's 'Visits to St. Elizabeth's,' in 'Ringing the Bells,'" *CP* 15 (1982): 37-47.

"Wading at Wellfleet"

Willard Spiegelman, "Elizabeth Bishop's 'Natural Heroism,'" *CentR* 22 (Winter 1978): 28-44.

BISHOP, JOHN PEALE

"Ballet"

S. C. Moore, *Expl* 23 (Oct. 1964): 12.

"Behavior of the Sun"

R. W. Stallman, *Expl* 5 (Oct. 1946): 6. Reprinted in *The Explicator Cyclopedia* 1:18-19.

R. W. Stallman, "The Poetry of John Peale Bishop," *Western Review* 11 (Autumn 1946): 15-16.

"Divine Nativity"

Joseph Frank, "Force and Form: A Study of John Peale Bishop," *SR* 55 (Winter 1947): 97-98.

"O Let Not Virtue Seek"

Frank, "Force and Form," 91-93.

"Perspectives Are Precipices"

R. W. Stallman, *Expl* 5 (Nov. 1946): 8. Reprinted in *The Explicator Cyclopedia* 1:19-20.

R. W. Stallman, "The Poetry of John Peale Bishop," *Western Review* 11 (Autumn 1946): 17-19.

Allan Tate, "A Note on Bishop's Poetry," *SoR* 1 (Autumn 1935): 362-63.

Tate, *Reactionary Essays on Poetry and Ideas*, 60-62. Reprinted in Tate, *On the Limits of Poetry*, 244-46.

"A Recollection"

R. W. Stallman, *Expl* 19 (April 1961): 43. Reprinted in *The Explicator Cyclopedia* 1:20-21.

"The Return"

Allan Tate, "A Note on Bishop's Poetry," *SoR* 1 (Autumn 1935): 361-62.

Tate, *Reactionary Essays on Poetry and Ideas*, 58-60. Reprinted in Tate, *On the Limits of Poetry*, 243-44.

"The Saints"

Joseph Frank, "Force and Form: A Study of John Peale Bishop," *SR* 55 (Winter 1947): 95-96.

"Southern Pines"

R. W. Stallman, *Expl* 4 (Apr. 1946): 46. Reprinted in *The Explicator Cyclopedia* 1:21-22.

R. W. Stallman, "The Poetry of John Peale Bishop," *Western Review* 11 (Autumn 1946): 10-12.

"Speaking of Poetry"

Deutsch, *Poetry in Our Time*, 191-93.

Joseph Frank, "Force and Form: A Study of John Peale Bishop," *SR* 55 (Winter 1947): 83-86.

"The Tree"

Joseph Frank, "Force and Form: A Study of John Peale Bishop," *SR* 55 (Winter 1947): 98-99.

"Twelfth Night"

Joseph Frank, "Force and Form: A Study of John Peale Bishop," *SR* 55 (Winter 1947): 79-80.

BISSETT, BILL

[Interview]

Maidie Hilmo, "Interview with Bill Bissett," *Essays on Canadian Writing* 32 (Summer 1986): 134-46.

"Blew Ointment"

Caroline Bayard, "Bill Bissett: Subversion et poésie concrete," *ELit* 19 (Fall 1986): 81-108.

"how do yu pik sum"

McCaffery, *North of Intention*, 93-106.

"The Semantic Attack: Grammar"

McCaffery, *North of Intention*, 93-106.

Sunday Work

McCaffery, *North of Intention*, 93-106.

Vancouver mainland ice & cold storage

McCaffery, *North of Intention*, 93-106.

"voices
thank yu   what"

McCaffery, *North of Intention*, 93-106.

BLACKBURN, PAUL

"The Net of Moon"

Michael Davidson, "'By ear, he sd': Audio-Tape and Contemporary Criticism," *Credences*, n.s. 1 (1981): passim.

BLACKMUR, R. P.

"Elegy for Five"

Bloom, *The Stock of Available Reality: R. P. Blackmur and John Berryman*, 83-85.

"Judas Priest," Sonnet III:
"Judas, Not Pilate, Had a Wakened Mind"

Tate, *Reason in Madness*, 175-79.

"Missa Vocis"

Donald A. Stauffer, "Genesis, of the Poet as Maker," in *Poets at Work*, 43-52.

"The Spear"

Tate, *Reason in Madness*, 174-75,

BLY, ROBERT

[Interview]

Mary Lammon, "Something Hard to Get Rid Of: An Interview with Robert Bly," *Ploughshares* 8 (1982): 11-23.

"Afternoon Sleep"

Nelson, *Robert Bly*, passim.

"Driving Toward the La Qui Parle River"

Lacey, *The Inner War*, 39-41.
Nelson, *Robert Bly*, passim.

"Hunting Pheasants in a Cornfield"

Nelson, *Robert Bly*, passim.

The Light Around the Body

Mersmann, *Out of the Vietnam Vortex: A Study of Poets and Poetry Against the War*, 113-57.

"Like the New Moon I Will Live My Life"

Lensing and Moran, *Four Poets and the Emotive Imagination*, 81.

"Meeting the Man Who Wants Me"

Michael Atkinson, "Robert Bly's *Sleepers Joining Hands*: Shadow and Self," *IowaR* 7 (Fall 1976): 145-48.

"Night Journey in the Cooking Pot"

Michael Atkinson, "Robert Bly's *Sleepers Joining Hands*: Shadow and Self,"
IowaR 7 (Fall 1976): 145-48.

"Return to Solitude"

Nelson, *Robert Bly*, passim.

Silence in the Snow Fields

Lawrence Kramer, "A Sensible Emptiness: Robert Bly and the Poetics of
Immanence," *ConL* 24 (Winter 1983): 449-62.

Sleepers Joining Hands

Michael Atkinson, "Robert Bly's *Sleepers Joining Hands*: Shadow and Self,"
IowaR 7 (Fall 1976): 138-41.

William V. Davis, "At the Edges of the Light: A Reading of Robert Bly's
Sleepers Joining Hands," in Jones and Daniels, *Of Solitude and Silence:
Writings on Robert Bly*, 250-67.

David Seal, "Waking to Sleepers Joining Hands," in Jones and Daniels, *Of
Solitude and Silence: Writings on Robert Bly*, 219-48.

"Talking All Morning"

Tom Hansen, "On Writing Poetry: Four Contemporary Poets," *CE* 44 (Mar.
1982): 265-73.

"The Teeth Mother Naked at Last"

Michael Atkinson, "Robert Bly's *Sleepers Joining Hands*: Shadow and Self,"
IowaR 7 (Fall 1976): 138-41.

Lawrence Kramer, "A Sensible Emptiness: Robert Bly and the Poetics of
Immanence," *ConL* 24 (Winter 1983): 449-62.

Lacey, *The Inner War*, 51-55.

N. F. Thornton, "Robert Bly's Poetry and the Haiku," *CLS* 20 (Spring 1983): 1-13.

This Body Is Made of Camphor and Gopherwood

William V. Davis, "Camphor and Gopherwood: Robert Bly's Recent Poems in Prose," *MPS* 11 (1982): 88-102.

"This Tree Will Be Here for a Thousand Years"

Lawrence Kramer, "A Sensible Emptiness: Robert Bly and the Poetics of Immanence," *ConL* 24 (Winter 1983): 449-62.

"Three Kinds of Pleasures"

Nelson, *Robert Bly*, passim.

"Watering the Horse"

Lacey, *The Inner War*, 38-39.

"With Pale Women in Maryland"

Victoria Frenkel Harris, "Relationship and Change: Text and Content of James Wright's 'Blue Teal Mother' and Robert Bly's 'With Pale Women in Maryland,'" *AmerP* 3 (Fall 1985): 43-55.

BOGAN, LOUISE

"Ad Castitatem"

Pope, *A Separate Vision*, passim.

"The Alchemist"

Diane Wood Middlebrook, "The Problem of the Woman Aritst: Louise Bogan, 'The Alchemist,'" in Collins, *Critical Essays on Louise Bogan*, 180-94.

BOGAN, LOUISE

"The Blue Estuaries"

Donna Dorian, "Knowledge Puffeth Up," *Parnassus* 12-13 (Spring/Winter 1985): 144-59.

"Body of This Death"

Deborah Pope, "Music in the Granite Hill," in Collins, *Critical Essays on Louise Bogan*, 146-66.

"Cassandra"

Diane Wood Middlebrook, "The Problem of the Woman Artist: Louise Bogan," in Collins, *Critical Essays on Louise Bogan*, 174-80.

"The Dream"

Perrine and Reid, *100 American Poems*, 146-47.

Pope, *A Separate Vision*, passim.

"The Exhortation"

Winters, *Forms of Discovery*, 279-81.

"Fifteenth Farewell"

Diane Wood Middlebrook, "The Problem of the Woman Artist: Louise Bogan," in Collins, *Critical Essays on Louise Bogan*, 174-80.

"Portrait of the Artist as a Young Woman"

Ruth Limmer, "Circumscriptions," in Collins, *Critical Essays on Louise Bogan*, 166-74.

"Psychiatrist's Recitative and Aria"

Sandra Cookson, "The Repressed Becomes the Poem: Landscape and Quest in Two Poems by Louise Bogan," in Collins, *Critical Essays on Louise Bogan*, 194-203.

"Putting to Sea"

Sandra Cookson, "The Repressed Becomes the Poem: Landscape and Quest in Two Poems by Louise Bogan," in Collins, *Critical Essays on Louise Bogan*, 194-203.

"Simple Autumnal"

Winters, *Forms of Discovery*, 278-79.

"Solitary Observations"

Daniels, *The Art of Reading Poetry*, 199-200.

"A Tale"

Pope, *A Separate Vision*, passim.

BOLLING, ROBERT

"Neanthe"

J. A. Leo Lamay, "Southern Colonial Grotesque: Robert Bolling's 'Neanthe,'" *MissQ* 35 (Spring 1982): 97-112.

BOOTH, PHILIP

"Letter from a Distant Land"

Rotella, *Three Contemporary Poets of New England*, 64-127.

BOWEN, ELIZABETH

"The Demon Lover"

D. V. Faustino, "Elizabeth Bowen's 'The Demon Lover': Psychosis or Seduction?" *SSF* 17 (1980): 483-87.

BOWERING, GEORGE

Allophanes

McCaffery, *North of Intention*, 131-42.

Kerrisdale Elegies

Smaro Kamboureli, "Stealing the Text: George Bowering's *Kerrisdale Elegies* and Dennis Colley's *Bloody Jack*," *CanL* 115 (Winter 1987): 9-23.

A Short Sad Book

L. K. MacKendrick, "The Comic, the Centripetal Text, and the Canadian Novel," *ESC* 10 (Sept. 1984): 343-56.

BOWERS, EDGAR

"Adam's Song to Heaven"

Helen P. Trimpi, "Contexts for 'Being,' 'Divinity,' and 'Self' in Valéry and Edgar Bowers," *SoR*, n.s. 13 (Winter 1977): 69-70, 72-80.

"The Astronomers of Mont Blanc"

Winters, *Forms of Discovery*, 284-86.

"Autumn Shade"

Helen P. Trimpi, "Contexts for 'Being,' 'Divinity,' and 'Self' in Valéry and Edgar Bowers," *SoR*, n.s. 13 (Winter 1977): 69-70, 72-80.

"Dark Earth and Summer"

Richard G. Stern, "The Poetry of Edgar Bowers," *ChiR* 11 (Autumn 1957): 73-75.

Winters, *Forms of Discovery*, 283-84.

"Grove and Building"

Helen P. Trimpi, "Contexts for 'Being,' 'Divinity,' and 'Self' in Valéry and Edgar Bowers," *SoR*, n.s. 13 (Winter 1977): 49-50.

"Oedipus at Colonus"

Helen P. Trimpi, "Contexts for 'Being,' 'Divinity,' and 'Self' in Valéry and Edgar Bowers," *SoR*, n.s. 13 (Winter 1977): 50-51.

"A Song for Rising"

Helen P. Trimpi, "Contexts for 'Being,' 'Divinity,' and 'Self' in Valéry and Edgar Bowers," *SoR*, n.s. 13 (Winter 1977): 81-82.

"The Stoic"

Winters, *Forms of Discovery*, 287-288.

"Variations on an Elizabethan Theme"

Helen P. Trimpi, "Contexts for 'Being,' Divinity,' and 'Self' in Valéry and Edgar Bowers," *SoR*, n.s. 13 (Winter 1977): 71-72.

BOYD, MARK A.

"Fra Bank to Bank, Fra Wood to Wood I Rin"

Winters, *Forms of Discovery*, 325-26.

BRAUN, RICHARD E.

"Against Nature"

Jerome Mazzaro, "Putting It Together: The Poetry of Richard Emil Braun," *MPS* 5 (Winter 1974): 256-58.

BRINNIN

"The Alps"

Daivd Daiches, "Some Notes on Contemporary American Poetry," in Rajan, *Modern American Poetry*, 113-14.

"The Fortunate Isles"

Beach, *Obsessive Images*, 136-37.

"Goodnight, When the Door Swings"

David Daiches, "Some Notes on Contemporary American Poetry," in Rajan, *Modern American Poetry*, 114.

"Islands: A Song"

Beach, *Obsessive Images*, 135-36.

"A Sail"

Beach, *Obsessive Images*, 166-68.

"Second Sight"

Beach, *Obsessive Images*, 168-69.

"Skin Diving in the Virgins"

Perrine and Reid, *100 American Poems*, 239.

"Views of the Favorite Colleges"

Sr. Mary Humiliata, I.H.M., *Expl* 14 (Jan. 1956): 20. Reprinted in *The Explicator Cyclopedia* 1:22-23.

John Theobald, "The World in a Cross Word," *Poetry* 71 (Nov. 1947): 82-90.

BROMIGE, DAVID

[Interview]

Barry Alpert, "Interview," *Vort* 3 (1973): 2-23.

Ends of the Earth

Michael Davidson, "The Dreamwork," *Vort* 3 (1973): 24-26.

Threads

Michael Davidson, "The Dreamwork," *Vort* 3 (1973): 24-26.

BRONK, WILLIAM

Silence or Metaphor

Robert Bertholf, "On William Bronk, His Silence and Metaphor," *Credences* 1 (1977): 34-41.

"We aren't even here but in a real house"

Dana Gioia, "Business and Poetry," *HudR* 36 (Spring 1983): 147-71.

BROOKE

"The Soldier"

Daniels, *The Art of Reading*, 270-72.

BROOKS, GWENDOLYN

[Interview]

Gloria T. Hull and Posey Gallagher, "Update on Part I: An Interview With Gwendolyn Brooks," *CLAJ* 21 (Sept. 1977): 19-40.

"A Bronzeville Mother Loiters in Mississippi, Meanwhile, A Mississippi Mother Burns Bacon"

Maria K. Mootry, *Expl* 42 (Summer 1984): 51-52.

"The Chicago Picasso"

William H. Hansell, "Aestheticism Versus Political Militancy in Gwendolyn Brooks' 'The Chicago Picasso' and 'The Wall,'" *CLAJ* 17 (Sept. 1973): 11-13.

"The Children of the Poor"

Hayden Carruth, *Poetry: A Critical Supplement*, Mar. 1949, 16-18.

"In the Mecca"

Haki R. Madhubuti, "Hard Words and Clear Songs: The Writing of Black Poetry," in *Tapping Potential: English and Language Arts for the Black Learner*, ed. Charlotte K. Brooks, Jerrie Cobb Scott, Miriam Chaplin et al. (Urbana: Black Caucus of National Council of Teachers of English, 1985), 168-75.

"A Light and Diplomatic Bird"

Hayden Carruth, *Poetry: A Critical Supplement*, Mar. 1949, 16-18.

"Old People Working"

William H. Hansell, "The Poet-Militant and Foreshadowing of a Black Mystique: Poems in the Second Period of Gwendolyn Brooks," *CP* 10 (Fall 1977): 37-45.

"Piano After War"

Alan C. Lupaek, *Expl* 36 (Summer 1978): 2-3.

"Riders"

William H. Hansell, "The Poet-Militant and Foreshadowing of a Black Mystique: Poems in the Second Period of Gwendolyn Brooks," *CP* 10 (Fall 1977): 37-45.

"Satin-Less"

R. B. Miller, "'Does Man Love Art?' The Humanistic Aesthetics of Gwendolyn Brooks," in *Black American Literature and Humanism*, 95-112.

Songs After Sunset

Erlene Stetson, "*Songs After Sunset* (1935-1936): The Unpublished Poetry of Gwendolyn Elizabeth Brooks," *CLAJ* 24 (Sept. 1980): 87-96.

"Sonnets"

Gladys Margaret Williams, "Gwendolyn Brooks's Way with the Sonnet," *CLAJ* 26 (Dec. 1982): 215-40.

"Spaulding and Francois"

William H. Hansell, "The Poet-Militant and Foreshadowing of a Black Mystique: Poems in the Second Period of Gwendolyn Brooks," *CP* 10 (Fall 1977): 37-45.

"The Sundays of Satin-Legs Smith"

Larry R. Andrews, "Ambivalent Clothes Imagery in Gwendolyn Brooks's 'The Sundays of Satin-Legs Smith,'" *CLAJ* 24 (Dec. 1980): 150-63.

"The Third Sermon on the Warpland"

William H. Hansell, "The Role of Violence in Recent Poems of Gwendolyn Brooks," *SBL* 5 (Summer 1974): 22-25.

"The Wall"

William H. Hansell, "Aestheticism Versus Political Militancy in Gwendolyn Brooks's 'The Chicago Picasso' and 'The Wall,'" *CLAJ* 17 (Sept. 1973): 13-15.

"We Real Cool"

Barbara B. Sims, *Expl* 34 (Apr. 1976): 58.

BROPHY, BRIGID

By Grand Central Station I Sat Down and Wept

Alice Van Wart, "*By Grand Central Station I Sat Down and Wept*: The Novel as Poem," *SCL* 11 (1986): 38-51.

BROUGHTON, JAMES

The Androgyne Journal

Robert Peters, "James Broughton" [Interview], in Leyland, *Gay Sunshine Interviews*, 2:35.

The Gift to Be Simple

Robert Peters, "James Broughton" [Interview], in Leyland, *Gay Sunshine Interviews*, 29-30, passim.

BROUMAS, OLGA

Beginning with O

M. J. Carruthers, "Revision of the Muse: Adrienne Rich, Audre Lorde, Judy Grahn, Olga Broumas," *HudR* 36 (Summer 1983): 293-322.

BROWN, HARRY

"Fourth Elegy: The Poet Compared to an Unsuccessful General"

Hayden Carruth, The Poet With Wounds," *Poetry* 71 (Jan. 1948): 217-21.

J. F. Nims, *Poetry: A Critical Supplement*, Jan. 1948, 2-12.

BROWN, THOMAS

"My Garden"

Daniels, *The Art of Reading Poetry*, 261.

BUCHANAN, ROBERT

"The Ballad of Judas Iscariot"

Cunningham, *Literature as a Fine Art: Analysis and Interpretation*, 98-99.

BUKOWSKI, CHARLES

"Dangling in the Tournefortia"

David E. James, "Poetry/Punk/Production: Some Recent Writing in L.A.," *MinnR*, n.s. 23 (Fall 1984): 127-48.

"fire station"

Russell T. Harrison, "An Analysis of Charles Bukowski's 'fire station,'" *CP* 18 (1985): 67-83.

BULLOCK, MICHAEL

Brambled Heart

Jack F. Stewart, "Image and Mood: Recent Poems by Michael Bullock," *CanL* 115 (Winter 1987): 107-21.

Poems on Green Paper

Jack F. Stewart, "Image and Mood: Recent Poems by Michael Bullock," *CanL* 115 (Winter 1987): 107-21.

Vancouver Moods

Jack F. Stewart, "Image and Mood: Recent Poems by Michael Bullock," *CanL* 115 (Winter 1987): 107-21.

BURKE, KENNETH

"Three Seasons of Love"

John Ciardi, "The Critic of Love," *Nation* 181 (Oct. 8, 1955): 307.

BURKE, SHARON

"People of the Gleaming City"

Ruthe T. Sheffey, "Rhetorical Structure in Contemporary Afro-American Poetry," *CLAJ* 24 (Sept. 1980): 97-107.

BUSH, BARNEY

My Horse and a Jukebox

Kenneth Lincoln, "Native American Literature: 'old like hills, like stars,'" in Baker, *Three American Literatures*, 133-35.

Lincoln, *Native American Renaissance*, passim.

BYNNER, WITTER

"Eden Tree"

R. P. Blackmur, "Versions of Solitude," *Poetry* 39 (Jan. 1932): 217-21.

CAGE, JOHN

Empty Words

John Cage, "Empty Words with Relevant Material," in Waldman and Webb, *Talking Poetics from Naropa Institute* 1:195-220.

Marjorie Perloff, "Unimpededness and Interpenetration: The Poetic of John Cage," *TriQ* 54 (Spring 1982): 76-88.

M. C. Richards, "John Cage and the Way of the Ear," *TriQ* 54 (Spring 1982): 110-21.

"For the Birds"

Joan Retallack, "High Adventures of Indeterminacy," *Parnassus* 11 (Spring/Summer 1983): 231-63.

HPSCHD

Andrew Stiller, "John Cage's *HPSCHD*," *Credences*, n.s. 1 (1981): passim.

CAMPBELL, JOSEPH

"The Dancer"

Clark, *Lyric Resonance*, 85-90.

CANE, MELVILLE

"April Flurry"

Melville Cane, "Snow: Themes with Variations," *ASch* 22 (Winter 1952-53): 101-2.

"Deep in Wagon-Ruts"

Melville Cane, "Snow: Theme with Variations," *ASch* 22 (Winter 1952-53): 97.

"Hither and Thither"

Melville Cane, "Snow: Theme with Variations," *ASch* 22 (Winter 1952-53): 99-101.

"Hopkinson"

Melville Cane, "Concerning 'Hopkinson,'" *University of Kansas City Review* 17 (Summer 1951): 288-93.

"January Garden"

Melville Cane, "Snow: Theme with Variations," *ASch* 22 (Winter 1952-53): 97-98.

"Last Night It Snowed"

Melville Cane, "Snow: Theme with Variations," *ASch* 22 (Winter 1952-53): 98-99.

"Presence of Snow"

Melville Cane, "Snow: Theme with Variations," *ASch* 22 (Winter 1952-53): 104-5.

"Snow in April"

Melville Cane, "Snow: Theme with Variations," *ASch* 22 (Winter 1952-53): 102-4.

"White Fog"

Melville Cane, "Snow: Theme with Variations," *ASch* 22 (Winter 1952-53): 96-97.

CARY, ALIVE

"Make Believe"

Cooper and Holmes, *Preface to Poetry*, 211-13.

CERVANTES, LORNA DEE

"Beneath the Shadow of the Freeway"

Norwood and Monk, *The Desert Is No Lady*, passim.

"Oaxaca"

Sánchez, *Contemporary Chicano Poetry*, 98.

"Refugee Ship"

Sánchez, *Contemporary Chicano Poetry*, 87, 98, 122.

"Visions of Mexico"

Sánchez, *Contemporary Chicano Poetry*, 94-97, 99-103.

•

CERVENKA, EXENE

"Adulterers Anonymous"

David E. James, "Poetry/Punk/Production: Some Recent Writing in L.A.," *MinnR*, n.s. 23 (Fall 1984): 127-48.

CHAPPELL, FRED

"Midquest"

R. T. Smith, "Fred Chappell's Rural Vigil and the Fifth Element in 'Midquest,'" *MissQ* 37 (Winter 1983-84): 31-38.

"River"

Donald Secreast, "Images of Impure Water in Chappell's *River*," *MissQ* 37 (Winter 1983-1984): 39-44.

CHEEVER, JOHN

"The Enormous Radio"

Christine W. Sizemore, "The Sweeney Allusion in John Cheever's 'Enormous Radio,'" *NConL* 7 (Sept. 1977): 9.

CHISOLM, HUGH

"Lament of the Lovers"

Leonard Unger, "Seven Poets," *SR* 56 (Winter 1948): 169.

CIARDI, JOHN

"Letter to Virginia Johnson"

Harvey Curtis Webster, "Humanism as the Father Face," *Poetry* 70 (June 1947): 146-50.

"Metropolitan Ice Co."

Hayden Carruth and John Ciardi, *Poetry: A Critical Supplement*, Apr. 1949, 15-18.

"The Size of Song"

Edward Cifelli, "The Size of John Ciardi's Song," *CEA* 36 (Nov. 1973): 22-27.

"Tenzone"

Edward J. Gallagher, *Expl* 27 (Dec. 1968): 28.

Laurence Perrine, *Expl* 28 (May 1970): 82.

"To Judith"

J. F. Nims, *Poetry: A Critical Supplement*, Feb. 1948, 10-16.

"To Judith Asleep"

Hayden Carruth, *Poetry: A Critical Supplement*, Apr. 1949, 18-19.

CLARK, DAVID R.

"The Bee Space"

Clark, *Lyric Resonance*, 210-11.

CLARK, DAVID R.

"Mountain Ash"

Clark, *Lyric Resonance*, 211-15.

"Robin"

Clark, *Lyric Resonance*, 204-6.

"Tree"

Clark, *Lyric Resonance*, 207-10.

CLARKE, GEORGE ELLIOTT

Saltwater Spirituals and Deeper Blues

M. Travis Lane, "An Impoverished Style: The Poetry of George Elliott Clarke," *CanPo* 16 (Spring/Summer 1985): 47-54.

CLIFTON, LUCILLE

"Admonitions"

Alicia Ostriker, "Dancing at the Devil's Party: Some Notes on Politics and Poetry," *CritI* (Spring 1987): 584-85.

COHEN, LEONARD

[Interview]

Robert Sward and Pat Keeney Smith, "An Interview with Leonard Cohen," *Malahat Review* 77 (Dec. 1986): 55-63.

"Death of a Lady's Man"

Ken Norris, "Healing Itself the Moment It Is Condemned: Cohen's 'Death of Lady's Man,'" *CanPo* 20 (Spring/Summer 1987): 51-60.

"Go by Brooks, Love"

Don Gutteridge, "The Affective Fallacy and the Student's Response to Poetry," *EJ* 61 (Feb. 1972): 217-21.

COLEMAN, WANDA

"Mad Dog Black Lady"

David E. James, "Poetry/Punk/Production: Some Recent Writing in L.A.," *MinnR*, n.s. 23 (Fall 1984): 127-48.

CONGDON, KIRBY

[Interview]

Maurice Kenny, "Kirby Congdon," in Leyland, *Gay Sunshine Interviews* 2:42-54.

Dream-Work (1970)

Maurice Kenny, "Kirby Congdon," in Leyland, *Gay Sunshine Interviews* 2:42-54.

"If the final winds were to come"

Maurice Kenny, "Kirby Congdon," in Leyland, *Gay Sunshine Interviews* 2:42-54.

COOLEY, DENNIS

Bloody Jack

Smaro Kamboureli, "Stealing the Text: George Bowering's *Kerrisdale Elegies* and Dennis Cooley's *Bloody Jack*," *CanL* 115 (Winter 1987): 9-23.

COOLIDGE, CLARK

The Maintains

Bernstein, *Content's Dream: Essays 1975-1984*, 259-65.

Space

Bernstein, *Content's Dream: Essays 1975-1984*, 259-65.
McCaffery, *North of Intention*, 21-22, 26-27.

COOPER, DENNIS

"The Tenderness of Wolves"

David E. Jones, "Poetry/Punk/Production: Some Recent Writing in L.A.,"
MinnR, n.s. 23 (Fall 1984): 127-48.

CORN, ALFRED

"A Call in the Midst of a Crowd"

Martin, *The Homosexual Tradition in American Poetry*, 208-17.

COULETTE, HENRI

[Interview]

Michael S. Harper, "Michael Harper Interviews Henri Coulette," *IowaR* 13
(Spring 1982): 62-84.

COWLEY, MALCOLM

[Interview]

Susan J. Shephard, "Talking with Malcolm Cowley," *Book Forum* 7 (1984):
11-12.

Warren Herendeen and Donald G. Parker, "An Interview with Malcolm Cowley," *VCom* 1 (Summer 1981): 9-22.

"The Long Voyage"

Perrine and Reid, *100 American Poems*, 172.

Perrine, *The Art of Total Relevance*, 122-24.

"The Source"

J. F. Nims, *Poetry: A Critical Supplement*, Apr. 1948: 12-13.

COXE, LOUIS O.

"Gunner's Mate"

Leonard Unger, "Seven Poets," *SR* 56 (Winter 1948): 160-61.

CRANE, HART

"The Air Plant"

O'Connor, *Sense and Sensibility in Modern Poetry*, 148.

Eric J. Sundquist, "Bringing Home the Word: Magic, Lies, and Silence in Hart Crane," *ELH* 44 (Summer 1977): 394-95.

"And Yet This Great Wink of Eternity"

Drew, *Directions in Modern Poetry*, 212-17.

"Atlantis"

Clark, *Lyric Resonance*, 141-45.

Friar and Brinnin, *Modern Poetry*, 453-55.

Eric J. Sundquist, "Bringing Home the Word: Magic, Lies, and Silence in Hart Crane," *ELH* 44 (Summer 1977): 392-93.

Vogler, *Preludes to Vision*, 191-94.

"At Melville's Tomb"

Brooks and Warren, *Understanding Poetry*, 477-82; rev. ed., 333-36.

Clark, *Lyric Resonance*, 152-58.

Hart Crane, quoted in *Hart Crane* by Brom Weber. Reprinted in Stallman, *The Critic's Notebook*, 242-47.

Eastman, *The Literary Mind*, 94-97.

Philip Furia, *Expl* 33 (May 1975): 73.

R. W. B. Lewis, "Crane's Visionary Lyric: The Way to *The Bridge*," *MR* 7 (Spring 1966): 242-48.

Harriet Monroe and Hart Crane, "A Discussion with Hart Crane," *Poetry* 29 (Oct. 1926): 34-41. Reprinted in Locke, Gibson, and Arms, *Readings for Liberal Education*, 3d ed., 229-34; 4th ed., 231-36; 5th ed., 214-19.

Peter J. Sheehan, "Hart Crane and the Contemporary Search," *EJ* 60 (Dec. 1971): 1212-13.

Richard Strier, "The Poetics of Surrender: An Exposition and Critique of New Critical Poetics," *CritI* 2 (Autumn 1975): 182-86.

"Ave Maria"

Friar and Brinnin, *Modern Poetry*, 451-52.

Vogler, *Preludes to Vision*, 149-53.

"Belle Isle"

Evelyn J. Hinz, "Hart Crane's 'Voyages' Reconsidered," *ConL* 13 (Summer 1972), 325-33.

"Black Tambourine"

Gray, *American Poetry*, 219-20.

Milne Holton, "'A Boudelairesque Thing': The Direction of Hart Crane's 'Black Tambourine,'" *Criticism* 9 (Summer 1967): 215-28.

Edward Kessler, *Expl* 29 (Sept. 1970): 4.

Peter J. Sheehan, "Hart Crane and the Contemporary Search," *EJ* 60 (Dec. 1971): 1210-11.

"The Bridge"

Joseph J. Arpad, "Hart Crane's Platonic Myth: The Brooklyn Bridge," *AL* 39 (Mar. 1967): 75-86.

Joeph Warren Beach, "The Cancelling Out--A Note on Recent Poetry," *Accent* 7 (Summer 1947): 245-46.

Blasing, *American Poetry: The Rhetoric of Its Forms*, 188-89, 197-99.

E. Brunner, *Splendid Failure: Hart Crane and the Making of "The Bridge"* (Urbana and Chicago: University of Illinois Press, 1985), passim.

Butterfield, *Modern American Poetry*, 127-41.

T. Chaffin, "Toward a Poetics of Technology: Hart Crane and the American Sublime," *SoR* 20 (Jan. 1984): 68-81.

Stanley K. Coffman, "Symbolism in *The Bridge*," *PMLA* 66 (Mar. 1951): 65-77.

R. L. Combs, *Hart Crane and the Psychology of Romanticism* (Memphis: Memphis State University Press), 42-107, 109-74.

Lawrence Dembo, "The Unfractioned Idiom of Hart Crane's *Bridge*," *AL* 27 (May 1955): 203-24.

Deutsch, *Poetry in Our Time*, 322-28.

Deutsch, *This Modern Poetry*, 141-48.

Dickie, *On the Modernist Long Poem*, 47-76.

Joseph Frank, "Hart Crane: American Poet," *SR* 62 (Winter 1949): 157-58.

Brewster Ghiselin, "Bridge into the Sea," *PR* 16 (July 1949): 679-686.

Gordon K. Grigsby, "Hart Crane's Doubtful Vision," *CE* 24 (Apr. 1963): 518-23.

Hoffman, *The Twenties*, 229-39.

J. Krauss, "'Times Square to Columbus Circle': The Dual Format of Hart Crane's *Bridge*," *ELWIU* 12, no. 2 (1985): 273-83.

Hilton Landry, "Of Prayer and Praise: The Poetry of Hart Crane," in Hoffman, *The Twenties*, 20-24.

James McMichael, "Hart Crane," *SoR* 8 (Apr. 1972): 290-309.

Martin, *The Homosexual Tradition in American Poetry*, passim.

Robert K. Martin, "Painting and Primitivism: Hart Crane and the Development of an American Expressionist Aesthetic," *Mosaic* 14 (Summer 1981): 49-62.

Howard Moss, "Disorder as Myth: Hart Crane's *The Bridge*," *Poetry* 62 (Apr. 1943): 32-45.

O'Connor, *Sense and Sensibility in Modern Poetry*, 19-25.

Pearce, *The Continuity of American Poetry*, 102-11.

V. Pemberton, "Hart Crane and Yvor Winters; Rebuttal and Review: A New Crane Letter," *AL* 50 (May 1978): 276-81.

Quinn, *The Metaphoric Tradition*, 147-65.

R. Ramsey, "A Poetics for *The Bridge*," *TCL* 26 (Fall 1980): 278-93

Rosenthal, *The Modern Poets*, 169-76.

Richard H. Rupp, "Hart Crane: Vitality as *Credo* in 'Atlantis,'" *MQ* 3 (Apr. 1962): 265-75.

M. Sharp, "Theme and Free Variation: The Scoring of Hart Crane's *The Bridge*," *AQ* 37 (Autumn 1981): 197-213.

Bernice Slote, "Structure of Hart Crane's *The Bridge*," *University of Kansas City Review* 24 (Spring 1958): 225-38. Reprinted in Miller, Shapiro, and Slote, *Start with the Sun*, 137-55.

Bernice Slote, "Transmutation in Crane's Imagery in *The Bridge*," *MLN* 73 (Jan. 1958): 15-23. Reprinted in Miller, Shapiro, and Slote, *Start with the Sun*, 155-65.

Alan Swallow, "Hart Crane," *The University of Kansas City Review* 16 (Winter 1949): 114, 116-18. Reprinted in Swallow, *An Editor's Essays of Two Decades*, 183-84, 189-92; in *University of Denver Quarterly* 1 (Spring 1967): 115-17.

Tate, *On the Limits of Poetry*, 228-37. First published in *Hound and Horn* and *Poetry*.

Tate, *Reactionary Essays on Poetry and Ideas*, 30-42. Reprinted in Zabel, *Literary Opinion in America*, rev. ed., 230-36.

John Untrecker, "The Architecture of *The Bridge*," *Wisconsin Studies in Contemporary Literature* 3 (Spring/Summer 1962): 5-20.

Albert Van Nostrand, "'The Bridge' and Hart Crane's 'Span of Consciousness,'" in Ludwig, *Aspects of American Poetry*, 173-202.

Thomas A. Vogler, "A New View of Hart Crane's *Bridge*," *SR* 73 (Summer 1965): 381-408.

Waggoner, *The Heel of Elohim*, 157-58, 171-90.

Wells, *New Poets from Old*, 116-28.

Yvor Winters, "The Progress of Hart Crane," *Poetry* 36 (June 1930): 153-65.

Yvor Winters, "The Significance of *The Bridge*, by Hart Crane," in *In Defense of Reason*, 577-603.

Gregory Woods, *Articulate Flesh: Male Homo-Eroticism and Modern Poetry* (New Haven: Yale University Press, 1987), passim.

"The Bridge of Estador"

Maurice Kramer, "Hart Crane's 'Reflexes,'" *TCL* 13 (Oct. 1967): 134.

"The Broken Tower"

Marius Bewley, "Hart Crane's Last Poem," *Accent* 19 (Spring 1959): 75-85.

Blasing, *American Poetry: The Rhetoric of Its Forms*, 192-93.

Henry Braun, "Hart Crane's 'The Broken Tower,'" *Boston University Studies in English* 5 (Autumn 1961): 167-77.

Friar and Brinnin, *Modern Poetry*, 449.

Muriel Rukeyser, *The Life of Poetry* (New York: A. A. Wyn, 1949), 32-33.

Eric J. Sundquist, "Bringing Home the Word: Magic, Lies, and Silence in Hart Crane," *ELH* 44 (Summer 1977): 395-96.

M. D. Uroff, "The Imagery of Violence in Hart Crane's Poetry," *AL* 43 (May 1971): 211-13.

"C 33"

Maurice Kramer, "Hart Crane's 'Reflexes,'" *TCL* 13 (Oct. 1967): 134.

"Cape Hatteras"

Brooks, Lewis, and Warren, *American Literature*, 2216-17.

Karl Shapiro, "The Meaning of the Discarded Poem," in Abbot, *Poets at Work*, 111-18.

Eric J. Sundquist, "Bringing Home the Word: Magic, Lies, and Silence in Hart Crane," *ELH* 44 (Summer 1977): 389-90.

Vogler, *Preludes to Vision*, 170-76.

"Chaplinesque"

Deutsch, *Poetry in Our Time*, 317-18.

Gray, *American Poetry*, 220-21.

Robert L. Perry, "Critical Problems in Hart Crane's 'Chaplinesque,'" *CP* 8 (Fall 1975): 23-27.

Frank Porter, "'Chaplinesque': An Explication," *EJ* 57 (Feb. 1968): 191-92, 195.

Sheehan, "Hart Crane and the Contemporary Search," *EJ* 60 (Dec. 1971): 1211-12.

"Cutty Sark"

Eric J. Sundquist, "Bringing Home the Word: Magic, Lies, and Silence in Hart Crane," *ELH* 44 (Summer 1977): 387-88.

Vogler, *Preludes to Vision*, 166-70.

"The Dance"

Clark, *Lyric Resonance*, 176-84.

James McMichael, "Hart Crane," *SoR* 8 (Apr. 1972): 300-309.

Eric J. Sundquist, "Bringing Home the Word: Magic, Lies, and Silence in Hart Crane," *ELH* 44 (Summer 1977): 383-86.

Vogler, *Preludes to Vision*, 162-65.

Winters, *Primitivism and Decadence*, 30-32. Reprinted in Winters, *Defense of Reason*, 44-45, 52; in Winters, *The Function of Criticism*, 295-98.

"Eternity"

M. D. Uroff, "The Imagery of Violence in Hart Crane's Poetry," *AL* 43 (May 1971): 209-10.

"The Fernery"

Robert L. Perry, "Critical Problems in Hart Crane's 'The Fernery,'" *Expl* 35 (Fall 1976): 3-5.

"Finale"

Brunner, *Splendid Failure*, 22-28.

"For the Marriage of Faustus and Helen"

Bruce Bassoff, *Expl* 31 (Mar. 1973): 53.

Bruce Bassoff, "Rhetorical Pressures in 'For the Marriage of Faustus and Helen,'" *CP* 5 (Fall 1972): 40-48.

Clark, *Lyric Resonance*, 159-73.

Roger Dickinson-Brown, *Expl* 31 (Apr. 1973): 66.

Joseph Frank, "Hart Crane: American Poet," *SR* 57 (Winter 1949): 155-56.

Gray, *American Poetry*, 221-24.

Will C. Jumper, *Expl* 17 (Oct. 1958): 8. Reprinted in *The Explicator Cyclopedia* 1:23-24.

Maurice Kramer, "Hart Crane's 'Reflexes,'" *TCL* 13 (Oct. 1967): 134-35.

Patricia McClintock, "A Reading of Hart Crane's 'For the Marriage of Faustus and Helen,'" *MSE* 1 (Fall 1967): 39-43.

Robert K. Martin, "Hart Crane's 'For the Marriage of Faustus and Helen': Myth and Alchemy," *CP* 9 (Spring 1976): 59-62.

Helge Normann Nilsen, "'Surrender to the Sensations of Urban Life': A Note on the Poetry of Hart Crane," *EA*, no. 3 (1981): 322-26.

Savage, *The Personal Principle*, 115-18.

Philip R. Yannella, "'Inventive Dust': The Metamorphoses of 'For the Marriage of Faustus and Helen,'" *ConL* 15 (Winter 1974): 102-22.

"The Harbor Dawn"

Edward Brunner, "'Your Hands Within My Hands Are Deeds': Poems of Love in *The Bridge*," *IowaR* 4 (Winter 1973): 112-18.

Friar and Brinnin, *Modern Poetry*, 452-53.

Helge Norman Nilsen, "'Surrender to the Sensations of Urban Life': A Note on the Poetry of Hart Crane," *EA* 3 (1981): 322-26.

Perrine and Reid, *100 American Poems*, 179-80.

Eric J. Sundquist, "Bringing Home the Word: Magic, Lies, and Silence in Hart Crane," *ELH* 44 (Summer 1977): 382-83.

Vogler, *Preludes to Vision*, 153-56.

"The Hurricane"

M. D. Uroff, "The Imagery of Violence in Hart Crane's Poetry," *AL* 43 (May 1971): 210-11.

"Indiana"

Vogler, *Preludes to Vision*, 165-66.

"Key West"

Kingsley Widmer, *Expl* 18 (Dec. 1959): 17. Reprinted in *The Explicator Cyclopedia* 1:24-25.

"Lachrymae Christi"

Blackmur, *The Double Agent*, 135-37. Reprinted in Blackmur, *Language as Gesture*, 312-14.

Blasing, *American Poetry: The Rhetoric of Its Forms*, 190-91.

Brunner, *Splendid Failure*, 59-71.

Barbara Herman, "The Language of Hart Crane," *SR* 58 (Winter 1950): 62-65.

Martin Staples Shockley, "Hart Crane's 'Lachrymae Christi,'" *University of Kansas City Review* 16 (Autumn 1949): 31-36. Reprinted in Engle and Carrier, *Reading Modern Poetry*, 321-28.

M. D. Uroff, "The Imagery of Violence in Hart Crane's Poetry," *AL* 43 (May 1971): 206-7.

Philip R. Yannella, "Toward Apotheosis: Hart Crane's Visionary Lyrics," *Criticism* 10 (Fall 1968): 317-20.

"Legend" (Introductory lyric to *White Buildings*)

Amtai F. Avi-ram, "*APO KOINOU* in Audre Lorde and the Moderns: Defining the Differences," *Callaloo* 9 (Winter 1986): 193-208.

Maurice Kramer, "Hart Crane's 'Reflexes,'" *TCL* 13 (Oct. 1967): 133-34.

M. D. Uroff, "The Imagery of Violence in Hart Crane's Poetry," *AL* 43 (May 1971): 203-4.

Philip R. Yannella, "Toward Apotheosis: Hart Crane's Visionary Lyrics," *Criticism* 10 (Fall 1968): 313-20.

"The Mango Tree"

Bernie Leggett, *Expl* 32 (Nov. 1973): 18.

Melvin E. Lyon, *Expl* 25 (Feb. 1967): 48.

"The Mermen"

Ribner and Morris, *Poetry*, 440-42.

"Moment Fugue"

Peter J. Sheehan, *Expl* 31 (May 1973): 78.

"The Moth that God Made Blind"

Norman D. Hinton and Lise Rodgers, "Hart Crane's 'The Moth that God Made Blind,'" *PLL* 16 (Summer 1980): 287-94.

"National Winter Garden"

Edward Brunner, "'Your Hands within My Hands Are Deeds': Poems of Love in *The Bridge*," *IowaR* (Winter 1973): 121-23.

Vogler, *Preludes to Vision*, 179-81.

"O Carib Isle!"

Friar and Brinnin, *Modern Poetry*, 449-50.

Eric J. Sundquist, "Bringing Home the Word: Magic, Lies, and Silence in Hart Crane," *ELH* 44 (Summer 1977): 393-94.

"Paraphrase"

Ben W. Griffith, Jr., *Expl* 13 (Oct. 1954): 5. Reprinted in *The Explicator Cyclopedia* 1:25-26.

"Passage"

Gene Koretz, *Expl* 13 (June 1955): 47. Reprinted in *The Explicator Cyclopedia* 1:27-28.

Maurice Kramer, "Hart Crane's 'Reflexes,'" *TCL* 13 (Oct. 1967): 136-37.

R. W. B. Lewis, "Crane's Visionary Lyric: The Way to *The Bridge*," *MR* 7 (Spring 1966): 227-32.

Rosenthal, *The Modern Poets*, 177-78.

M. D. Uroff, "The Imagery of Violence in Hart Crane's Poetry," *AL* 43 (May 1971): 208-9.

John R. Willingham and Virginia Moseley, *Expl* 13 (June 1955): 47. Reprinted in *The Explicator Cyclopedia* 1:26-27.

"Possessions"

Brunner, *Splendid Failure*, 28-34.

Swallow, "Hart Crane," 113. Reprinted in Swallow, *An Editor's Essays of Two Decades*, 182-83.

"Poster" (from "Voyages")

Evelyn J. Hinz, "Hart Crane's 'Voyages' Reconsidered," *ConL* 13 (Summer 1972): 319-23.

"Praise for an Urn"

Swallow, "Hart Crane," 115. Reprinted in Swallow, *An Editor's Essays of Two Decades*, 185-86.

Van Doren, *Introduction to Poetry*, 103-7.

"Proem: To Brooklyn Bridge"

Edward Brunner, "'Your Hands within My Hands Are Deeds': Poems of Love in *The Bridge*," *IowaR* 4 (Winter 1973): 108-11.

Friar and Brinnin, *Modern Poetry*, 427-28, 450-51.

Eric J. Sundquist, "Bringing Home the Word: Magic, Lies, and Silence in Hart Crane," *ELH* (Summer 1977): 379-81.

"Quaker Hill"

Eric J. Sundquist, "Bringing Home the Word: Magic, Lies, and Silence in Hart Crane," *ELH* (Summer 1977): 376.

Stephanie A. Tirgley, "Hart Crane's 'Quaker Hill': A Plea for a Positive Perspective," *ELN* 22, no. 1 (1984): 55-61.

Vogler, *Preludes to Vision*, 182-85.

"Recitative"

Maurice Kramer, "Hart Crane's 'Reflexes,'" *TCL* 13 (Oct. 1967): 134-35.

M. D. Uroff, "Hart Crane's 'Recitative,'" *CP* 3 (Spring 1970): 22-27.

M. D. Uroff, "The Imagery of Violence in Hart Crane's Poetry," *AL* 43 (May 1971): 205.

Yannella, "Toward Apotheosis: Hart Crane's Visionary Lyrics," *Criticism* 10 (Fall 1968): 322-23.

"Repose of Rivers"

Clark, *Lyric Resonance*, 148-51.

R. W. B. Lewis, "Crane's Visionary Lyric: The Way to *The Bridge*," *MR* 7 (Spring 1966): 249-53.

Rosenheim, *What Happens in Literature*, 140-60.

Sanders, *The Discovery of Poetry*, 11-12.

"The Return"

A. Grossman, "Hart Crane and Poetry: A Consideration of Crane's Intense Poetics with Reference to 'The Return,'" *ELH* 48 (Winter 1981): 841-79.

Thomas E. Sanders, *Expl* 10 (Dec. 1951): 20. Reprinted in *The Explicator Cyclopedia* 1:128-29.

M. D. Uroff, "The Imagery of Violence in Hart Crane's Poetry," *AL* 43 (May 1971): 211.

"The River"

Perrine and Reid, *100 American Poems*, 177-78.

Vogler, *Preludes to Vision*, 160-62.

"The Sad Indian"

John R. Scarlett, *Expl* 29 (Apr. 1971): 69.

"The Sea Raised Up"

R. J. Reisling, "Some Perils of Textual Corruption: A Return to a Consideration of Hart Crane's 'The Sea Raised Up . . . ,'" *JML* 12 (Mar. 1985): 175-82.

"Southern Cross"

Edward Brunner, "'Your Hands within My Hands Are Deeds': Poems of Love in *The Bridge*," *IowaR* (Winter 1973): 123-25.

Vogler, *Preludes to Vision*, 177-79.

"Three Songs"

Eric J. Sundquist, "Bringing Home the Word: Magic, Lies, and Silence in Hart Crane," *ELH* 44 (Summer 1977): 390-91.

John R. Willingham, "'Three Songs' of Hart Crane's *The Bridge*: A Reconsideration," *AL* 27 (Mar. 1955): 64-68.

"The Tunnel"

Robert K. Martin, *Expl* 34 (Oct. 1975): 16.

Helge Normann Nilsen, "'Surrender to the Sensations of Urban Life': A Note on the Poetry of Hart Crane," *EA,* no. 3 (1981): 322-26.

Vogler, *Preludes to Vision*, 185-91.

"Van Winkle"

Eric J. Sundquist, "Bringing Home the Word: Magic, Lies, and Silence in Hart Crane," *ELH* 44 (Summer 1977): 382-83.

Vogler, *Preludes to Vision*, 156-60.

"Virginia"

Edward Brunner, "'Your Hands within My Hands Are Deeds': Poems of Love in *The Bridge*," *IowaR* 4 (Winter 1973): 118-21.

Vogler, *Preludes to Vision*, 156-60.

"Voyages"

Blasing, *American Poetry: The Rhetoric of Its Forms*, 194-96.

Friar and Brinnin, *Modern Poetry*, 455-56.

Maurice Kramer, "Six Voyages of a Derelict Seer," *SR* 73 (Summer 1965): 410-23.

H. C. Morris, "Crane's 'Voyages' as a Single Poem," *Accent* 14 (Autumn 1954): 291-99.

Rosenthal, *The Modern Poets*, 179-82.

Philip R. Yannella, "Toward Apotheosis: Hart Crane's Visionary Lyrics," *Criticism* 10 (Fall 1968): 324-33.

"Voyages" I

Evelyn J. Hinz, "Hart Crane's 'Voyages' Reconsidered," *ConL* 13 (Summer 1972): 323-25, 327-29.

"Voyages" II

Brooks, Lewis, and Warren, *American Literature*, 2211.

Clark, *Lyric Resonance*, 138-40.

Robert A. Day, "Image and Idea in 'Voyages II,'" *Criticism* 7 (Summer 1965): 224-34.

Deutsch, *Poetry in Our Time*, 319-21.

Judith S. Friedman and Ruth Perlmutter, *Expl* 19 (Oct. 1960): 4. Reprinted in *The Explicator Cyclopedia* 1:31-32.

John T. Irwin, "Naming Names: Hart Crane's 'Logic of Metaphor,'" *SoR* 11 (Apr. 1975): 286-89.

O'Connor, *Sense and Sensibility in Modern Poetry*, 73-75.

A. Poulin, Jr., *Expl* 28 (Oct. 1969): 15.

Sidney Richman, "Hart Crane's 'Voyages II': An Experiment in Redemption," *Wisconsin Studies in Contemporary Literature* 3 (Spring/Summer 1962): 65-78.

Max F. Schulz, *Expl* 14 (Apr. 1956): 46. Reprinted in *The Explicator Cyclopedia* 1:32-33.

Richard Strier, "The Poetics of Surrender: An Exposition and Critique of New Critical Poetics," *CritI* 2 (Autumn 1975): 187-88.

Unger and O'Connor, *Poems for Study*, 637-41.

"Voyages" V

Evelyn J. Hinz, "Hart Crane's 'Voyages' Reconsidered," *ConL* 13 (Summer 1972): 328.

"Voyages" VI

Brooks, Lewis, and Warren, *American Literature*, 2212.

Eveyln J. Hinz, "Hart Crane's 'Voyages' Reconsidered," *ConL* 13 (Summer 1972): 329-33.

M. D. Uroff, "Hart Crane's 'Voyages VI,' Stanza 6," *ELN* 8 (Sept. 1970): 46-48.

Charles C. Walcutt, *Expl* 4 (May 1946): 53. Reprinted in *The Explicator Cyclopedia* 1:33-34.

James Ziggerell, *Expl* 13 (Nov. 1954): 7. Reprinted in *The Explicator Cyclopedia* 1: 29-30.

"The Wine Menagerie"

Blackmur, *The Double Agent*, 130-34. Reprinted in Blackmur, *Language as Gesture*, 309-12; in Stallman, *The Critic's Notebook*, 106-10.

Brunner, *Splendid Failure*, 71-79. Reprinted in Maurice Kramer, "Hart Crane's 'Reflexes,'" *TCL* 13 (Oct. 1967): 136.

R. W. B. Lewis, "Crane's Visionary Lyric," *MR* 7 (Spring 1966): 233-39.

Philip R. Yannella, "Toward Apotheosis: Hart Crane's Visonary Lyrics," *Criticism* 10 (Fall 1968): 320-22.

G. R. Zeck, "Hart Crane's *The Wine Menagerie*," *AI* 36 (Fall 1979): 291-305.

CRAPSEY

"Niagara"

Sanders, *The Discovery of Poetry*, 75-76.

"November Night"

Sanders, *The Discovery of Poetry*, 79-90.

"Song: I Make My Shroud, but No One Knows--"

Sanders, *The Discovery of Poetry*, 328-33.

"Suzanna and the Elders"

Sanders, *The Discovery of Poetry*, 76-77.

"Triad"

Daniels, *The Art of Reading Poetry*, 53.
Sanders, *The Discovery of Poetry*, 79.

CRAWFORD, ISABELLA VALANCY

"The Canoe"

Frank Bessai, "The Ambivalence of Love in the Poetry of Isabella Valancy Crawford," *QQ* 77 (Autumn 1970): 411-12.

""The Dark Stag"

Frank Bessai, "The Ambivalence of Love in the Poetry of Isabella Valancy Crawford," *QQ* 77 (Autumn 1970): 408-9.

"The Deacon's Fate"

Robert Alan Burns, "Isabella Valancy Crawford's Poetic Technique," *SCL* 10 (1985): 53-80.

"Esther"

Robert Alan Burns, "Isabella Valancy Crawford's Poetic Technique," *SCL* 10 (1985): 53-80.

"The Lily Bed"

Frank Bessai, "The Ambivalence of Love in the Poetry of Isabella Valancy Crawford," *QQ* 77 (Autumn 1970): 409-10.

"Love, Stay for Me"

Robert Alan Burns, "Isabella Valancy Crawford's Poetic Technique," *SCL* 10 (1985): 53-80.

"Malcolm's Katie"

Kenneth Radu, "Patterns of Meaning: Isabella Crawford's 'Malcolm's Katie,'" *DR* 57 (Summer 1977): 322-31.

"Old Spense"

Robert Alan Burns, "Isabella Valancy Crawford's Poetic Technique," *SCL* 10 (1985): 53-80.

"The Rolling Pin"

Robert Alan Burns, "Isabella Valancy Crawford's Poetic Technique," *SCL* 10 (1985): 53-80.

"Two Songs"

Robert Alan Burns, "Isabella Valancy Crawford's Poetic Technique," *SCL* 10 (1985): 53-80.

"The Waterlily"

Robert Alan Burns, "Isabella Valancy Crawford's Poetic Technique," *SCL* 10 (1985): 53-80.

CREELEY, ROBERT

[Interview]

"Conversation with Robert Creeley," *Gamut* 12 (Spring/Summer 1984): 20-32.

"After Lorca"

Von Hallberg, *American Poetry and Culture, 1945-1980*, passim.

"The Box"

Cynthia Dubin Edelberg, "Creeley's Orphan Lines: The Rhythmic Character of the Sequences," *Sagetrieb* 1 (Winter 1982): 143-62.

"The Business"

Von Hallberg, *American Poetry and Culture, 1945-1980*, passim.

The Charm

George Butterick, "Robert Creeley and the Tradition," *Sagetrieb* 1 (Winter 1982): 119-34.

Paul, *The Lost America of Love*, passim.

"Chasing the Bird"

George Butterick, "Robert Creeley and the Tradition," *Sagetrieb* 1 (Winter 1982): 119-34.

"A Day Book"

Bernstein, *Content's Dream: Essays 1975-1984*, 292-304.

Paul, *The Lost America of Love*, passim.

"The Dishonest Mailman"

Charles Altieri, "The Unsure Egoist: Robert Creeley and the Theme of Nothingness," *ConL* 13 (Spring 1972): 169-70.

"The Farm"

Cynthia Dubin Edelberg, "Creeley's Orphan Lines: The Rhythmic Character of the Sequences," *Sagetrieb* 1 (Winter 1982): 143-62.

"The Flower"

Charles Altieri, "The Unsure Egoist: Robert Creeley and the Theme of Nothingness," *ConL* 13 (Spring 1972): 167-68.

Jerry R. Bacon, "Closure in Robert Creeley's Poetry," *MPS* 8 (Winter 1977): 234-35.

"For Benny and Sabina"

Cynthia Dubin Edelberg, "Creeley's Orphan Lines: The Rhythmic Character of the Sequences," *Sagetrieb* 1 (Winter 1982): 143-62.

For Love

George Butterick, "Robert Creeley and the Tradition," *Sagetrieb* 1 (Winter 1982): 119-34.

"For W. C. W."

Charles Altieri, "The Unsure Egoist: Robert Creeley and the Theme of Nothingness," *ConL* 13 (Spring 1972): 174-75.

"Le Fou"

Jerry R. Bacon, "Closure in Robert Creeley's Poetry," *MPS* 8 (Winter 1977): 232-33.

"Four"

Peter Halter, "Dialogue for the Sister Arts: Number-Poems and Number-Paintings in America, 1920-70," *ES* 63 (1982): 207-19.

"Hart Crane"

George Butterick, "Robert Creeley and the Tradition," *Sagetrieb* 1 (Winter 1982): 119-34.

Hello

Cynthia Dubin Edelberg, "Creeley's Orphan Lines: The Rhythmic Character of the Sequences," *Sagetrieb* 1 (Winter 1982): 143-62.

"If You"

Dirk Stratton, "If Is to Is: Robert Creeley's 'If You,'" *Sagetrieb* 3 (Spring 1984): 105-9.

"I Know a Man"

Charles Altieri, "The Unsure Egoist: Robert Creeley and the Theme of Nothingness," *ConL* 13 (Spring 1972): 163-64.

Lee Bartlett, *Expl* 41 (Fall 1983): 53.

Kenner, *A Homemade World*, 184-85.

William T. Lawlor, "Creeley's 'I Know a Man': A Metaphysical Conceit," *IowaR* 15 (Spring/Summer 1985): 173-75.

W. Prunty, "Emaciated Poetry," *SR* 93 (Winter 1985): 78-94.

"In London"

Cynthia Dubin Edelberg, "Creeley's Orphan Lines: The Rhythmic Character of the Sequences," *Sagetrieb* 1 (Winter 1982): 143-62.

"The Innocence"

Allen Barry Cameron, "'Love Comes Quietly': The Poetry of Robert Creeley," *ChiR* 19 (1967): 24.

"The Kind of Act Of"

Cid Corman, "A Requisite Commitment," *Poetry* 83 (Mar. 1954): 340-42.

"The Language"

Charles Altieri, "The Unsure Egoist: Robert Creeley and the Theme of Nothingness," *ConL* 13 (Spring 1972): 176-77.

"Lida"

George Butterick, "Robert Creeley and the Tradition," *Sagetrieb* 1 (Winter 1982): 119-34.

"Love Comes Quietly"

Allen Barry Cameron, "'Love Comes Quietly': The Poetry of Robert Creeley," *ChiR* 19 (1967): 98-99.

"Mabel: A Story"

Bernstein, *Content's Dream: Essays 1975-1984*, 292-304.

CREELEY, ROBERT

"La Noche"

Allen Barry Cameron, "'Love Comes Quietly': The Poetry of Robert Creeley," *ChiR* 19 (1967): 100.

"A Piece"

Cynthia Dubin Edelberg, "Creeley's Orphan Lines: The Rhythmic Character of the Sequences," *Sagetrieb* 1 (Winter 1982): 143-62.

Pieces

Cynthia Dubin Edelberg, "Creeley's Orphan Lines: The Rhythmic Character of the Sequences," *Sagetrieb* 1 (Winter 1982): 143-62.

Jed Rasula, "Placing *Pieces*," *Sagetrieb* 1 (Winter 1982): 163-69.

"Prayer to Hermes"

Cynthia Dubin Edelberg, "Creeley's Orphan Lines: The Rhythmic Character of the Sequences," *Sagetrieb* 1 (Winter 1982): 143-62.

"Presences"

Stephen Fredman, *Poet's Prose: The Crisis in American Verse* (Cambridge: Cambridge University Press, 1983), passim.

"Quick-Step"

W. Prunty, "Emaciated Poetry," *SR* 93 (Winter 1985): 78-94.

"The Rhyme"

Charles Altieri, "The Unsure Egoist: Robert Creeley and the Theme of Nothingness," *ConL* 13 (Spring 1972): 164-65.

"Something"

Von Hallberg, *American Poetry and Culture*, passim.

"Still Life or . . . "

George Butterick, "Robert Creeley and the Tradition," *Sagetrieb* 1 (Winter 1982): 119-34.

"They"

Charles Altieri, "The Unsure Egoist: Robert Creeley and the Theme of Nothingness," *ConL* 13 (Spring 1972): 184-85.

Cynthia Dubin Edelberg, "Creeley's Orphan Lines: The Rhythmic Character of the Sequences," *Sagetrieb* 1 (Winter 1982): 143-62.

"Thinking"

Altieri, *Self and Sensibility in Contemporary American Poetry*, passim.

"The Three Ladies"

George Butterick, "Robert Creeley and the Tradition," *Sagetrieb* 1 (Winter 1982): 119-34.

"A Wicker Basket"

Carroll, *The Poem in Its Skin*, 31-38.

"Zero

Charles Altieri, "The Unsure Egoist: Robert Creeley and the Theme of Nothingness," *ConL* 13 (Spring 1972): 182-83.

CULLEN, COUNTEE

"Incident"

Perrine and Reid, *100 American Poems*, 191.

"The Shroud of Color"

Ronald Primeau, "Countee Cullen and Keats's 'Vale of Soul-Making,'" *PLL* 12 (Winter 1975): 78-80.

CUMMINGS, E. E.

"262"

Nat Henry, *Expl* 21 (May 1963): 72.

"275"

Nat Henry, *Expl* 20 (Apr. 1962): 63. Reprinted in *The Explicator Cyclopedia* 1:48.

"303 (nor woman)"

Nat Henry, *Expl* 22 (Sept. 1963): 2.

"305"

Nat Henry, *Expl* 20 (Feb. 1962): 49. Reprinted in *The Explicator Cyclopedia* 1:49.

W. Yeaton Wagener, *Expl* 21 (Oct. 1962): 18.

"All in Green Went My Love Riding"

William V. Davis, "Cummings' 'All in Green Went My Love Riding,'" *CP* 3 (Fall 1970): 65-67.

Will C. Jumper, *Expl* 26 (Sept. 1967): 6.

Cora Robey, *Expl* 27 (Sept. 1968): 2.

Barry Sanders, *Expl* 25 (Nov. 1966): 23.

"among these red pieces of"

John Arthos, "The Poetry of E. E. Cummings," *AL* 14 (Jan. 1943): 386-87.

John Peale Bishop, "The Poems and Prose of E. E. Cummings," *SoR* 4 (Summer 1938): 176-77.

Eastman, *The Literary Mind*, 59-62.

Riding and Graves, *A Survey of Modernist Poetry*, 84-89.

"anyone and noone"

Clark, *Lyric Resonance*, 187-94.

"anyone lived in a pretty how town"

Herbert C. Barrows, Jr., and William R. Steinhoff, *Expl* 9 (Oct. 1950): 1. Abridged in Gwynn, Condee, and Lewis, *The Case for Poetry*, 95. Reprinted in *The Explicator Cyclopedia* 1:35-36.

Arthur Carr, *Expl* 11 (Nov. 1952): 6. Abridged in Gwynn, Condee, and Lewis, *The Case for Poetry*, 95-96. Reprinted in *The Explicator Cyclopedia* 1:36-37.

James P. Dougherty, "Language as a Reality in E. E. Cummings," *BuR* 16 (May 1968): 119-22.

James Paul Gee, "Anyone's: A View of Language and Poetry Through an Analysis of 'anyone lived in a pretty how town,'" *Lang&S* 16 (Spring 1983): 123-37.

George Haines, IV, " : : 2 : 1--The World and E. E. Cummings," *SR* 59 (Spring 1951): 216-17.

Perrine and Reid, *100 American Poems*, 153-55.

Charles L. Squier, *Expl* 25 (Dec. 1966): 37.

Theo Steinmann, "The Semantic Rhythm in 'anyone lived in a pretty how town,'" *CP* 11 (Fall 1978): 71-79.

Chad Walsh, *Doors into Poetry*, 132-33.

Robert C. Walsh, *Expl* 22 (May 1964): 72.

Stallman and Watters, *The Creative Reader*, 886-87.

"(applaws)"

Joseph Axelrod, "Cummings and Phonetics," *Poetry* 65 (Nov. 1944): 88-94.

Karl Shapiro, "Prosody as the Meaning," *Poetry* 73 (Mar. 1949): 338-40 and passim.

"because you go away i give roses"

Riding and Graves, *A Survey of Modernist Poetry*, 60-64.

"Bells"

John W. Crowley, "Visual-aural Poetry: The Typography of E. E. Cummings," *CP* 5 (Fall 1972): 51-54.

"! blac"

S. V. Baum, "E. E. Cummings: The Technique of Immediacy," *SAQ* 53 (Jan. 1954): 87-88.

"bright"

Robert M. McIlvaine, *Expl* 30 (Sept. 1971): 6.

"Buffalo Bill's/Defunct"

Adam Berkeley, "'Buffalo Bill's Defunct,'" *CEA* 29 (Mar. 1967): 13-14.

Louis J. Budd, *Expl* 11 (June 1953): 55. Reprinted in *The Explicator Cyclopedia* 1:37-38.

Earl J. Diaz, "'Buffalo Bill's Defunct,'" *CEA* 24 (Mar. 1967): 14.

Earl J. Diaz, "e. e. cummings and Buffalo Bill," *CEA* 29 (Dec. 1966): 6-7.

Norman Friedman and David Ray, "Pan and Buffalo Bill," *CE* 23 (May 1962): 672.

Londa Bradley Funkhouser, "Accoustical Rhythms in Cummings' 'Buffalo Bill's,'" *JML* 7 (Apr. 1979): 219-42.

David Ray, "The Irony of E. E. Cummings," *CE* 23 (Jan. 1962): 282, 287-90.

Rosenthal, *The Modern Poets*, 148-49.

John E. Unterecker, "Buffalo Bill Revisited," *CE* 29 (Apr. 1967): 1.

"by little accurate saints thickly which tread"

Y. Renan, "'Angelfaces Clustered like Bright Lice': Comic Elements in Modernist Writing," *CL* 35 (Summer 1983): 247-61.

"Chansons Innocentes I: in just-spring"

Brooks, *A Shaping Joy*, 93-94.

Marvin Felheim, *Expl* 14 (Nov. 1955): 11. Reprinted in *The Explicator Cyclopedia* 1:38-39.

R. D. Mayo, *English "A" Analyst*, no. 2, 1-4. Reprinted in Engle and Carrier, *Reading Modern Poetry*, 133-36.

Sanders, *The Discovery of Poetry*, 243-46.

C. Steven Turner, *Expl* 24 (Oct. 1965): 18.

"Crepuscule"

Richard S. Kennedy, "E. E. Cummings: The Emergent Styles, 1916," *JML* 7 (Apr. 1979): 175-204.

"darling! because my blood can sing"

Frankenberg, *Invitation to Poetry*, 281-82.

"death is more than certain"

Norman Friedman, "Diction, Voice, and Tone: The Poetic Language of E. E. Cummings," *PMLA* 62 (Dec. 1957): 1057-58.

Riding and Graves, *A Survey of Modernist Poetry*, 244-47.

"floatfloafloflf"

Richard Crowder, *Expl* 16 (Apr. 1958): 41. Reprinted in *The Explicator Cyclopedia* 1:47-48.

"goodbye Betty, don't remember me"

Rosenthal, *The Modern Poets*, 150-51.

"the greedy, the people"

Perrine and Reid, *100 American Poems*, 156-57.

"La Guerre" I

William R. Osborne, *Expl* 24 (Nov. 1965): 28.

"him"

M. A. Cohen, "Cummings and Freud," *AL* 55 (Dec. 1983): 591-610.

"I"

James E. White, *Expl* 21 (Sept. 1962): 4.

"i am a little church (no great cathedral)"

Rushworth Kidder, "Picture into Poem: The Genesis of Cummings' 'i am a little church,'" *ConL* 21 (1980): 315-30.

"if everything happens that can't be done"

Norman Friedman, "Diction, Voice and Tone: The Poetic Language of E. E. Cummings," 1050-51.

James M. Reid, John Ciardi, and Laurence Perrine, *Poetry: A Closer Look* (New York: Harcourt, Brace & World, 1963), 45-49. Reprinted in Perrine *The Art of Total Relevance*, 70-73.

"if up's the word; and a world grows greener"

Perrine and Reid, *100 American Poems*, 151-52.

"(IM)C-A-T(MO)"

Vincent L. Heinrichs, *Expl* 27 (Apr. 1969): 59.

"Impression"

Adams, *The Contexts of Poetry*, 4-8.

"in heavenly realms of hellas"

Laurence Perrine, "Cummings's 'in heavenly realms of hellas,'" *NConL* 1 (Jan. 1971): 9.

"it's/so damn sweet when anybody--"

David R. Clark, *Expl* 22 (Feb. 1964): 48.

"i will be/moving in the Street of her"

Richard Gid Powers, *Expl* 28 (Feb. 1970): 54.

Theodore Spencer, "Technique as Joy," *[Harvard] Wake* 5 (Spring 1946): 25-27.

"Jehovah Buried, Satan Dead"

Perrine and Read, *100 American Poems*, 148-50.

"a kike is the most dangerous"

John Arthos, "The Poetry of E. E. Cummings," *AL* 14 (Jan. 1943): 385-86.

M. L. Rosenthal, "Cummings and Hayes: Mr. Joy and Mr. Gloom," *New Republic* 123 (18 Sept. 1950): 18.

CUMMINGS, E.E.

"kind)"

Guy Rotella, "Cummings' 'kind)' and Whitman's Astronomer," *CP* 18, nos. 1-2: 39-46.

Paul O. Williams, *Expl* 23 (Sept. 1964): 4.

"let's, from some loud unworld's most rightful wrong"

Mary S. Mattfield, *Expl* 26 (Dec. 1967): 32.

"listen"

William E. Thompson, "Intensity: An Essential Element in E. E. Cummings' Aesthetic Theory and Practice," *UWR* 16, no. 2 (1982): 18-33.

"Luck Means Finding"

Edward A. Levenston, *Expl* 34 (Jan. 1976): 36.

"a man who had fallen among thieves"

Bloom, Philbrick, and Blistein, *The Order of Poetry*, 96-98.

"Memorabilia"

Cynthia Barton, *Expl* 22 (Dec. 1963): 26.

H. Seth Finn, *Expl* 29 (Jan. 1971): 42.

Ben W. Griffith, Jr., *Expl* 12 (May 1954): 47. Reprinted in *The Explicator Cyclopedia* 1:40.

Clyde S. Kilby, *Expl* 12 (Nov. 1953): 15. Reprinted in *The Explicator Cyclopedia* 1:39-40.

"Morsel Miraculous"

Valerie Meilotes Arms, "A Catholic Reading of Cummings' 'Morsel Miraculous,'" *JML* 7 (Apr. 1979): 292-94.

"mortals)"

George Haines, IV, " : : 2 : 1--The World and E. E. Cummings," *SR* 59 (Spring 1951): 218-21.

"my father moved through dooms of love"

James P. Dougherty, "Language as a Reality in E. E. Cummings," *BuR* 16 (May 1968): 117-19.

Gray, *American Poetry*, 216-17.

George Haines, IV, " : : 2 : 1--The World and E. E. Cummings," *SR* 59 (Spring 1951): 215-16.

Orm Overland, "E. E. Cummings' 'my father moved through dooms of love': A Measure of Achievement," *ES* 54 (Apr. 1973): 141-47.

"my sweet old etcetera"

Fred E. H. Schroeder, "Obscenity and Its Function in the Poetry of E. E. Cummings," *SR* 63 (July/Sept. 1965): 472-73.

"next to of course god america i"

William V. Davis, "Cummings' 'next to of course god america i,'" *CP* 3 (Spring 1970), 14-15.

Friedman and McLaughlin, *Poetry: An Introduction to Its Form and Art*, 96-97.

"Nobody Loses All the Time"

William V. Davis, "Cummings' 'Nobody Loses All the Time,'" *AN&Q* 9 (Apr. 1971): 119-20.

'no man, if men are gods"

Frankenberg, *Invitation to Poetry*, 74.

CUMMINGS, E.E.

"nonsun blob a"

Richard Gunter, "Sentence and Poem," *Style* 5 (Winter 1971): 26-36.

"The Noster Was a Ship of Swank"

Luther S. Luedtke, *Expl* 26 (Mar. 1968): 59.

"no time ago"

William V. Davis, "Cummings' 'no time ago,'" *Research Studies* 41 (Sept. 1973): 205-7.

Norman Friedman, "Diction, Voice, and Tone: The Poetic Language of E. E. Cummings," *PMLA* 62 (Dec. 1957): 1058.

"(one!)"

George C. Brauer, Jr., *Expl* 16 (Dec. 1957): 14. Reprinted in *The Explicator Cyclopedia* 1:4.

Louis C. Rus, *Expl* 15 (Mar. 1957): 40. Reprinted in *The Explicator Cyclopedia* 1:40-41.

"lxl"

Jack Steinberg, *Expl* 8 (Dec. 1949): 17. Reprinted in *The Explicator Cyclopedia* 1:46-47.

"one's not half two"

Norman Friedman, "Diction, Voice, and Tone: The Poetic Language of E. E. Cummings," *PMLA* 62 (Dec. 1957): 1041.

"o pr"

Sheridan Baker, "Cummings and Catullus," *MLN* 74 (Mar. 1959): 231-34.

"the people who"

G. J. Weinberger, "E. E. Cummings' 'the people who,'" *Research Studies* 39 (Dec. 1971): 313-15.

"pity this busy monster, manunkind"

John Britton, *Expl* 18 (Oct. 1959): 5. Reprinted in *The Explicator Cyclopedia* 1:41-42.

James W. Gargano, *Expl* 20 (Nov. 1961): 21. Reprinted in *The Explicator Cyclopedia* 1:42.

Nat Henry, *Expl* 27 (May 1969): 68.

"poem" ("love's function is to fabricate unknownness")

Clark, *Lyric Resonance*, 195-99.

Gerald Levin, *Expl* 17 (Dec. 1958): 18. Reprinted in *The Explicator Cyclopedia* 1:42-43.

"Portrait"

Brooks and Warren, *Understanding Poetry*, 296-98; rev. ed., 158-60.

"raise the shade"

William Heyen, "In Consideration of Cummings," *SHR* 7 (Spring 1973): 138-39.

"r-p-o-p-h-e-s-s-a-g-r"

Helen Bevington, *When Found Make a Verse of* (New York: Simon and Schuster, 1961), 36-37.

Sam Hynes, *Expl* 10 (Nov. 1951): 9.

Rosenthal, *The Modern Poets*, 147-48.

CUMMINGS, E.E.

"Silence" (Poem 40 of *95 Poems*)

Rosenthal, *The Modern Poets*, 146-47.

"since feeling is first"

Heyen, "In Consideration of Cummings," *SHR* 7 (Spring 1973): 132-34.

"the sky was"

John Arthos, "The Poetry of E. E. Cummings," *AL* 14 (Jan. 1943): 383-85.

"so little he is"

Frankenberg, *Pleasure Dome*, 176-77.

"Sonnet Entitled How to Run the World"

Gary Lane, *Expl* 31 (Sept. 1972): 7.

Michael L. Lasser, *Expl* 24 (Jan. 1966): 44.

"Space Being (don't forget to remember) Curved"

Richard B. Vowles, *Expl* 9 (Oct. 1950), 3. Reprinted in *The Explicator Cyclopedia* 1:43.

"Sunset"

Riding and Graves, *A Survey of Modernist Poetry*, 12-28.

"ta" (*Collected Poems*, 52)

S. V. Baum, "E. E. Cummings: The Technique of Immediacy," *SAQ* 53 (Jan. 1954): 83-84.

G. R. Wilson, Jr., *Expl* 31 (Nov. 1977): 18.

"That Which We Who're Alive IN SPITE of Mirrors"

Edith A. Everson, *Expl* 32 (Mar. 1974): 55.

"these children singing in a stone a"

Nat Henry, *Expl* 13 (June 1955): 51. Reprinted in *The Explicator Cyclopedia* 1:45.

Edwin M. Moseley, *Expl* 9 (Oct. 1950): 2. Reprinted in *The Explicator Cyclopedia* 1:43-44.

"a thrown a"

S. V. Baum, "E. E. Cummings: The Technique of Immediacy," *SAQ* 53 (Jan. 1954): 85-86.

"Twin Obsessions"

Rushworth Kidder, "'Twin Obsessions': The Poetry and Painting of E. E. Cummings," *GaR* 32 (Summer 1978): 342-68.

"up into the silence of the green"

John Arthos, "The Poetry of E. E. Cummings," *AL* 14 (Jan. 1943): 385-86.

"the way to hump a cow is not"

Fred E. H. Schroeder, "Obscenity and its Function in the Poetry of E. E. Cummings," *SR* 63 (July/Sept. 1965): 385-86.

"what a proud dreamhorse pulling (smooth-loomingly) through"

Frankenberg, *Invitation to Poetry*, 257-60.

M. Pagini, "The case of Cummings," *Poetics Today*, no. 3, 6:357-73.

CUMMINGS, E.E.

"what if a much of a which of a wind"

Laurel Maureen O'Neal, *Expl* 32 (Sept. 1973): 6.

Stephen E. Whicher, *Expl* 12 (Nov. 1953): 14. Reprinted in *The Explicator Cyclopedia* 1:45-46.

"when faces called flowers float out of the ground"

Alan M. Nadel, *Expl* 32 (Feb. 1974): 47.

"when god decided to invent"

Norman Friedman, "Cummings Posthumous," *JML* 7 (Apr. 1979): 295-322.

"When God Lets My Body Be"

Doris Dundas, *Expl* 29 (May 1971): 79.

")when what hugs stopping earth than silent is"

G. J. Weinberger, "Cummings' ')when what hugs stopping earth than silent is,'" *Research Studies* 41 (June 1973): 136-39.

"when you are silent, shining host by guest"

G. J. Weinberger, "E. E. Cummings's Benevolent God: A Reading of 'when you are silent, shining host by guest,'" *PLL* 16 (Winter 1974): 70-75.

"whipporwill this"

Don Jobe, *Expl* 42 (Fall 1983): 48.

"who are these (wraith a clinging with a wraith)"

Norman Friedman, "Diction, Voice, and Tone: The Poetic Language of E. E. Cummings," *PMLA* 62 (Dec. 1957): 1047.

"yes is a pleasant country"

Gary Lane, *Expl* 31 (Oct. 1972): 11.

CUNNINGHAM, J. V.

"The Chase"

John Williams, "J. V. Cunningham: The Major and the Minor," *ArQ* 6 (Summer 1950): 140-41.

"Doctor Drink Epigram #1"

Pinsky, *The Situation of Poetry: Contemporary Poetry and Its Traditions*, 136-39.

"Meditation on a Statistical Method"

Yvor Winters, "The Poetry of J. V. Cunningham," *TCL* 6 (Jan. 1961): 163-64.

"Passion"

John Williams, "J. V. Cunningham: The Major and the Minor," *ArQ* 6 (Summer 1950): 142-44.

"Reason and Nature"

Winters, *Forms of Discovery*, 301-3.

"Timor Dei"

John Williams, "J. V. Cunningham: The Major and the Minor," *ArQ* 6 (Summer 1950): 137-39.

"To the Reader"

Winters, *Forms of Discovery*, 300-301.

Yvor Winters, "The Poetry of J. V. Cunningham," *TCL* 6 (Jan. 1961): 161.

"To What Stangers, What Welcome"

Frances W. Kaye, "The West as Desolation: J. V. Cunningham's 'To What Strangers, What Welcome,'" *SoR* 11 (Oct. 1975): 820-24.

DALE, PETER

"Wildflower"

Ian Haig, "Commentary," *Agenda* 9 (Winter 1971): 37.

DAVIDSON, DONALD

"The Ninth Part of Speech"

Lawrence Dessommes, "The Epistemological Implications in 'The Ninth Part of Speech,'" *MissQ* 27 (Winter 1973-74): 21-32.

"The Tall Men"

Louis D. Rubin, Jr., "The Concept of Nature in Modern Southern Poetry," *AQ* 9 (Spring 1957): 65-67.

Rubin, *The Wary Fugitives--Four Poets and the South*, 136-86.

DAVIES, ROBINSON

"Orchestra: A Poem Dancing"

M. Brown, "'Errours Endlesse Traine': On Turning Points and the Dialectical Imagination," *PMLA* 99 (Jan. 1984): 9-25.

DAVIS, CATHERINE

"Beware, Old Scrounger"

Helen P. Trimpi, "The Theme of Loss in the Earlier Poems of Catherine Davis and Edgar Bowers," *SoR* 9 (July 1973): 602-3.

"The Last Step"

Helen P. Trimpi, "The Theme of Loss in the Earlier Poems of Catherine Davis and Edgar Bowers," *SoR* 9 (July 1973): 606-9.

"The Leaves"

Helen P. Trimpi, "The Theme of Loss in the Earlier Poems of Catherine Davis and Edgar Bowers," *SoR* 9 (July 1973): 597-98.

"The Narrow House"

Helen P. Trimpi, "The Theme of Loss in the Earlier Poems of Catherine Davis and Edgar Bowers," *SoR* 9 (July 1973): 609-10.

DAVISON, PETER

"Not Forgotten"

Rotella, *Three Contemporary Poets of New England*, 128-87.

DE HOYOS, ANGELA

"La Gran Ciudad"

Norwood and Monk, *The Desert Is No Lady*, passim.

"Hermano"

Norwood and Monk, *The Desert Is No Lady*, passim.

DENBY, WILLIAM

"#17"

Ted Berrigan, "The Business of Writing Poetry," in Waldman and Webb, *Talking Poetics from Naropa Institute* 1:58-59.

DENNEY, REUEL

"The Rememberer"

Hayden Carruth, *Poetry: A Critical Supplement*, Apr. 1949, 11-14.

DENNIS, CARL

"The Veteran"

Charles Altieri, "Sensibility, Rhetoric, and Will: Some Tensions in Contemporary Poetry," *ConL* 23 (Fall 1982): 451-79.

DENT, PETER

"Movement (For F. C.)"

Eileen Labrom, "Commentary," *Agenda* 9 (Winter 1971): 33.

DEUTSCH, BABETTE

"Visit to the Zoo"

Frank Jones, *Poetry: A Critical Supplement*, Nov. 1949, 11-14.

DICKEY, JAMES

"Adultery"

Constance Pierce, "Dickey's 'Adultery': A Ritual of Renewal," *CP* 9 (Fall 1976): 67-69.

"Approaching Prayer"

H. L. Weatherby, "The Way of Exchange in James Dickey's Poetry," *SR* 74 (July/Sept. 1966): 672-73.

"A Dog Sleeping on My Feet"

H. L. Weatherby, "The Way of Exchange in James Dickey's Poetry," *SR* 74 (July/Sept. 1966): 669-72.

"The Driver"

Charles C. Tucker, "Knowledge Up, Down, and Beyond: Dickey's 'The Driver' and 'Falling,'" *CEA* 38 (May 1976): 5-7.

H. L. Weatherby, "The Way of Exchange in James Dickey's Poetry," *SR* 74 (July/Sept. 1966): 675.

"The Eye-Beaters"

Joyce Carol Oates, "Out of Stone into Flesh: The Imagination of James Dickey," *MPS* 5 (Autumn 1974): 136-37.

"Falling"

Charles C. Tucker, "Knowledge Up, Down, and Beyond: Dickey's 'The Driver' and 'Falling,'" *CEA* 38 (May 1987): 7-10.

Vernon, *The Garden and the Map: Schizophrenia in Twentieth Century Literature and Culture*, passim.

"The Firebombing"

Ross Bennet, "'The Firebombing': A Reappraisal," *AL* 52 (Nov. 1980): 430-48.

Joyce Carol Oates, "Out of Stone into Flesh: The Imagination of James Dickey," *MPS* 5 (Autumn 1974): 113-18.

"The Heaven of Animals"

Carroll, *The Poem in Its Skin*, 43-49.

Nelson Hathcock, "The Predator, the Prey, and the Poet in Dickey's 'Heaven of Animals,'" *CP* 18 (1985): 47-56.

William Heyen, ed., "A Conversation with James Dickey," *SoR* 9 (Winter 1973): 142-45.

"In Pursuit from Under"

Daniel L. Guillory, "Water Magic in the Poetry of James Dickey," *ELN* 8 (Dec. 1970): 135.

"The Lifeguard"

Perrine and Reid, *100 American Poems*, 279-80.

"Mary Sheffield"

Daniel L. Guillory, "Water Magic in the Poetry of James Dickey," *ELN* 8 (Dec. 1970): 132.

"Orpheus Before Hades"

David C. Berry, "Harmony with the Dead: James Dickey's Descent into the Underworld," *SoQ* 12 (Apr. 1974): 234-35.

"The Other"

Harold Bloom, "James Dickey: From 'The Other' through *The Early Motion*," *SoR* 21 (Jan. 1985): 63-78.

"The Owl King"

Daniel L. Guillory, "Water Magic in the Poetry of James Dickey," *ELN* 8 (Dec. 1970): 133-34.

"The Performance"

William Heyen, ed., "A Conversation with James Dickey," *SoR* 9 (Winter 1973): 136-38.

"The Rain Guitar"

Robert Peters, "The Phenomenon of James Dickey, Currently," *WHR* 34 (Spring 1980): 159-66.

"Sled Burial, Deam Ceremony"

William Heyen, ed., "A Conversation with James Dickey," *SoR* 9 (Winter 1973): 149-50.

"Turning Away"

Joyce Carol Oates, "Out of Stone into Flesh: The Imagination of James Dickey," *MPS* 5 (Autumn 1974): 139-42.

The Zodiac

Linda Mizejewski, "Shamanism toward Confessionalism: James Dickey, Poet," *GaR* 32 (Summer 1978): 409-19.

Francis E. Skipp, "James Dickey's *The Zodiac*: The Heart of the Matter," *CP* 14 (1981): 1-10.

DiPALMA, RAY

"Codocil"

McCaffery, *North of Intention*, 16-20.

DOBYNS, STEPHEN

Black Dog, Red Dog

Mary Karr, "Stephen Dobyns: *Black Dog, Red Dog*," *APR* 15 (Mar./Apr. 1986): 20-22.

H. D. (HILDA DOOLITTLE)

By Avon River

Susan Stanford Frieman, "'Remembering Shakespeare Always, But Remembering Him Differently': H. D.'s *By Avon River*," *Sagetrieb* 2 (Fall 1983): 45-70.

"The Flowering of the Rod"

Joyce Lorraine Beck, "Dea, Awakening: A Reading of H. D.'s *Trilogy*," *SJS* 8 (Spring 1982): 59-70.

"Good Frend" [sic]

Susan Stanford Frieman, "'Remembering Shakespeare Always, But Remembering Him Differently': H. D.'s *By Avon River*," *Sagetrieb* 2 (Fall 1983): 45-70.

"The Guest"

Susan Stanford Frieman, "'Remembering Shakespeare Always, But Remembering Him Differently': H. D.'s *By Avon River*," *Sagetrieb* 2 (Fall 1983): 45-70.

"Helen"

Ostriker, *Stealing the Language*, 223.

"Helen in Egypt"

R. B. DuPlessis, "Romantic Thralldom in H. D.," *ConL* 20 (Spring 1979): 178-203.

L. M. Feibert, "From Semblance to Selfhood: The Evolution of Woman in H. D.'s Neo-Epic 'Helen in Egypt,'" *ArQ* 36 (1980): 165-75.

Susan Friedman, "Creating a Woman's Mythology: H. D.'s 'Helen in Egypt,'" *WS* 5 (1977): 163-97.

A. Gepi, "Hilda in Egypt," *SoR* 18 (Spring 1982): 233-50.

Elizabeth Hirsh, "*New Eyes*: H. D., Modernism, and the Psychoanalysis of Seeing," *L&P* 32, no. 3 (1986): 1-10.

"Helios and Athene"

Adalaide Morris, "Reading H. D.'s 'Helios and Athene,'" *IowaR* 12 (Spring/Summer 1981): 155-63.

"Hermetic Definition"

Vincent Quinn, "H. D.'s 'Hermetic Definition': The Poet as Archetypal Mother," *ConL* 18 (Winter 1977): 51-61.

"Oread"

Daniels, *The Art of Reading Poetry*, 198-99.

Willis D. Jacobs, *Expl* 10 (May 1952): 45. Reprinted in *The Explicator Cyclopedia* 1:88.

Juhasz, *Metaphor and Poetry*, 25-26.

Macklin Thomas, "Analysis of the Experience in Lyric Poetry," *CE* 9 (Mar. 1948): 320.

H. D.

Palimpsest

Deborah Kelley Kloepfer, "Fishing the Murex Up: Sense and Resonance in H. D.'s *Palimpsest*," *ConL* 27 (1986): 553-73.

"The Pool"

Daniels, *The Art of Reading Poetry*, 196-97. Reprinted in Stageberg and Anderson, *Poetry as Experience*, 29.

"Red Roses for Bronze"

R. P. Blackmur, "The Lesser Satisfaction," *Poetry* 41 (Nov. 1932): 94-100.

"Sagesse"

Vincent Quinn, "H. D.'s 'Hermetic Definition': The Poet as Archetypal Mother," *ConL* 18 (Winter 1977): 51-61.

"Sea Gods"

Ostriker, *Writing Like a Woman*, 12-13.

"Tribute to the Angel"

Joyce Lorraine Beck, "Dea, Awakening: A Reading of H. D.'s *Trilogy*," *SJS* 8 (Spring 1982): 59-70.

Trilogy

Susan Gubar, "The Echoing Spells of H. D.'s *Trilogy*," *ConL* 19 (Spring 1978): 196-218.

Melody M. Zajdel, "H. D.'s *Trilogy* as a Feminist Response to Masculine Modernism," *Sagetrieb* 5 (Spring 1986): 7-13.

"Walls Do Not Fall"

Joyce Lorraine Beck, "Dea, Awakening: A Reading of H. D.'s *Trilogy*, *SJS* 8 (Spring 1982): 59-70.

H. H. Watts, "H. D. and the Age of Myth," *SR* 56 (Spring, 1948): 287-303.

Watts, *Hound and Quarry*, 210-21.

"Winter Love (Espérance)"

Susan Friedman, "Who Buried H. D.? A Poet, Her Critics, and Her Place in 'The Literary Tradition,'" *CE* 36 (Mar. 1975): 808-11.

Vincent Quinn, "H. D.'s 'Hermetic Definition': The Poet as Archetypal Mother," *ConL* 18 (Winter 1977): 51-61.

DORN, EDWARD

[Interview]

Barry Alpert, "Ed Dorn," *Vort* 1 (Fall 1972): 2-19.

Edward Dorn, "Strumming Language," in Waldman and Webb, *Talking Poetics from Naropa Institute* 1:83-95.

Tandy Sturgeon, "An Interview with Ed Dorn," *ConL* 27 (Spring 1986): 1-16.

Stephen Fredman, "Roadtesting the Language: An Interview with Edward Dorn," *Documents for New Poetry* 1 (1978): n.p.

"Death while Journeying"

Von Hallberg, *American Poetry and Culture, 1945-1980*, passim.

Gunslinger

Donald Davie, "Ed Dorn and the Treasures of Comedy," *Vort* 1 (Fall 1972): 2-19.

Hello La Jolla

Sherman Paul, *The Lost America of Love*, passim.

Alan Golding, "Edward Dorn's 'Pontificatory Use of the Art': *Hello La Jolla* and *Yellow Lola*," in Wesling, *Internal Resistance: The Poetry of Ed Dorn*, 208-34.

Kathryn Shevelow, "Reading Edward Dorn's *Hello La Jolla* and *Yellow Lola*," *Sagetrieb* 2 (Fall 1983): 99-109.

"Idaho Out"

Laurie Ricou, "Prairie Poetry and Metaphors of Plain/s Space," *GPQ* 3 (Spring 1983): 109-19.

Recollections of Gran Apachería

Paul Dresman, "Internal Resistances: Edward Dorn on the American Indian," in Wesling, *Internal Resistance: The Poetry of Ed Dorn*, 87-112.

Slinger

Michael Davidson, "To Eliminate the Draw: Edward Dorn's *Slinger*," *AL* 53 (Nov. 1981): 443-64.

Michael Davidson, "To Eliminate the Draw: Narrative and Language in *Slinger*," in Wesling, *Internal Resistance: The Poetry of Ed Dorn*, 113-49.

Alan Golding, "History, Mutation, and the Mutation of History in Edward Dorn's *Slinger*," *Sagetrieb* 6 (Spring 1987): 7-20.

William J. Lockwood, "Art Rising to Clarity: Edward Dorn's Compleat *Slinger*," in Wesling, *Internal Resistance: The Poetry of Ed Dorn*, 150-207.

Yellow Lola

Alan Golding, "Edward Dorn's 'Pontificatory Use of the Art': *Hello, La Jolla* and *Yellow Lola*," in Wesling, *Internal Resistance: The Poetry of Ed Dorn*, 208-34.

Kathryn Shevelow, "Reading Edward Dorn's *Hello La Jolla* and *Yellow Lola,*" *Sagetrieb* 2 (Fall 1983): 99-109.

DOVE, RITA

"Dusting"

John Shoptaw, Review of *Thomas and Beulah, BALF* 21 (Fall 1987): 335-41.

Thomas and Beulah

John Shoptaw, Review of *Thomas and Beulah, BALF* 21 (Fall 1987): 335-41.

DUBIE, NORMAN

"Indian Summer"

John Bensko, "Reflexive Narration in Contemporary American Poetry: Some Examples from Mark Strand, John Ashbery, Norman Dubie, and Louis Simpson," *JNT* 16 (Spring 1986): 81-96.

"The Scythes"

John Bensko, "Reflexive Narration in Contemporary American Poetry: Some Examples from Mark Strand, John Ashbery, Norman Dubie, and Louis Simpson," *JNT* 16 (Spring 1986): 81-96.

DUNCAN, ROBERT

[Interview]

Michael Andre Bernstein and Burton Hatlen, "Interview with Robert Duncan," *Sagetrieb* 4 (Fall/Winter 1985): 87-135.

Jack R. Cohen, "The Poetry of Unevenness: An Interview with Robert Duncan," *Credences* 3 (Spring 1985): 91-111.

Jack R. Cohen and Thomas J. O'Donnell, "An Interview with Robert Duncan," *ConL* 21 (1980): 513-48.

Robert Duncan, "Warp and Woof: Notes from a Talk," in Waldman and Webb, *Talking Poetics from Naropa Institute* 1:1-10.

"An African Elegy"

Faas, *Young Robert Duncan*, 151-54.

"At the Loom"

Michael Davidson, "'From the Latin *Speculum*': The Modern Poet as Philologist," *ConL* 28 (Summer 1987): 187-205.

Bending the Bow

Dennis Cooley, "Robert Duncan's Green Wor[l]ds," *Credences*, no. 8/9 [vol. 3] (Mar. 1980): 152-60.

Mark Johnson, "Robert Duncan's 'Momentous Inconclusions,'" *Sagetrieb* 2 (Fall 1983): 71-84.

Mersmann, *Out of the Vietnam Vortex: A Study of Poets and Poetry against the War*, 159-204.

Sherman Paul, *The Lost America of Love*, passim.

Caesar's Gate

Carl D. Esbjornson, "Tracking the Soul's Truth: Robert Duncan's Revisioning of the Self in *Caesar's Gate*," *Sagetrieb* 4 (Fall/Winter 1985): 257-72.

"The Continent"

Nathaniel Mackey, "The World-Poem in Microcosm: Robert Duncan's 'The Continent,'" *ELH* 47 (1980): 595-618.

"Earth's Winter Song"

Dennis Cooley, "Robert Duncan's Green Wor[l]ds," *Credences*, no. 8/9 [vol. 3] (Mar. 1980): 152-60.

"The Fire"

Dennis Cooley, "Robert Duncan's Green Wor[l]ds," *Credences*, no. 8/9 [vol. 3] (Mar. 1980): 152-60.

Ground Work

Michael Andre Bernstein, "Robert Duncan: Talent and the Individual Tradition," *Sagetrieb* 4 (Fall/Winter 1985): 177-90.

George Butterick, "Seraphic Predator: A First Reading of Robert Duncan's *Ground Work*," *Sagetrieb* 4 (Fall/Winter 1985): 177-90.

T. Parkinson, "Robert Duncan's *Ground Work*," *SoR* 21 (Winter 1985): 52-62.

"Heavenly City, Earthly City"

Faas, *Young Robert Duncan*, 220-22.

"The Homosexual in Society"

Faas, *Young Robert Duncan*, 149-52.

"I Am a Most Fleshly Man"

Norman M. Finkelstein, "Robert Duncan: Poet of the Law," *Sagetrieb* 2 (Spring 1983): 75-88.

"The Law I Love Is Major Mover"

Norman M. Finkelstein, "Robert Duncan: Poet of the Law," *Sagetrieb* 2 (Spring 1983): 75-88.

"The Mirror"

Faas, *Young Robert Duncan*, 230.

The Opening of the Field

Dennis Cooley, "Robert Duncan's Green Wor[l]ds," *Credences* 8/9 [vol. 3] (Mar. 1980): 152-60.

Norman M. Finkelstein, "Robert Duncan: Poet of the Law," *Sagetrieb* 2 (Spring 1983): 75-88.

Joseph G. Kronick, "Robert Duncan and the Truth that Lies in Myth," *Sagetrieb* 4 (Fall/Winter 1985): 191-207.

Sherman Paul, *The Lost America of Love*, passim.

"A Poem Beginning with a Line from Pindar"

Michael Heller, "The True Epithalamium," *Sagetrieb* 3 (Spring 1984): 77-88.

Thurley, *The American Moment--American Poetry in the Mid-Century*, 139-55.

"The Propositions, 2"

Eniko Bollobas, "Potencies of Words: A Grammetrical Reading of Robert Duncan's 'The Propositions, 2,'" *Lang&S* 19 (1986): 219-32.

Roots and Branches

Norman M. Finkelstein, "Robert Duncan: Poet of the Law," *Sagetrieb* 2 (Spring 1983): 75-86.

Mark Johnson, "Robert Johnson's 'Momentous Inconclusions,'" *Sagetrieb* 2 (Fall 1983): 71-84.

Joseph G. Kronick, "Robert Duncan and the Truth that Lies in Myth," *Sagetrieb* 4 (Fall/Winter 1985): 191-207.

Sherman Paul, *The Lost America of Love*, passim.

"Such Is the Sickness"

Thurley, *The American Moment--American Poetry in the Mid-Century*, 139-55.

"The Torso"

Martin, *The Homosexual Tradition in American Poetry*, 171-79.

"Where We Are, 1-12"

Thomas Gardner, "'Where We Are': A Reading of Passages 1-12," *Sagetrieb* 4 (Fall/Winter 1985): 285-306.

EBERHART, RICHARD

"Experience Evoked"

Seamus Cooney, *Expl* 32 (Jan. 1974): 39.

Richard Eberhart, *Expl* 32 (May 1974): 76.

"From Letter I"

J. F. Nims, *Poetry: A Critical Supplement*, Apr. 1948, 11.

"The Fury of Aerial Bombardment"

Jo Allen Bradham, *Expl* 22 (May 1964): 71.

Ciardi, *How Does a Poem Mean?*, 999-1002.

"Grave Piece"

Richard Eberhart, *Expl* 6 (Feb. 1948): 23. Reprinted in Engel and Carrier, *Reading Modern Poetry*, 273-74; in *The Explicator Cyclopedia* 1:89-90.

"The Groundhog"

Abad, *A Formal Approach to Lyric Poetry*, 54-59.

Aerol Arnold, *Expl* 15 (Oct. 1956): 3. Reprinted in *The Explicator Cyclopedia* 1:90-91.

Harry J. Cargas, *Daniel Berrigan and Contemporary Protest Poetry* (New Haven: College and University Press, 1972), 23-26.

Deutsch, *Poetry in Our Time*, 216-17.

Sydney Mendel, *Expl* 17 (June 1959): 64. Reprinted in *The Explicator Cyclopedia* 1:91-92.

Perrine and Reid, *100 American Poems*, 193-94.

Rosenthal, *The Modern Poets*, 247.

M. L. Rosenthal, "Three Poets in Focus," *New Republic* 125 (10 Dec. 1951): 27.

Wright, *The Poet in the Poem*, 55-57.

"Hardening into Print"

Gutiérrez, *The Maze in the Mind and the World: Labyrinths in Modern Literature*, passim.

"The Horse Chestnut Tree"

Perrine and Reid, *100 American Poems*, 195-96.

"The Incomparable Light"

Gutiérrez, *The Maze in the Mind and the World*, passim.

"I Walked Out to the Graveyard to See the Dead"

Richard Eberhart in Friar and Brinnin, *Modern Poetry*, 458-59.

"Light from Above"

Gutiérrez, *The Maze in the Mind and the World*, passim.

"Meditation"

J. L. Sweeney and I. A. Richards [Letters], *Furioso* 1 (Spring 1940): 42-43.

"On a Squirrel Crossing the Road in Autumn, New England"

Perrine and Reid, *100 American Poems*, 196-98.

"Opulence"

Gutiérrez, *The Maze in the Mind and the World*, passim.

"Orchard"

Mills, *Contemporary American Poetry*, 19-20.

"Seals, Terns, Time"

Richard Eberhart, *Expl* 30 (Dec. 1971): 29.
Alvin Sullivan, *Expl* 30 (Dec. 1971): 29.

"Throwing the Apple"

Richard F. Bauerle, *Expl* 27 (Nov. 1968): 21.

"Ur Burial"

Richard F. Bauerle, *Expl* 16 (Apr. 1958): 38. Reprinted in *The Explicator Cyclopedia* 1:92-93.

Richard Eberhart, *Expl* 16 (May 1958): 48. Reprinted in *The Explicator Cyclopedia* 1:92-93.

"The Young Hunter"

Richard Eberhart, *Expl* 6 (Feb. 1948): 24. Reprinted in *The Explicator Cyclopedia* 1:93-94.

EDSON, RUSSELL

"One Wonders"

Alberta T. Turner, "Implied Metaphor: A Problem in Evaluating Contemporary Poetry," *IowaR* 5 (Winter 1974): 116-17.

ELIOT, T. S.

"The Ad-dressing of Cats"

Felix Clowder, "The Bestiary of T. S. Eliot," *PrS* 34 (Spring 1960): 35-36.

"Animula"

Melvin W. Askew, "Form and Process in Lyric Poetry," *SR* 72 (Spring 1964): 281-99.

T. A. Stroud, *Expl* 28 (Oct. 1969): 14.

"Ariel Poems"

Richard Sylvia, *Expl* 45 (Fall 1986): 41-42.

"Ash Wednesday"

Blackmur, *The Double Agent*, 190-96. Reprinted in Blackmur, *Language as Gesture*, 168-71.

Gwenn R. Boardman, "'Ash Wednesday': Eliot's Lenten Mass Sequence," *Renascence* 15 (Autumn 1962): 28-36.

A. P. Brady, *Lyricism in the Poetry of T. S. Eliot* (Port Washington: Kennikat Press, 1978), passim.

Cleanth Brooks and Robert Penn Warren, "The Reading of Modern Poetry," *American Review* 7 (Feb. 1937): 445-46.

Paul J. Dolan, "'Ash Wednesday': A Catechumenical Poem," *Renascence* 19 (Summer 1967): 198-207.

Daniel N. Dwyer, S.J., *Expl* 9 (Oct. 1950): 5. Reprinted in *The Explicator Cyclopedia* 1:95.

F. Peter Dzwonkoski, Jr., "'The Hollow Men' and 'Ash Wednesday': Two Dark Nights," *ArQ* 30 (Spring 1974): 23-42.

Genevieve W. Foster, "Archetypal Imagery of T. S. Eliot," *PMLA* 60 (June 1945): 580-82.

Vincent Freimarck, *Expl* 9 (Oct. 1950): 6. Reprinted in *The Explicator Cyclopedia* 1:94-95.

Friar and Brinnin, *Modern Poetry*, 465-72.

Nancy D. Hargrove, "Landscape as Symbol in T. S. Eliot's 'Ash Wednesday,'" *ArQ* 30 (Spring 1974): 53-62.

Hugh Kenner, "Eliot's Moral Dialectic," *HudR* 2 (Autumn 1949): 439-46.

J. M. Kertzer, "T. S. Eliot and the Problem of Will," *MLQ* 45 (Dec. 1984): 373-94.

Leavis, *New Bearings in English Poetry*, 117-28.

Sr. M. Cleophas, "'Ash Wednesday': *The Purgatorio* in Modern Mode," *CL* 11 (Fall 1959): 329-39.

Miller, *Poets of Reality*, 182-84.

George Monteiro, "T. S. Eliot and Stephen Foster," *Expl* 45 (Spring 1987): 44-45.

Theodore Morrison, "'Ash Wednesday': A Religious History," *NEQ* 11 (June 1938): 266-86.

Pottle, *The Idiom of Poetry*, 89-91; rev. ed. (1946), 96-99.

B. Rajan, "The Overwhelming Question," *SR* 74 (Jan./Mar. 1966): 368-70.

John N. Sero, "Landscape and Voice in T. S. Eliot's Poetry," *CentR* 26 (Winter 1982): 33-50.

Eleanor M. Sickels, *Expl* 9 (Oct. 1950): 4.

Sr. Margaret Patrice Slattery, "Structural Unity in Eliot's 'Ash Wednesday,'" *Renascence* 20 (Spring 1968): 147-52.

Gordon Symes, "T. S. Eliot and Old Age," *Fortnightly* 169 (Mar. 1951): 188-91.

Allen Tate, "Irony and Humility," *Hound and Horn* 4 (Jan./Mar. 1931): 290-97.

Tate, *Reactionary Essays on Poetry and Ideas*, 210-20. Reprinted in Tate, *On the Limits of Poetry*, 344-49.

M. Thormahlen, "Dry Bones Can Harm No One: Ezekiel 37 in *The Waste Land* 5 and 'Ash Wednesday' 2," *ES* 65 (Feb. 1984): 37-47.

Tschumi, *Thought in Twentieth-Century English Poetry*, 144-46.

D. N. Tobin, *The Presence of the Past: T. S. Eliot's Victorian Inheritance* (Ann Arbor: UMI Research, 1983), 55-72.

Leonard Unger, "Notes on 'Ash Wednesday,'" *SoR* 4 (Spring 1939): 745-70.

Unger, *The Man in the Name*, 141-66.

Leonard Unger, "T. S. Eliot's Images of Awareness," *SR* 74 (Jan./Mar. 1966): 207, 211-12.

Leonard Unger, "T. S. Eliot's Rose Garden: A Persistent Theme," *SoR* 7 (Spring 1942): 675-76.

Eugene Webb, *The Dark Dove: The Sacred and Secular in Modern Literature* (Seattle and London: University of Washington Press, 1975), 203-20.

William Carlos Williams, "The Fatal Blunder," *Quarterly Review of Literature* 2 (1944): 125-26.

Carl Wooten, "The Mass: 'Ash Wednesday' 's Objective Correlative," *ArQ* 17 (Spring 1961): 31-42.

"Aunt Helen"

Abad, *A Formal Approach to Lyric Poetry*, 159-60, 164.

"The Boston Evening Transcript"

W. C. Brown, "'A Poem Should Not Mean But Be,'" *University of Kansas City Review* 15 (Autumn 1948): 61-62.

"Burbank with a Baedeker: Bleistein with a Cigar"

Robert F. Goheen, "'Burbank with a Baedeker': The Third Stanza," *SR* 61 (Winter 1953): 109-19.

L. G. Locke, *Expl* 3 (May 1945): 53. Reprinted in *The Explicator Cyclopedia* 1:95-96.

James Longenbach, "Guarding the Horned Gates: History and Interpretation in the Early Poetry of T. S. Eliot," *ELH* 52 (1985): 503-30.

Riding and Graves, *A Survey of Modernist Poetry*, 235-42.

Theodore Spencer, "The Poetry of T. S. Eliot," *Atlantic Monthly* 151 (Jan. 1933): 61-62.

Richard C. Turner, "Burbank and Grub-Street: A Note on T. S. Eliot and Swift," *ES* 52 (Aug. 1971): 347-48.

Jane Worthington, "The Epigraphs to the Poetry of T. S. Eliot," *AL* 21 (Mar. 1949): 6-7.

"The Burial of the Dead"

Mutlu Konuk Blasing, "*The Waste Land*: Gloss and Glossary," *Essays in Literature* 9 (Spring 1982): 97-106.

"Burnt Norton"

Mother Mary Anthony, "Verbal Pattern in 'Burnt Norton I,'" *Criticism* 2 (Winter 1960): 81-89.

C. A. Bodelson, "Two 'Difficult' Poems by T. S. Eliot," *ES* 34 (Feb. 1953): 17-21.

Daiches and Charvat, *Poems in English*, 741-42.

Elizabeth Drew, in Locke, Gibson, and Arms, *Readings for Liberal Education*, 3d ed., 216-22. Reprinted from Drew, *T. S. Eliot: The Design of His Poetry* (New York: Charles Scribner's Sons, 1950), 151-62; 4th ed., 218-24; 5th ed., 200-207.

Drew and Sweeney, *Directions in Modern Poetry*, 138-40.

Barbara Everett, "A Visit to Burnt Norton," *CritQ* 16 (Autumn 1974): 199-224.

Friar and Brinnin, *Modern Poetry*, 461-65.

C. O. Gardner, "Some Reflections on the Opening of 'Burnt Norton,'" *CritQ* 12 (Winter 1970): 326-29.

Harvey Gross, "Music and the Analogue of Feeling: Some Notes on Eliot and Beethoven," *CentR* (Summer 1959): 272-74.

Leavis, *Education and the University*, 94-98.

F. R. Leavis, "Eliot's Later Poetry," *Scrutiny* 11 (Summer 1942): 65-67.

ELIOT, T.S.

A. O. Lewis, Jr., *Expl* 8 (Nov. 1949): 9. Reprinted in *The Explicator Cyclopedia* 1:98-99.

Mack, Dean, and Frost, *Modern Poetry*, 15-16.

Walter J. Ong, "'Burnt Norton' in St. Louis," *AL* 33 (Jan. 1962): 522-26.

Mark Reisenberg, "A Footnote to *Four Quartets*," *AL* 21 (Nov. 1949): 342-44.

Linda Bradley Salamon, "The Orchestration of 'Burnt Norton II,'" *UTQ* 45 (Fall 1975): 51-66.

Schneider, *Poems and Poetry*, 498-99.

C. T. Thomas, "Eliot's 'Burnt Norton,' lines 16-23," *Expl* 38 (Spring 1980): 14-15.

Tschumi, *Thought in Twentieth-Century English Poetry*, 149-54.

Unger, *The Man in the Name*, 177-81.

Leonard Unger, "T. S. Eliot's Rose Garden: A Persistent Theme," *SoR* 7 (Spring 1942): 677-81.

Philip Wheelwright, "The Burnt Norton Trilogy," *Chimera* 1 (1942): 7-18.

Jane Worthington, "The Epigraphs to the Poetry of T. S. Eliot," *AL* 21 (Mar. 1949): 16-17.

"Cape Ann"

Erik Arne Hansen, "T. S. Eliot's 'Landscapes,'" *ES* 50 (Aug. 1969): 374-76.

"A Cooking Egg"

Drew, *Discovering Poetry*, 113-15.

Peckham and Chatham, *Word, Meaning, Poem*, 320-22.

Richards, *Principles of Literary Criticism*, 293-94.

Grover Smith, Jr., "Getting Used to T. S. Eliot," *EJ* 49 (Jan. 1960): 8-9.

Sherna S. Vinograd, "The Accidental: A Cue to Structure in Eliot's Poetry," *Accent* 9 (Summer 1949): 231-32.

Jane Worthington, "The Epigraphs to the Poetry of T. S. Eliot," *AL* 21 (Mar. 1949): 9-10.

"Coriolan"

Edwards, *Imagination and Power*, 197-203.

Feder, *Ancient Myth in Modern Poetry*, 312-15.

Donald F. Theall, "Traditional Satire in Eliot's 'Coriolan,'" *Accent* 11 (Autumn 1951): 194-206.

"The Cultivation of Christmas Trees"

Hugh Kenner, "A Plea for Metrics," *Poetry* 86 (Apr. 1955): 42-45.

"Dans le Restaurant"

William Arrowsmith, "Daedal Harmonies: A Dialogue on Eliot and the Classics," *SoR* 13 (Winter 1977): 1-47.

Jeanne Flood, "T. S. Eliot's 'Dans le Restaurant,'" *AI* 33 (Summer 1976): 155-73.

Frankenberg, *Pleasure Dome*, 72-76.

Unger, *The Man in the Name*, 169-71.

Leonard Unger, "T. S. Eliot's Rose Garden: A Persistent Theme," *SoR* 7 (Spring 1942): 669-71.

"The Death of Saint Narcissus"

V. Mahaffey, "'The Death of Saint Narcissus' and 'Ode': Two Suppressed Poems by T. S. Eliot," *AL* 50 (Jan. 1979): 604-12.

"The Death of the Duchess"

James Longenbach, "Guarding the Horned Gates: History and Interpretation in the Early Poetry of T. S. Eliot," *ELH* 52 (1985): 503-30.

"A Dedication to My Wife"

Leonard Unger, "T. S. Eliot's Images of Awareness," *SR* 74 (Jan./Mar. 1966): 222-24.

ELIOT, T.S.

"The Dry Salvages"

Ackroyd, *T. S. Eliot*, 262-65, 328-29.

Stephen J. Adams, "T. S. Eliot's So-Called Sestina: A Note on 'The Dry Salvages,'" II, *ELN* 15 (1978): 203-207.

John D. Boyd, S.J., "The Dry Salvages: Topography as Symbol," *Renascence* 20 (Spring 1968): 119-32.

John Bugge, "Rhyme as Onomatopoeia in 'The Dry Salvages,'" *PLL* 10 (Summer 1974): 312-16.

Jack L. Davis, "Transcendental Vision in 'The Dry Salvages,'" *ESQ* 62 (Winter 1971): 38-44,

F. Peter Dzwonkoski, Jr., "Time and the River, Time and the Sea: A Study of T. S. Eliot's 'Dry Salvages,'" *CimR* 30 (Jan. 1975): 48-57.

Harvey Gross, "Music and the Analogue of Feeling: Notes on Eliot and Beethoven," *CentR* 3 (Summer 1959): 277.

Leavis, *Education and the University*, 99-103.

F. R. Leavis, "Eliot's Later Poetry," *Scrutiny* 11 (Summer 1942): 68-71.

Audrey T. Rodgers, "The Mythic Perspective of Eliot's 'The Dry Salvages,'" *ArQ* 30 (Spring 1974): 81-93.

Unger, *The Man in the Name*, 186-88.

Leonard Unger, "T. S. Eliot's Rose Garden: A Persistent Theme," *SoR* 7 (Spring 1942): 687-89.

Waggoner, *The Heel of Elohim*, 91-99.

Philip Wheelwright, "The Burnt Norton Trilogy," *Chimera* 1 (1942): 7-18.

"East Coker"

Beaty and Matchett, *Poetry: From Statement to Meaning*, 235-36.

Curtis Bradsford, "Footnotes to *East Coker*: A Reading," *SR* 52 (Jan./Mar. 1944): 169-75.

D. Bosley Brotman, "T. S. Eliot: The Music of Ideas," *UTQ* 18 (Oct. 1948): 22-29.

Anita Gandolfo, *Expl* 39 (Summer 1981): 24-25.

Harvey Gross, "Music and the Analgoue of Feeling: Notes on Eliot and Beethoven," *CentR* 3 (Summer 1959): 274-75.

H. W. Hausermann, "'East Coker' and *The Family Reunion*," *Life and Letters* 8 (Oct. 1945): 32-38.

Jack Kligerman, "An Interpretation of T. S. Eliot's 'East Coker,'" *ArQ* 18 (Summer 1962): 101-12.

Scott, *Rehearsals of Discomposure*, 237-43.

F. J. Smith, "A Reading of 'East Coker,'" *Thought* 21 (June 1946): 272-86.

James Johnson Sweeney, "East Coker: A Reading," *SoR* 6 (Spring 1941): 771-91.

Unger, *The Man in the Name*, 185-86.

Leonard Unger, "T. S. Eliot's Rose Garden: A Persistent Theme," *SoR* 7 (Spring 1942): 686-87.

The Family Reunion

A. Wertheim, "The Modern British Homecoming Play," *CompD* 19 (Summer 1985): 151-92.

"La Figlia che Piange"

Edward A. Geary, "T. S. Eliot and the *Fin-de-siècle*," *RMR* 40, no. 1 (1986): 21-33.

Jean Hagstrum, *English "A" Analyst*, no. 3, 1-7.

Vernon Hall, Jr., *Expl* 5 (Nov. 1946): 16.

Martin Scofield, "'A gesture and a pose': T. S. Eliot's Images of Love," *CritQ* 18 (Autumn 1976): 11-14.

Jane Worthington, "The Epigraphs to the Poetry of T. S. Eliot," *AL* 21 (Mar. 1949): 4-5.

"The Fire Sermon"

Blasing, *American Poetry: The Rhetoric of Its Forms*, 44.

ELIOT, T.S.

"For Ralph Hodgson Esgre"

Stanford S. Apseloff, "T. S. Eliot and Ralph Hodgson Esgre," *JML* 10 (June 1983): 342-46.

"Four Quartets"

Ackroyd, *T. S. Eliot*, 262-66, 268-72.

Frances O. Austin, "ING Forms in 'Four Quartets,'" *ES* 63 (Feb. 1982): 23-31.

P. Barry, "Making Sense of Syntax, Perhaps: A Reply to Frances Austin's 'ING Forms in 'Four Quartets,'" *ES* 65 (Feb. 1984): 36-38.

Ole Bay-Peterson, "T. S. Eliot and Einstein: The Fourth Dimension in the 'Four Quartets,'" *ES* 66 (1985): 143-55.

Joseph Beaver, *Expl* 11 (Mar. 1953): 37. Reprinted in *The Explicator Cyclopedia* 1:97-98.

William Bisset, "The Argument of T. S. Eliot's 'Four Quarters,'" *UTQ* 15 (Jan. 1946): 115-26.

Blackmur, *Language as Gesture*, 192-220.

R. P. Blackmur, "Unappeasable and Peregrine: Behavior and the 'Four Quartets,'" *Thought* 26 (Spring 1951): 50-76.

Blasing, *American Poetry: The Rhetoric of Its Forms*, 48-49.

Bornstein, *Transformations of Romanticism*, 154-60.

Bowra, *The Creative Experiment*, 22-23.

John M. Bradbury, "'Four Quartets': The Structural Symbolism," *SR* 59 (Spring 1951): 254-70.

A. P. Brady, *Lyricism in the Poetry of T. S. Eliot* (Port Washington: Kennikat, 1979), passim.

Curtis B. Bradsford, "Journeys to Byzantium," *VQR* 25 (Spring 1949): 216-24.

R. L. Brett, "Mysticism and Incarnation in 'Four Quartets,'" *English* 16 (Autumn 1966): 94-99.

Brett, *Reason and Imagination*, 119-35.

Jewel Spears Brooker, "F. H. Bradley's Doctrine of Experience in T. S. Eliot's 'The Waste Land' and 'Four Quartets,'" *MP* 77 (Nov. 1979): 146-57.

Frank Bunch Brown, "'The Progress of the Intellectual Soul': Eliot, Pascal, and 'Four Quartets,'" *JML* 10 (Mar. 1983): 26-39.

P. H. Butler, "'Four Quartets': Some yes-buts to Dr. Leavis," *CritQ* 18 (Spring 1976): 31-40.

R. Caspar, "'All Shall Be Well': Prototypica: Symbols of Hope," *JHI* 42 (Jan./Mar. 1981): 139-50.

Merrel D. Clubb, Jr., "The Heraclitean Element in Eliot's 'Four Quartets,'" *PQ* 40 (Jan. 1961): 19-33.

Ethel F. Cornwell, *The "Still Point,"* 17-61.

Elizabeth S. Dallas, "Canon Cancrizans and the 'Four Quartets,'" *CL* 17 (Summer 1965): 193-208.

Donald Davie, "T. S. Eliot: The End of an Era," *TC* 159 (Apr. 1956): 350-62.

Vivian De Sola Pinto, *Crisis in English Poetry*, 180-84.

Deutsch, *Poetry in Our Time*, 164-67, 170-72, 177-80.

Arnold P. Drew, "Hints and Guesses in 'Four Quartets,'" *University of Kansas City Review* 20 (Spring 1954): 171-75.

R. W. Flint, "The 'Four Quartets' Reconsidered," *SR* 56 (Winter 1948): 69-81.

Joseph Frank, "Force and Form: A Study of John Peale Bishop," *SR* 55 (Winter 1947): 102-3.

Frankenberg, *Pleasure Dome*, 98-117.

Friar and Brinnin, *Modern Poetry*, 426-27, 459-61.

B. H. Fussell, "Structural Methods in 'Four Quartets,'" *ELH* 22 (Sept. 1955): 201-8.

Paul Fussell, Jr., "The Gestic Symbolism of T. S. Eliot," *ELH* 22 (Sept. 1955): 201-8.

Helen L. Gardner, "'Four Quartets': A Commentary." Reprinted in Stallman, *Critiques*, 181-97.

Frederick Glaysher, "T. S. Eliot and 'The horror! The horror!'" *Modern Age* 28 (Fall 1984): 339-48.

L. Gordon, *Eliot's Early Years* (New York: Oxford University Press, 1977), passim.

Harvey Gross, "Music and the Analogue of Feeling: Notes on Eliot and Beethoven," *CentR* 3 (Summer 1959): 276-77, 282-88.

N. D. Hargrove, *Landscape as Symbol in the Poetry of T. S. Eliot* (Jackson: University of Mississippi Press, 1978), passim.

A. Kennedy, "The Speaking 'I' in 'Four Quartets,'" *ES* 60 (Apr. 1978): 166-75.

George A. Knox, "Quest for the Word in Eliot's 'Four Quartets,'" *ELH* 18 (Dec. 1951): 310-21.

Karl Malkoff, "Eliot and Elytis: Poet of Time, Poet of Space," *CL* 36 (Summer 1984): 238-57.

Sr. Mary Gerard, "Eliot of the Circle and John of the Cross," *Thought* 34 (Spring 1959): 107-27.

James E. Miller, Jr., "Whitman and Eliot: The Poetry of Mysticism," *SWR* 43 (Spring 1958): 114-23.

Arthur Mizener, "To Meet Mr. Eliot," *SR* 65 (Winter 1957): 45-49.

T. Morrissey, "'Intimate and Unidentifiable': The Voices of Fragmented Reality in the Poetry of T. S. Eliot," *CentR* 22 (1978): 1-27.

William T. Moynihan, "Character and Action in 'The Four Quartets,'" *Mosaic* 6 (Fall 1972): 203-28.

George L. Musacchio, "A Note on the Fire-Rose Synthesis of T. S. Eliot's 'Four Quartets,'" *ES* 45 (June 1964): 238.

David Perkins, "Rose Garden to Midwinter Spring: Achieved Faith in the 'Four Quartets,'" *MLQ* 23 (Mar. 1962): 41-45.

M. Gilbert Porter, "Narrative Stance in *Four Quartets*: Choreography and Commentary," *University of Kansas City Review* 26 (Autumn 1969): 57-66.

Quinn, *The Metamorphic Tradition*, 143-47.

B. Rajan," The Overwhelming Question," *SR* 74 (Jan./Mar. 1966): 370-72.

Thomas R. Rees, "The Orchestration of Meaning in T. S. Eliot's 'Four Quartets,'" *JAAC* 28 (Fall 1969): 63-69.

Julia M. Reibetanz, "Accentual Forms in Eliot's Poetry from *The Hollow Men* to 'Four Quartets,'" *ES* 65 (Aug. 1984): 334-49.

Julia M. Reibetanz, "Traditional Meters in 'Four Quartets,'" *ES* 56 (Oct. 1975): 409-20.

Rosenthal, *The Modern Poets*, 88-89, 94-103.

John N. Serio, "Landscape and Voice in T. S. Eliot's Poetry," *CentR* 26 (Winter 1982): 33-50.

James P. Sexton, "Four Quartets and the Christian Calendar," *AL* 43 (May 1971): 279-81.

T. B. Shepherd, "The *Four Quartets* Re-examined," *London Quarterly and Holborn Review* 175 (July 1950): 228-39.

Gordon Symes, "T. S. Eliot and Old Age," *Fortnightly* 169 (Mar. 1951):192-93.

Leonard Unger, *Eliot's Compound Ghost: Influence and Confluence* (University Park: Pennsylvania State University Press, 1982), passim.

Leonard Unger, "T. S. Eliot's Image of Awareness," *SR* 74 (Jan./Mar. 1966): 212-15.

Robert D. Wagner, "The Meaning of Eliot's Rose Garden," *PMLA* 69 (Mar. 1954): 22-33.

Watts, *Hound and Quarry*, 226-38.

A. Kingsley Weatherhead, "'Four Quartets': Setting Love in Order," *Wisconsin Studies in Contemporary Literature* 3 (Spring-Summer 1962): 32-49.

Eugene Webb, *The Dark Dove: The Sacred and Secular in Modern Literature* (Seattle: University of Washington Press, 1975), 221-36.

Morris Weitz, "T. S. Eliot: Time as a Mode of Salvation," *SR* 60 (Winter 1952): 49-52, 55-64.

Wheelwright, *The Burning Fountain*, 332-36, 350-64.

George T. Wright, "Eliot Written in a Country Churchyard: *The Elegy* and 'Four Quartets,'" *ELH* 43 (Summer 1976): 227-43.

Woodward, *At Last, the Real Distinguished Thing: The Late Poems of Eliot, Pound, Stevens, and Williams*, passim.

"Gerontion"

James Applewhite, *Seas and Inland Journeys: Landscape and Consciousness from Wordsworth to Roethke* (Athens: University of Georgia, 1985), passim.

R. P. Blackmur, "T. S. Eliot," *Hound and Horn* 1 (Mar. 1928): 201-3.

D. S. Bonds, "The House of Mirrors: Language in Eliot's 'Gerontion,'" *CollL* 9 (Winter 1982): 44-53.

Jewel Spears Brooker, "The Structure of Eliot's 'Gerontion': An Interpretation Based on Bradley's Doctrine of the Systematic Nature of Truth," *ELH* 46 (1979): 314-40.

Brooks, Lewis, and Warren, *American Literature*, 2107-11.

Alec Brown, "The Lyric Impulse in the Poetry of T. S. Eliot," *Scrutiny* 2:7-12.

Robert M. Brown and Joseph B. Yokelson, *Expl* 15 (Feb. 1957): 31. Reprinted in *The Explicator Cyclopedia* 1:103-4.

Taylor Culbert, *Expl* 17 (Dec. 1958): 20. Reprinted in *The Explicator Cyclopedia* 1:104-5.

David Daiches, "Some Aspects of T. S. Eliot," *CE* 9 (Dec. 1947): 117-20.

Daiches and Charvat, *Poems in English*, 738-40.

Edgar F. Daniels, *Expl* 17 (May 1959): 58. Reprinted in *The Explicator Cyclopedia* 1:106.

Douglas, Lamson, and Smith, *The Critical Reader*, 125-30.

Drew and Sweeney, *Directions in Modern Poetry*, 42-44.

F. Dye, *Expl* 18 (Apr. 1960): 39. Reprinted in *The Explicator Cyclopedia* 1:102-3.

William R. Eshelman, *Expl* 4 (Apr. 1946): 44. Reprinted in *The Explicator Cyclopedia* 1:99-101.

Feder, *Ancient Myth in Modern Poetry*, 308-11.

Armin Paul Frank, *Expl* 30 (Mar. 1972): 53.

Frankenberg, *Pleasure Dome*, 51-56.

G. S. Fraser, *TLS*, June 11, 1970.

Friar and Brinnin, *Modern Poetry*, 497-98.

Clark Griffith, *Expl* 21 (Feb. 1963): 46.

Harvey Gross, "'Gerontion' and the Meaning of History," *PMLA* 73 (June 1958): 299-304.

Robert B. Kaplan and Richard J. Wall, *Expl* 19 (Mar. 1961): 36. Reprinted in *The Explicator Cyclopedia* 1:106-7.

Elsie Leach, "'Gerontion' and Marvell's 'The Garden,'" *ELN* 13 (Sept. 1975): 45-48.

Leavis, *New Bearings on English Poetry*, 79-87.

Mack, Dean, and Frost, *Modern Poetry*, 22.

John M. Major, "Eliot's 'Gerontion' and *As You Like It*," *MLN* 74 (Jan. 1959): 29-31.

Arthur Mizener, "To Meet Mr. Eliot," *SR* (Winter 1957): 42-44.

George Monteiro, *Expl* 18 (Feb. 1960): 30. Reprinted in *The Explicator Cyclopedia* 1:105-6.

Myrtle P. Pope, *Expl* 6 (May 1948), 16. Reprinted in *The Explicator Cyclopedia* 1:101.

Frederick A. Pottle, *Expl* 4 (June 1946): 55.

B. Rajan, "The Overwhelming Question," *SR* 74 (Jan./Mar. 1966): 365-67.

John Crowe Ransom, "Gerontion," *SR* 74 (Spring 1966): 389-414.

Rosenthal, *The Modern Poets*, 85-88.

Rosenthal and Smith, *Exploring Poetry*, 638-44.

E. San Juan, Jr., "Form and Meaning in 'Gerontion,'" *Renascence* 22 (Spring 1970): 115-26.

Daniel R. Schwarz, "The Unity of Eliot's 'Gerontion': The Failure of Meditation," *BuR* 19 (Spring 1971): 55-76.

John N. Sero, "Landscape and Voice in T. S. Eliot's Poetry," *CentR* 26 (Winter 1982): 33-50.

Grover Smith, *Expl* 7 (Feb. 1949): 26. Reprinted in *The Explicator Cyclopedia* 1:101-2.

Gordon Symes, "T. S. Eliot and Old Age," *Fortnightly* 169 (Mar. 1951): 189-90.

Allen Tate, "Poetry Modern and Unmodern: A Personal Recollection," *HudR* 21 (Summer 1968): 258-60.

Zohreh Tawakuli Sullivan, "Memory and Meditative Structure in T. S. Eliot's Early Poetry," *Renascence* 29 (Winter 1977): 102-5.

Unger, *The Man in the Name*, 172-73.

Leonard Unger, "T. S. Eliot's Rose Garden: A Persistent Theme," *SoR* 7 (Spring 1942): 672-673.

Sherna S. Vinograd, "The Accidental: A Clue to Structure in Eliot's Poetry," *Accent* 9 (Summer 1949): 233-35.

Wheelwright, *The Burning Fountain*, 336-38.

Mervyn W. Williamson, "T. S. Eliot's 'Gerontion,'" *University of Texas Studies in English* 36 (1957): 111-26.

ELIOT, T.S.

Jane Worthington, "The Epigraphs to the Poetry of T. S. Eliot," *AL* 21 (Mar. 1949): 5-6.

"Gus: The Theatre Cat"

Priscilla Preston, "A Note on T. S. Eliot and Sherlock Holmes," *MLR* 54 (Oct. 1959): 399.

"The Hippopotamus"

Abad, *A Formal Approach to Lyric Poetry*, 306-7.

Herbert Marshall McLuhan, *Expl* 2 (May 1944): 50. Reprinted in *The Explicator Cyclopedia* 1:107.

Christine Meyer, *Expl* 8 (Oct. 1949): 6. Reprinted in *The Explicator Cyclopedia* 1:108.

Bruce Ross, "Mysteries of the Broad Backed Church: T. S. Eliot's 'The Hippopotamus,'" *CP* 15, no. 1 (1979): 11-18.

Robert Sprich, "Theme and Structure in Eliot's 'The Hippopotamus,'" *CEA* 31 (Apr. 1969): 8.

Francis Lee Utley, *Expl* 3 (Nov. 1944): 10. Reprinted in *The Explicator Cyclopedia* 1:1107-8.

Jane Worthington, "The Epigraphs to the Poetry of T. S. Eliot," *AL* 21 (Mar. 1949): 10-11.

"The Hollow Men"

D. Albright, *Lyricality in English Literature* (Lincoln and London: University of Nebraska Press, 1985), passim.

Donald R. Benson, "Eliot's and Conrad's Hollow Men," *CEA* 29 (Jan. 1967): 10.

R. P. Blackmur, "T. S. Eliot," *Hound and Horn* 1 (Mar. 1928): 203-5.

A. P. Brady, *Lyricism in the Poetry of T. S. Eliot* (Port Washington: Kennikat Press, 1978), passim.

Harold F. Brooks, "Between *The Waste Land* and the First Ariel Poems: 'The Hollow Men,'" *English* 16 (Autumn 1966): 89-93.

Drew and Sweeney, *Directions in Modern Poetry*, 134-36.

F. Peter Dzwonkoski, Jr., "'The Hollow Men' and *Ash Wednesday*: Two Dark Nights," *ArQ* 30 (Spring 1974): 16-23.

Feder, *Ancient Myth in Modern Poetry*, 232-36.

Robert F. Fleissner, *Expl* 42 (Summer 1984): 40-41.

Genevieve W. Foster, "Archetypal Imagery of T. S. Eliot," *PMLA* 60 (June 1945): 576-78.

Paul Fussell, Jr., "The Gestic Symbolism of T. S. Eliot," *ELH* 22 (Sept. 1955): 198-203.

Everett A. Gillis, "The Spiritual Status of T. S. Eliot's Hollow Men," *TSLL* 2 (Winter 1961): 464-75.

Everett A. Gillis, Lawrence V. Ryan, and Friederich W. Strothman, "Hope for Eliot's Hollow Men?" *PMLA* 75 (Dec. 1960): 635-38.

E. Hay, "T. S. Eliot's Virgil: Dante," *JEGP* 82 (Jan. 1983): 50-65.

J. G. Keogh, "Eliot's 'Hollow Men' as Graveyard Poetry," *Renascence* 21 (Spring 1969): 115-18.

Robert S. Kinsman, *Expl* 8 (Apr. 1950): 48. Reprinted in *The Explicator Cyclopedia* 1:108-9.

Sydney J. Krauss, "Hollow Men and False Horses," *TSLL* 2 (Winter 1961): 368-377.

Miller, *Poets of Reality*, 180-82.

J. M. Reibetanz, "Accentual Forms in Eliot's Poetry from 'The Hollow Men' to *Four Quartets*," *ES* 65 (Aug. 1984): 334-49.

M. L. Rosenthal, *Sailing into the Unknown: Yeats, Pound, and Eliot* (New York: Oxford University Press, 1978), 45-66.

Lawrence V. Ryan and Friedrich W. Strothman, "Hope for T. S. Eliot's 'Empty Men,'" *PMLA* 32 (Sept. 1968): 426-32.

Charles Sanders, *Expl* 38 (Summer 1980): 8-9.

Grover Smith, Jr., "Getting Used to T. S. Eliot," *EJ* 49 (Jan. 1960): 9.

Gordon Symes, "T. S. Eliot and Old Age," *Fortnightly* 159 (Mar. 1951): 191-92.

John B. Vickery, "Eliot's Poetry: The Quest and the Way" (Part 1), *Renascence* 10 (Autumn 1957): 8-9.

ELIOT, T.S.

Jane Worthington, "The Epigraphs to the Poetry of T. S. Eliot," *AL* 21 (Mar. 1949): 14-15.

"Humoresque"

J. J. Soldo, "T. S. Eliot and Jules LaFargue," *AL* 55 (May 1983): 137-50.

"Hysteria"

Henry Christian, "Thematic Development in T. S. Eliot's 'Hysteria,'" *TCL* 7 (July 1960): 76-80.

"Jellicle Cats"

Felix Clowder, "The Bestiary of T. S. Eliot," *PrS* 34 (Spring 1960): 31-33.

"Journey of the Magi"

R. D. Brown, "Revelation in T. S. Eliot's 'Journey of the Magi,'" *Renascence* 24 (Spring 1972): 136-40.

E. F. Burgess, *Expl* 42 (Summer 1984): 36.

Margaret Church, *Expl* 18 (June 1960): 55. Reprinted in *The Explicator Cyclopedia* 1:110-11.

Michael P. Dean, *Expl* 37 (Summer 1979): 9-10.

Drew, *Poetry: A Modern Guide*, 237-40.

Genevieve W. Foster, "Archetypal Imagery of T. S. Eliot," *PMLA* 60 (June 1945): 578-80.

Rosemary Franklin, "The Satisfactory Journey of Eliot's Magus," *ES* 49 (Dec. 1968): 559-61.

D. A. Harris, "Language, History, and Text in Eliot's 'Journey of the Magi,'" *PMLA* 95 (October 1980): 838-56.

Perrine and Reid, *100 American Poems*, 133-34.

T. A. Smailes, *Expl* 29 (Nov. 1970): 18.

John Howard Wills, *Expl* 12 (Mar. 1954): 32. Reprinted in *The Explicator Cyclopedia* 1:109-10.

"Landscape" series [1934-1935]

Erik Arne Hansen, "T. S. Eliot's 'Landscapes,'" *ES* 50 (Aug. 1969): 370-73.

N. D. Hargrove, *Landscape as Symbol in the Poetry of T. S. Eliot* (Jackson: University of Mississippi Press, 1978), passim.

John N. Serio, "Landscape and Voice in T. S. Eliot's Poetry," *CentR* 26 (Winter 1982): 33-50.

"Lines to Ralph Hodgson Esgre"

Robert H. Sykes, *Expl* 30 (May 1972): 79.

"Little Gidding"

Ackroyd, *T. S. Eliot*, 263-66.

Brooks, Lewis, and Warren, *American Literature*, 2130-37.

E. Hay, "T. S. Eliot's Virgil: Dante," *JEGP* 82 (Jan. 1983): 50-65.

F. O. Matthiessen, "Eliot's Quartets," *KR* 5 (Spring 1943): 173-75.

M. L. Rosenthal, *Sailing into the Unknown: Yeats, Pound, and Eliot* (New York: Oxford University Press, 1978): 162-79.

Rosenthal and Smith, *Exploring Poetry*, 696-704.

John Shand, "Around 'Little Gidding,'" *The Nineteenth Century and After* 136 (Sept. 1944): 120-32.

James Johnson Sweeney, "'Little Gidding': Introductory to a Reading," *Poetry* 62 (July 1943): 216-23.

"The Love Song of J. Alfred Prufrock"

Ackroyd, *T. S. Eliot*, passim.

Adams, *Strains of Discord*, 112-13.

Charles Altieri, "Objective Image and Act of Mind in Modern Poetry," *PMLA* 91 (Jan. 1976): 106-7.

Russell Ames, "Decadence in the Art of T. S. Eliot," *Science and Society* 16 (Summer 1952): 198-221.

Roy P. Basler, "Psychological Pattern in 'The Love Song of J. Alfred Prufrock,'" in *Twentieth Century English*, ed. William S. Knickerbocker (New York: The Philosophical Library, 1946), 384-400. Reprinted in Basler, *Sex, Symbolism, and Psychology in Literature*, 203-21.

M. L. Baumann, "Let Us Ask 'What Is It?'" *AQ* 37 (Spring 1981): 47-58.

Vereen M. Bell, "A Reading of 'Prufrock,'" *ES* 50 (Supplement 1969): lxviii-lxxiv.

R. P. Blackmur, "T. S. Eliot," *Hound and Horn* 1 (Mar. 1928): 209-12.

Blasing, *American Poetry: The Rhetoric of Its Forms*, 37-40.

Margaret Morton Blum, "The Fool in 'The Love Song of J. Alfred Prufrock,'" *MLN* (June 1957): 424-26.

Bornstein, *Transformation of Romanticism*, 130-34.

Jon Bracker, *Expl* 25 (Nov. 1966): 21.

Brooks, Lewis, and Warren, *American Literature*, 2099-102.

Brooks and Warren, *Understanding Poetry*, 589-96; rev. ed., 433-44. Reprinted in Stallman and Walters, *The Creative Reader*, 881-85.

Gordon Browning, *Expl* 31 (Feb. 1973): 49.

Chatman, *An Introduction to the Language of Poetry*, 32-33.

R. G. Collingwood, *The Principles of Art* (Oxford: Oxford University Press, 1938), 310-11.

N. R. Comley, "From Narcissus to Tiresias: T. S. Eliot's Use of Metamorphosis," *MLR* 74 (1979): 281-86.

Robert G. Cook, "Emerson's 'Self-Reliance,' Sweeney and Prufrock," *AL* 42 (May 1970): 223-26.

Jay Dougherty, *Expl* 42 (Summer 1984): 38-40.

Ian S. Dunn, *Expl* 22 (Sept. 1963): 1.

Daniel N. Dwyer, S. J., *Expl* 9 (Mar. 1951): 38.

Paul Engle, "Why Modern Poetry?" *CE* 15 (Oct. 1953): 8.

Engle and Carrier, *Reading Modern Poetry*, 167-74.

Barbara Everett, "In Search of Prufrock," *CritQ* 16 (Summer 1974): 101-21.

Feder, *Ancient Myth in Modern Poetry*, 219-22,

Clifford J. Fish, *Expl* 8 (June 1950), 62. Reprinted in *The Explicator Cyclopedia* 1:111-12.

Robert F. Fleissner, "Prufrock's Peach," *Research Studies* 44 (June 1976): 121-25.

Robert F. Fleissner, "Prufrock's 'Ragged Claws,'" *ES* 53 (June 1972): 247-48.

Frankenberg, *Pleasure Dome*, 40-42, 45-49.

John Halverson, "Prufrock, Freud, and Others," *SR* 76 (Autumn 1968): 571-88.

Versa R. Harvey, "T. S. Eliot's 'The Love Song of J. Alfred Prufrock,'" *IEY* 6 (Fall 1961): 29-31.

Eugene Hollahan, "A Structural Dantean Parallel in Eliot's 'The Love Song of J. Alfred Prufrock,'" *AL* 42 (Mar. 1970): 91-93.

James L. Jackson, *Expl* 18 (May 1960): 48. Reprinted in *The Explicator Cyclopedia* 1:113-14.

Willis D. Jacobs, "T. S. Eliot's 'The Love Song of J. Alfred Prufrock,'" *Rocky Mountain Modern Language Association Bulletin* 8 (Oct. 1954): 5-6.

Jerome, *Poetry: Premeditated Art*, 164-68.

Kenner, *The Pound Era*, passim.

Hugh Kenner, "Prufrock of St. Louis," *PrS* 31 (Spring 1957): 24-30.

James F. Knapp, "Eliot's 'Prufrock' and the Form of Modern Poetry," *ArQ* 30 (Spring 1974): 5-14.

Langbaum, *The Poetry of Experience*, 189-92, 197, 200-202.

Frederick W. Locke, "Dante and T. S. Eliot's 'Prufrock,'" *MLN* 78 (Jan. 1963): 51-59.

Robert McNamara, "'Prufrock' and the Problem of Literary Narcissism," *ConL* 27 (Fall 1986): 357-77.

Minor Wallace Major, "A St. Louisan's View of Prufrock," *CEA* 23 (Mar. 1961): 5.

Joseph Margolis, "On Prufrock," in Wain, *Interpretations*, 183-93.

Miller, *Poets of Reality*, 138-41.

Conny Nelson, "T. S. Eliot, Michelangelo, and John Webster," *RS* 38 (Dec. 1970): 304-6.

Perrine and Reid, *100 American Poems*, 110-12.

John C. Pope, "Prufrock and Raskolnikov," *AL* 17 (Nov. 1945): 213-30; 18 (Jan. 1947): 319-21.

Lyall H. Powers, *Expl* 14 (Mar. 1956): 39. Reprinted in *The Explicator Cyclopedia* 1:113.

Edward Proffitt, "Bald Narcissus: The Drowning of J. Alfred Prufrock," *NConL* 8 (Nov. 1978): 3-4.

R. Rajan, "The Overwhelming Question," *SR* 74 (Jan./Mar. 1966): 362-64.

John Crowe Ransom, "Gerontion," *SR* 74 (Apr./June 1966): 391-94.

Rosenthal and Smith, *Exploring Poetry*, 376-77.

Thomas C. Rumble, "Some Grail Motifs in Eliot's 'Prufrock,'" in *Studies in American Literature*, ed. Waldo McNeir and Leo B. Levy (Baton Rouge: Louisiana State University Press, 1960), 95-103.

Charles Sanders, "'Beyond the Language of the Living': The Voice of T. S. Eliot," *TCL* 27 (Winter 1981): 376-98.

Schneider, *Poems and Poetry*, 491-95.

Martin Scofield, "'A gesture and a pose': T. S. Eliot's Images of Love," *CritQ* 18 (Autumn 1976): 9-11.

C. M. Shanahan, "Irony in LaForgue, Corbière, and Eliot," *MP* 53 (Nov. 1955): 119.

Kathleen A. Sherfick, *Expl* 46 (Fall 1987): 43.

Robert C. Slack, "Victorian Literature as It Appears to Contemporary Students," *CE* 22 (Feb. 1961): 345-47.

Gerald Smith, *Expl* 21 (Oct. 1962): 10.

Grover Smith, Jr., "Getting Used to T. S. Eliot," *EJ* 49 (Jan. 1960): 6-7.

J. J. Soldo, "T. S. Eliot and Jules LaForgue," *AL* 55 (May 1983): 137-50.

William J. Stuckey, *Expl* 20 (Sept. 1961): 10.

Zohreh Tawakuli Sullivan, "Memory and Meditative Structure in T. S. Eliot's Early Poetry," *Renascence* 29 (Winter 1977): 94-100.

Stanley Sultan, "Tradition and the Individual Talent in 'Prufrock,'" *JML* 12 (Mar. 1985): 77-90.

Gordon Symes, "T. S. Eliot and Old Age," *Fortnightly* 169 (Mar. 1951): 188-89.

Thomas and Brown, *Reading Poems: An Introduction to Critical Study*, 698-700.

Tschumi, *Thought in Twentieth-Century English Poetry*, 127-32.

W. A. Turner, "The Not So Coy Mistress of J. Alfred Prufrock," *SAQ* 54 (Oct. 1955): 516-22.

John Virtue, *Expl* 13 (Nov. 1954): 10. Reprinted in *The Explicator Cyclopedia* 1:112-13.

Charles C. Walcutt, "Eliot's 'The Love Song of J. Alfred Prufrock,'" *CE* 19 (Nov. 1957): 71-72.

Leon Waldoff, "Prufrock's Defenses and Our Responses," *AI* 26 (Summer 1969): 182-93.

Walsh, *Doors into Poetry*, 118-26, 130.

Arthur E. Waterman, *Expl* 17 (June 1959): 67. Reprinted in *The Explicator Cyclopedia* 1:114.

Weitz, *Philosophy of the Arts*, 94-107, 145.

Morris Weitz, "T. S. Eliot: Time as a Mode of Salvation," *SR* 60 (Winter 1952): 53-54.

Wheeler, *The Design of Poetry*, 17-40, 168-71, 274.

Robert White, *Expl* 20 (Nov. 1961): 19.

Arthur Wormhoudt, "A Psychoanalytic Interpretation of 'The Love Song of J. Alfred Prufrock,'" *Perspective* 2 (Winter 1949): 109-17.

Jane Worthington, "The Epigraphs to the Poetry of T. S. Eliot," *AL* 21 (Mar. 1949): 1-2.

"Macavity: The Mystery Cat"

Priscilla Preston, "A Note on T. S. Eliot and Sherlock Holmes," *MLR* 54 (Oct. 1959): 398-99.

"Marina"

Richard Abel, "The Influence of St. John Perse on T. S. Eliot," *ConL* 14 (Spring 1973): 235-37.

W. J. Barnes, "T. S. Eliot's 'Marina,'" *University of Kansas City Review* 29 (Summer 1963): 297-305.

Michael Black, "The Musical Analogy," *English* 25 (Summer 1976): 125-32.

Elspeth Cameron, "T. S. Eliot's 'Marina': An Exploration," *QQ* 77 (Summer 1970): 180-89.

Daiches and Charvat, *Poems in English*, 741.

Deutsch, *Poetry in Our Time*, 175.

Paul J. Dolan, "Eliot's 'Marina': A Reading," *Renascence* 21 (Summer 1969): 203-6, 222.

Genevieve W. Foster, "Archetypal Imagery of T. S. Eliot," *PMLA* 60 (June 1945): 582-83.

Leavis, *Education and the University*, 90-92.

F. R. Leavis, "Eliot's Later Poetry, *Scrutiny* 11 (Summer 1942): 61-63.

Leavis, *New Bearings in English Poetry*, 129-31.

Martin Scofield, "'A gesture and a pose': T. S. Eliot's Images of Love," *CritQ* 18 (Autumn 1976): 22-25.

Jane Worthington, "The Epigraphs to the Poetry of T. S. Eliot," *AL* 21 (Mar. 1949): 15-16.

"Mr. Apollinax"

Alec Brown, "The Lyric Impulse in the Poetry of T. S. Eliot," *Scrutinies* 2:29-31.

John Coakley, "T. S. Eliot's 'Mr. Appollinax' and Frost's 'The Demiurge's Laugh,'" *Expl* 45 (Fall 1986): 42-45.

Grover Smith, Jr., "Getting Used to T. S. Eliot," *EJ* 49 (Jan. 1960): 8.

Floyd C. Watkins, "T. S. Eliot's Mysterious 'Mr. Apollinax,'" *Research Studies* 38 (Sept. 1970): 193-200.

Jane Worthington, "The Epigraphs to the Poetry of T. S. Eliot," *AL* 21 (Mar. 1949): 3-4.

"Mr. Eliot's Sunday Morning Service"

Abad, *A Formal Approach to Lyric Poetry*, 332-36.

Anselm Atkins, "Mr. Eliot's Sunday Morning Parody," *Renascence* 21 (Autumn 1968): 41-43, 54.

Orvid Shulenberger, *Expl* 10 (Feb. 1952): 29. Reprinted in *The Explicator Cyclopedia* 1:114-15.

Floyd C. Watkins, "T. S. Eliot's Painter of the Umbrian School," *AL* 36 (Mar. 1964): 72-75.

Jane Worthington, "The Epigraphs to the Poetry of T. S. Eliot," *AL* 21 (Mar. 1949): 11-12.

Murder in the Cathedral

W. J. McGill, "Voices in the Cathedral: The Chorus in Eliot's *Murder in the Cathedral*," *MD* 23 (Sept. 1980): 292-96.

J. Pike, "Liturgy and Time in Counterpoint: A View of T. S. Eliot's *Murder in the Cathedral*," *MD* 23 (Sept. 1980): 277-91.

"The Naming of Cats"

Felix Clowder, "The Bestiary of T. S. Eliot," *PrS* 34 (Spring 1960): 34-35.

"New Hampshire"

Brendon Galvin, "A Note on T. S. Eliot's 'New Hampshire' as a Lyric Poem," *MSE* 1 (Fall 1967): 44-45.

Eric Arne Hansen, "T. S. Eliot's 'Landscapes,'" *ES* 50 (Aug. 1969): 365-67.

"Ode of Dejection"

E. P. Bollier, "T. S. Eliot's 'Lost' 'Ode of Dejection,'" *BuR* 16 (Mar. 1968): 1-17.

V. Mahaffey, "'The Death of Saint Narcissus' and 'Ode': Two Suppressed Poems by T. S. Eliot," *AL* 50 (Jan. 1978): 604-12.

"Old Deuteronomy"

Felix Clowder, "The Bestiary of T. S. Eliot," *PrS* 34 (Spring 1960): 33-34.

ELIOT, T.S.

"Old Possum's Book of Practical Cats"

Felix Clowder, "The Bestiary of T. S. Eliot," *PrS* 34 (Spring 1960): 36-37.

"Polyphiloprogenitive"

Dana Gioia, "Business and Poetry," *HudR* 36 (Spring 1983): 147-71.

"Portrait of a Lady"

Sar de Saussure Davis, "Two Portraits of a Lady: Henry James and T. S. Eliot," *ArQ* 32 (Autumn 1976): 367-80.

Richard J. Giannone, "Eliot's 'Portrait of a Lady' and Pound's 'Portrait d'une Femme,'" *TCL* 5 (Oct. 1959): 131-34.

C. M. Shanahan, "Irony in LaForgue, Corbiere, and Eliot," *MP* 53 (Nov. 1955): 123-24.

Patricia Meyer Spacks, "In Search of Sincerity," *CE* 29 (May 1968): 599-601.

W. A. Turner, "The Not So Coy Mistress of J. Alfred Prufrock," *SAQ* 54 (Oct. 1955): 517-18.

Leonard Unger, "T. S. Eliot's Images of Awareness," *SR* 74(Jan./Mar. 1966): 209-11, 217-18.

Philip Waldron, "T. S. Eliot, Mr. Whiteside, and 'The Psychobiographical Approach,'" *SoRA* 6 (June 1973): 138-41.

Jane Worthington, "The Epigraphs to the Poetry of T. S. Eliot," *AL* 21 (Mar. 1949): 2-3.

"Preludes"

J. H. Johnston, *The Poet and the City: A Study in Urban Perspectives* (Athens: University of Georgia Press, 1980), passim.

Miller, *Poets of Reality*, 144-45, 172-73.

T. Morrissey, "'Intimate and Unidentifiable': The Voices of Fragmented Reality in the Poetry of T. S. Eliot," *CentR* 22 (Winter 1978): 1-27.

Perrine and Reid, *100 American Poems*, 105.

Grover Smith, Jr., "Getting Used to T. S. Eliot," *EJ* 49 (Jan. 1960): 6.

Walsh, *Doors into Poetry*, 27-30.

"Rannoch, by Glencoe"

Erik Arne Hansen, "T. S. Eliot's 'Landscapes,'" *ES* 50 (Aug. 1969): 373-74.

"The Return"

Kenner, *The Mechanic Muse*, 44-54.

"Rhapsody on a Windy Night"

Cleanth Brooks and Robert Penn Warren, "The Reading of Modern Poetry," *American Review* 7 (Feb. 1937): 442-45.

William Harmon, "T. S. Eliot's Raids on the Inarticulate," *PMLA* 91 (May 1976): 452-53.

J. H. Johnston, *The Poet and the City: A Study in Urban Perspectives* (Athens: University of Georgia Press, 1984), passim.

Miller, *Poets of Reality*, 146.

Rosenthal, *The Modern Poets*, 6-7.

Zohreh Tawakuli Sullivan, "Memory and Meditative Structure in T. S. Eliot's Early Poetry," *Renascence* 29 (Winter 1977): 101-2.

"A Song for Simeon"

Malcolm S. Glass, "T. S. Eliot: Christian Poetry through Liturgical Allusion," in Hoffman, *The Twenties*, 42-45.

Hugh Kenner, "Eliot's Moral Dialectic," *HudR* 2 (Autumn 1949): 424-28.

"Sweeney Agonsites"

Ackroyd, *T. S. Eliot*, 145-48 and passim.

Morris Freedman, "Jazz Rhythms and T. S. Eliot," *SAQ* 51 (July 1952): 420-23, 428-32.

Morris Freedman, "The Meaning of T. S. Eliot's Jew," *SAQ* 55 (Apr. 1956): 200-201.

Charles L. Holt, "On Structure and 'Sweeney Agonistes,'" *MD* 10 (May 1967): 43-47.

Sears Jayne, "Mr. Eliot's Agon," *PQ* 34 (Oct. 1955): 395-414.

William V. Spanos, "'Wanna Go Home, Baby?': 'Sweeney Agonsites' as Drama of the Absurd," *PMLA* 85 (Jan. 1970): 8-20.

"Sweeney among the Nightingales"

Cleanth Brooks, "T. S. Eliot as a 'Modernist' Poet," in Brady, Palmer, and Price, *Literary Theory and Structure,* 366-69.

Brooks, Lewis, and Warren, *American Literature*, 2104-5.

James Davidson, "The End of Sweeney," *CE* 27 (Feb. 1966): 400-403.

Deutsch, *Poetry in Our Time*, 168-70.

Elizabeth Drew, abridged in *The Case for Poetry*, 133-35, from *T. S. Eliot: The Design of His Poetry* (New York: Charles Scribner's Sons, 1949), 44-46.

Elizabeth Rudisill Homann, *Expl* 17 (Feb. 1959): 34. Reprinted in *The Explicator Cyclopedia* 1:117-18.

Stanley E. Hyman, "Poetry and Criticism: T. S. Eliot," *ASch* 30 (Winter 1961): 43-55.

Charles Kaplan, "Eliot Among the Nightingales: Fair and Foul," *New Mexico Quarterly Review* 24 (Summer 1954): 228.

Leo Kerschbaum and Roy P. Basler, *Expl* 2 (Dec. 1943): 18. Reprinted in *The Explicator Cyclopedia* 1:115-16.

P. G. Mudford, "'Sweeney among the Nightingales,'" *EIC* 19 (July 1969): 285-90.

J. Ower, "Pattern and Value in 'Sweeney among the Nightingales,'" *Renascence* 23 (Spring 1971): 151-58.

M. Pittock, "Poet and Narrator in 'Sweeney among the Nightingales,'" *EIC* 30 (Jan. 1980): 29-41.

Stauffer, *The Nature of Poetry*, 78-80. Abridged in Gwynn, Condee, and Lewis, *The Case for Poetry*, 135.

Charles C. Walcutt, *Expl* 2 (Apr. 1944): 48. Reprinted in *The Explicator Cyclopedia* 1:116-17.

George Williamson, abridged in Gwynn, Condee, and Lewis, *The Case for Poetry*, 133, from *A Reader's Guide to T. S. Eliot* (New York: Noonday Press, 1953), 97-98.

Jane Worthington, "The Epigraphs to the Poetry of T. S. Eliot," *AL* 21 (Mar. 1949): 13.

"Sweeney Erect"

William Arrowsmith, "The Poem as Palimpsest: A Dialogue on Eliot's 'Sweeney Erect,'" *SoR* (Jan. 1981): 17-68.

Chatman, *An Introduction to the Language of Poetry*, 67-73.

Robert G. Cook, "Emerson's 'Self-Reliance,' Sweeney and Prufrock," *AL* 42 (May 1970): 222-23.

Arthur Mizener, "To Meet Mr. Eliot," *SR* 65 (Winter 1957): 41-42.

Glen W. Singer, *Expl* 34 (Sept. 1975): 7.

Charles Child Walcutt, *Expl* 35 (Winter 1976): 31-32.

Jane Worthington, "The Epigraphs to the Poetry of T. S. Eliot," *AL* 21 (Mar. 1949): 7-9.

"Triumphal March" (from the unfinished "Coriolan")

Daniels, *The Art of Reading Poetry*, 406-9.

F. R. Leavis, "Eliot's Later Poetry," *Scrutiny* 11 (Summer 1942): 63-64.

Lewis, *Education and the University*, 92-93.

"Usk"

Erik Arne Hansen, "T. S. Eliot's 'Landscapes,'" *ES* 50 (Aug. 1969): 370-73.

"Virginia"

Erik Arne Hansen, "T. S. Eliot's 'Landscapes,'" *ES* 50 (Aug. 1969): 367-70.

ELIOT, T.S.

"The Waste Land"

Ackroyd, *T. S. Eliot*, 117-19.

Conrad Aiken, "An Anatomy of Melancholy," *SR* 74 (Jan./Mar. 1966): 188-96.

Robert J. Andreach, *"Paradise Lost* and the Christian Configuration of *The Waste Land*," *PLL* 5 (Summer 1969): 296-309.

James Applewhite, *Seas and Inland Journeys: Landscape and Consciousness from Wordsworth to Roethke* (Athens: University of Georgia Press, 1985), passim.

John Ross Baker, *Expl* 14 (Jan. 1956): 27. Reprinted in *The Explicator Cyclopedia* 1:124.

Belgion, *Reading for Profit*, 258-86, passim.

A. F. Beringause, "Journey through *The Waste Land*," *SAQ* 56 (Jan. 1957): 79-90.

C. Berryman, *From Wilderness to Wasteland: The Trial of the Puritan God in the American Imagination* (Port Washington: Kennikat Press, 1979), 182-86, 193-95.

J. Bishop, "A Handful of Words: The Credibility of Language in *The Waste Land*," *TSLL* 27 (Summer 1985): 154-77.

R. P. Blackmur, "T. S. Eliot," *Hound and Horn* 1 (Mar. 1928): 190-96.

Blasing, *American Poetry: The Rhetoric of Its Forms*, 45-46.

William Blissett, "Wagner in *The Waste Land*," in *The Practical Vision: Essays in English Literature in Honour of Flora Roy*, ed. Jane Campbell and James Doyle (Waterloo, Ontario: Wilfrid Laurier University Press, 1978), 1-85.

M. M. Boaz, "Musical and Poetic Analogues in T. S. Eliot's *The Waste Land* and Igor Stravinsky's *The Rite of Spring*," *CentR* 24 (Spring 1980): 218-31.

Bodkin, *Archetypal Patterns in Poetry*, 310-15.

L. Boone, "Tiresias and The Man from Somewhere," *SAQ* 79 (Autumn 1980): 398-407.

Bowra, *The Creative Experiment*, 159-88.

A. P. Brady, *Lyricism in the Poetry of T. S. Eliot* (Port Washington: Kennikat Press, 1979), passim.

Jewel Spears Brooker, "F. H. Bradley's Doctrine of Experience in T. S. Eliot's *The Waste Land* and 'Four Quartets,'" *MP* 77 (Nov. 1979): 146-57.

Cleanth Brooks, "*The Waste Land*: An Analysis," *SoR* 3 (Summer 1937): 106-36. Reprinted in Brooks and Warren, *Understanding Poetry*, rev. ed., 645-67.

Brooks, Lewis, and Warren, *American Literature*, 2118-27.

Alec Brown, "The Lyric Impulse in the Poetry of T. S. Eliot," *Scrutiny* 2:34-48.

Oscar Cargill, "Death in a Handful of Dust," *Criticism* 11 (Summer 1969): 275-96.

Richard Chase, "The Sense of the Present," *KR* 7 (Spring 1945): 225-31.

N. R. Comley, "From Narcissus to Tiresias: T. S. Eliot's Use of Metamorphosis," *MLR* 74 (1979): 281-86.

Albert Cook, *Expl* 6 (Oct. 1947): 7. Reprinted in *The Explicator Cyclopedia* 1:125.

C. B. Cox, "T. S. Eliot at the Cross-Roads," *CritQ* 12 (Winter 1970): 307-10, 316-19.

David Craig, *The Real Foundations: Literature and Social Change* (London: Chatto & Windus, 1973), 195-212.

B. B. Creekmore, "The Tarot Fortune in *The Waste Land*," *ELH* 49 (Winter 1982): 909-28.

Daiches, *The Place of Meaning in Poetry*, 49-55.

Robert Gorham Davis et al., "The New Criticism," *ASch* 20 (Spring 1951): 225-26.

Robert A. Day, "The 'City Man' in the Waste Land: The Geography of Reminiscence," *PMLA* 80 (June 1965): 285-91.

Patrick Deane, "A Line of Complicity: Baudelaire--T. S. Eliot--Adrienne Rich," *CRevAS* 18 (Winter 1987): 463-81.

De Sola Pinto, *Crisis in English Poetry*, 170-74.

Deutsch, *Poetry in Our Time*, 160-64.

Deutsch, *This Modern Poetry*, 118-27.

Dickie, *On the Modernist Long Poem*, 18-46.

Marjorie Donker, "*The Waste Land* and the *Aeneid*," *PMLA* 89 (Jan. 1974): 164-73.

Drew and Sweeney, *Directions in Modern Poetry*, 40-44 and passim.

Barbara Everett, "Eliot in and out of *The Waste Land*," *CritQ* 17 (Spring 1975): 7-30.

B. Everett, "Eliot's Marianne: *The Waste Land* and Its Poetry of Europe," *RES* 31 (Feb. 1980): 41-53.

William J. Farrell, "*The Waste Land* as Rhetoric," *Renascence* 22 (Spring 1970): 127-40.

Feder, *Ancient Myth in Modern Poetry*, 128-35, 222-31.

Rene E. Fortin, *Expl* 21 (Dec. 1962): 32.

Genevieve W. Foster, "Archetypal Imagery of T. S. Eliot," *PMLA* 60 (June 1945), 571-76.

D. C. Fowler, "*The Waste Land*: Mr. Eliot's 'Fragments,'" *CE* 14 (Jan. 1953): 234-35.

Frankenberg, *The Pleasure Dome*, 64-77.

Friar and Brinnin, *Modern Poetry*, 425-26, 472-97.

A. L. French, "Criticism and *The Waste Land*," *SoRA* 1 (1964): 69-81.

Paul Fussell, Jr., "The Gestic Symbolism of T. S. Eliot," *ELH* 22 (Sept. 1955): 194-211.

Sally M. Gall, "Domestic Monologues: The Problem of 'Voice' in Contemporary American Poetry," *MR* 23 (Autumn 1982): 489-503.

A. M. Gibbs, "Mr. French's Mr. Eliot," *SoRA* 1 (1964): 82-85.

William M. Gibson, "Sonnets in T. S. Eliot's *The Waste Land*," *AL* 32 (Jan. 1961): 465-66.

Frederick Glaysher, "T. S. Eliot and 'The horror! The horror!'" *Modern Age* 28 (Fall 1984): 339-48.

L. Gordon, *Eliot's Early Years* (New York: Oxford University Press, 1977), passim.

J. Guillory, "The Ideology of Canon-Formation: T. S. Eliot and Cleanth Brooks," *CritI* 10 (Sept. 1983): 173-98.

N. D. Hargrove, *Landscape as Symbol in the Poetry of T. S. Eliot* (Jackson: University of Mississippi Press, 1978), passim.

William Harmon, "T. S. Eliot's Raids on the Inarticulate," *PMLA* 91 (May 1976): 453-54.

Peter L. Hays, "Eliot's *The Waste Land*," *Expl* 42 (Summer 1984): 36-37.

Hoffman, *The Twenties*, 291-303.

J. H. Johnston, *The Poet and the City: A Study in Urban Perspectives* (Athens: University of Georgia Press, 1984), passim.

Florence Jones, "T. S. Eliot among the Prophets," *AL* 38 (Nov. 1966): 285-303.

Kenner, *The Mechanic Muse*, 29-36.

Kenner, *The Pound Era*, passim.

G. W. Knight, "Thoughts on *The Waste Land*," *University of Denver Quarterly* 7 (Summer 1972): 1-13.

Herbert Kunst, *Expl* 23 (May 1965): 74.

Herbert Kunst, "What's the Matter with One-Eyed Riley?" *CL* 17 (Fall 1975): 289-98.

Jacob Korg, "Modern Art Techniques in *The Waste Land*," *JAAC* 18 (June 1966), 456-63.

Dale Kramer, *Expl* 24 (Apr. 1966): 74.

Robert Langbaum, *The Mysteries of Identity: A Theme in Modern Literature* (New York: Oxford University Press, 1977), 88-105.

Nancy K. Lawlor, "Eliot's Use of Rhyming Quatrains in *The Waste Land*," *Poet and Critic* 4 (Fall 1967): 29-37.

Leavis, *New Bearings in English Poetry*, 90-114.

Paul Lewis, "Life By Water: Characterization and Salvation in *The Waste Land*," *Mosaic* 2 (Summer 1978): 81-90.

J. Logenbach, "Guarding the Horned Gates: History and Interpretation in the Early Poetry of T. S. Eliot," *ELN* 52 (Summer 1985): 503-27.

John Lucas and William Myers, "II. *The Waste Land* Today," *EIC* 19 (Apr. 1969): 193-209.

Mack, Dean, and Frost, *English Masterpieces*, vol. 7, *Modern Poetry*, 21.

Juliet McLauchlan, "Allusion in *The Waste Land*," *EIC* 19 (Oct. 1969): 454-60.

Marshall McLuhan, "Pound, Eliot, and the Rhetoric of *The Waste Land*," *NLH* 10 (Spring 1978): 557-80.

Florence Marsh, "The Desert-Ocean: 'The Ancient Mariner' and *The Waste Land*," *EIC* 9 (Apr. 1959): 126-33.

William H. Marshall, *Expl* 17 (Mar. 1959): 42. Reprinted in *The Explicator Cyclopedia* 1:124-25.

Peter A. Martin, "'Son of Man' in the Book of Ezekiel and T. S. Eliot's *The Waste Land*," *ArQ* 33 (Autumn 1977): 197-15.

P. Marudanayagam, *Expl* 45 (Fall 1986): 45-47.

Timothy Materer, "Chantecler in *The Waste Land*," *N&Q* 24 (Oct. 1977): 451.

Giorgio Melchiori, "Echoes in *The Waste Land*," *ES* 32 (Feb. 1951): 1-11.

James D. Merritt, *Expl* 23 (Dec. 1964): 31.

Milton Miller, "What the Thunder Meant," *ELH* 36 (June 1969): 440-54.

Marion Montgomery, "The Awful Daring: The Self Surrendered in *The Waste Land*," *ArQ* 30 (Spring 1974): 43-52.

Charles Moorman, "Myth and Organic Unity in *The Waste Land*," *SAQ* 57 (Spring 1958): 194-203.

L. K. Morris, "Marie, Marie, Hold on Tight," *PR* (Mar./Apr. 1954): 231-33.

J. Mitchell Morse, "A Fascist Cryptogram in *The Waste Land*," *JML* 9 (May 1982): 315-16.

J. I. Morse, "T. S. Eliot in 1921: Toward the Dissociation of Sensibility," *WHR* 30 (Winter 1976): 31-40.

Max Nanny, "'Cards Are Queer': A New Reading of the Tarot in *The Waste Land*," *ES* 62 (Aug. 1981): 335-47.

Max Nanny, "*The Waste Land*: A Menippean Satire?" *ES* 66 (1985): 526-35.

George W. Nitchie, "Eliot's Borrowing: A Note," *MR* 6 (Winter/Spring 1965): 403-6.

Gabriela Notola, "*The Waste Land*: Symbolism and Structure," *L&P* 18 (1968): 205-12.

Palmer, *Post-Victorian Poetry*, 312-22.

Pearce, *The Continuity of American Poetry*, 306-12.

M. C. Pecheux, "In Defense of 'Death By Water,'" *ConL* 20 (Summer 1978): 339-53.

Marion Perret, "Eliot, the Naked Lady, and the Missing Link," *AL* 46 (Nov. 1974): 289-303.

Perrine and Reid, *100 American Poems*, 130-32.

John Peter, "A New Interpretation of *The Waste Land* (1952) with Postscript (1969)," *EIC* 19 (Apr. 1969): 140-75.

Sanford Pinsker, "Eliot's 'Falling Towers' and the Death of Language: A Note on *The Waste Land*," *CP* 10 (Fall 1977): 75.

Sidney Poger, "Eliot's *The Waste Land*," *Expl* 36 (Winter 1978): 8-10.

Linda Ray Pratt, "The Holy Grail: Subversion and Revival of Tradition in Tennyson and T. S. Eliot," *VP* 11 (Winter 1973): 307-21.

William H. Pritchard, "I. Reading *The Waste Land* Today," *EIC* 19 (Apr. 1969): 176-92.

Quinn, *The Metamorphic Tradition*, 130-42.

B. Rajan, "The Overwhelming Question," *SR* 74 (Jan./Mar. 1966): 367-68.

John Crowe Ransom, "The Inorganic Muses," *KR* 5 (Spring 1943): 298-300.

D. F. Rauber, "The Notes on *The Waste Land*," *ELN* 7 (June 1970): 287-94.

Paul C. Ray, "On Fragments and Fragmentation," *WHR* 34 (Summer 1980): 223-32.

Julia M. Reibetanz, "Accentual Forms in Eliot's Poetry from *The Hollow Men* to *Four Quartets*," *ES* 65 (Aug. 1984): 334-49.

Lee J. Richmond, *Expl* 30 (Nov. 1971): 23.

Riding and Graves, *A Survey of Modernist Poetry*, 50-58.

Jean-Paul Riquelme, "Withered Stumps of Time: Allusion, Reading, and Writing in *The Waste Land*," *University of Denver Quarterly* 15 (Winter 1981): 90-110.

Audrey T. Rodgers, "'He do the police in different voices': The Design of *The Waste Land*," *CollL* 1 (Winter 1974): 48-63.

William N. Rogers II, "'Laquearia' in *The Waste Land*," *AN&Q* 13 (Mar. 1975): 105-6.

Rosenthal, *The Modern Poets*, 88-94.

M. L. Rosenthal, *Sailing into the Unknown: Yeats, Pound, and Eliot* (New York: Oxford University Press, 1978), 183-88.

Charles Sanders, "'Beyond the Language of the Living': The Voice of T. S. Eliot," *TCL* 27 (Winter 1981): 376-98.

Charles Sanders, *Expl* 39 (Spring 1981): 29-80.

Charles Sanders, "*The Waste Land*: The Last Minstrel Show?" *JML* 8 (1980): 23-38.

Harry M. Schwalb, *Expl* 11 (Apr. 1953): 46.

Delmore Schwartz, "T. S. Eliot as the International Hero," *PR* 12 (Spring 1945): 200-206.

Scott, *Rehearsals of Discomposure*, 203-25.

John N. Sero, "Landscape and Voice in T. S. Eliot's Poetry," *CentR* 26 (Winter 1982): 33-50.

C. M. Shanahan, "Irony in LaForgue, Corbière, and Eliot," *MP* 53 (Nov. 1955): 125-27.

Philip Sicke, "The Belladonna: Eliot's Female Archetype in *The Waste Land*," *TCL* 30 (Winter 1984): 420-31.

Irene Simon, "Echoes in *The Waste Land*," *ES* 34 (Apr. 1953): 64-72.

William V. Spanos, "Repetition in *The Waste Land*: A Phenomenological De-Struction," *Boundary* 7 (Spring 1979): 225-85.

Theodore Spencer, "The Poetry of T. S. Eliot," *Atlantic Monthly* 151 (Jan. 1933): 64-65.

Erwin R. Steinberg, "*Mrs. Dalloway* and T. S. Eliot's Personal Waste Land," *JML* 10 (Mar. 1983): 3-25.

Ronald Tamplin, "*The Tempest* and *The Waste Land*," *AL* 39 (Nov. 1967): 352-72.

Tate, *On the Limits of Poetry*, 299-302, 344-45. First published in *Hound and Horn* and *American Review*.

Thomas and Brown, *Reading Poems: An Introduction to Critical Study*, 716-31, 749-51.

D. Trotter, "Modernism and Empire: Reading *The Waste Land*," *CritQ* 28 (Spring 1985): 143-53.

Tschumi, *Thought in Twentieth-Century English Poetry*, 132-44.

Turco, *Visions and Revisions of American Poetry*, 85-94.

Leonard Unger, "T. S. Eliot's Images of Awareness," *SR* 74 (Jan./Mar. 1966): 202-3.

M. D. Uroff, "*The Waste Land*: Metatext," *CentR* 24 (Spring 1980): 148-66.

John B. Vickery, "Eliot's Poetry: The Quest and the Way" (Part 1), *Renascence* 10 (Autumn 1957): 5-8.

Charles Child Walcutt, Introduction to *The Explicator Cyclopedia* 1:xv.

Helen Watson-Williams, "The Blackened Wall: Notes on Blake's 'London' and Eliot's *The Waste Land*," *English* 10 (Summer): 181-84.

Margaret C. Weirick, "Myth and Water Symbolism in T. S. Eliot's *The Waste Land*," *Texas Quarterly* 10 (Spring 1967): 97-104.

Peter A. Weiss, *Expl* 40 (Spring 1982): 45-46.

Wheelwright, *The Burning Fountain*, 338-51.

George Williamson, "The Structure of *The Waste Land*," *MP* 47 (Feb. 1950): 191-206.

Edmund Wilson, *Axel's Castle*, 104-11. Reprinted in Zabel, *Literary Opinion in America*, 186-93; rev. ed., 213-18.

Winters, *The Anatomy of Nonsense*, 162-67. Reprinted in Wilson, *In Defense of Reason*, 497-501.

Ellen Wiznitzer, "Legends of Lil: The Repressed Thematic Center of *The Waste Land*," *WS* 13 (Dec. 1986): 87-102.

Jane Worthington, "The Epigraphs to the Poetry of T. S. Eliot," *AL* 21 (Mar. 1949): 13-14.

"The Waste Land I, The Burial of the Dead"

Beatty and Matchett, *Poetry: From Statement to Meaning*, 71-77.

Lyman A. Cotten, *Expl* 9 (Oct. 1950): 7. Reprinted in *The Explicator Cyclopedia* 1:121.

Patrick Deane, "A Line of Complicity: Baudelaire--T. S. Eliot--Adrienne Rich," *Canadian Review of American Studies* 18 (Winter 1987): 463-81.

Lyle Glazier, *Expl* 8 (Feb. 1950): 26. Reprinted in *The Explicator Cyclopedia* 1:118-19.

Lysander Kemp, *Expl* 7 (June 1949): 60. Reprinted in *The Explicator Cyclopedia* 1:121.

Lysander Kemp, *Expl* 8 (Feb. 1950): 27. Reprinted in *The Explicator Cyclopedia* 1:122.

ELIOT, T.S.

Anthony Low, "The Friendly Dog: Eliot and Hardy," *AN&Q* 12 (Mar. 1974): 106-8.

Eleanor M. Sickels, *Expl* 9 (Oct. 1950): 4. Reprinted in *The Explicator Cyclopedia* 1:119.

Ray Smith, *Expl* 9 (Oct. 1950): 8. Reprinted in *The Explicator Cyclopedia* 1:121-22.

Willie T. Weathers, *Expl* 9 (Feb. 1951): 31. Reprinted in *The Explicator Cyclopedia* 1:119-20.

"The Waste Land II, A Game of Chess"

Drew, *Discovering Poetry*, 119-20.

Empson, *Seven Types of Ambiguity* (1947), 77-78.

Harry M. Schwalb, *Expl* 11 (Apr. 1953): 46. Reprinted in *The Explicator Cyclopedia* 1:123-24.

Eleanor M. Sickels, *Expl* 7 (Dec. 1948): 20. Reprinted in *The Explicator Cyclopedia* 1:123.

"The Waste Land III, The Fire Sermon"

E. Huberman, "St. Magnus Visited," *MR* 21 (Spring 1980): 109-18.

"The Waste Land IV, Death by Water"

Grover Smith, "Observations, on Eliot's 'Death by Water,'" *Accent* 6 (Summer 1946): 257-63.

"The Waste Land V, What the Thunder Said"

R. P. Blackmur, "T. S. Eliot," *Hound and Horn* 1 (Mar. 1928): 197-201.

M. E. Gerander and K. S. Narayana Rao, "*The Waste Land* and the *Upanishads*: What Does the Thunder Say?" *IndL* 14 (Mar. 1971): 85-98.

"Whispers of Immortality"

R. P. Blackmur, "T. S. Eliot," *Hound and Horn* 1 (Mar. 1928): 207-8.

Cleanth Brooks, "T. S. Eliot as a 'Modernist' Poet," in Brady, Palmer, and Price, *Literary Theory and Structure*, 365-66.

Brooks, Lewis, and Warren, *American Literature*, 2105-6.

Empson, *Seven Types of Ambiguity* (1947), 78-79.

V. Forrest-Thompson, *Poetic Artifice: A Theory of Twentieth-Century Poetry* (New York: St. Martin's, 1978), 83-87.

Sr. M. Cleophas, R.S.M., *Expl* 8 (Dec. 1949): 22. Reprinted in *The Explicator Cyclopedia* 1:126-27.

Victor Strandberg, *Expl* 17 (May 1959): 53. Reprinted in *The Explicator Cyclopedia* 1:127-28.

Chares C. Walcutt, *Expl* 7 (Nov. 1948): 11. Reprinted in *The Explicator Cyclopedia* 1:125-26.

ENGLE, PAUL

"America Remembers"

Robert G. Ahearn, "The American West: An Enduring Mirage?" *Colorado Quarterly* 26 (Autumn 1977): 3-16.

ESHLEMAN, CLAYTON

"Hades in Manganese"

David E. James, "Poetry/Punk/Production: Some Recent Writing in L.A.," *MinnR*, n.s. 23 (Fall 1984): 127-48.

EVANS, MARI

"I Am a Black Woman"

Solomon Edwards, "Affirmation in the Works of Mari Evans," in Evans, *Black Woman Writers*, 190-200.

EVERSON, WILLIAM (BROTHER ANTINOUS)

"A Canticle to the Waterbirds"

Elder, *Imagining the Earth: Poetry and the Vision of Nature*, passim.

"Jacob and the Angel"

Lacey, *The Inner War*, 99-101.

"The Residual Years"

Joe Marusiak, "Where We Might Meet Each Other: An Appreciation of Galway Kinnell and William Everson," *LitR* 24 (Spring 1981): 355-70.

"The Veritable Years"

Joe Marusiak, "Where We Might Meet Each Other: An Appreciation of Galway Kinnell and William Everson," *LitR* 24 (Spring 1981): 355-70.

EWING, SAMUEL

"American Miracle"

Irving N. Rothman, "Structure and Theme in Samuel Ewing's Satire, the 'American Miracle,'" *AL* 40 (Nov. 1968): 294-308.

FEARING, KENNETH

"Ad"

Walsh, *Doors into Poetry*, 56-57.

"The Face at the Bar Room Mirror"

J. F. Nims, *Poetry: A Critical Supplement*, Oct. 1947, 16-17.

"Green Light"

Macha Rosenthal, "The Meaning of Kenneth Fearing's Poetry," *Poetry* 64 (July 1944): 211-12.

Rosenthal, *The Modern Poets*, 237-38.

"Obituary"

Macha Rosenthal, "The Meaning of Kenneth Fearing's Poetry," *Poetry* 64 (July 1944): 214.

"Portrait"

Perrine and Reid, *100 American Poems*, 185-86.

"Radio Blues"

Macha Rosenthal, "The Meaning of Kenneth Fearing's Poetry," *Poetry* 64 (July 1944): 220.

"What If Mr. Jesse James Should Someday Die?"

Macha Rosenthal, "The Meaning of Kenneth Fearing's Poetry," *Poetry* 64 (July 1944): 214-15.

"Yes, the Serial Will Be Continued"

Walter Gierasch, "Reading Modern Poetry," *CE* 2 (Oct. 1940): 34-35.

FERLINGHETTI, LAWRENCE

[Interview]

"A Conversation: Lawrence Ferlinghetti," *Another Chicago Mag* 16 (1986): 118-30.

"*Pulpsmith* Interviews Lawrence Ferlinghetti," *Pulpsmith* 4 (Autumn 1984): 132-42.

"Autobiography"

Michael Skau, "The Poet as Form: Ferlinghetti's Songs of Myself," *CP* 20 (1987): 57-61.

"Bickford's Buddha"

Michael Skau, "The Poet as Form: Ferlinghetti's Songs of Myself," *CP* 20 (1987): 57-61.

"A Coney Island of the Mind"

Br. Edward Kent, O.S.F., "Daredevil Poetics: Ferlinghetti's Definition of a Poet," *EJ* 59 (Dec. 1970): 1243-44, 1251.

"Great American Waterfront Poem"

Michael Skau, "The Poet as Form: Ferlinghetti's Songs of Myself," *CP* 20 (1987): 57-61.

"Mock Confessional"

Michael Skau, "The Poet as Form: Ferlinghetti's Songs of Myself," *CP* 20 (1987): 57-61.

"Overheard Conversation"

Michael Skau, "The Poet as Form: Ferlinghetti's Songs of Myself," *CP* 20 (1987): 57-61.

"The Third World"

Michael Skau, "The Poet as Form: Ferlinghetti's Songs of Myself," *CP* 20 (1987): 57-61.

"True Confessional"

Michael Skau, "The Poet as Form: Ferlinghetti's Songs of Myself," *CP* 20 (1987): 57-61.

"Truth Is Not the Secret of a Few"

Michael Skau, "The Poet as Form: Ferlinghetti's Songs of Myself," *CP* 20 (1987): 57-61.

FIELD, EDWARD

"After the Moonwalk"

Ronald Weber, "The View from Space: Notes on Space Exploration and Recent Writing," *GaR* 33 (Summer 1979): 280-96.

FIELD, EUGENE

"Little Boy Blue"

Laurence Perrine, "Are Tears Made of Sugar or Salt?" *IEY* (Fall 1963): 19-21.

Laurence Perrine, *The Art of Total Relevance*, 125-29.

FIELDS, JAMES T.

"The Captain's Daughter"

Daniels, *The Art of Reading Poetry*, 85-88.

FINCH, ROBERT

"The Statue"

William Walsh, "The Shape of Canadian Poetry," *SR* 87 (Jan./Mar. 1979): 73-95.

"This Rose You Gave Me"

George Johnston, "Diction in Poetry," *CanL* 97 (Summer 1983): 39-44.

"Weather"

William Walsh, "The Shape of Canadian Poetry," *SR* 87 (Jan./Mar. 1979): 73-95.

FLANAGAN, BOB

"The Kid Is the Man"

David E. James, "Poetry/Punk/Production: Some Recent Writing in L.A.," *MinnR*, n.s. 23 (Fall 1984): 127-48.

FORCHÉ, CAROLYN

[Interview]

"Yale's Younger Poets: Interview with Chester Kerr, Stanley Kunitz, Carolyn Forché," *Book Forum* 2 (1976): 367-68, 370, 386.

The County Between Us

Judith Gleason, "The Lesson of Bread," *Parnassus* 10 (Spring/Summer 1982): 9-21.

"Gathering the Tribes"

Eleanor Lerman, "Tribal World of Carolyn Forché," *Book Forum* 2 (1976): 396-99.

"The Morning Baking"

Judith Gleason, "The Lesson of Bread," *Parnassus* 10 (Spring/Summer 1982): 9-21.

"Return"

Judith Gleason, "The Lesson of Bread," *Parnassus* 10 (Spring/Summer 1982): 9-21.

FORD, MICHAEL

"The World Is a Suburb of Los Angeles"

David E. James, "Poetry/Punk/Production: Some Recent Writing in L.A.," *MinnR*, n.s. (Fall 1984): 127-48.

FRANCIS, ROBERT

"The Big Tent"

J. F. Nims, *Poetry: A Critical Supplement*, Nov. 1948, 17-18.

FRANKENBERG, LLOYD

"I, Lazarus"

Nelson Algren, "Lloyd Frankenberg's Poems," *Poetry* 56 (Apr. 1940): 47-48.

FROST, FRANCES

"Cradle Song"

John Ciardi, "Sensitivity without Discipline," *Nation* 179 (Dec. 4, 1954): 490-92.

FROST, ROBERT

"Accidentally on Purpose"

Claude M. Simpson, "Robert Frost and Man's 'Royal Role,'" in Ludwig, *Aspects of American Poetry*, 135-36.

Robert B. Thompson, *Expl* 36 (Winter 1978): 17.

"Acquainted with the Night"

Malcolm Brown, "The Sweet Crystalline Cry," *Western Review* 16 (Summer 1952): 266.

Robert F. Fleissner, *Expl* 37 (Fall 1978): 11-13.

Joseph H. Friend, "Teaching the 'Grammar of Poetry,'" *CE* 27 (Feb. 1966): 363-65.

Nat Henry, *Expl* 35 (Spring 1977): 28-29.

Wallace Martin, *Expl* 26 (Apr. 1968): 64.

Laurence Perrine, *Expl* 25 (Feb. 1967): 50.

Laurence Perrine, *Expl* 37 (Fall 1978): 13-14.

"After Apple-Picking"

Brooks, *Modern Poetry and the Tradition*, 114-16.

Brooks and Warren, *Understanding Poetry*, rev. ed., 389-97.

Cardwell, *Readings, from the Americas*, 776-77.

Reginald L. Cook, "Frost as a Parablist," *Accent* 10 (Autumn 1949): 36.

Peter W. Dowell, "Counter-Images and Their Function in the Poetry of Robert Frost," *TSL* 14 (1969): 18-20.

Joe M. Ferguson, Jr., *Expl* 22 (Mar. 1964): 53.

Hadas, *Form, Cycle, Infinity*, passim.

George Monteiro, *Expl* 30 (Mar. 1972): 62.

P. M. Paton, "Robert Frost: 'The fact is the sweetest dream that labor knows,'" *AL* 53 (Mar. 1981): 43-55.

William B. Stein, "'After Apple-Picking': Echoic Parody," *University of Kansas City Review* 35 (Summer 1969): 301-5.

Wallace, *God Be with the Clown: Humor in American Poetry*, passim.

"All Revelation"

Peter L. Hays, "Frost and the Critics: More Revelation on 'All Revelation,'" *ELN* 18, no. 4 (1980): 283-90.

"And All We Call American"

Claude M. Simpson, "Robert Frost and Man's 'Royal Role,'" in Ludwig, *Aspects of American Poetry*, 126-28.

"America Is Hard to See"

Leslie Lee Francis, "Robert Frost and the Majesty of Stones upon Stones," *JML* 9 (Winter 1981/1982): 3-26.

"Away!"

Richard Eberhart, "Robert Frost in the Clearing," *SoR* 11 (Spring 1975): 264-66.

"The Axe-Helve"

James R. Vitelli, "Robert Frost: The Contrarieties of Talent and Tradition," *NEQ* 47 (Sept. 1974): 363-64.

Floyd C. Watkins, "The Poetry of the Unsaid--Robert Frost's Narrative and Dramatic Poems," *Texas Quarterly* 15 (Winter 1972): 90-92.

"The Bear"

H. H. Watts, "Robert Frost and the Interrupted Dialogue," *AL* 27 (Mar. 1955): 76-77.

Winters, *The Function of Criticism*, 166-67.

"Beech"

Harold E. Toliver, *Pastoral: Forms and Attitudes* (Berkeley and London: University of California Press, 1971): 338-40.

"Bereft"

Clark Griffith, "Frost and the American View of Nature," *AQ* 20 (Spring 1968): 32-34.

"Birches"

Hadas, *Form, Cycle, Infinity*, passim.

Jeffrey Hart, "Frost and Eliot," *SR* 84 (July/Sept. 1976): 435-37.

Lewis H. Miller, Jr., "The Poet as Swinger: Fact and Fancy in Robert Frost," *Criticism* 16 (Winter 1947): 59-63.

P. M. Paton, "Robert Frost: 'The fact is the sweetest dream that labor knows,'" *AL* 53 (Mar. 1981): 43-55.

Perrine and Reid, *100 American Poems*, 35-36.

J. O. Perry, "The Dialogue of Voices in Robert Frost's Poems," *SAQ* 81 (Spring 1982): 214-29.

"The Birthplace"

Peter W. Dowell, "Counter-Images and Their Function in the Poetry of Robert Frost," *TSL* 14 (1969): 17-18.

"The Black Cottage"

Peter W. Dowell, "Counter-Images and Their Function in the Poetry of Robert Frost," *TSL* 14 (1969): 27-28.

Hadas, *Form, Cycle, Infinity*, passim.

"Bond and Free"

Mordecai Marcus, "Robert Frost's 'Bond and Free': Structure and Meaning," *CP* 8 (Spring 1975): 61-64.

"A Boy's Will"

Donald T. Haynes, "The Narrative Unity of *A Boy's Will*," *PMLA* 87 (May 1972): 452-64.

"Brown's Descent"

Walter Gierasch, *Expl* 11 (June 1953): 60. Reprinted in *The Explicator Cyclopedia* 1:128-29.

"The Census-Taker"

Hadas, *Form, Cycle, Infinity*, passim.

"The Cocoon"

Richard Poirier, "Soundings for Home: Frost's Poetry of Extravagance and Return," *GaR* 31 (Summer 1977): 299-300.

"Come In"

Brooks, Purser, and Warren, *An Approach to Literature*, 4th ed., 426.

Deutsch, *Poetry in Our Time*, 75-76.

Robert Kern, "Toward a New Nature Poetry," *CentR* 19 (Summer 1975): 208-10.

Robert Ornstein, *Expl* 15 (June 1957): 61. Reprinted in *The Explicator Cyclopedia* 1:129.

"A Concept Self-Conceived"

Joseph Kau, *Expl* 35 (Spring 1977): 19.

"The Death of the Hired Man"

C. M. Bowra, "Reassessments I: Robert Frost," *Adelphi* 27 (Nov. 1950), 46-64.

Robert P. Tristram Coffin, Untitled Review, *AL* 14 (Jan. 1943): 438-39.

C. C. Cunningham, *Literature as a Fine Art: Analysis and Interpretation*, 106-10.

Bess C. Hopkins, "A Study of 'The Death of the Hired Man,'" *EJ* 43 (Apr. 1954): 175-76.

Jerome, *Poetry: Premeditated Art*, 196-207.

Fritz H. Oehlschlaeger, "The Consecration of Home: Robert Frost's 'The Death of the Hired Man,'" *ELWIU* 11 (Spring 1984): 105-12.

Perrine and Reid, *100 American Poems*, 31-33.

V. Vogt, "Narrative and Drama in the Lyric: Robert Frost's Strategic Withdrawal," *CritI* 5 (Spring 1979): 529-51.

Charles C. Walcutt, *Expl* 3 (Oct. 1944): 7. Reprinted in *The Explicator Cyclopedia* 1:129-30.

"The Demiurge's Laugh"

Walter Blair, *The Literature of the United States* 2:933.

Robert F. Fleissner, "Frost's Response to Keats' Risibility," *BSUF* 11 (Winter 1970): 40-43.

"Departmental"

Mario L. D'Avanzo, "Frost's 'Departmental' and Emerson: A Further Range of Satire," *CP* 10 (Fall 1977): 67-69.

"Desert Places"

Ronald Bieganowski, *Expl* 38 (Fall 1979): 20-21.

R. P. Blackmur, "The Instincts of a Bard," *Nation* 142 (June 24, 1936): 819.

Brooks and Warren, *Understanding Poetry*, 193-94; rev. ed., 87-88.

W. C. Brown, "A Poem Should Not Mean But Be," *University of Kansas City Review* 15 (Autumn 1948): 62-63.

Chatman, *An Introduction to the Language of Poetry*, 11-13.

Friedman and McLaughlin, *Poetry: An Introduction to Its Form and Art*, 29-32, 51-53, 70-74, 93-95, 118-20, 143-48, 162-64, 179-81.

Charles B. Hand, "The Hidden Terror of Robert Frost," *EJ* 58 (Nov. 1969): 1166-68.

Carol M. Lindner, "Robert Frost: Dark Romantic," *ArQ* 29 (Autumn 1973): 243-44.

Lewis H. Miller, Jr., "Two Poems of Winter," *CE* 28 (Jan. 1967): 314-16.

"Design"

Gareth Cordery, *Expl* 41 (Spring 1983): 45-47.

Drew, *Poetry: A Modern Guide*, 186-88.

Jere K. Huzzard, *Expl* 42 (Summer 1984): 26-27.

Randall Jarrell, "To the Laodiceans," *KR* 14 (Autumn 1952): 543-45.

Jerome, *Poetry: Premeditated Art*, 54-57.

Carol M. Lindner, "Robert Frost: Dark Romantic," *ArQ* 29 (Autumn 1973): 240-43.

Laurence Perrine, *Expl* 42 (Winter 1984): 16.

Perrine and Reid, *100 American Poems*, 46-47.

L. R. Pratt, "Robert Frost and the Limits of Thought," *ArQ* 36 (Autumn 1980): 240-60.

"Devotion"

Walter Gierasch, *Expl* 10 (May 1952): 50. Reprint *The Explicator Cyclopedia* 1:130

"Directive"

Marie Borroff, "Robert Frost's New Testament: Language and the Poem," *MP* 69 (Aug. 1971): 50-53.

Margaret M. Blum, "Robert Frost's 'Directive': A Theological Reading," *MLN* 76 (June 1961): 524-25.

Pearlanna Briggs, *Expl* 21 (May 1963): 71.

Clark, *Lyric Resonance*, 106-17.

James M. Cox, "Robert Frost and the Edge of the Clearing," *VQR* 35 (Winter 1959): 85-87.

Deutsch, *Poetry in Our Time*, 75.

Dickinson, *Suggestions for Teachers of "Introduction to Literature*," 42.

James P. Dougherty, "Robert Frost's 'Directive' to the Wilderness," *AQ* 18 (Summer 1966): 208-19.

Drew, *Poetry: A Modern Guide*, 229-33.

Elder, *Imagining the Earth: Poetry and the Vision of Nature*, passim.

Mildred E. Hartsock, *Expl* 16 (Apr. 1958): 42. Reprinted in *The Explicator Cyclopedia* 1:130-31.

Anne K. Juhnke, "Religion in Robert Frost's Poetry: The Play for Self-Possession," *AL* 36 (May 1964): 163-64.

V. Y. Kantak, "Poetic Ambiguity in Frost," *WHR* 28 (Winter 1974): 42-44.

George Knox, "A Backward Motion toward the Source," *Personalist* 47 (Summer 1966): 365-81.

Robert Peters, "The Truth of Frost's 'Directive,'" *MLN* 75 (Jan. 1960): 29-32.

R. Wakefield, *Robert Frost and the Opposing Lights of the Hour* (New York: Peter Lang, 1985), passim.

Gregory Waters, "'Directive': Frost's Magical Mystery Tour," *CP* 9 (Spring 1976): 33-38.

"The Discovery of the Madeiras"

Yvor Winters, "Robert Frost: Or, The Spiritual Drifter as Poet," *SR* 56 (Autumn 1948): 593-94. Reprinted in Winters, *The Function of Criticism*, 184-85.

"Doom to Doom"

Claude M. Simpson, "Robert Frost and Man's 'Royal Role,'" in Ludwig, *Aspects of American Poetry*, 128-29.

"The Draft Horse"

Eben Bass, "Frost's Poetry of Fear," *AL* 43 (Jan. 1972): 613-15.

Margaret M. Blum, *Expl* 24 (May 1966): 79.

Paul Burrell, *Expl* 25 (Mar. 1967): 60.

Frederick L. Gwynn, "Analysis and Synthesis of Frost's 'The Draft Horse,'" *CE* 26 (Dec. 1964): 223-25.

Laurence Perrine, *Expl* 24 (May 1966): 79.

Sandra W. Tomlinson, *Expl* 42 (Summer 1984): 28-29.

"A Dream Pang"

R. Wakefield, *Robert Frost and the Opposing Lights of the Hour* (New York: Peter Lang, 1985), passim.

"Dust of Snow"

Norbert Artzt, "The Poetry Lesson," *CE* 32 (Apr. 1971): 740-42.

Linda Bradley Funkhouser, "Acoustic Rhythm in Frost's 'Dust of Snow,'" *Lang&S* 14 (Fall 1981): 287-303.

Edgar H. Knapp, *Expl* 28 (Sept. 1969): 9.

Elizabeth Nitchie, "The Language of Men," *CentR* 3 (Winter 1959): 193-94.

Laurence Perrine, *Expl* 29 (Mar. 1971): 61.

Laurence Perrine, "Frost's 'Dust of Snow,'" *NConL* 12 (May 1982): 2-4.

H. G. Widdowson, *Stylistics and the Teaching of Literature* (London: Longman Group, 1975), 38-39, 104-107.

"The Egg and the Machine"

Peter W. Dowell, "Counter-Images and Their Function in the Poetry of Robert Frost," *TSL* 14 (1969): 23-25.

Yvor Winters, "Robert Frost: Or, The Spiritual Drifter as Poet," *SR* 56 (Autumn 1948): 577-78. Reprinted in Winters, *The Function of Criticism*, 170-71; in Zabel, *Literary Opinion in American*, rev. ed., 425-26.

"An Empty Threat"

Laurence Perrine, *Expl* 30 (Apr. 1972): 63.

"Etherealizing"

Todd M. Lieber, "Robert Frost and Wallace Stevens: 'What to Make of a Diminished Thing,'" *AL* 47 (Mar. 1975): 75-76.

"Far-away Meadow" (in "The Last Mowing")

Toliver, *Pastoral: Forms and Attitudes*, 359-60.

"The Fear"

Eben Bass, "Frost's Poetry of Fear," *AL* 43 (Jan. 1972): 611-12.

Laurence Perrine, "Frost's 'The Fear': Unfinished Sentences, Unanswered Questions," *CollL* 11 (Spring 1984): 125-33.

"The Figure in the Doorway"

Peter W. Dowell, "Counter-Images and Their Function in the Poetry of Robert Frost," *TSL* 14 (1969): 22-23.

Richard Poirier, "Soundings for Home: Frost's Poetry of Extravagance and Return," *GaR* 31 (Summer 1977): 303-4.

"Fire and Ice"

Michael West, "Versifying Thoreau: Frost's 'The Quest of the Purple Fringed' and 'Fire and Ice,'" *ELN* 16 (1978): 40-46.

"Fireflies in the Garden"

Robert F. Fleissner, *Expl* 39 (Summer 1981): 26-27.

"Forgive, O Lord"

Richard Eberhart, "Robert Frost in the Clearing," *SoR* 11 (Spring 1975): 263-64.

"For Once, Then Something"

Helen Bacon, "Dialogue of the Poets: *Mens Animi* and the Renewal of Words," *MR* 19 (Summer 1978): 319-34.

Charles B. Hands, "The Hidden Terror of Robert Frost," *EJ* 58 (Nov. 1969): 1162-64.

Dan G. Hoffman, *Expl* 9 (Nov. 1950): 17. Reprinted in *The Explicator Cyclopedia* 1:131-32.

Judson Jerome, "Six Senses of the Poet," *Colorado Quarterly* 10 (Winter 1962): 225-40.

L. R. Pratt, "Robert Frost and the Limits of Thought," *ArQ* 36 (Autumn 1980): 240-60.

"Gathering Leaves"

Laurence Perrine, "Frost's 'Gathering Leaves,'" *CEA* 34 (Nov. 1971): 29.

"Ghost House"

Dennis Vail, *Expl* 30 (Oct. 1971): 11.

"The Gift Outright"

Hamida Bosmajian, "R. Frost's 'The Gift Outright': Wish and Reality in History and Poetry," *AQ* 22 (Spring 1970): 95-105.

Raymond D. Gozzi, *Expl* 41 (Spring 1983): 44-45.

Kreuzer, *Elements of Poetry*, 154-55.

Albert J. von Frank, *Expl* 38 (Fall 1971): 22-23.

"Going for Water"

Joseph J. Comprone, "Play and the 'Aesthetic State,'" *MSE* 1 (Spring 1967): 24-26.

"The Grindstone"

Reginald L. Cook, "Frost as Parablist," *Accent* 10 (Autumn 1949): 37-38.

"Happiness Makes up in Height"

W. G. O'Donnell, "Robert Frost and New England: A Revaluation," *YR* 37 (Summer 1948): 698-712.

"A Hillside Thaw"

Wallace, *God Be with the Clown: Humor in American Poetry*, passim.

"The Hill Wife"

Floyd C. Watkins, "The Poetry of the Unsaid--Robert Frost's Narrative and Dramatic Poems," *Texas Quarterly* 15 (Winter 1972): 92-94.

"Home Burial"

Abad, *A Formal Approach to Lyric Poetry*, 81-93.

Eben Bass, "Frost's Poetry of Fear," *AL* 43 (Jan. 1972): 608-9.

Randall Jarrell, "Robert Frost's 'Home Burial,'" in Allen, *The Moment of Poetry*, 99-132.

Laurence J. Sasso, Jr., "Robert Frost: Love's Questions," *NEQ* 42 (Mar. 1969): 100-102.

Robert H. Swennes, "Man and Wife: The Dialogue of Contraries in Robert Frost's Poetry," *AL* 42 (Nov. 1970): 366-67.

R. Wakefield, *Robert Frost and the Opposing Lights of the Hour* (New York: Peter Lang, 1985), passim.

Floyd C. Watkins, "The Poetry of the Unsaid--Robert Frost's Narrative and Dramatic Poems," *Texas Quarterly* 15 (Winter 1972): 86-87, 89-90.

Laurence Perrine, *Expl* 34 (Feb. 1976): 48.

"In Hardwood Groves"

Steve Gowler, *Expl* 40 (Spring 1982): 48.

"In the Home Stretch"

Darrel Abel, *Expl* 45 (Winter 1987): 37-39.

Richard Foster, "Leaves Compared with Flowers: A Reading in Robert Frost's Poems," *NEQ* 46 (Sept. 1973): 411-12.

"In Time of Cloudburst"

Peckham and Chatman, *Word, Meaning, Poem*, 254-60.

"Into My Own"

Wallace, *God Be with the Clown: Humor in American Poetry*, passim.

"In White and Design"

David Hiatt, *Expl* 28 (Jan. 1970): 41.

"Iris by Night"

P. M. Cubeta, "Robert Frost and Edward Thomas: Two Soldier Poets," *NEQ* 52 (June 1979): 147-76.

"I Will Sing You One-O"

Anna K. Juhnke, "Religion in Robert Frost's Poetry: The Play for Self-Possession," *AL* 36 (May 1964): 154-55.

Laurence Perrine, "Frost's 'Iris by Night,'" *CP* 12 (Spring 1979): 35-43.

"Kitty Hawk"

Helen Bacon, "Dialogue of Poets: *Mens Animi* and the Renewal of Words," *MR* 19 (Summer 1978): 319-34.

Laurence Goldstein, "'Kitty Hawk' and the Question of American Destiny," *IowaR* 9 (Winter 1978): 41-49.

Claude M. Simpson, "Robert Frost and Man's 'Royal Role,'" in Ludwig, *Aspects of American Poetry*, 136-47.

"The Last Mowing"

Walter Gierasch, *Expl* 10 (Feb. 1952): 25. Reprinted in *The Explicator Cyclopeida* 1:132-33.

Yvor Winters, "Robert Frost: Or, The Spiritual Drifter as Poet," *SR* 56 (Autumn 1948): 589-90. Reprinted in Winters, *The Function of Criticism*, 181-82; in Zabel, *Literary Opinion in America*, rev. ed., 434-35.

"A Leaf Treader"

Brooks, Purser, and Warren, *An Approach to Literature*, 4th ed., 423-24.

"Leaves Compared with Flowers"

Richard Foster, "Leaves Compared with Flowers: A Reading in Robert Frost's Poems," *NEQ* 46 (Sept. 1973): 422-23.

"The Lesson for Today"

Yvor Winters, "Robert Frost: Or, The Spiritual Drifter as Poet," *SR* 56 (Autumn 1948): 585-586. Reprinted in Winters, *The Function of Criticism*, 177-78; in Zabel, *Literary Opinion in America*, rev. ed., 431-32.

"A Line-Storm Song"

Perrine and Reid, *100 American Poems*, 44-45.

"The Literate Farmer and the Planet Venus," *NConL* 5 (Mar. 1975): 10-13.

"Locked Out: As Told to a Child"

Eben Bass, "Frost's Poetry of Fear," *AL* 43 (Jan. 1972): 610-11.

"A Lone Striker"

Frederick L. Gwynn, "Poetry Crisis at Corning," *CEA* 15 (Dec. 1953): 1, 3.

Harold H. Watts, "Robert Frost and the Interrupted Dialogue," *AL* 27 (Mar. 1955): 77-78.

"Love and a Question"

Michael J. Collins, "A Note on Frost's 'Love and a Question,'" *CP* 8 (Spring 1975): 57-58.

Laurence Perrine, "The Dilemma in Frost's 'Love and a Question,'" *CP* 5 (Fall 1972): 5-8.

"The Lovely Shall Be Choosers"

W. L. Lerner, *Expl* 13 (Apr. 1955): 39. Reprinted in *The Explicator Cyclopedia* 1:134.

Elizabeth Nitchie, *Expl* 13 (Apr. 1955): 39. Reprinted in *The Explicator Cyclopedia* 1:133-34.

Edward Schwartz, *Expl* 13 (Oct. 1954): 3. Reprinted in *The Explicator Cyclopedia* 1:133.

"Maple"

John Morris, "The Poet as Philosopher: Robert Frost," *MQR* 11 (Spring 1972): 127-28.

"A Masque of Mercy"

Roberta F. S. Borkat, "The Bleak Landscape of Robert Frost," *MQ* 16 (Summer 1975): 453-57.

Sr. Mary Jeremy Finnegan, O. P., "Frost's 'Masque of Mercy,'" *Catholic World* 186 (Feb. 1958): 358-61.

W. R. Irwin, "The Unity of Frost's Masques," *AL* 32 (Nov. 1960): 302-12.

Anna K. Juhnke, "Religion in Robert Frost's Poetry: The Play for Self-Possession," *AL* 36 (May 1964): 161-63.

Laurence Perrine, "A Set of Notes for Frost's Two Masques," *RALS* 7 (Autumn 1977): 125-33.

D. Bradley Sullivan, "'Education by Poetry' in Robert Frost's Masques," *PLL* 22 (1986): 312-21.

"A Masque of Reason"

Roberta F. S. Borkat, "The Bleak Landscape of Robert Frost," *MQ* 16 (Summer 1975): 453-67.

H. C. Hatfield, *Expl* 4 (Nov. 1945): 9. Reprinted in *The Explicator Cyclopedia* 1:134-35.

W. R. Irwin, "The Unity of Frost's Masques," *AL* 32 (Nov. 1960): 302-12.

Anna K. Juhnke, "Religion in Robert Frost's Poetry: The Play for Self-Possession," *AL* 36 (May 1964): 160-61.

Laurence Perrine, "A Set of Notes for Frost's Two Masques," *RALS* 7 (Autumn 1977): 125-33.

D. Bradley Sullivan, "'Education by Poetry' in Robert Frost's Masques," *PLL* 22 (1986): 312-21.

Ruth Todasco, "Dramatic Characterization in Frost: 'A Masque of Reason,'" *University of Kansas City Review* 29 (Mar. 1963): 227-30.

H. H. Waggoner, *Expl* 4 (Mar. 1946): 32. Reprinted in *The Explicator Cyclopedia* 1:135.

"Meeting and Passing"

Laurence J. Sasso, Jr., "Robert Frost: Love's Question," *NEQ* 42 (Mar. 1969): 106-7.

Thomas Shalvey, S.J., "Valéry and Frost: Two Views of Subjective Reality," *Renascence* 11 (Summer 1959): 188.

"Mending Wall"

George Arms and Nat Henry, *Expl* 37 (Spring 1979): 30-32.

Joseph Warren Beach, "Robert Frost," *YR* 43 (Winter 1953): 210-11.

Marie Borroff, "Robert Frost's New Testament: Language and the Poem," *MP* 69 (Aug. 1971): 37-44.

J. K. Bowen, "The *Persona* in Frost's 'Mending Wall': Mended or Amended," *CEA* 31 (Nov. 1968): 14.

John C. Broderick, *Expl* 14 (Jan. 1956): 24. Reprinted in *The Explicator Cyclopedia* 1:135-36.

Joseph J. Comprone, "Play and the 'Aesthetic State,'" *MSE* 1 (Spring 1967): 26-28.

A. R. Coulthard, *Expl* 45 (Winter 1987): 40-42.

Deutsch, *This Modern Poetry*, 42-44.

S. L. Dragland, *Expl* 25 (Jan. 1967): 39.

Carson Gibb, *Expl* 20 (Feb. 1962): 48. Reprinted in *The Explicator Cyclopedia* 1:136-37.

Hadas, *Form, Cycle, Infinity*, passim.

Jeremy Hawthorn, *Identity and Relationship: A Contribution to Marxist Theory of Literary Criticism* (London: Lawrence & Wishart, 1973): 78-82.

Edward Jayne, "Up against the 'Mending Wall': The Psychoanalysis of a Poem by Frost," *CE* 34 (Apr. 1973): 934-51.

Frank Lentricchia, "Experience as Meaning: Robert Frost's 'Mending Wall,'" *CEA* 34 (May 1972): 8-12.

George Monteiro, "Robert Frost's Linked Analogies," *NEQ* 46 (Sept. 1973): 466-68.

George Monteiro, "Unlinked Myth in Frost's 'Mending Wall,'" *CP* 7 (Fall 1974): 10-11.

Marion Montgomery, "Robert Frost and His Use of Barriers: Man vs. Nature Toward God," *SAQ* 57 (Summer 1958): 349-50.

F. Oehlschlaeger, "Fences Make Neighbors: Process, Identity, and Ego in Robert Frost's 'Mending Wall,'" *ArQ* 40 (Autumn 1984): 242-54.

William H. Pritchard, "The Grip of Frost," *HudR* 29 (Summer 1976): 190-92.

Rosenthal and Smith, *Exploring Poetry*, 5-6.

Barton Levi St. Armand, *Expl* 41 (Fall 1982): 47-48.

Thomas Shalvey, S.J., "Valéry and Frost: Two Views of Subjective Reality," *Renascence* 11 (Summer 1959): 187.

R. Wakefield, *Robert Frost and the Opposing Lights of the Hour* (New York: Peter Lang, 1985), passim.

Wallace, *God Be with the Clown: Humor in American Poetry*, passim.

William S. Ward, "Lifted Pot Lids and Unmended Walls," *CE* 27 (Feb. 1966), 428-29.

Charles N. Watson, Jr., "Frost's Wall: The View from the Other Side," *NEQ* 44 (Dec. 1971): 653-56.

Wheeler, *The Design of Poetry*, 53.

Douglas L. Wilson, "The Other Side of the Wall," *IowaR* 10 (Winter 1979): 65-75.

"Moon Compasses"

Robert F. Fleissner, *Expl* 32 (May 1974): 66.

Roger L. Slakey, *Expl* 37 (Fall 1978): 22-23.

"The Most of It"

Helen Bacon, "Dialogue of Poets: *Mens Animi* and the Renewal of Words," *MR* 19 (Summer 1978): 319-34.

Pinsky, *The Situation of Poetry: Contemporary Poetry and Its Traditions*, 65-68.

Richard Poirier, "Soundings for Home: Frost's Poetry of Extravagance and Return," *GaR* 31 (Summer 1977): 304-12.

L. R. Pratt, "Robert Frost and the Limits of Thought," *ArQ* 36 (Autumn 1980): 240-60.

William H. Pritchard, "The Grip of Frost," *HudR* 29 (Summer 1976): 200-203.

Thomas Shalvey, S.J., "Valéry and Frost: Two Views of Subjective Reality," *Renascence* 11 (Summer 1959): 188.

Yvor Winters, "Robert Frost: Or, The Spriritual Drifter as Poet," *SR* 56 (Autumn 1948): 591-92. Reprinted in Winters, *The Function of Criticism*; in Zabel, *Literary Opinion in America*, rev. ed., 435-36.

"The Mountain"

Laurence Perrine, "Frost's 'The Mountain': Concerning Poetry," *CP* 4 (Spring 1971): 5-11.

"Mowing"

Ethel Beach-Viti, *Expl* 40 (Summer 1982): 45-46.

Marie Borroff, "Robert Frost's New Testament: Language and the Poem," *MP* 69 (Aug. 1971): 46-47.

Seymour Chatman, "Robert Frost's 'Mowing': An Inquiry into Prosodic Structure," in *Discussions of Poetry: Rhythm and Sound*, ed. George Hemphill (Boston: D. C. Heath & Co., 1961), 85-92.

Lewis H. Miller, Jr., "The Poet as Swinger: Fact and Fancy in Robert Frost," *Criticism* 16 (Winter 1974): 64-67.

P. M. Paton, "Robert Frost: 'The fact is the sweetest dream that labor knows,'" *AL* 53 (Mar. 1981): 43-55.

Toliver, *Pastoral: Forms and Attitudes*, 344-45.

"Nature's First Green Is Gold"

Southworth, *Some Modern American Poets*, 84-85.

"The Need of Being Versed in Country Things"

Brooks, Purser, and Warren, *An Approach to Literature*, 3d ed., 346-47; 4th ed., 344-45.

Hadas, *Form, Cycle, Infinity*, passim.

"Neither Out Far Nor in Deep"

Harold H. Corbin, Jr., and Cecilia Hennel Hendricks, *Expl* 1 (May 1943): 58. Reprinted in *The Explicator Cyclopedia* 1:137.

Clark Griffith, "Frost and the American View of Nature," *AQ* 20 (Spring 1968): 30-32.

Cecilia Hennel Hendricks, *Expl* 1 (May 1943): 58. Reprinted in *The Explicator Cyclopedia* 1:137-38.

Randall Jarrell, "To the Laodiceans," *KR* 14 (Autumn 1952): 539-40.

D. J. Lepore, "Robert Frost--The Middle Ground: An Analysis of 'Neither Out Far Nor In Deep,'" *EJ* 53 (Mar. 1964): 215-16.

Laurence Perrine, *Expl* 7 (Apr. 1949): 46. Reprinted in *The Explicator Cyclopedia* 1:138.

R. W. Stallman, "The Position of Poetry Today," *EJ* 46 (May 1957): 247-48.

"Never Again Would Birds' Song Be the Same"

C. Perri, "Knowing and Playing: The Literary Text and the Trope Allusion," *AI* 41 (Summer 1984): 117-28.

Richard Poirier, "Soundings for Home: Frost's Poetry of Extravagance and Return," *GaR* 31 (Summer 1977): 313-14.

"New Hampshire"

Jeffrey Hart, "Frost and Eliot," *SR* 84 (July/Sept. 1976): 429-32.

Laurence Perrine, *Expl* 39 (Spring 1981): 38-39.

James R. Vitelli, "Robert Frost: The Contrarieties of Talent and Tradition," *NEQ* 47 (Sept. 1974): 361-62.

"La Noche Triste"

Leslie Lee Francis, "Robert Frost and the Majesty of Stones upon Stones," *JML* 9 (Winter 1981/1982): 3-26.

"Not All There"

Morton W. Bloomfield, "The Two Cognitive Dimensions of the Humanities," *Daedalus* 99 (Spring 1970): 256-67.

Robert F. Fleissner, *Expl* 31 (Jan. 1973): 33.

"Nothing Gold Can Stay"

Charles R. Anderson, *Expl* 22 (Apr. 1964): 63.

Warren Beck, "Poetry's Chronic Disease," *EJ* 33 (Sept. 1944): 363.

Laurence Perrine, *Expl* 42 (Fall 1983): 38-39.

Walter Sutton, "The Contextualist Dilemma--or Fallacy?" *JAAC* 17 (Dec. 1958): 225-26.

"October"

Southworth, *Some Modern American Poets*, 69-71.

"The Oft-Repeated Dream"

Felver and Nurmi, *Poetry: An Introduction and Anthology*, 78-79.

"An Old Man's Winter Night"

Charles G. Davis, *Expl* 27 (Nov. 1968): 19.

"On a Tree Fallen across the Road"

Peter W. Dowell, "Counter-Images and Their Function in the Poetry of Robert Frost," *TSL* 14 (1969): 25-27.

"Once by the Pacific"

Brian Barbour, *Expl* 37 (Summer 1979): 18-19.

C. Hines Edwards, Jr., *Expl* 39 (Summer 1981): 28-29.

Robert F. Fleissner, *Expl* 40 (Summer 1982): 46-47.

Robert Fleissner, "Robert Frost's 'Once by the Pacific': The Moorish Genesis," *CLAJ* 23 (Dec. 1979): 160-71.

Clark Griffith, "Frost and the American View of Nature," *AQ* 20 (Spring 1968): 34-36.

Laurence Perrine, *Expl* 41 (Spring 1983): 44.

D. S. J. Parsons, "Night of Dark Intent," *PLL* 6 (Spring 1970): 205-10.

Judith P. Saunders, *Expl* 39 (Summer 1981): 29-31.

Van Doren, *Introduction to Poetry*, 77-80.

Wallace, *God Be with the Clown: Humor in American Poetry*, passim.

"Once More Brevity"

Claude M. Simpson, "Robert Frost and Man's 'Royal Role,'" in Ludwig, *Aspects of American Poetry*, 130-32.

"Once Looking up by Chance at the Constellations"

Carl M. Lindner, "Robert Frost: Dark Romantic," *ArQ* 29 (Autumn 1973): 238-40.

L. R. Pratt, "Robert Frost and the Limits of Thought," *ArQ* 36 (Autumn 1980): 240-60.

"One or Two"

Herbert Marks, "The Counter-Intelligence of Robert Frost," *YR* 71 (July 1982): 554-78.

"On the Heart's Beginning to Cloud the Mind"

Richard Poirier, "Soundings for Home: Frost's Poetry of Extravagance and Return," *GaR* 31 (Summer 1977): 301-3.

"Out, Out--"

Abad, *A Formal Approach to Lyric Poetry*, 233-34.

Marie Borroff, "Robert Frost's New Testament: Language and the Poem," *MP* 69 (Aug. 1971): 47-48.

William S. Doxey, *Expl* 29 (Apr. 1971): 70.

Archibald Henderson, Robert Frost's 'Out, Out--,'" *AI* 34 (Spring 1977): 12-27.

William J. Kelley, *Expl* 38 (Spring 1980): 12-13.

Valerie Rosendord and William Freedman, *Expl* 34 (Fall 1980): 10-11.

Satin, *Reading Poetry*, 1021-23.

Peter J. Schakel, *Expl* 40 (Summer 1982): 47-48.

Weldon Thornton, *Expl* 25 (May 1967): 71.

"The Oven Bird"

C. F. Burgess, *Expl* 20 (Mar. 1962): 59. Reprinted in *The Explicator Cyclopedia* 1:138-39.

C. R. B. Combellack, *Expl* 22 (Nov. 1963): 17.

Jerry A. Herndon, *Expl* 28 (Apr. 1970): 64.

William G. Lambdin, *Expl* 31 (Sept. 1972): 3.

William R. Osborne, *Expl* 26 (Feb. 1968): 47.

Van Doren, *Introduction to Poetry*, 73-77.

"The Pasture"

William Freedman, *Expl* 29 (May 1971): 80.

Rod W. Horton and Lawrence Thompson, *CEA* 11 (Feb. 1949): 4-5.

William S. Long, "Frost," *CEA* 10 (Nov. 1948): 4.

Fritz Oehlschlaeger, "Robert Frost's 'The Pasture': A Reconsideration," *CP* 16 (1983): 1-9.

"The Pauper Witch of Grafton"

Mordecai Marcus, "The Whole Pattern of Robert Frost's 'Two Witches': Contrasting Psycho-Sexual Modes," *L&P* 26 (1976): 75-78.

"Pod of the Milkweed"

Laurence Perrine, "Frost's 'Pod of the Milkweed,'" *Notes on Modern American Literature* 5 (Winter 1981): item 5.

179

"A Prayer in Spring"

Laurence Perrine, *The Art of Total Relevance*, 111-18.

"Provide, Provide"

Randall Jarrell, "To the Laodiceans," *KR* 14 (Autumn 1952): 541-42.

K. E. Marre, "Some Uses of Irony in Robert Frost's Poetry," *University of Dayton Review* 16 (Winter 1983/1984): 83-88.

Laurence Perrine, "Frost's 'Provide, Provide,'" *NConL* 8 (Mar. 1978): 8-9.

"Putting in the Seed"

Daniel R. Barnes, *Expl* 31 (Apr. 1973): 59.

Hadas, *Form, Cycle, Infinity*, passim.

"Quandary"

Thomas K. Hearn, Jr., "Making Sweetbreads Do: Robert Frost and Moral Empiricism," *NEQ* 49 (Mar. 1976): 73-75.

"The Quest of the Purple Fringed"

George Monteiro, "Frost's Quest for the 'Purple Fringed,'" *ELN* 13 (1976): 204-6.

Michael West, "Versifying Thoreau: Frost's 'The Quest of the Purple Fringed' and 'Fire and Ice,'" *ELN* 16 (1978): 40-46.

"Range-Finding"

Peter W. Dowell, "Counter-Images and Their Function in the Poetry of Robert Frost," *TSL* 14 (1969): 20-22.

Daniel Mansell, *Expl* 24 (Mar. 1966): 63.

"Reluctance"

Dickinson, *Suggestions for Teachers of "Introduction to Literature,"* 40.

"Revelation"

Laurence Perrine, *Expl* 42 (Fall 1983): 36-38.

"The Road Not Taken"

William B. Bache, "Rationalization in Two Frost Poems," *BSUF* 11 (Winter 1970): 33-34.

Patrick F. Bassett, *Expl* 39 (Spring 1981): 41-43.

Daniels, *The Art of Reading Poetry*, 347-49.

Robert W. French, "Reading Frost: 'The Road Not Taken,'" *EngR* 26 (Spring 1975): 91-93.

Ben W. Griffith, Jr., *Expl* 12 (June 1954): 55. Reprinted in *The Explicator Cyclopedia* 1:139-40.

Thomas Elwood Hart, "Frost's 'The Road Not Taken': Text Structure and Poetic Theory," *Lang&S* 17 (Winter 1984): 3-43.

R. G. Malbone, *Expl* 24 (Nov. 1965): 27.

Laurence Perrine, *Expl* 19 (Feb. 1961): 28. Reprinted in *The Explicator Cyclopedia* 1:140.

Laurence Perrine, "Teaching Ambiguity: Some Roads Not to Be Taken," *English in Texas* 8 (Summer 1977): 78-80.

John Oliver Perry, "The Dialogue of Voices in Robert Frost's Poems," *SAQ* 81 (Spring 1982): 214-29.

Eleanor M. Sickels, *Expl* 19 (Feb. 1961): 28. Reprinted in *The Explicator Cyclopedia* 1:140-41.

Southworth, *Some Modern American Poets*, 74-75.

Walsh, *Doors into Poetry*, 52-53.

"The Rose Family"

Laurence Perrine, *Expl* 26 (Jan. 1968): 43.

"The Runaway"

Charles B. Hands, "The Hidden Terror of Robert Frost," *EJ* 58 (Nov. 1969): 1165-66.

Mark Van Doren, "The Permanence of Robert Frost," *ASch* 5 (Spring 1936): 190-98.

"Sand Dunes"

Laurence Perrine, *Expl* 14 (Mar. 1956): 38. Reprinted in *The Explicator Cyclopedia* 1:141.

R. W. Stallman, "The Position of Poetry Today," *EJ* 46 (May 1957): 246-47.

"The Self-Seeker"

Laurence Perrine, "The Sense of Frost's 'The Self-Seeker,'" *CP* 7 (Fall 1974): 5-8.

R. Wakefield, *Robert Frost and the Opposing Lights of the Hour* (New York: Peter Lang, 1985, passim.

"A Semi-Revolution"

Chatman, *An Introduction to the Language of Poetry*, 66-67.

"A Servant to Servants"

Donald Jones, "Kindred Entanglements in Frost's 'A Servant to Servants," *PLL* 2 (Spring 1966): 150-61.

Floyd C. Watkins, "The Poetry of the Unsaid--Robert Frost's Narrative and Dramatic Poems," *Texas Quarterly* 15 (Winter 1972): 88-89.

"The Silken Tent"

Walter Gierasch, *Expl* 30 (Sept. 1971): 10.

Herbert Marks, "The Counter-Intelligence of Robert Frost," *YR* 71 (July 1982): 554-78.

"Sitting by a Bush in Broad Sunlight"

Harry Modean Campbell, *Expl* 5 (Dec. 1946): 18. Reprinted in *The Explicator Cyclopedia* 1:142.

"Snow"

Eben Bass, "Frost's Poetry of Fear," *AL* 43 (Jan. 1972): 604-5.

"A Soldier"

P. M. Cubeta, "Robert Frost and Edward Thomas: Two Soldier Poets," *NEQ* 52 (June 1979): 147-76.

Wheeler, *The Design of Poetry*, 171-72.

"The Sound of Trees"

Hadas, *Form, Cycle, Infinity*, passim.

"The Span of Life"

Brown and Olmstead, *Language and Literature*, 187-88.

Ciardi, *How Does a Poem Mean?*, 994-95.

Laurence Perrine, *Expl* 37 (Summer 1979): 4.

"Spring Pools"

C. R. B. Combellack, *Expl* 30 (Nov. 1971): 27.

Hadas, *Form, Cycle, Infinity*, passim.

Edward Stone, *A Certain Morbidness: A View of American Literature* (Carbondale: Southern Illinois University Press, 1969), 70-84.

David Toor, *Expl* 28 (Nov. 1969): 28.

"A Star in a Stoneboat"

Leslie Lee Francis, "Robert Frost and the Majesty of Stones Upon Stones," *JML* 9 (1981/1982): 3-26.

"Stopping by Woods on a Snowy Evening"

Abad, *A Formal Approach to Lyric Poetry*, 51-54.

James Armstrong, "The Death Wish in 'Stopping by Woods,'" *CE* 25 (Mar. 1964): 440, 445.

Beaty and Matchett, *Poetry: From Statement to Meaning*, 7-8.

Blair and Gerber, *Better Reading 2: Literature*, 156-57.

Brooks, *A Shaping Joy*, xv-xvii.

Brown and Olmstead, *Language and Literature*, 142-48, 150-55.

Ciardi, *How Does a Poem Mean?* 671-76.

John Ciardi, "Robert Frost: The Way to Poem," *Saturday Review* 41 (12 Apr. 1958): 13-15. Reprinted in *Harbrace College Reader*, ed. Mark Schorer, Phylip Durham, and Everett L. Jones (New York: Harcourt, Brace & Co., 1959), 444-56.

Cooper and Homes, *Preface to Poetry*, 605-7. Reprinted in Locke, Gibson, and Arms, *Readings for Liberal Education*, 510-512; 3d ed., 182-84; 4th ed., 182-85; 5th ed., 162-65; in Stallman and Watters, *The Creative Reader*, 840-42; in Engle and Carrier, *Reading Modern Poetry*, 1-4.

Herbert R. Coursen, Jr., "The Ghost of Christmas Past: 'Stopping by Woods on a Snowy Evening,'" *CE* 24 (Dec. 1962): 236-38.

James M. Cox, "Robert Frost and the Edge of the Clearing," *VQR* 35 (Winter 1959): 82-84.

Daniels, *The Art of Reading Poetry*, 16-18. Reprinted Stallman and Watters, *The Creative Reader*, 857-78.

Virginia Faulkner, "More Frosting on the Woods," *CE* 24 (Apr. 1963): 560-561.

Robert F. Fleissner, "Stopping Yet Again by Frost's Woods," *RS* 45 (Mar. 1977): 45-49.

Bernhard Frank, *Expl* 40 (Summer 1982): 43-45.

Charles B. Hands, "The Hidden Terror of Robert Frost," *EJ* 58 (Nov. 1969): 1164-65.

Nat Henry, *Expl* 32 (Jan. 1974): 33.

Nat Henry, *Expl* 37 (Fall 1978): 37-38.

Selwyn Kittredge, "'Stopping By Woods on a Snowy Evening'--Without Tugging at the Reins," *EngR* 23 (Fall 1972): 37-39.

Charles A. McLaughlin, "Two Views of Poetic Unity," *University of Kansas City Review* 22 (Summer 1956): 312-15.

Perrine, *Sound and Sense*, 117-18, 124-25. Reprinted 2d edition, 126-27, 136-37.

Perrine and Reid, *100 American Poems*, 24-26.

John Oliver Perry, "The Dialogue of Voices in Robert Frost's Poems," *SAQ* 81 (Spring 1982): 214-29.

Stanley Poss, "Low Skies, Some Clearing, Local Frost," *NEQ* 41 (Sept. 1968): 438-42.

E. H. Rosenberry, "Toward Notes for 'Stopping by Woods': Some Classical Analogs," *CE* (Apr. 1963): 526-28.

W. H. Shurr, "Once More to the 'Woods': A New Point of Entry into Frost's Most Famous Poem," *NEQ* 47 (Dec. 1974): 584-94.

Elmer F. Suderman, "The Frozen Lake in Frost's 'Stopping by Woods on a Snowy Evening,'" *BSUF* 11 (Winter 1970), 22.

Anya Taylor, "A Frost Debt to Beddoes," *ELN* 13, no. 4 (1976): 291-92.

Unger and O'Connor, *Poems for Study*, 597-600.

Charles Child Walcutt, "Interpreting the Symbol," *CE* 14 (May 1953): 450.

Richard Wilbur, "Poetry's Debt to Poetry," *HudR* 26 (Summer 1973): 292-93.

Earl Wilcox, *Expl* 27 (Sept. 1968): 7.

"Storm Fear"

Carl M. Lindner, "Robert Frost: Dark Romantic," *ArQ* 29 (Autumn 1973): 236-38.

"The Subverted Flower"

Howard Munford, *Expl* 17 (Jan. 1959): 31. Reprinted in *The Explicator Cyclopedia* 1:144-45.

Donald B. Stauffer, *Expl* 15 (Mar. 1957): 38. Reprinted in *The Explicator Cyclopedia* 1:142-44.

"The Telephone"

Laurence Perrine, "Frost's 'The Telephone,'" *NConL* 10 (May 1980): 11-12.

"The Thatch"

Clark, *Lyric Resonance*, 117-33.

Hadas, *Form, Cycle, Infinity*, passim.

Laurence J. Sasso, Jr., Robert Frost: Love's Question," *NEQ* 42 (Mar. 1969): 102-4.

"To Earthward"

Brooks, Purser, and Warren, *An Approach to Literature*, 4th ed., 425.

Wilbur S. Scott, *Expl* 16 (Jan. 1958): 23. Reprinted in *The Explicator Cyclopedia* 1:145.

"To E.T."

P. M. Cubeta, "Robert Frost and Edward Thomas: Two Soldier Poets," *NEQ* 52 (June 1979): 147-76.

"To the Thawing Wind"

Bruce Stillians, *Expl* 31 (Dec. 1972): 31.

"Tree at My Window"

Hadas, *Form, Cycle, Infinity*, passim.

R. W. Stallman, "The Position of Poetry Today," *EJ* 46 (May 1957): 248-49.

"Trespass"

Marjorie Cook, "The Complexity of Boundaries: 'Trespass' by Robert Frost," *NConL* 5 (Jan. 1975): 2-5.

"The Tuft of Flowers"

George Monteiro, "Robert Frost's Linked Analogies," *NEQ* 46 (Sept. 1973): 464-66.

Laurence Perrine, *Expl* 42 (Fall 1983): 36.

Laurence Perrine, "Four Forms of Metaphor," *CE* 33 (Nov. 1971): 131-32. Reprinted in *The Art of Total Relevance*, 55-56.

Thomas Shalvey, S.J., "Valéry and Frost: Two Views of Subjective Reality," *Renascence* 11 (Summer 1959): 187-88.

William S. Waddell, Jr., "Aphorism in Robert Frost's 'The Tuft of Flowers': The Sound of Certainty," *CP* 13 (Spring 1980): 41-44.

Sr. Mary Anthony Weinig, "A Note on Robert Frost's 'Tuft of Flowers,'" *CP* 2 (Spring 1969): 79.

"Two Look at Two"

Frances Helphinstine, *Expl* 39 (Summer 1981): 31-33.

Laurence J. Sasso, Jr., "Robert Frost: Love's Question," *NEQ* 42 (Mar. 1969): 105-6.

"Two Tramps in Mud Time"

Abad, *A Formal Approach to Lyric Poetry*, 185-86, 232-33.

William B. Bache, "Rationalization in Two Frost Poems," *BSUF* 11 (Winter 1970): 34-35.

Blair, *The Literature of the United States* 2:940.

Albert Braverman and Bernard Einbond, *Expl* 29 (Nov. 1970): 25.

D. Bromwich, "Wordsworth, Frost, Stevens and the Poetic Vocation," *SIR* 21 (Spring 1982): 87-100.

Brooks, *Modern Poetry and the Tradition*, 112-13.

Joseph J. Comprone, "Play and the 'Aesthetic State,'" *MSE* 1 (Spring 1967): 28-29.

Richard Foster, "Leaves Compared with Flower: A Reading in Robert Frost's Poems," *NEQ* 46 (Sept. 1973): 418-20.

Charles Kaplan, *Expl* 12 (June 1954): 51. Reprinted in *The Explicator Cyclopedia* 1:145-46.

Laurence Perrine, "'Two Tramps in Mud Time' and the Critics," *AL* 44 (Jan. 1973): 671-76.

Floyd C. Watkins, "The Poetry of the Unsaid--Robert Frost's Narratives and Dramatic Poems," *Texas Quarterly* 15 (Winter 1972): 96-97.

George F. Whicher, "Frost at Seventy," *ASch* 14 (Autumn 1945): 412-14.

"Unharvested"

Toliver, *Pastoral: Forms and Attitudes*, 346-48.

"The Vanishing Red"

C. M. Bowra, "Reassessments I: Robert Frost," *Adelphi* 27 (Nov. 1950): 46-64.

"The Vantage Point"

Wallace, *God Be with the Clown: Humor in American Poetry*, passim.

"The Vindictives"

Leslie Lee Francis, "Robert Frost and the Majesty of Stones Upon Stones," *JML* 9 (1981/1982): 3-26.

"West-Running Brook"

Joseph Warren Beach, "Robert Frost," *YR* 43 (Winter 1953): 212.

Richard D. Lord, "Frost and Cyclicism," *Renascence* 10 (Autumn 1957): 20-25, 31.

Patrick Morrow, "The Greek Nexus in Robert Frost's 'West-Running Brook,'" *Personalist* 49 (Winter 1968): 24-33.

Laurence Perrine, *Expl* 35 (Summer 1977): 26-27.

Laurence J. Sasso, Jr., "Robert Frost: Love's Question," *NEQ* 42 (Mar. 1969): 98-100.

Robert H. Swennes, "Man and Wife: The Dialogue of Contraries in Robert Frost's Poetry," *AL* 42 (Nov. 1970): 369-71.

H. H. Watts, "Robert Frost and the Interrupted Dialogue," *AL* 27 (Mar. 1955), 70-74 and passim.

H. T. Webster, *Expl* 8 (Feb. 1950): 32. Reprinted in *The Explicator Cyclopedia* 1:146-48.

"White-Tailed Hornet"

Laurence Perrine, "A House for Frost's 'White-Tailed Hornet,'" *NConL* 10 (Jan. 1980): 3.

"Wild Grapes"

Helen Bacon, "For Girls: From 'Birches' to 'Wild Grapes,'" *YR* 67 (Oct. 1977): 13-29.

Hadas, *Form, Cycle, Infinity*, passim.

Laurence Perrine, "Letting Go with the Heart: Frost's 'Wild Grapes,'" *Notes on Modern American Literature* 2 (Summer 1978): item 20.

"A Wishing Well"

A. R. Ferguson, "Frost, Sill, and 'A Wishing Well,'" *AL* 33 (Nov. 1961): 370-73.

Claude M. Simpson, "Robert Frost and Man's 'Royal Role,'" in Ludwig, *Aspects of American Poetry*, 133-35.

"The Witch of Coos"

Eben Bass, "Frost's Poetry of Fear," *AL* 43 (Jan. 1972): 612-613.

J. J. Joyce, "Robert Frost's 'The Witch of Coos': A Matter of Choice," *CollL* 10 (Spring 1983): 189-93.

Mordecai Marcus, "The Whole Pattern of Robert Frost's 'Two Witches': Contrasting Psycho-Sexual Modes," *L&P* 26 (1976): 69-74.

Perrine and Reid, *100 American Poems*, 41-43.

Fred C. Schutz, *Expl* 33 (Nov. 1974): 19.

Camille Slights and William Slights, *Expl* 27 (Feb. 1969): 40.

Thomas R. Thornburg, "Mother's Private Ghost: A Note on Frost's 'The Witch of Coos,'" *BSUF* 11 (Winter 1970): 16-20.

Floyd C. Watkins, "The Poetry of the Unsaid--Robert Frost's Narrative and Dramatic Poems," *Texas Quarterly* 15 (Winter 1970): 96.

"A Witness Tree"

Alvin S. Ryan, *Expl* 7 (Mar. 1949): 39. Reprinted in *The Explicator Cyclopedia* 1:148.

"The Wood-Pile"

Ferman Bishop, *Expl* 18 (June 1960): 58. Reprinted in *The Explicator Cyclopedia* 1:148-49.

Brooks, *Modern Poetry and the Tradition*, 113-14.

Brooks, Purser, and Warren, *An Approach to Literature*, 453-54; 3d ed., 305-7; 4th ed., 421-23.

Alexander C. Kern, *Expl* 28 (Feb. 1970): 49.

Laurence Lerner, "An Essay on Pastoral," *EIC* 20 (July 1970): 275-77.

Laurence Lerner, *The Uses of Nostalgia: Studies in Pastoral Poetry* (New York: Schocken Books, 1972), 11-13.

Lewis H. Miller, Jr., "The Poet as Swinger: Fact and Fancy in Robert Frost," *Criticism* 16 (Winter 1974): 67-72.

Robert D. Narveson, "On Frost's 'The Wood-Pile,'" *EJ* 57 (Jan. 1968): 39-40.

Laurence Perrine, "On Frost's 'The Wood-Pile,'" *Notes on Modern American Literature* 6 (Spring/Summer 1982): item 1.

Richard Poirier, "Soundings for Home: Frost's Poetry of Extravagance and Return," *GaR* 31 (Summer 1977): 288-92.

R. Wakefield, *Robert Frost and the Opposing Lights of the Hour* (New York: Peter Lang, 1985), passim.

"A Young Birch"

Mario L. D'Avanzo, "Frost's 'A Young Birch': A Thing of Beauty," *CP* 3 (Fall 1970): 69-70.

GARDNER, ISABELLA

"Summer Remembered"

Perrine and Reid, *100 American Poems*, 236-37.

"The Widow's Yard"

Carroll, *The Poem in Its Skin*, 51-62.

GARRIGUE, JEAN

"Dialog for Belvedere"

Joseph Warren Beach, "The Cancelling Out--A Note on Recent Poetry," *Accent* 7 (Summer 1947): 246-48.

GASPARINI, LEN

"Il Sangue" [Blood]

Alexandre L. Amprimoz and Dennis F. Essar, "La Poétique de la mort: La Poésie italo-canadienne et italo-québécoise aujourd'hui," *SCL* 12 (1987): 161-76.

GAUVREAU, CLAUDE

Jappements à la Lune

McCaffery, *North of Intention*, 170-77.

GHISELIN, BREWSTER

"Bath of Aphrodite"

Brewster Ghiselin, "The Birth of a Poem," *Poetry* 69 (Oct. 1946): 30-43. Reprinted in Locke, Gibson, and Arms, *Readings for Liberal Education*, 3d ed., 239-46.

"Gull in the Great Basin"

Ray B. West, *Writing in the Rocky Mountains* (Lincoln: University of Nebraska Press, 1947), 58-59.

"Poetry"

Dave Smith, "The Poetry of Brewster Ghiselin," *WHR* 35 (Autumn 1981): 162-65.

"The Vision of Adam"

Dave Smith, "The Poetry of Brewster Ghiselin," *WHR* 35 (Autumn 1981): 162-65.

GIBBS, BARBARA

"Dry Canyon, September"

Hayden Carruth, *Poetry: A Critical Supplement*, Jan. 1949, 16.

"In a Garden," I and II

Hayden Carruth, *Poetry: A Critical Supplement*, Jan. 1949, 14-16.

GIBSON, WALKER

"Billiards"

Abbe, *You and Contemporary Poetry*, 40-41.

"Thaw"

Abbe, *You and Contemporary Poetry*, 39.

GINSBERG, ALLEN

[Interview]

Linda Hamalian, "Allen Ginsberg in the Eighties," *LitR* 29 (Spring 1986): 293-300.

Portugués, "On Drugs," "On Mantras," "On Tibetan Buddhism," in *The Visionary Poetics of Allen Ginsberg*, 109-63.

Robert Stewart, "Sacred Speech: A Conversation with Allen Ginsberg," *NewL* 54 (Fall 1987): 72-86.

"Howl"

Steven K. Hoffman, "Lowell, Berryman, Roethke, and Ginsberg: The Communal Function of Confessional Poetry," *LitR* 22 (Spring 1979): 329-41.

Mersmann, *Out of the Vietnam Vortex*, 31-76.

Portugués, *The Visionary Poetics of Allen Ginsberg*, 44-46, 74-81, 85-89.

Thurley, *The American Moment--American Poetry in the Mid-Century*, 172-86.

"Kaddish"

Darryl Pinckney, "The May King," *Parnassus* 10 (Spring/Summer 1982): 99-116.

Portugués, *The Visionary Poetics of Allen Ginsburg*, 38-40, 45-53, 80-82.

"Love Poem on Theme by Whitman"

Darryl Pinckney, "The May King," *Parnassus* 10 (Spring/Summer 1982): 99-116.

"Mind Breaths"

Jay Dougherty, "From Society to Self: Ginsberg's Inward Turn in 'Mind Breaths,'" *Sagetrieb* 6 (Spring 1987): 81-92.

"On Reading Wm Blake's Poem 'The Sick Rose'"

Portugués, *The Visionary Poetics of Allen Ginsberg*, 42-62 and passim.

Planet News

Martin, *The Homosexual Tradition in American Poetry*, 165-70.

"Psalm"

Portugués, *The Visionary Poetics of Allen Ginsberg*, 30-31 and passim.

"Witchita Vortex Sutra"

Portugués, *The Visionary Poetics of Allen Ginsburg*, 82-83.

GIOVANNI, NIKKI

[Interview]

A. Elder, "A MELUS Interview: Nikki Giovanni," *MELUS* 9 (Winter 1982): 61-75.

Claudia Tate, "Nikki Giovanni," in *Black Women Writers at Work*, ed. Claudia Tate (New York: Continuum, 1983), 60-78.

"Beautiful Black Men (with compliments and
apologies to all not mentioned by name)"

Juhasz, *Naked and Fiery Forms*, 158-59.

"Ego-Tripping"

Ruthe T. Sheffey, "Rhetorical Structure in Contemporary Afro-American
Poetry," *CLAJ* 24 (Sept. 1980): 97-107.

"Rain"

Juhasz, *Naked and Fiery Forms*, 164-65.

"Revolutionary Dreams"

Juhasz, *Naked and Fiery Forms*, 167-68.

GLASCO, JOHN

"The Burden of Junk"

William Walsh, "The Shape of Canadian Poetry," *SR* 87 (Jan./Mar. 1979): 73-
95.

GLÜCK, LOUISE

"Clara Hopes for a Lie"

Charles Altieri, "Sensibility, Rhetoric, and Will: Some Tensions in
Contemporary Poetry," *ConL* 23 (Fall 1982): 451-79.

"Descending Figure"

A. Fisher, "Construction of a Self," *PrS* 56 (Fall 1982): 93-98.

"First Goodbye"

Charles Altieri, "Sensibility, Rhetoric, and Will: Some Tensions in Contemporary Poetry," *ConL* 23 (Fall 1982), 451-79.

GONZALEZ, REBECCA

"South Texas Summer Rain"

Norwood and Monk, *The Desert Is No Lady*, passim.

GRAHAM

"The White Threshold"

Leonie Adams, "First Poems of Celebration," *Poetry* 82 (Aug. 1953): 275-76.

GRAHN, JUDY

"The Work of a Common Woman

Mary J. Carruthers, "The Re-Vision of the Muse: Adrienne Rich, Audre Lord, Judy Grahn, Olga Broumas," *HudR* 36 (1983): 293-322.

Leonie Adams, "The First Poems of Celebration," *Poetry* 82 (Aug. 1953): 275-76.

GREGORY, HORACE

"Bridgewater Jones: Impromptu in a Speakeasy"

Robert K. Morris, "The Resurrected Vision: Horace Gregory's Thirties Poems," *MPS* 4 (Spring 1973): 82-83.

"Chorus for Survival"

Robert K. Morris, "The Resurrected Vision: Horace Gregory's Thirties Poems," *MPS* 4 (Spring 1973): 96-99.

"O Metaphysical Head"

Robert K. Morris, "The Resurrected Vision: Horace Gregory's Thirties Poems," *MPS* 4 (Spring 1973): 81-82.

"O Mors Aeterna"

Robert K. Morris, "The Resurrected Vision: Horace Gregory's Thirties Poems," *MPS* 4 (Spring 1973): 84-85.

"Under the Stone I Saw Them Flow" (from *Chorus for Survival*)

Walter Gierasch, "Reading Modern Poetry," *CE* 2 (Oct. 1940): 33-34.

Walter Gierasch, *Expl* 3 (June 1945): 63. Reprinted in *The Explicator Cyclopedia* 1:149-50.

GRIFFIN, SUSAN

Woman and Nature

Lauter, *Women as Mythmakers*, chap. 8, passim.

HACKER, MARILYN

"Why We Are Going Back to Paradise"

Karen Alkalay-Gut, "The Lesbian Imperative in Poetry," *CP* 24 (1983): 209-11.

HALL, DONALD

[Interview]

David Hamilton, "An Interview with Donald Hall," *IowaR* 15 (Winter 1985): 1-17.

"The Body of Politics"

Perrine and Reid, *100 American Poems*, 273-74.

"Cold Water"

Ralph J. Mills, Jr., "Donald Hall's Poetry," *IowaR* 2 (Winter 1971): 108-11.

"Exile"

Ralph J. Mills, Jr., "Donald Hall's Poetry," *IowaR* 2 (Winter 1971): 85-86.

Goatfoot, Milktongue, Twinbird

Tom Hansen, "On Writing Poetry: Four Contemporary Poets," *CE* 44 (Mar. 1982): 265-73.

"The Grass"

Ralph J. Mills, Jr., "Donald Hall's Poetry," *IowaR* 2 (Winter 1971): 98-99.

"The Snow"

Ralph J. Mills, Jr., "Donald Hall's Poetry," *IowaR* 2 (Winter 1971): 96-98.

"The Stump"

Ralph J. Mills, Jr., "Donald Hall's Poetry," *IowaR* 2 (Winter 1971): 102-4.

"Swan"

Ralph J. Mills, Jr., "Donald Hall's Poetry," *IowaR* 2 (Winter 1971): 117-20.

"Wedding Party"

Ralph J. Mills, Jr., "Donald Hall's Poetry," *IowaR* 2 (Winter 1971): 86-87.

"Wells"

Ralph J. Mills, Jr., "Donald Hall's Poetry," *IowaR* 2 (Winter 1971): 105-6.

HALL, HAZEL

"Lingerie"

Beth Bentley, "Mirror in the Shadows: Hazel Hall 1886-1924," *CP* 13 (Fall 1980): 7-12.

HALLEY, ANNE

"Dear God, the Day Is Grey"

Perrine and Reid, *100 American Poems*, 288-89.

HANDSPRING, HIRAM

"Mulatas per Gentes"

J. Roger Dave, "The Poetry Handspring," *IowaR* 13 (Spring 1982): 53-61.

HARPER, FRANCES WATKINS

"Aunt Chloe" poems (from *Sketches of Southern Life*)

Patricia Hill, "Frances W. Harper's Aunt Chloe Poems from *Sketches of Southern Life*: Antithesis to the Plantation Literary Tradition," *MissQ* 34 (Fall 1981): 403-13.

HARPER, MICHAEL

[Interview]

David Lloyd, "Interview with Michael S. Harper," *TriQ* 65 (Winter 1986): 119-28.

"Alice"

Joseph A. Brown, S.J., "Their Long Scars Touch Ours: A Reflection on the Poetry of Michael Harper," *Callaloo* 9 (Winter 1986): 209-20.

"Dear John, Dear Coltrane"

Joseph A. Brown, S.J., "Their Long Scars Touch Ours: A Reflection on the Poetry of Michael Harper," *Callaloo* 9 (Winter 1986): 209-20.

"A Narrative of the Life and Times of John Coltrane:
Played By Himself"

Joseph A. Brown, S.J., "Their Long Scars Touch Ours: A Reflection on the Poetry of Michael Harper," *Callaloo* 9 (Winter 1986): 209-20.

Nightmare Begins Responsibility

Joseph A. Brown, S.J., "Their Long Scars Touch Ours: A Reflection on the Poetry of Michael Harper," *Callaloo* 9 (Winter 1986): 209-20.

"Reuben, Reuben"

Joseph A. Brown, S.J., "Their Long Scars Touch Ours: A Reflection on the Poetry of Michael Harper," *Callaloo* 9 (Winter 1986): 209-20.

HART, RICHARD

"Letter from Madrid"

J. F. Nims, *Poetry: A Critical Supplement*, Jan. 1948, 13.

HARTOG, DIANA

[Interview]

Constance Rooke, "Getting into Heaven: An Interview with Diana Hartog, Paulette Jiles, and Sharon Thesen," *Malahat Review* 83 (Summer 1988): 5-52.

Candy from Strangers

Brian Edwards, "Dis-Closures: Diana Hartog's Surprises in Half-Light," *Malahat Review* 83 (Summer 1988): 176-83.

Smaro Kamboureli, "Under 'the nib of Poe's pen': Tropics of Love in Diana Hartog's Poetry," *Malahat Review* 83 (Summer 1988): 161-75.

"MAN"

Smaro Kamboureli, "Under 'the nib of Poe's pen': Tropics of Love in Diana Hartog's Poetry," *Malahat Review* 83 (Summer 1988): 161-75.

Matinee Light

Smaro Kamboureli, "Under 'the nib of Poe's pen': Tropics of Love in Diana Hartog's Poetry," *Malahat Review* 83 (Summer 1988): 161-75.

"The Muse Is All Exactitude"

Smaro Kamboureli, "Under 'the nib of Poe's pen': Tropics of Love in Diana Hartog's Poetry," *Malahat Review* 83 (Summer 1988): 161-75.

"The Third Muse"

Smaro Kamboureli, "Under 'the nib of Poe's pen': Tropics of Love in Diana Hartog's Poetry," *Malahat Review* 83 (Summer 1983): 161-75.

HASS, ROBERT

"Meditation at Lagunitas"

Charles Altieri, "Sensibility, Rhetoric, and Will: Some Tensions in Contemporary Poetry," *ConL* 23 (Fall 1982): 451-79.

HAYDEN, ROBERT

Angle of Ascent

Hatcher, *From the Auroral Darkness: The Life and Poetry of Robert Hayden*, passim.

Wilburn Williams, Jr., "Covenant of Timelessness & Time: Symbolism & History in Robert Hayden's *Angle of Ascent*," *MR* 18 (Winter 1977): 732-33. Reprinted in *Chant of Saints: A Gathering of Afro-American Art, Literature, and Scholarship*, ed. Michael Harper and Robert B. Stepto (Urbana: University of Illinois Press, 1979), 79-80.

"The Black Spear"

Reginald Gibbons, "Robert Hayden in the 1940's," *TriQ* 62 (Winter 1985): 177-86.

"The Diver"

Maurice J. O'Sullivan, Jr., "The Mask of Allusion in Robert Hayden's 'The Diver,'" *CLAJ* 17 (Sept. 1973): 85-92.

Wilburn Williams, Jr., "Covenant of Timelessness & Time: Symbolism & History in Robert Hayden's *Angle of Ascent*," *MR* 18 (Winter 1977): 732-33. Reprinted in *Chant of Saints: A Gathering of Afro-American Art, Literature, and Scholarship*, ed. Michael Harper and Robert B. Stepto (Urbana: University of Illinois Press, 1979), passim.

"Frederick Douglass"

Fred M. Fetrow, "Robert Hayden's 'Frederick Douglass,' Form and Meaning in a Modern Sonnet," *CLAJ* 17 (Sept. 1973): 79-84.

"Full Moon"

Wilburn Williams, Jr., "Covenant of Timelessness & Time: Symbolism & History in Robert Hayden's *Angle of Ascent*," *MR* 18 (Winter 1977): 743-45.

"Middle Passage"

Howard Faulkner, "Transformed by Sleeps of Flight: The Poetry of Robert Hayden," *CLAJ* 21 (Dec. 1977): 290.

Fred M. Fetrow, "Middle Passage: Robert Hayden's Anti-Epic," *CLAJ* 22 (June 1979): 304-18.

Vera M. Kutzinski, "Changing Permanences: Historical and Literary Revisionism in Robert Hayden's 'Middle Passage,'" *Callaloo* 9 (Winter 1986): 171-83.

"The Peacock Room"

Wilburn Williams, Jr., "Covenant of Timelessness & Time: Symbolism & History in Robert Hayden's *Angle of Ascent*," *MR* 18 (Winter 1977): 746-47. Reprinted in *Chant of Saints: A Gathering of Afro-American Art, Literature, and Scholarship*, ed. Michael Harper and Robert B. Stepto (Urbana: University of Illinois Press, 1979), passim.

"The Rabbi"

Wilburn Williams, Jr. "Covenant of Timelessness and Time: Symbolism & History in Robert Hayden's *Angle of Ascent*," *MR* 18 (Winter 1977): 741-42. Reprinted in *Chant of Saints: A Gathering of Afro-American Art, Literature, and Scholarship*, ed. Michael Harper and Robert B. Stepto (Urbana: University of Illinois Press, 1979), passim.

HAYES, ALFRED

"The Shrunken Head"

J. F. Nims, *Poetry: A Critical Supplement*, Nov. 1948, 7-8.

HECHT, ANTHONY

"Ostia Antica"

Nicholas Joost, *Expl* 20 (Oct. 1961): 13. Reprinted in *The Explicator Cyclopedia* 1:154.

"The Venetian Vespers"

B. Howard, "Seeker after Law," *PrS* 55 (Winter 1982): 84-88.

HELWIG, DAVID

"The Best Name of Silence"

D. G. Jones, "David Helwig's New Timber: Notes on 'The Best Name of Silence,'" *QQ* 81 (Summer 1974): 202-14.

HENDERSON, ALICE CORBIN

Red Earth

Norwood and Monk, *The Desert Is No Lady*, passim.

The Spinning Women of the Sky

Norwood and Monk, *The Desert Is No Lady*, passim.

HILBERRY, CONRAD

"Hamster Cage"

Margaret A. Larson, "Instructive Destructive," *EJ* 61 (Apr. 1972): 508-9.

HILL, GEOFFREY

"Brand"

Ricks, *The Force of Poetry*, 319-55.

"Tenebrae"

Ricks, *The Force of Poetry*, 319-55.

HIRSCHMAN, JACK

[Untitled]

Gitenstein, *Apocalyptic Messianism and Contemporary Jewish-American Poetry*, 49-51.

HITCHCOCK, GEORGE

"Scattering Flowers"

Cary Nelson, "Whitman in Vietnam: Poetry and History in Contemporary America," *MR* 16 (Winter 1975): 55-71.

HOGAN, LINDA

[Interview]

Bruchac, "To Take Care of Life: An Interview with Linda Hogan," *Survival This Way*, 119-33.

Bo Scholer, "'A Heart Made Out of Crickets': An Interview with Linda Hogan," *JEthS* 16 (Spring 1988): 107-17.

"Heartland"

Bo Scholer, "'A Heart Made Out of Crickets': An Interview with Linda Hogan," *JEthS* 16 (Spring 1988): 107-17.

"The Sand Roses"

Bo Scholer, "'A Heart Made Out of Crickets': An Interview with Linda Hogan," *JEthS* 16 (Spring 1988): 107-17.

"Spontaneous Combustion"

Bo Scholer, "'A Heart Made Out of Crickets': An Interview with Linda Hogan," *JEthS* 16 (Spring 1988): 107-17.

HOLLANDER, JOHN

Spectral Emanations

David Lehman, "The Sound and Sense of the Sleight-of-Hand-Man," *Parnassus* 12 (Fall/Winter 1984): 190-212.

Joseph Parisi, "Homing In," *Shenandoah* 30 (1979): 99-107.

HOLMES, JOHN

"Herself"

Doris Holmes, *Expl* 28 (May 1970): 77.

HOPE, A. D.

"Agony Column"

Laurence Perrine, "A. D. Hope's 'Agony Column,'" *NConL* 2 (May 1972): 2-3.

HOSKINS, JOHN

"Absence"

Brooks, *Modern Poetry and the Tradition*, 22-24.

Cleanth Brooks, Jr., "Three Revolutions in Poetry," *SoR* 1 (Autumn 1935): 330.

Williamson, *The Proper Wit of Poetry*, 16-18.

"Of the Loss of Time"

Williamson, *The Proper Wit of Poetry*, 14-15.

HOWARD, RICHARD

"Waiting for Ada"

Thomas Woll, "Stasis within Flux: Richard Howard's Findings," *MPS* 4 (Winter 1973): 263-64.

HOWES, BARBARA

"The Heart of Europe"

Hayden Carruth, *Poetry: A Critical Supplement*, Feb. 1949: 7-8.

"In the Cold Country"

Hayden Carruth, *Poetry: A Critical Supplement*, Feb. 1949, 3-7.

"Portrait of an Artist"

Hayden Carruth, *Poetry: A Critical Supplement*, Feb. 1949, 9.

HUGHES, LANGSTON

"Daybreak in Alabama"

R. Baxter Miller, "'A Mere Poem': 'Daybreak in Alabama,' A Resolution to Langston Hughes's Theme of Music and Art," *Obsidian II: Black Literature in Review* 2 (Summer 1976): 30-37.

A. Rampersad, "The Origins of Poetry in Langston Hughes," *SoR* 21 (Summer 1985): 695-705.

"Fine Clothes to the Jew"

Arnold Rampersad, "Langston Hughes's *Fine Clothes to the Jew*," *Callaloo* 9 (Winter 1986): 144-58.

Dellita L. Martin, "Langston Hughes's Uses of the Blues," *CLAJ* 22 (Dec. 1978): 151-59.

"Five Live Their Own Life"

Thomas L. Franke, "The Art of Verbal Performance: A Stylistic Analysis of Langston Hughes," *Lang&S* 19 (1986): 377-87.

"A House in Texas"

Dona Hoilman, "A Red Southwestern House for a Black Midwestern Poet," *CP* 13 (Fall 1980): 55-61.

"Jitney"

R. Barksdale, "Langston Hughes: His Times and His Humanistic Techniques," in Miller, *Black American Literature and Humanism*, 8-26.

"Prayer Meeting"

Arnold Rampersad, "Langston Hughes's *Fine Clothes to the Jew*," *Callaloo* 9 (Winter 1986): 144-58.

"Theme for English B"

Gary F. Scharnhorst, *Expl* 32 (Dec. 1973): 27.

"The Weary Blues"

Arnold Rampersad, "Langston Hughes's *Fine Clothes to the Jew*," *Callaloo* 9 (Winter 1986): 144-58.

HUGO, RICHARD

[Interview]

Thomas Gardner, "An Interview with Richard Hugo," *ConL* 22 (Spring 1981): 139-52.

"December 24 and George McBride is Dead"

Paul J. Lindholdt, "Richard Hugo's Language: The Poem as Obsessive Musical Deed," *CP* 16 (1983): 67-75.

"Duwamish"

Paul J. Lindholdt, "Richard Hugo's Language: The Poem as Obsessive Musical Deed," *CP* 16 (1983): 67-75.

"The Triggering Town"

Tom Hansen, "On Writing Poetry: Four Contemporary Poets," *CE* 44 (Mar. 1982): 265-73.

"West Marginal Way"

Paul J. Lindholdt, "Richard Hugo's Language: The Poem as Obsessive Musical Deed," *CP* 16 (1983): 67-75.

IGNATOW, DAVID

[Interview]

Leif Sjoberg, "An Interview with David Ignatow," ConL 28 (Summer 1987): 143-62.

Facing the Tree

Paul Zweig, "David Ignatow," *APR* 5 (Jan./Feb. 1976): 29-30.

Selected Poems

Paul Zweig, "David Ignatow," *APR* 5 (Jan./Feb. 1976): 29-30.

INEZ, COLETTE

[Interview]

Jim Gorman, "An Interview with Colette Inez," *Parnassus* 7 (1978): 210-23.

IRBY, KENNETH

[Interview]

Barry Alpert, "Ken Irby," *Vort* 3 (Summer 1973): 52-69.

Catalpa

David Bromige, "Ken Irby's *Catalpa*," *Credences* 3 (Feb. 1979): 101-3.

George Butterick, "Ken Irby's *Catalpa*: The Discontinuous, Dendritic Narrative of a Journey," *Credences* 3 (Feb. 1979): 104-7.

Reginald Gibbons, "Musings on *Catalpa*," *Credences* 3 (Feb. 1979): 108-12.

Paul Kahn, "Irby's Later Poetry," *Credences* 3 (Feb. 1979): 97-100.

Thomas Meyer, "Our Neglected Study: Irby's *Catalpa* Considered Obliquely," *Credences* 3 (Feb. 1979): 29-38.

George Quasha, "Brief, Enigmatized Reflections on Irby After Circumambulating *Catalpa* in a Long, Recorded, Suppressed Conversation," *Credences* 3 (Feb. 1979): 118-20.

Jed Rasula, "On Ken Irby," *Credences* 3 (Feb. 1979): 40-55.

"Jed Smith and the Way"

Eric Mottram, "'Restlessness and Patience': The Poetry of Kenneth Irby," *Credences* 3 (Feb. 1979): 128-41.

Kansas-New Mexico

Kenneth Irby, "A Note on *Kansas-New Mexico*--For Ed Grier and Rog Gridley," *Credences* 3 (Feb. 1979): 56-61.

Eric Mottram, "'Restlessness and Patience': The Poetry of Kenneth Irby," *Credences* 3 (Feb. 1979): 128-41.

Relations

Mark Karlins, "The American Pastoral," *Credences* 3 (Feb. 1979): 20-24.

Eric Mottram, "'Restlessness and Patience': The Poetry of Kenneth Irby," *Credences* 3 (Feb. 1979): 128-41.

"Some Morning Music Fragments"

Eric Mottram, "'Restlessness and Patience': The Poetry of Kenneth Irby," *Credences* 3 (Feb. 1979): 128-41.

To Max Douglas

Eric Mottram, "'Restlessness and Patience': The Poetry of Kenneth Irby," *Credences* 3 (Feb. 1979): 128-41.

JACOBSEN, JOSEPHINE

[Interview]

Karla M. Hammond, "Poets on Poetry: An Interview with Josephine Jacobsen," *Bennington Review* 2 (Sept. 1978): 23-26.

Jacqueline Tavernier-Courbin and R. G. Rollins, "Interview with Josephine Jacobsen," *Thalia* 2 (1979): 5-15.

JARAMILLO, CLEOFRAS M.

Romance of a Little Village Girl

Norwood and Monk, *The Desert Is Not a Lady*, passim.

JARRELL, RANDALL

"The Black Swan"

Quinn, *The Metaphoric Tradition*, 186-88.

"Burning the Letters"

Mark I. Goldman, "The Politics of Poetry: Randall Jarrell's War," *SAQ* 86 (Spring 1987): 127.

Quinn, *The Metaphoric Tradition*, 198-99.

"A Camp in a Prussian Forest"

W. S. Graham, "It All Comes Back to Me Now," *Poetry* 72 (Sept. 1948): 306.

Perrine and Reid, *100 American Poems*, 229-30.

Stephen Spender, "Randall Jarrell's Landscape," *Nation* 166 (May 1 1948): 476.

"The Dead Wingman"

Mark I. Goldman, "The Politics of Poetry: Randall Jarrell's War," *SAQ* 86 (Spring 1987): 127.

"The Death of the Ball Turret Gunner"

Patrick F. Bessett, "Jarrell's 'The Death of the Ball Turret Gunner,'" *Expl* 36 (Spring 1978): 20-21.

David K. Cornelius, *Expl* 35 (Spring 1977): 3.

Levin M. Dawson, *Expl* 31 (Dec. 1972): 29.

George V. Griffith, "Jarrell's 'The Death of the Ball Turret Gunner,'" *Expl* 40 (Fall 1981): 62.

Patrick J. Horner, "Jarrell's 'The Death of the Ball Turret Gunner,'" *Expl* 36 (Summer 1978): 9-10.

Isabel C. Hungerford, "The Interpretation of Poetry," *JAAC* 13 (Mar. 1955): 353-54.

Kreuzer, *Elements of Poetry*, 146-48.

David Ray, "The Lightning of Randall Jarrell," *PrS* 35 (Spring 1961): 45-52.

Rosenthal, *The Modern Poets*, 245.

Rosenthal and Smith, *Exploring Poetry*, 547-49.

Bruce Weigl, "An Autobiography of a Nightmare," *Field* 35 (Fall 1986): 19-20.

C. D. Wright, "Mission of the Surviving Gunner, *Field* 35 (Fall 1986): 23-29.

"Eighth Air Force"

Cleanth Brooks, "Irony as a Principle of Structure," in Zabel, *Literary Opinion in America*, rev. ed., 738-41.

Brooks, Purser, and Warren, *An Approach to Literature*, 3d ed., 397-99; 4th ed., 396-98.

Frances C. Ferguson, "Randall Jarrell and the Flotations of Voice," *GaR* 28 (Fall 1974): 436-38.

"The Emancipators"

Mordecai and Erin Marcus, *Expl* 16 (Feb. 1958): 26. Reprinted in *The Explicator Cyclopedia* 1:196-98.

"Field and Forest"

Marianne Boruch, "Rhetoric and Mystery," *Field* 35 (Fall 1986): 64-67.

"The Girl Dreams That She Is Giselle"

Quinn, *The Metamorphic Tradition*, 188-91.

"Hohensalzburg"

Hayden Carruth, *Poetry: A Critical Supplement*, Apr. 1949, 1-10.

Quinn, *The Metamorphic Tradition*, 174-75, 178-81.

"Hope"

Perrine and Reid, *100 American Poems*, 231-33.

"The House in the Wood"

David Walker, "The Shape on the Bed," *Field* 35 (Fall 1986): 64-67.

Robert Weisberg, "Randall Jarrell: The Integrity of His Poetry," *CentR* 17 (Summer 1973): 251-52.

"A Hunt"

Weisberg, "Randall Jarrell: The Integrity of His Poetry," *CentR* 17 (Summer 1973): 248-50.

"Jerome"

Frances C. Ferguson, "Randall Jarrell and the Flotations of Voice," *GaR* 28 (Fall 1974): 431-35.

Jeffrey Meyers, "Randall Jarrell: The Paintings in the Poems," *SoR* 20 (Apr. 1984): 300-315.

"King's Hut"

Quinn, *The Metamorphic Tradition*, 192-93.

"The Knight, Death, and the Devil"

Jeffrey Meyers, "Randall Jarrell: The Paintings in the Poems," *SoR* 20 (Apr. 1984): 300-315.

Little Friend, Little Friend

Mark I. Goldman, "The Politics of Poetry: Randall Jarrel's War," *SAQ* 86 (Spring 1987): 130.

"Losses"

James L. Jackson, *Expl* 19 (Apr. 1961): 49.

"The Lost World"

Patricia Rodgers Black, "The Atom Bomb: Jarrell's Dream-Work in 'The Lost World,'" *MissQ* 39 (Winter 1985/1986): 31-40.

Robert Weisberg, "Randall Jarell: The Integrity of His Poetry," *CentR* 17 (Summer 1973): 244-47.

"Love in Its Separate Being"

Joseph Warren Beach, "The Cancelling Out--A Note on Recent Poetry," *Accent* 7 (Summer 1947): 248-49.

"The Metamorphosis"

Quinn, *The Metamorphic Tradition*, 200-201.

"Money"

Dana Goia, "Business and Poetry," *HudR* 36 (Spring 1983): 147-71.

"Moving"

Fred Chappell, "The Longing to Belong," *Field* 35 (Fall 1986): 23-29.

"The Night Before the Night Before Christmas"

Quinn, *The Metamorphic Tradition*, 182-85.

"Nestus Gurley"

David Young, "Day for Night," *Field* 35 (Fall 1986): 46-49.

"The Old and the New Masters"

Jeffrey Meyers, "Randall Jarrell: The Paintings in the Poems," *SoR* 20 (Apr. 1984): 300-315.

"On the Railway Platform"

Beach, *Obsessive Images*, 178-82.

"A Quilt Pattern"

Quinn, *The Metamorphic Tradition*, 193-95.

"A Rhapsody on Irish Themes"

Quinn, *The Metamorphic Tradition*, 191.

"Seele im Raum"

Russell Fowler, "Randall Jarrell's 'Eland': A Key to Motive and Technique in His Poetry," *IowaR* 5 (Spring 1974): 119-23.

Bertrand R. Richards, *Expl* 33 (Nov. 1974): 22.

David St. John, "'Seele im Raum,'" *Field* 35 (Fall 1986): 33-36.

"The Sleeping Beauty: Variation of the Prince"

Quinn, *The Metamorphic Tradition*, 175-77.

"Soldiers"

Mark I. Goldman, "The Politics of Poetry: Randall Jarrell's War," *SAQ* 86 (Spring 1987): 131.

"Soul"

Quinn, *The Metamorphic Tradition*, 172-73.

"Thinking of the Lost World"

Robert Weisberg, "Randall Jarrell: The Integrity of His Poetry," *CentR* 17 (Summer 1973): 252-55.

"The Truth"

Ralph Burns, "The Plain Truth in 'The Truth,'" *Field* 35 (Fall 1986): 39-42.

"The Venetian Blind"

Quinn, *The Metamorphic Tradition*, 191-92.

"A War"

Mark I. Goldman, "The Politics of Poetry: Randall Jarrell's War," *SAQ* 86 (Spring 1987): 132.

"A Well-to-do-Invalid"

Robert Weisberg, "Randall Jarrell: The Integrity of His Poetry," *CentR* 17 (Summer 1973): 242-43.

JEFFERS, LANCE

[Interview]

Doris L. Laryea, "A Black Poet's Vision: An Interview with Lance Jeffers," *CLAJ* 26 (June 1983): 422-33.

JEFFERS, ROBINSON

"Apology for Bad Dreams"

Wyatt, *The Fall into Eden*, 174-85.

"Boats in a Fog"

Jessica Hueter, "Beauty as Participation," *RJN* (1987): 20-21.

"Continent's End"

Brian Salzman, "Cycle and Equinox," *RJN* (1987): 10-11.

"The Cycle"

Wyatt, *The Fall into Eden*, 174-85.

"Christmas Card"

Deutsch, *Poetry in Our Time*, 21-22.

"Divinely Superfluous Beauty"

Douglas T. Kartub, "The Carmel Landscape," *RJN* (1987): 12-13.

"Evening Ebb"

Didi Shuff, "An Ambience," *RJN* (1987): 18-19.

"Fire on the Hills"

George Arms, *Expl* 1 (May 1943): 59. Reprinted in *The Explicator Cyclopedia* 1:198-99.

"Fog"

Scott Coombs, "Nirvana Rejected," *RJN* (1987): 14-15.

"Give Your Heart to the Hawks"

Frajam Taylor, "The Enigma of Robinson Jeffers: II, The Hawk and the Stone," *Poetry* 55 (Oct. 1939): 39-44.

David C. Dougherty, "The Epic Conventions of Robinson Jeffers," *MHLS* 7 (1984): 45-56.

"Greater Grandeur"

J. F. Nims, *Poetry: A Critical Supplement*, Oct. 1947, 5-6.

"The Hanged God"

Didi Shuff, "Prophet of the Self-Tormented God," *RJN* (1987): 24-25.

"Hands"

Scott Coombs, "Formal Reciprocity," *RJN* (1987): 22-23.

"Hurt Hawks"

Gray, *American Poetry*, 205.

"Invocation"

Wyatt, *The Fall into Eden*, 174-85.

"Margrave"

Waggoner, *The Heel of Elohim*, 121-29.

"Meditation on Saviours"

W. S. Johnson, "The 'Saviour' in the Poetry of Robinson Jeffers," *AL* 15 (May 1943): 163-64.

"Nova"

Perrine and Reid, *100 American Poems*, 91-92.

"Ocean"

Perrine and Reid, *100 American Poems*, 89-90.

"The Purse-Seine"

Butterfield, *Modern American Poetry*, 93-109.

Perrine and Reid, *100 American Poems*, 93-94.

Rosenthal, *The Modern Poets*, 157-58.

Roan Stallion (verse novel)

Gray, *American Poetry*, 201-5.

Karl Keller, "California, Yankees, and the Death of God: The Allegory in Jeffers' *Roan Stallion*," *TSLL* 12 (Spring 1970): 111-20.

Patrick D. Murphy, "Reclaiming the Novel: Robinson Jeffers' Verse Novels," *WAL* 22 (Aug. 1987): 125-48.

"Self-Criticism in February"

William H. Nolte, "Robinson Jeffers Redivivus," *GaR* 32 (Summer 1978): 429-34.

"Science"

Delmore Schwartz, "The Enigma of Robinson Jeffers: I, Sources of Violence," *Poetry* 55 (Oct. 1939): 34-38.

"Shine, Perishing Republic"

Jessica Hueter, "A Patriot's Lament," *RJN* (1987): 26-27.

Walsh, *Doors into Poetry*, 30-31.

"Solstice"

Terry Beers, *Expl* 42 (Summer 1984): 34-35.

"Still the Mind Smiles"

Larry Maddox, "Vantage Points," *RJN* (1987): 16-17.

Tamar (verse novel)

David C. Dougherty, "The Epic Conventions of Robinson Jeffers," *MHLS* 7 (1984): 45-56.

Patrick D. Murphy, "Reclaiming the Novel: Robinson Jeffers' Verse Novels," *WAL* 22 (Aug. 1987): 125-48.

"To the House"

Bryan Nichols, "Ecologic Consistency," *RJN* (1987): 8-9.

"To the Stone-Cutters"

Wyatt, *The Fall into Eden*, 174-85.

The Women at Point Sur

Frederic I. Carpenter, "Robinson Jeffers Today: Beyond Good and Beneath Evil," *AL* 41 (Mar. 1977): 86-96.

Wyatt, *The Fall into Eden*, 174-85.

JILES, PAULETTE

[Interview]

Constance Rooke, "Getting into Heaven: An Interview with Diana Hartog, Paulette Jiles, and Sharon Thesen," *Malahat Review* 83 (Summer 1988): 5-52.

Celestial Navigation

Dennis Cooley, "'we will try to act like human beings': *Celestial Navigation* as Anti-Authoritarian," *Malahat Review* 83 (Summer 1988): 127-37.

Waterloo Express

Lane M. Travis, "Travelling With St. Theresa: The Poetry of Paulette Jiles," *ECW* 10 (1978): 61-72.

JOHNSTON, GEORGE

[Interview]

William Blissett, "Three Talks with George Johnston," *Malahat Review* 78 (1987): 37-51.

"Cathleen Sweeping"

Harvey De Roo, "*Happy Enough*: The Poetry of George Johnston," *Malahat Review* 78 (1987): 106-31.

"The Cruising Auk"

Harvey De Roo, "*Happy Enough*: The Poetry of George Johnston," *Malahat Review* 78 (1987): 106-31.

"Happy Enough"

Harvey De Roo, "*Happy Enough*: The Poetry of George Johnston," *Malahat Review* 78 (1987): 106-31.

"The Pool"

Harvey De Roo, "*Happy Enough*: The Poetry of George Johnston," *Malahat Review* 78 (1987): 106-31.

The Saga of Gisli (translation)

Peter Foote, "How It Strikes a Philologist: George Johnston's Translation of Saga Prose," *Malahat Review* 78 (1987): 92-97.

Taking a Grip

Harvey De Roo, "*Happy Enough*: The Poetry of George Johnston," *Malahat Review* 78 (1987): 106-31.

"War on the Periphery"

Harvey De Roo, "*Happy Enough*: The Poetry of George Johnston," *Malahat Review* 78 (1987): 106-31.

JORDAN, JUNE

"Critical and Well-Beloved Friends and Comrades"

Peter Erickson, "The Love Poetry of June Jordan," *Callaloo* 9 (Winter 1986): 221-35.

"Directed by Desire"

Peter Erickson, "The Love Poetry of June Jordan," *Callaloo* 9 (Winter 1986): 221-35.

"Fibrous Ruin"

Peter Erickson, "The Love Poetry of June Jordan," *Callaloo* 9 (Winter 1986): 221-35.

"Fragments from a Parable (of the 1950s)"

Peter Erickson, "The Love Poetry of June Jordan," *Callaloo* 9 (Winter 1986): 221-35.

"On New Year's Eve"

Peter Erickson, "The Love Poetry of June Jordan," *Callaloo* 9 (Winter 1986): 221-35.

Passion

Peter Erickson, "The Love Poetry of June Jordan," *Callaloo* 9 (Winter 1986): 221-35.

"Poem about My Rights"

Peter Erickson, "The Love Poetry of June Jordan," *Callaloo* 9 (Winter 1986): 221-35.

JUSTICE, DONALD

"Beyond the Hunting Woods"

Mary Grosselink de Jong, "Musical Possibilities: Music, Memory, and Composition in the Poetry of Donald Justice," *CP* 18 (1985): 57-66.

KAHN, HANNAH

"Ride a Wild Horse"

Sanders, *The Discovery of Poetry*, 165-67.

KAUFMAN, WALLACE

"Smethport, Pennsylvania"

K. Crowhurst, "Comment," *Agenda* 9 (Winter 1971): 35.

KEES, WELDON

"Aspects of Robinson"

D. Gioia, "The Achievement of Weldon Kees," in *Weldon Kees: A Critical Introduction*, ed. J. Elledge (Metuchen and London: Scarecrow, 1985), 76-92.

"The Image Robinsonian"

J. Elledge, "'The Image Robinsonian': Weldon Kees' Robinson Sequence," in *Weldon Kees: A Critical Introduction*, ed. J. Elledge (Metuchen and London: Scarecrow, 1985), 76-92.

"The Locusts, the Plaza, the Room"

J. F. Nims, *Poetry: The Critical Supplement*, Oct. 1947, 10-11.

KELLEY, ROBERT

"The Centerfielder"

D. Barone, "Under the Silence of the Unfinished Work," *Boundary* 10 (Winter 1982): 115-34.

KENNEDY, X. J.

"Nude Descending a Staircase"

Ronald A. Sharp, "Kennedy's 'Nude Descending a Staircase,'" *Expl* 37 (Spring 1979): 2-3

KEROUAC, JACK

Mexico City Blues

Armand B. Chartier, "Jack Kerouac, franco-americain," *Revue d'Histoire Littéraire du Québec et du Canada Française* 12 (Summer/Autumn 1986): 83-96.

Michael Powell, "The Locomotive Poetic of Jack Kerouac's *Mexico City Blues*," *NMAL* 9 (Fall 1985): item B.

KILMER, JOYCE

"Trees"

Brooks and Warren, *Understanding Poetry*, 387-91. Rev. ed., 274-78.

Jeffrey Fleece, "Further Notes on a 'Bad' Poem," *CE* 12 (Mar. 1951): 314-20.

KINNELL, GALWAY

[Interview]

Thomas Gardner, "An Interview with Galway Kinnell," *CP* 20 (1979): 423-33.

"The Bear"

William V. Davis, "The Rank Flavor of Blood: Galway Kinnell's 'The Bear,'" *NConL* 7 (Mar. 1977): 4-6.

John Hobbs, Galway Kinnell's 'The Bear': Dream and Technique," *MPS* 5 (Winter 1974): 237-50.

J. T. Ledbetter, *Expl* 33 (Apr. 1975): 63.

"The Book of Nightmares"

Thomas A. Gardner, "An Interview with Galway Kinnell," *ConL* 20 (1979): 423-33.

"The Descent"

Ralph J. Mills, "A Reading of Galway Kinnell: Part 1," *IowaR* 1 (Winter 1970): 78-82.

"Easter"

Ralph J. Mills, "A Reading of Galway Kinnell: Part 1," *IowaR* 1 (Winter 1970): 72-73.

"First Communion"

Ralph J. Mills, "A Reading of Galway Kinnell: Part 1," *IowaR* 1 (Winter 1970): 68-69.

"First Song"

James R. Hurt, *Expl* 20 (Nov. 1961): 23. Reprinted in *The Explicator Cyclopedia* 1:203-4.

Gene H. Koretz, *Expl* 15 (Apr. 1957): 43. Reprinted in *The Explicator Cyclopedia* 1:202-3.

Melvin Walker LaFollette, *Expl* 14 (Apr. 1956): 48. Reprinted in *The Explicator Cyclopedia* 1:201-2.

"How Many Nights"

Philip L. Gerber and Robert J. Gemmett, "Deeper Than Personality: A Conversation with Galway Kinnell," *IowaR* 1 (Spring 1970): 125-26.

"The Name Bearing the Initial of Christ into the New World"

Joe Marusiak, "'Where We Might Meet Each Other': An Appreciation of Galway Kinnell and William Everson," *LitR* 24 (Spring 1981): 355-70.

"The Porcupine"

Thomas Gardner, "An Interview with Galway Kinnell," *ConL* 20 (1979): 423-33.

Ralph J. Mills, "A Reading of Galway Kinnell: Part 2," *IowaR* 1 (Spring 1970): 117-19.

"Seven Streams of Nevis"

Ralph J. Mills, "A Reading of Galway Kinnell: Part 1," *IowaR* 1 (Winter 1970): 73-76.

"Song of Myself"

Thomas Gardner, "An Interview with Galway Kinnell," *ConL* 20 (1979): 423-33.

"Spindrift"

Linda Wagner, "Spindrift: The World in a Seashell," *CP* 8 (Spring 1975): 5-9.

"The Supper After the Last"

Ralph J. Mills, "A Reading of Galway Kinnell: Part 1," *IowaR* 1 (Winter 1970): 82-86.

"The Thief"

Ralph J. Mills, "A Reading of Galway Kinnell: Part 2," *IowaR* 1 (Spring 1970): 115-17.

"To Christ Our Lord"

Ralph J. Mills, "A Reading of Galway Kinnell: Part 1," *IowaR* 1 (Winter 1970): 70-71.

"Vapor Trail Reflected in the Frog Pond"

Philip L. Gerber and Robert J. Gemmett, eds., "Deeper Than Personality: A Conversation with Galway Kinnell," *IowaR* 1 (Spring 1970): 129-31.

"Where the Track Vanishes"

Ralph J. Mills, "A Reading of Galway Kinnell: Part 1," *IowaR* 1 (Winter 1970): 76-78.

KINSELLA, THOMAS

"Downstream"

Clark, *Lyric Resonance*, 91-102.

"First Light"

Bruce Kellner, "The Wormwood Poems of Thomas Kinsella," *WHR* 26 (Summer 1972): 225-27.

"Navigators"

Dickinson, *Suggestions for Teachers of "Introduction to Literature,"* 53.

KIYOOKA, ROY

"The Fontainebleau Dream Machine"

Eva-Marie Krooler, "Roy Kiyooka's 'The Fontainebleau Dream Machine': A Reading," *CanL* 113/114 (Summer 1987): 47-58.

KLEIN, ABRAHAM MOSES

"The Rocking Chair"

William Walsh, "The Shape of Canadian Poetry," *SR* 87 (Jan./Mar. 1979): 73-95.

KLOEFKORN, WILLIAM

"loony"

Mark Sanders, "Measurements of Compatibility in Contemporary Nebraska Poetry: The Verse of William Kloefkorn, Ted Kooser, and Don Welch," *CP* 13 (Fall 1980): 65-72.

KNIGHT, ETHERIDGE

"2 Poems for Black Relocation Centers"

Ashby Bland Crowder, "Etheridge Knight: Two Fields of Combat," *CP* 16 (1983): 23-25.

KOOSER, TED

"In the Corners of Fields"

Mark Sanders, "Measurements of Compatibility in Contemporary Nebraska Poetry: The Verse of William Kloefkorn, Ted Kooser, and Don Welch," *CP* 13 (Fall 1980): 65-72.

"Tom Balls's Barn"

Mark Sanders, "Measurements of Compatibility in Contemporary Nebraska Poetry: The Verse of William Kloefkorn, Ted Kooser, and Don Welch," *CP* 13 (Fall 1980): 65-72.

KROETSCH, ROBERT

Advice to My Friends

Paul Hjartarson, "Discourse of the Other," *CanL* 115 (Winter 1987): 135-38.

Gone Indian

L. K. MacKendrick, "The Comic, the Centripetal Text, and the Canadian Novel," *ESC* 10 (Sept. 1984): 343-56.

The Ledger

D. G. Jones, "Canadian Poetry: Roots & New Directions," *Credences*, n.s. 2 (Fall/Winter 1983): 254-75.

"Seed Catalog"

Laurie Ricou, "Prairie Poetry and Metaphors of Plain/s [sic] Space," *GPQ* 3 (Spring 1983): 109-19.

The Studhorse Man

L. K. MacKendrick, "The Comic, the Centripetal Text, and the Canadian Novel," *ESC* 10 (Sept. 1984): 343-56.

KUMIN, MAXINE

[Interview]

Karla Hammond, "An Interview with Maxine Kumin," *WHR* 33 (Winter 1979): 1-15.

"A Family Man"

D. Pope, *A Separate Vision*, passim.

"The Retrieval System"

Philip Booth, "Maxine Kumin's Survival," *APR* 7 (Nov./Dec. 1978): 18-19.

Sybil P. Estess, "Past Halfway: 'The Retrieval System,' by Maxine Kumin," *IowaR* 10 (1979): 99-109.

"A Voice From the Roses"

D. Pope, *A Separate Vision*, passim.

KUNITZ, STANLEY

[Interview]

"Yale's Younger Poets: Interview with Chester Kerr, Stanley Kunitz, Carolyn Forché," *Book Forum* 2 (1976): passim.

"Among the Gods"

George P. Elliott, "The Poetry of Stanley Kunitz," *Accent* 18 (Autumn 1958): 270.

"Careless Love"

George P. Elliott, "The Poetry of Stanley Kunitz," *Accent* 18 (Autumn 1958): 268-69.

"Geometry of Moods"

Mills, *Contemporary American Poetry*, 37-39.

"Hermetic Poem"

Mills, *Contemporary American Poetry*, 39-40.

"Journal for My Daughter"

Marjorie G. Perloff, "The Testing of Stanley Kunitz," *IowaR* 3 (Winter 1972): 94-99.

"Night Letter"

Mills, *Contemporary American Poetry*, 44-47.

"Prophecy on Lethe"

Robert Weisberg, "Stanley Kunitz: The Stubborn Middle Way," *MPS* 6 (Spring 1975): 67-69.

"The Science of the Night"

Mills, *Contemporary American Poetry*, 33-35.

"The Scourge"

Robert Weisberg, "Stanley Kunitz: The Stubborn Middle Way," *MPS* 6 (Spring 1975): 65-66.

"The Surgeons"

Mills, *Contemporary American Poetry*, 41-43.

"The Testing-Tree"

Cynthia Davis, "Stanley Kunitz's 'The Testing-Tree,'" *CP* 8 (Spring 1975): 43-46.

LANIER, SIDNEY

"Corn"

Edd Winfield Parks, "Lanier as Poet," in Ghodes, *Essays on American Literature*, 189-90.

"The Marshes of Glynn"

Philip Graham, "Sidney Lanier and the Pattern of Contrast," *AQ* 11 (Winter 1959): 506-7.

Edd Winfield Parks, "Lanier as Poet," in Ghodes, *Essays on American Literature*, 196-98.

Owen J. Reaner, "Lanier's 'The Marshes of Glynn' Revisited," *MissQ* 23 (Winter 1969/1970): 57-63.

Robert H. Ross, "'The Marshes of Glynn': A Study of Symbolic Obscurity," *AL* 32 (Jan. 1961): 403-16.

R. P. Warren, "The Blind Poet: Sidney Lanier," *American Review* 2 (Nov. 1933): 42-45.

LATTIMORE, RICHARD

"Witness to Death"

Ford T. Swetnam, *Expl* 25 (Mar. 1967): 59.

LAUGHLIN, JAMES

"Go West Young Man"

Laurence Perrine, *Expl* 28 (Mar. 1970): 61.

LAYTON, IRVING

"A Tall Man Executes a Jig"

Lee Briscoe Thompson and Deborah Black, "The Dance of a Pot-bellied Poet: Explorations into 'A Tall Man Executes a Jig,'" *CP* 12 (Fall 1979): 33-43.

LEA, SYDNEY

"The Feud"

Sydney Lea, "On 'The Feud,'" *KanQ* 15 (Fall 1983): 97-103.

LEE, DENNIS

Civil Elegies

D. G. Jones, "Canadian Poetry: Roots & New Directions," *Credences*, n.s. 2 (Fall/Winter 1983): 254-75.

LEE, DON L.

"But He Was Cool, Or: He Even Stopped for Green Lights"

Ann Colley, "Don L. Lee's 'But He Was Cool, Or: He Even Stopped for Green Lights': An Example of the New Black Aesthetic," *CP* 4 (Fall 1971): 20-27.

LE PAN, DOUGLAS

"Image of Silenus"

James Reaney, "The Third Eye," *CanL* 3 (1960). Reprinted in Woodcock, *Choice of Critics*, 156-68.

LeSUEUR, MERIDEL

"Behold Me! Touch Me!"

Gelfant, *Women Writing in America: Voices in Collage*, 83.

"Behold this and always love it!"

Gelfant, *Women Writing in America: Voices in Collage*, 77.

"For the White Poets Who Would Be Indians"

Gelfant, *Women Writing in America: Voices in Collage*, 88.

"I Hear You Singing in the Barley Ripe"

Gelfant, *Women Writing in America: Voices in Collage*, 90.

LEVERTOV, DENISE

"The Absence"

Pope, *A Separate Vision: Isolation in Contemporary Women's Poetry*, passim.

"Artist to Intellectual"

Elder, *Imagining the Earth*, passim.

"Cancion"

Lauter, *Women as Mythmakers*, chap. 8, passim.

"The Dead"

Denise Levertov, "On the Malice of Innocence: Poetry in the Classroom," *The APR* 1 (Nov./Dec. 1972): 44.

"The Dogwood"

Pope, *A Separate Vision*, 84-115.

"During the Eichmann Trial"

Sophia B. Blaydes, "Metaphors of Life and Death in the Poetry of Denise Levertov and Sylvia Plath," *DR* 57 (Autumn 1977): 494-506.

"The Earthwoman and the Waterwoman"

Pope, *A Separate Vision*, passim.

"The Five Day Rain"

Baker, *Syntax in English Poetry, 1870-1830*, 151-53.

"The Garden Wall"

Carol A. Kyle, "Every Step on Arrival: *Six Variations* and the Musical Structure of Denise Levertov's Poetry," *CentR* 17 (Summer 1973): 291-92.

"Hurricane Watch"

Lauter, *Women as Mythmakers*, chap. 8, passim.

"The Illustrious Ancestors"

Lacey, *The Inner War*, 111-13.

"Losing Track"

M. L. Rosenthal, "Dynamics of Form and Motive in Some Representative Twentieth-Century Lyric Poems," *ELH* 37 (Mar. 1970): 139-41.

"The Malice of Innocence"

Carol A. Kyle, "Every Step an Arrival: *Six Variations* and the Musical Structure of Denise Levertov's Poetry," *CentR* 17 (Summer 1973): 294-95.

"May Our Right Hands Lose Their Cunning"

Elder, *Imagining the Earth*, passim.

"The 90th Year"

Denise Levertov, "The 90th Year," in *Fifty Contemporary Poets: The Creative Process*, ed. Alberta T. Turner (New York: David McKay Co., 1977), 193-201.

"Pleasures"

Diana Suzman, "Inside and Outside in the Poetry of Denise Levertov," *CritQ* 22 (Spring 1980): 57-68.

"The Pulse"

Lauter, *Women as Mythmakers*, chap. 8, passim.

"Relearning the Alphabet"

Mersmann, *Out of the Vietnam Vortex: A Study of Poets and Poetry against the War*, 77-112.

"Revolutionary"

Juhasz, *Naked and Fiery Forms*, 81.

"Six Variations"

Carol A. Kyle, "Every Step an Arrival: *Six Variations* and the Musical Structure of Denise Levertov's Poetry," *CentR* 17 (Summer 1973): 281-89.

"The Snake"

Johanna R. Brent et al., "Poem Opening: An Invitation to Transactive Criticism," *CE* 40 (1978): 2-16.

"Song for Ishtar"

Ostriker, *Stealing the Language*, 220.

"Staying Alive"

Paul A. Lacey, "The Poetry of Political Anguish," *Sagetrieb* 4 (Spring 1985): 61-71.

Cary Nelson, "Whitman in Vietnam: Poetry and History in Contemporary America," *MR* 16 (Winter 1975): 55-71.

Lorrie Smith, "Songs of Experience: Denise Levertov's Political Poetry," *ConL* 27 (Summer 1986): 212-32.

"A Stir in the Air"

Carol A. Kyle, "Every Step an Arrival: *Six Variations* and the Musical Structure of Denise Levertov's Poetry," *CentR* 17 (Summer 1973): 292-93.

"The Stonecarver's Poem"

Marjorie Pryse, "'The Stonecarver's Poem'--A Linguistic Interpretation," *Lang&S* 7 (Winter 1974): 62-71.

To Stay Alive

Nancy J. Sisko, "*To Stay Alive*: Levertov's Search for a Revolutionary Poetry," *Sagetreib* 5 (Fall 1986): 47-60.

"The Tulips"

Sophia B. Blaydes, "Metaphors of Life and Death in the Poetry of Denise Levertov and Sylvia Plath," *DR* 57 (Autumn 1977): 494-506.

"The Whirlwind"

Pope, *A Separate Vision*, passim.

"The Wings"

Pope, *A Separate Vision*, passim.

"With Eyes at the Back of Our Heads"

Mills, *Contemporary American Poetry*, 194-96.

LEVINE, PHILIP

[Interview]

Irv Broughton, "An Interview with Philip Levine," *WHR* 32 (Spring 1978): 139-63.

"Ashes"

Joseph Parisi, "Homing In," *Shenandoah* 30 (1979): 99-107.

"They Feed They Lion"

Joe Jackson, *Expl* 41 (Summer 1983): 56-58.

LEVINE, PHILIP

"Years from Somewhere"

Joseph Parisi, "Homing In," *Shenandoah* 30 (1970): 99-107.

LIEBERMAN, LAURENCE

God's Measurements

Michael McFee, "Gaijin's Measurements," *Parnassus* 11 (Fall/Winter 1983): 367-77.

Dave Smith, "Castles, Elephants, Buddhas: Some Recent American Poetry," *APR* 10 (May/June 1981): 37-42.

The Mural of Wakeful Sleep

"Culture and Poetry: The Mural at Its Best," *Chariton Review* 12 (Fall 1986): 82-86.

LEWIS, ALUN

"Ha, Ha! Among the Trumptets"

Ralph Huston, "The Broken Arch: A Study of the Poetry of Alun Lewis," *Adelphi* 28 (1951): 403-13.

LEWIS, JAMES F.

"Dawn in the Study"

Mary Graham Lund, *Expl* 18 (Nov. 1959): 12. Reprinted in *The Explicator Cyclopedia* 1:205.

"In Memoriam"

Marh Graham Lund, *Expl* 18 (Jan. 1960): 23. Reprinted in *The Explicator Cyclopedia* 1:205-6.

LIMÓN, JOSÉ

"Frost in the Rio Grande Valley"

Albert Trevino, "'Frost in the Rio Grande Valley' by José Limón," *EJ* 66 (Mar. 1977): 69.

LINDSAY, VACHEL

"Abraham Lincoln Walks at Midnight"

Perrine and Reid, *100 American Poems*, 25.

"The Congo"

A. J. Bader, "Lindsay Explains 'The Congo,'" *PQ* 27 (Apr. 1948): 190-92.

Walter Blair, *The Literature of the United States* 2:946.

Perrine and Reid, *100 American Poems*, 61-64.

Austin Warren, "The Case of Vachel Lindsay," *Accent* 6 (Summer 1946): 237.

"The Jazz Age"

J. E. Hallwas, "Poetry and Prophecy: Vachel Lindsay's 'The Jazz Age,'" *Illinois Quarterly* 40 (Fall 1977): 30-37.

"The Santa Fe Trail"

Richard E. Amacher, *Expl* 5 (Mar. 1947): 33. Reprinted in *The Explicator Cyclopedia* 1:206-7.

Richard E. Amacher, "Off 'The Santa Fe Trail,'" *AL* 20 (Nov. 1948): 337.

A. L. Bader, "Vachel Lindsay and 'The Santa Fe Trail,'" *AL* 19 (Jan. 1948): 360-62.

LISTER, R. P.

"Target"

Laurence Perrine, "The Importance of Tone in the Interpretation of Literature," *CE* 24 (Feb. 1963): 391-92.

LIVESAY, DOROTHY

[Interview]

Doug Beardsley and Rosemary Sullivan, "An Interview with Dorothy Livesay," *CanPo* 3 (1978): 87-97.

"The Two Seasons" (in *Collected Poems*)

Debbie Foulks, "Livesay's Two Seasons of Love," *CanL* 74 (Autumn 1977): 63-73.

LOGAN, JOHN

"Big Sur: Partington"

Charles Altieri, "Poetry as Resurrection: John Logan's Structures of Metaphysical Solace," *MPS* 3 (1972): 211-13.

"A Century Piece for Poor Heine"

Carroll, *The Poem in Its Skin*, 116-36.

"Lines for Michael in the Picture"

Charles Altieri, "Poetry as Resurrection: John Logan's Structures of Metaphysical Solace," *MPS* 3 (1972): 219-20.

"The Picnic"

Charles Altieri, "Poetry as Resurrection: John Logan's Structures of Metaphysical Solace," *MPS* 3 (1972): 205-7.

"The Rescue"

Charles Altieri, "Poetry as Resurrection: John Logan's Structures of Metaphysical Solace," *MPS* 3 (1972): 195-98.

"Shore Scene"

Charles Altieri, "Poetry as Resurrection: John Logan's Structures of Metaphysical Solace," *MPS* 3 (1972): 207-8.

"A Trip to Four or Five Towns"

Charles Altieri, "Poetry as Resurrection: John Logan's Structures of Metaphysical Solace," *MPS* 3 (1972): 203-5.

LORDE, AUDRE

"Afterimages"

Amtai F. Avi-ram, "*APO KOINOU* in Audre Lorde and the Moderns: Defining the Differences," *Callaloo* 9 (Winter 1986): 193-208.

The Black Unicorn

Mary Carruthers, "The Re-Vision of the Muse: Adrienne Rich, Audre Lorde, Judy Grahn, Olga Broumas," *HudR* 36 (Summer 1983): 293-322.

Joan Martin, "The Unicorn Is Black: Audre Lorde in Retrospect," in Evans, *Black Women Writers*, 277-91.

"Coal"

Joan Martin, "The Unicorn is Black: Audre Lorde in Retrospect," in Evans, *Black Women Writers*, 277-91.

"From the House of Yemanja"

Amtai F. Avi-ram, "*APO KOINOU* in Audre Lorde and the Moderns: Defining the Differences," *Callaloo* 9 (Winter 1986): 193-208.

"Hard Love Rock #II"

Amtai F. Avi-ram, "*APO KOINOU* in Audre Lorde and the Moderns: Defining the Differences," *Callaloo* 9 (Winter 1986): 193-208.

"Now"

Amtai F. Avi-ram, "*APO KOINOU* in Audre Lorde and the Moderns: Defining the Differences," *Callaloo* 9 (Winter 1986): 193-208.

LOWELL, AMY

Fir-Flower Tablets

Kenner, *The Pound Era*, 291-98.

"Magnolia Gardens"

Thomas Brown, "The 'Little Controversy' Over *Magenta*: Amy Lowell and the South Carolinians," *ELN* 22 (1984): 62-66.

"Meeting-House Hill"

Brooks, Lewis, and Warren, *American Literature*. 2056-57.

"Night Clouds"

Cooper and Holmes, *Preface to Poetry*, 141-42.

"Patterns"

Brooks and Warren, *Understanding Poetry*, 139-43; rev. ed., 58-61.

Perrine and Reid, *100 American Poems*, 51-52.

"Sunshine"

Daniels, *The Art of Reading Poetry*, 196-97.

"Written Pictures"

Kenner, *The Pound Era*, 291-98.

LOWELL, ROBERT

"Adam and Eve"

Mills, *Contemporary American Poetry*, 144-46.

"After Surprising Conversions"

John Akey, *Expl* 9 (June 1951): 53. Reprinted in *The Explicator Cyclopedia* 1:209.

G. Giovanni, *Expl* 9 (June 1951): 53. Reprinted in *The Explicator Cyclopedia* 1:207-8.

John McCluhan, *Expl* 9 (June 1951): 53. Reprinted in *The Explicator Cyclopedia* 1:208.

Roy Harvey Pearce, *Expl* 9 (June 1951): 53. Reprinted in *The Explicator Cyclopedia* 1:209.

Dallas E. Wiebe, "Mr. Lowell and Mr. Edwards," *Wisconsin Studies in Contemporary Literature* 3 (Spring/Summer 1962): 26-29.

"As a Plane Tree by the Water"

De Sales Standerwick, "Notes on Robert Lowell," *Renanscence* 8 (Winter 1955): 80.

"At the Indian Killer's Grave"

De Sales Standerwick, "Notes on Robert Lowell," *Renascence* 8 (Winter 1955): 78-79.

Austin Warren, "A Double Discipline," *Poetry* 70 (Aug. 1947): 265.

"Between the Porch and the Altar"

Marius Bewley, "Aspects of Modern American Poetry," *Scrutiny* 17 (Mar. 1951): 345-47.

Rosenthal, *The Modern Poets*, 228-29.

Thomas Vogler, "Robert Lowell: Payment Gat He Nane," *IowaR* 2 (Summer 1971): 78-82.

"Beyond the Alps"

Clauco Cambon, "Dea Roma and Robert Lowell," *Accent* 20 (Winter 1960): 51-61.

Gray, *American Poetry*, 243-45.

Mills, *Contemporary American Poetry*, 149-51.

"Caligula"

Joan Bobbitt, "Lowell and Plath: Objectivity and the Confessional Mode," *ArQ* 33 (Autumn 1977): 312-13.

"The Cathedral"

Raymond D. Gozzi, *Expl* 45 (Spring 1987): 28-30.

"Charles River"

Katherine T. Wallingford, "Robert Lowell's Poetry of Repetition," *AL* 57 (Oct. 1985): 424-33.

"Children of Light"

Rosenthal, *The Modern Poets*, 227-28.

"Colloquy in Black Rock"

Richard J. Fein, "*Lord Weary's Castle* Revisited," *PMLA* 89 (Jan. 1974): 39.

Mills, *Contemporary American Poetry*, 139-41.

"Commander Lowell 1887-1950"

George McFadden, "'Life Studies'--Robert Lowell's Comic Breakthrough," *PMLA* 90 (Jan. 1975): 100.

"Day By Day"

Donald Hall, "Robert Lowell and the Literature Industry," *GaR* 32 (Spring 1978): 7-12.

"The Death of the Sheriff"

Thomas Vogler, "Robert Lowell: Payment Gat He Nane," *IowaR* (Summer 1971): 84-90.

"The Dolphin"

Steven Gould Axelrod, "Lowell's 'The Dolphin' as a 'Book of Life,'" *ConL* 18 (Autumn 1977): 473-74.

Christopher Butler, "Robert Lowell: From *Notebook* to 'The Dolphin,'" *YES* 8 (1978): 141-56.

"The Drinker"

Marie Borroff, "Words, Language, and Form," in Brady, Palmer, and Price, *Literary Theory and Structure*, 71-73.

Reginald Dyck, *Expl* 40 (Winter 1982): 7-9.

"Dunbarton"

J. G. Barry, "Robert Lowell's 'Confessional' Image of an Age: Theme and Language in Poetic Form," *ArielE* 12 (Jan. 1981): 51-58.

George McFadden, "'Life Studies'--Robert Lowell's Comic Breakthough," *PMLA* 90 (Jan. 1975): 100.

Phillips, *The Confessional Poets*, 27-29.

"During Fever"

J. G. Barry, "Robert Lowell's 'Confessional' Image of an Age: Theme and Language in Poetic Form," *ArielE* 12 (Jan. 1981): 51-58.

George McFadden, "'Life Studies'--Robert Lowell's Comic Breakthough," *PMLA* 90 (1975): 102-3.

"The Exile's Return"

Peter P. Remaley, "The Quest for Grace in Robert Lowell's *Lord Weary's Castle*," *Renascence* 28 (Spring 1976): 115-19.

"Ezra Pound"

Lawrence Kramer, "The Wodwo Watches the Water Clock: Language in Postmodern British and American Poetry," *ConL* 18 (Summer 1977), 326-28.

"Fall Weekend at Milgate"

Anthony Manousos, "Falling Asleep over *The Aeneid*: Lowell, Freud, and the Classics," *CLS* 21 (Spring 1984): 16-29.

Vanessa Ryder, "Passion Flowers and Humming Birds," *Salmagundi* 37 (Spring 1977), 106-11.

"Father's Bedroom"

George McFadden, "'Life Studies'--Robert Lowell's Comic Breakthrough," *PMLA* 90 (Jan. 1975): 101.

"The First Sunday in Lent"

Mills, *Contemporary American Poetry*, 136-38.

"Fishnet"

Stephen Gould Axelrod, "Lowell's *The Dolphin* as a 'Book of Life,'" *ConL* 18 (Autumn 1977): 461-64.

"For Sale"

J. G. Barry, "Robert Lowell's 'Confessional' Image of an Age: Theme and Language in Poetic Form," *ArielE* 12 (Jan. 1981): 51-58.

George McFadden, "'Life Studies'--Robert Lowell's Comic Breakthrough,'" *PMLA* 90 (Jan. 1975): 101.

"For the Union Dead"

W. Bedford, "The Morality of Form in the Poetry of Robert Lowell," *ArielE* 9 (Jan. 1978): 3-17.

Marie Borroff, "Words, Language, and Form," in Brady, Palmer, and Price, *Literary Theory and Structure*, 73-74.

Paul C. Doherty, "The Poet as Historian: 'For the Union Dead,' by Robert Lowell," *CP* 1 (Fall 1968): 37-40.

Steven K. Hoffman, "Lowell, Berryman, Roethke, and Ginsberg: The Communal Function of Confessional Poetry," *LitR* 22 (Spring 1979): 329-41.

David Holbrook, *Lost Bearings in English Poetry* (London: Vision Press, 1977): 48-57.

Jerome, *Poetry: Premeditated Art*, 343-47.

Perrine and Reid, *100 American Poems*, 247.

W. Nelles, "Saving the State in Lowell's 'For the Union Dead,'" *AL* 55 (Dec. 1983): 639-42.

Thurley, *The American Moment: American Poetry in the Mid-Century*, 71-90.

"Grandparents"

J. G. Barry, "Robert Lowell's 'Confessional' Image of an Age: Theme and Language in Poetic Form," *ArielE* 12 (Jan. 1981): 51-58.

Hayden, *Inside Poetry Out*, passim.

George McFadden, "'Life Studies'--Robert Lowell's Comic Breakthrough," *PMLA* 90 (Jan. 1975): 100.

Mills, *Contemporary American Poetry*, 153-55.

"Hawthorne"

Thomas Woodson, "Robert Lowell's 'Hawthorne,' Yvor Winters and the American Literary Tradition," *AQ* 19 (Fall 1967): 575-82.

"High Blood"

Joan Bobbitt, "Lowell and Plath: Objectivity and the Confessional Mode," *ArQ* 33 (Autumn 1977): 314.

"Home after Three Months Away"

J. G. Barry, "Robert Lowell's 'Confessional' Image of an Age: Theme and Language in Poetic Form," *ArielE* 12 (Jan. 1981): 51-58.

Sr. Madeline DeFrees, "Pegasus and Six Blind Indians," *EJ* 59 (Oct. 1970): 935-37.

George McFadden, "'Life Studies'--Robert Lowell's Comic Breakthrough," *PMLA* 90 (Jan. 1975): 103-4.

Phillips, *The Confessional Poets*, 35-37.

"In Memory of Arthur Winslow"

Marjorie Perloff, "Death by Water: The Winslow Elegies of Robert Lowell," *ELH* 34 (Mar. 1967): 117-24.

Stanley M. Wiersma, *Expl* 30 (Oct. 1971): 12.

"July in Washington"

Edwards, *Imagination and Power*, 221-24.

"Land of Unlikeness"

Steven K. Hoffman, "Lowell, Berryman, Roethke, and Ginsberg: The Communal Function of Confessional Poetry," *LitR* 22 (Spring 1979): 329-41.

Life Studies

W. Bedford, "The Morality of Form in the Poetry of Robert Lowell," *ArielE* 9 (Jan. 1978): 3-17.

Richard Y. Fein, "The Life of *Life Studies*," *LitR* 23 (Spring 1980): 325-38.

Burton Raffel, "Robert Lowell's *Life Studies*," *LitR* 23 (Spring 1980): 293-325.

Lord Weary's Castle

Steven K. Hoffman, "Lowell, Berryman, Roethke, and Ginsberg: The Communal Function of Confessional Poetry," *LitR* 22 (Spring 1979): 329-41.

Bruce Michelson, "Randall Jarrell and Robert Lowell: The Making of *Lord Weary's Castle*," *ConL* 26 (Winter 1985): 402-25.

"Man and Wife"

Marjorie Perloff, "Realism and the Confessional Mode of Robert Lowell," *ConL* 11 (Autumn 1970): 472-82.

Phillips, *The Confessional Poets*, 38-39.

"Mary Winslow"

John J. McAleer, *Expl* 18 (Feb. 1960): 29. Reprinted in *The Explicator Cyclopedia* 1:209-10.

"Memories of West Street and Lepke"

J. G. Barry, "Robert Lowell's 'Confessional' Image of an Age: Theme and Language in Poetic Form," *ArielE* 12 (Jan. 1981): 51-58.

George Lensing, "'Memories of West Street and Lepke': Robert Lowell's Associative Mirror," *CP* 3 (Fall 1970): 23-26.

George McFadden, "'Life Studies'--Robert Lowell's Comic Breakthough," *PMLA* 90 (Jan. 1975): 104.

"The Mills of the Kavanaughs"

Martha George Meek, *Expl* 38 (Winter 1980): 46-47.

"Mother Marie Therese"

De Sales Standerwick, "Notes on Robert Lowell," *Renascence* 8 (Winter 1955): 81-82.

"Mr. Edwards and the Spider"

Perrine and Reid, *100 American Poems,* 243-44.

Dallas E. Wiebe, "Mr. Lowell and Mr. Edwards," *Wisconsin Studies in Contemporary Literature* 3 (Spring/Summer 1962): 21-26.

"My Last Afternoon with Uncle Devereux Winslow"

J. G. Barry, "Robert Lowell's 'Confessional' Image of an Age: Theme and Language in Poetic Form," *ArielE* 12 (Jan. 1981): 51-58.

Richard James Calhoun, *Expl* 23 (Jan. 1965): 38.

Martha Carlson-Bradley, "Lowell's 'My Last Afternoon with Uncle Devereux Winslow': The Model for Bishop's 'First Death in Nova Scotia,'" *CP* 19 (1986): 117-31.

George McFadden, "'Life Studies'--Robert Lowell's Comic Breakthrough," *PMLA* 90 (Jan. 1975): 98-100.

Marjorie Perloff, "Death by Water: The Winslow Elegies of Robert Lowell," *ELH* 34 (Mar. 1967): 130-36.

Phillips, *The Confessional Poets*, 24-26.

"Napoleon Crosses the Berezina"

De Sales Standerwick, "Notes on Robert Lowell," *Renascence* 8 (Winter 1955): 79.

"Near the Ocean"

G. S. Fraser, "'Near the Ocean,'" *Salmagundi* 37 (Spring 1977): 77-83.

Steven K. Hoffman, "Lowell, Berryman, Roethke, and Ginsberg: The Communal Function of Confessional Poetry," *LitR* 22 (Spring 1979): 329-41.

"The Neo-Classical Urn"

Joan Bobbitt, "Lowell and Plath: Objectivity and the Confessional Mode," *ArQ* 33 (Autumn 1977): 313.

"Nostalgia de la Boue"

Paul Schwaber, "Robert Lowell in Mid-Career," *WHR* 25 (Autumn 1971): 348-50.

Notebooks

W. Bedford, "The Morality of Form in the Poetry of Robert Lowell," *ArielE* 9 (Jan. 1978): 3-17.

Christopher Butler, "Robert Lowell: From *Notebook* to *The Dolphin*," *YES* 8 (1978): 141-56.

Steven K. Hoffman, "Lowell, Barryman, Roethke, and Ginsberg: The Communal Function of Confessional Poetry," *LitR* 22 (Spring 1979): 239-41.

"A Prayer for My Grandfather to Our Lady"

Marius Bewley, "Apects of Modern American Poetry," *Scrutiny* 17 (Mar. 1951): 344-45.

"The Public Garden"

Rudolph L. Nelson, "A Note on the Evolution of Robert Lowell's 'The Public Garden,'" *AL* 41 (Mar. 1969): 108-10.

"The Quaker Graveyard in Nantucket"

Philip Cooper, *Expl* 38 (Summer 1980): 43.

Paul J. Dolan, "Lowell's Quaker Graveyard: Poem and Tradition," *Renascence* 21 (Summer 1969): 171-80, 194.

H. Dubrow, "The Marine in the Garden: Pastoral Elements in Lowell's 'Quaker Graveyard,'" *PQ* 62 (Spring 1983): 127-45.

Paul Engle, "Five Years of Pulitzer Poets," *EJ* 38 (Feb. 1949): 64.

Friar and Brinnin, *Modern Poetry*, 520-21.

Philip Furia, "'Is, the Whited Monster': Lowell's Quaker Graveyard Revisited," *TSLL* 17 (Winter 1976): 837-54.

Mills, *Contemporary American Poetry*, 141-44.

Marjorie Perloff, "Death by Water: The Winslow Elegies of Robert Lowell," *ELH* 34 (Mar. 1967): 124-30.

Sr. Mary Therese Rink, "The Sea in Lowell's 'Quaker Graveyard in Nantucket,'" *Renascence* 20 (Autumn 1967): 39-43.

Rosenthal, *The Modern Poets*, 229-30.

De Sales Standerwick, "Notes on Robert Lowell," *Renascence* 8 (Winter 1955): 76-78.

"Robert Frost"

Andy J. Moore, "Frost--and Lowell--at Midnight," *SoQ* 15 (Apr. 1977): 291-96.

"Sailing Home from Rapallo"

George McFadden, "'Life Studies'--Robert Lowell's Comic Breakthrough," *PMLA* 90 (Jan. 1975): 101-2.

"Skunk Hour"

Richard J. Fein, "The Life of *Life Studies*," *LitR* 23 (Spring 1980): 326-38.

George McFadden, "'Life Studies'--Robert Lowell's Comic Breakthrough," *PMLA* 90 (Jan. 1975): 105.

Phillips, *The Confessional Poets*, 40-42.

"The Slough of Despond"

Thomas Vogler, "Robert Lowell: Payment Gat He Nane," *IowaR* 2 (Summer 1971): 82-83.

"Soft Wood"

Marjorie Perloff, "Death by Water: The Winslow Elegies of Robert Lowell," *ELH* 34 (Mar. 1967): 136-40.

"'Sunthin' in the Pastoral Line"

John C. Broderick, "Lowell's ''Sunthin' in the Pastoral Line,'" *AL* 31 (May 1959): 163-72.

"Terminal Days at Beverly Farms"

George McFadden, "'Life Studies'--Robert Lowell's Comic Breakthough," *PMLA* 90 (Jan. 1975): 101.

"To Speak of Woe That Is in Marriage"

George McFadden, "'Life Studies'--Robert Lowell's Comic Breakthough," *PMLA* 90 (Jan. 1975): 105.

"Ulysses and Circe"

Robert Fitzgerald, "Aiaia and Ithaca: Notes on a New Lowell Poem," *Salmagundi* 37 (Spring 1977): 25-31.

"'Walking in the Blue"

J. G. Barry, "Robert Lowell's 'Confessional' Image of an Age: Theme and Language in Poetic Form," *ArielE* 12 (Jan. 1981): 51-58.

George McFadden, "'Life Studies'--Robert Lowell's Comic Breakthrough," *PMLA* 90 (Jan. 1975): 103.

Mills, *Contemporary American Poetry*, 156-58.

Phillips, *The Confessional Poets*, 33-35.

"The Washers of the Shroud"

John Q. Anderson, "Lowell's 'The Washers of the Shroud' and the Celtic Legend of the Washer of the Lord," *AL* 35 (Nov. 1963): 361-63.

"Where the Rainbow Ends"

Marius Bewley, "Aspects of Modern American Poetry," *Scrutiny* 17 (Mar. 1951): 343-44.

Randall Jarrell, "From the Kingdom of Necessity," *Nation* 164 (Jan. 18, 1947): 74-75.

Peter R. Remaley, "The Quest for Grace in Robert Lowell's *Lord Weary's Castle*," *Renascence* 28 (Spring 1976): 120-22.

De Sales Standerwick, "Notes on Robert Lowell," *Renascence* 8 (Winter 1955): 80-81.

LOY, MINA

The Last Lunar Baedeker

Contance Hunting, "The Morality of Mina Loy," *Sagetrieb* 2 (Spring 1983): 133-39.

Virginia Kouidis, untitled review, *Credences*, n.s. 2 (Summer 1982): 125-30.

"Lions' Jaws"

Constance Hunting, "The Morality of Mina Loy," *Sagetreib* 2 (Spring 1983): 133-39.

LUCE, G. H.

"Climb Cloud, and Pencil all the Blue"

Richards, *Practical Criticism*, 131-44 and passim.

LUHAN, MABEL

Edge of Taos Desert

Norwood and Mark, *The Desert Is No Lady*, passim.

Winter in Taos

Norwood and Mark, *The Desert Is No Lady*, passim.

LUNCH, LYDIA

"Adulterers Anonymous"

David E. James, "Poetry/Punk/Production: Some Recent Writing in L.A.," *MinnR*, n.s. 23 (Fall 1984): 127-48.

MacDONALD, CYNTHIA

"Departure"

R. L. Widmann, "The Poetry of Cynthia MacDonald," *CP* 7 (Spring 1974): 24-26.

"Inventory"

R. L. Widman, "The Poetry of Cynthia MacDonald," *CP* 7 (Spring 1974): 21-24.

"Objets d'Art"

R. L. Widman, "The Poetry of Cynthia MacDonald," *CP* 7 (Spring 1974): 20-21.

"(W)holes"

Dave Smith, "Castles, Elephants, Buddhas: Some Recent American Poetry," *APR* 10 (May/June 1981): 37-42.

McINERNEY, BRIAN

"The World"

Bernstein, *Content's Dream: Essays 1975-1984*, 68-70.

McKAY, CLAUDE

[Interview]

Isaac I. Elimimian, "Theme and Technique in Claude McKay's Poetry," *CLAJ* 25 (Dec. 1981): 203-11.

"If We Must Die"

Robert A. Lee, "On Claude McKay's 'If We Must Die,'" *CLAJ* 18 (Dec. 1974): 216-21.

MacLEISH, ARCHIBALD

"L'An Trentiesme de Mon Eage"

Richard E. Amacher, *Expl* 6 (Apr. 1948): 42. Reprinted in *The Explicator Cyclopedia* 1:213-14.

". . . & Forty-Second Street"

Ivar L. Myhr, *Expl* 3 (Apr. 1945): 47. Reprinted in *The Explicator Cyclopedia* 1:211.

"Ars Poetica"

David J. Kessler, "Resolution in 'Ars Poetica,'" *CP* 10 (Spring 1977): 73.

Sanders, *The Discovery of Poetry*, 49-52.

Victor P. Staudt, "'Ars Poetica' and the Teacher," *CE* 19 (Oct. 1957): 28-29.

Stauffer, *The Nature of Poetry*, 121-25. Reprinted in Engle and Carrier, *Reading Modern Poetry*, 99-101.

Harry R. Sullivan, "MacLeish's 'Ars Poetica,'" *EJ* 56 (Dec. 1967): 1280-83.

"'Dover Beach'--A Note to That Poem"

Kreuzer, *Elements of Poetry*, 183-89, 191-92.

James Zigerell, *Expl* 17 (Mar. 1959): 38. Reprinted in *The Explicator Cyclopedia* 1:210-11.

"Dr. Sigmund Freud Discovers the Sea Shell"

Perrine and Reid, *100 American Poems*, 161-62.

"Einstein"

Hoffman, *The Twenties*, 287-88.

Waggoner, *The Heel of Elohim*, 143-46.

"Eleven"

Deutsch, *Poetry in Our Time*, 147.

"The End of the World"

Perrine and Reid, *100 American Poems*, 163.

"Epistle to Be Left in the Earth"

Waggoner, *The Heel of Elohim*, 146-48.

"The Hamlet of A. MacLeish"

Waggoner, *The Heel of Elohim*, 141-43.

"Hypocrite Auteur"

Nicholas Joost, *Expl* 11 (May 1953): 47. Reprinted in *The Explicator Cyclopedia* 1:211-13.

"Lines for an Interment"

Kreuzer, *Elements of Poetry*, 141-43.

"Memorial Rain"

Brooks, *Modern Poetry and the Tradition*, 122-24.

J. Walsh, *American War Literature, 1914 to Vietnam* (New York: St. Martin's, 1982), passim.

"Men"

Brooks, *Modern Poetry and the Tradition*, 117-18.

"'Not Marble nor the Gilded Monuments'"

Beaty and Matchett, *Poetry: From Statement to Meaning*, 187-92.

"Pony Rock"

Gerald Sanders, *Expl* 2 (Oct. 1943): 8. Reprinted in *The Explicator Cyclopedia* 1:214.

"Voyage to the Moon"

Ronald Weber, "The View from Space: Notes on Space Exploration and Recent Writing," *GaR* 33 (Summer 1979): 280-96.

"You, Andrew Marvell"

Brooks, *Modern Poetry and the Tradition*, 122.

Brown and Olmstead, *Language and Literature*, 194-97.

Guy A. Cardwell, *Readings from the Americas* (New York: Ronald Press Co., 1947), 790-91.

Drew, *Poetry: A Modern Guide*, 104-5.

Louis L. Martz, "The Teachings of Poetry," in Gordon and Noyes, *Essays on the Teaching of English*, 249-52.

Perrine, *Sound and Sense*, 68-69. Reprinted in 2d ed., 74-75.

Perrine and Reid, *100 American Poems*, 159-60.

MAC LOW, JACKSON

[Interview]

Barry Alpert, *Vort* 3 (1975): 3-33.

Asymmetries

McCaffery, *North of Intention*, 222-26.

Stanzas for Iris Lezak

Bernstein, *Content's Dream: 1975-1984*, 252-58.

Robert Vas Dias, "Taking Chances with Meaning," *Vort* 3 (1975): 78-83.

Steve McCaffrey, "A Letter Regarding Jackson Mac Low," *Vort* 3 (1975): 59-63.

Eric Mottram, "Composition of the Magus: The Art of Jackson Mac Low," *Vort* 3 (1975): 3-33.

MACPHERSON, JAY

"Anagogic Man"

James Reaney, "The Third Eye," *CanL* 3 (1960). Reprinted in Woodcock, *A Choice of Critics*, 156-68.

The Boatman

James Reaney, "The Third Eye," *CanL* 3 (1960). Reprinted in Woodcock, *A Choice of Critics*, 156-68.

"Eve in Reflection"

D. G. Jones, "The Sleeping Giant," *CanL* 26 (1965). Reprinted in Woodcock, *A Choice of Critics*, 3-24.

"The Fisherman"

James Reaney, "The Third Eye," *CanL* 3 (1960). Reprinted in Woodcock, *A Choice of Critics*, 156-68.

MAGEE, J. G.

"High Flight"

Stageberg and Anderson, *Poetry as Experience*, 4.

MALLALIEU, H. B.

"Lines from Europe"

J. F. Nims, *Poetry: A Critical Supplement*, Apr. 1947, 14-16.

MARKHAM

"The Man with the Hoe"

Lynn H. Harris, *Expl* 3 (Mar. 1945): 41. Reprinted in *The Explicator Cyclopedia* 1:215.

MARLATT, DAPHNE

Steveston

Douglas Barbour, "The Phenomenological I: Daphne Marlatt's *Steveston*," in *Figures in a Ground*, ed. Frank Bessai and R. Jackel (Saskatoon: Western Producer Prairie Books, 1978), 178-79.

Chris Hall, "Two Poems of Place: Williams' *Paterson* and Marlatt's *Steveston*," *CRevAS* 15 (Summer 1984): 141-57.

D. G. Jones, "Canadian Poetry: Roots & New Directions," *Credences*, n.s. 2 (Fall/Winter 1983): 254-75.

MELTZER, DAVID

"Abulafia"

Gitenstein, *Apocalyptic Messianism and Contemporary Jewish-American Poetry*, 44-46, 106-8.

17 insects can die in your heart

David E. James, "Poetry/Punk/Production: Some Recent Writing in L.A.," *MinnR*, n.s. 23 (Fall 1984): 127-48.

MEREDITH, WILLIAM

"Battlewagon"

Dudley Fitts, "Meredith's Second Volume," *Poetry* 73 (Nov. 1948): 114-15.

Hazard the Painter

N. Herrington, "'The Language of the Tribe': William Meredith's Poetry," *SWR* (Winter 1982): 1-17.

"A Korean Woman Seated by a Wall"

N. Herrington, "'The Language of the Tribe': William Meredith's Poetry," *SWR* (Winter 1982): 1-17.

"Stages"

N. Herrington, "The Language of the Tribe': William Meredith's Poetry," *SWR* (Winter 1982): 1-17.

"Walter Jenk's Bath"

N. Herrington, "'The Language of the Tribe': William Meredith's Poetry," *SWR* (Winter 1982): 1-17.

"Wedding Song"

Duddley Fitts, "Meredith's Second Volume," *Poetry* 73 (Nov. 1948): 111-13.

"The Wreck of the Thresher"

N. Herrington, "'The Language of the Tribe': William Meredith's Poetry," *SWR* (Winter 1982): 1-17.

Rotella, *Three Contemporary Poets of New England*, 6-63.

MERRILL, JAMES

"After the Fire"

Moffett, *James Merrill*, passim.

The Book of Ephraim

D. Kalstone, *Five Temperaments* (New York: Oxford University Press, 1977), passim.

J. D. McClatchy, "Lost Paradises," *Parnassus* 5 (Fall/Winter 1976): 308-14.

The Changing Light at Sandover

Bruce Bawer, "A Summoning of Spirits: James Merrill and Sandover," *New Criterion* 2 (June 1984): 35-42.

D. L. McDonald, "Merrill and Freud: The Psychopathology of Eternal Life," *Mosaic* 19 (Fall 1986): 159-72.

James E. Miller, "Whitman's Leaves and The American 'Lyric-Epic,'" in Fraistat, *Poems in Their Place*, 289-307.

Moffett, *James Merrill*, passim.

Edmund White, "The Inverted Type: Homosexuality as a Theme in James Merrill's Prophetic Books," in *Literary Visions of Homosexuality*, ed. Stuart Kellogg (New York: Haworth, 1983), 47-52.

"Days of 1935"

Moffett, *James Merrill*, passim.

"Days of 1964"

Moffett, *James Merrill*, passim.

"Days of 1971"

Moffett, *James Merrill*, passim.

Divine Comedies, Part One

Moffett, *James Merrill*, passim.

"Dreams about Clothes"

Stephen Yenser, "Feux d'Artifice," *Poetry* 122 (June 1973): 164-65.

"18 West 11th Street"

Richard Saez, "James Merrill's Oedipal Fire," *Parnassus* 3 (Fall/Winter 1974): 174-82.

"From the Cupola"

Moffett, *James Merrill*, passim.

"In Nine Sleep Valley"

Richard Pevear, "Poetry Chronicle," *HudR* 26 (Spring 1973): 201-3.

Mirabel

Charles Berger, "Merrill and Pynchon: Our Apocalyptic Scribes," in Lehman and Berger, *James Merrill*, 282-97.

Charles Berger, "*Mirabel*: Conservative Epic," in Bloom, *James Merrill*, 181-88.

"Mirror"

Von Hallberg, *American Poetry and Culture, 1945-1980*, passim.

"Mornings in a New House"

Moffett, *James Merrill*, passim.

Scripts for the Pageant

Stephen Yenser, "The Name of God: *Scripts for the Pageant*," in Lehman and Berger, *James Merrill*, 246-81.

"The Summer People"

Moffett, *James Merrill*, passim.

"Syrinx"

Stephen Yenser, "Feux d'Artifice," *Poetry* 122 (June 1973): 166-67.

"The Thousand and Second Night"

Moffett, *James Merrill*, passim.

Von Hallberg, *American Poetry and Culture, 1945-1980*, passim.

MERTON, THOMAS

"St. Malachy"

Hayden Carruth, *Poetry: A Critical Supplement*, Feb. 1949, 10-13.

MERWIN, W. S.

[Interview]

David L. Elliott, "An Interview with W. S. Merwin," *ConL* 29 (Spring 1988): 1-25.

[Interview]

Ed Folsom and Cary Nelson, "'Fact Has Two Faces': An Interview with W. S. Merwin," *IowaR* 13 (Winter 1982): 30-66.

MERWIN, W.S.

"The Annunciation"

John Vogelsang, "Toward the Great Language: W. S. Merwin," *MPS* 3 (1972): 102-5.

"The Asians Dying"

Cary Nelson, "Whitman in Vietnam: Poetry and History in Contemporary America," *MR* 16 (Winter 1975): 55-71.

"Beginning"

Carole Kyle, "A Riddle for the New Year: Affirmation in W. S. Merwin," *MPS* 4 (Winter 1973): 302-3.

Cary Nelson, "The Resources of Failure: W. S. Merwin's Deconstructive Career," *Boundary* 5 (Winter 1977): 589-593.

The Carrier of Ladders

L. Folson, "Approaches and Removals: W. S. Merwin's Encounter with Whitman's America," *Shenandoah* 29 (Spring 1978): 57-73.

"December among the Vanished"

Cary Nelson, "The Resources of Failure: W. S. Merwin's Deconstructive Career," *Boundary* 5 (Winter 1977): 585-86.

"Evening with Loe Shore and Cliffs"

Kenneth Andersen, "The Poetry of W. S. Merwin," *TCL* 16 (Oct. 1970): 281-82.

"Folk Art"

Cary Nelson, "The Resources of Failure: W. S. Merwin's Deconstructive Career," *Boundary* 5 (Winter 1977): 594-95.

"For Now"

John Vogelsang, "Toward the Great Language: W. S. Merwin," *MPS* 3 (1972): 107-10.

"For the Anniversary of My Death"

Jacob Ramsey, "The Continuities of W. S. Merwin: 'What Has Escaped Us We Bring with Us,'" *MR* 14 (Summer 1973): 588-89.

"In a Clearing"

John Vogelsang, "Toward the Great Language: W. S. Merwin," *MPS* 3 (1972): 112-13.

"In the Time of the Blossoms"

John Vogelsang, "Toward the Great Language: W. S. Merwin," *MPS* 3 (1972): 113-14.

"Learning a Dead Language"

John Vogelsang, "Toward the Great Language: W. S. Merwin," *MPS* 3 (1972): 105-7.

"Lemuel's Blessing"

Carroll, *The Poem in Its Skin*, 142-52.

The Lice

L. Folsom, "Approaches and Removals: W. S. Merwin's Encounter with Whitman's America," *Shenandoah* 29 (Spring 1978): 57-73.

H. Lazer, "For a Coming Extinction: A Reading of W. S. Merwin's *The Lice*," *ELH* 49 (Spring 1982): 262-85.

MERWIN, W.S.

"Memory of Spring"

John Vogelsang, "Toward the Great Language: W. S. Merwin," *MPS* 3 (1972): 114.

Evan Watkins, *The Critical Act: Criticism and Community* (New Haven: Yale University Press, 1978), 224.

"Odysseus"

Cheri Colby Davis, "Merwin's Odysseus," *CP* 8 (Spring 1975): 25-27.

"The Port"

Cheri Colby Davis, "Time and Timelessness in the Poetry of W. S. Merwin," *MPS* 6 (Winter 1975): 229-31.

"The Prodigal Son"

John Vogelsang, "Toward the Great Language: W. S. Merwin," *MPS* 3 (1972): 99-105.

"Psalm: Our Fathers"

John Vogelsang, "Toward the Great Language: W. S. Merwin," *MPS* 3 (1972): 116-18.

"Signs"

John Vogelsang, "Toward the Great Language: W. S. Merwin," *MPS* 3 (1972): 115.

"Under Black Leaves"

Cherri Colby Davis, "Time and Timelessness in the Poetry of W. S. Merwin," *MPS* 6 (Winter 1975): 232-35.

"Whenever I Go There"

Pinsky, *The Situation of Poetry: Contemporary Poetry and Its Traditions*, 92-95.

"When You Go Away"

Jan B. Gordon, "The Dwelling of Disappearance: W. S. Merwin's *The Lice*," *MPS* 3 (1972): 129-30.

METCALFE, JAMES

"Pray in May"

Perrine, *The Art of Total Relevance*, 111-18.

MEYERS, THOMAS

[Interview]

John Browning, "Jonathan Williams and Thomas Meyers," in Leyland, *Gay Sunshine Interviews* 2:279-88.

MILLAY, EDNA ST. VINCENT

"Euclid Alone Has Looked on Beauty Bare"

Bradford A. Booth, *Expl* 6 (Oct. 1947): 5. Reprinted in *The Explicator Cyclopedia* 1:223.

Cooper and Holmes, *Preface to Poetry*, 46-53.

Arthur Dickson, *Expl* 3 (Dec. 1944): 23. Reprinted in *The Explicator Cyclopedia* 1:222-23.

Arthur Dickson, *Expl* 6 (May 1948): 49. Reprinted in *The Explicator Cyclopedia* 1:223-24.

Drew and Sweeney, *Directions in Modern Poetry*, 207-8. Reprinted in Douglas, Lamson, Smith, *The Critical Reader*, 110-11.

Carl A. Niemeyer and Robert M. Gay, *Expl* 1 (Nov. 1942): 16.

"God's World"

Sanders, *The Discovery of Poetry*, 132-38.

"Memorial to D. C.: Elegy"

Walter Gierasch, *Expl* 2 (May 1944): 23. Reprinted in *The Explicator Cyclopedia* 1:224.

"Oh, Oh, You Will Be Sorry for that Word"

Perrine and Reid, *100 American Poems*, 165-66.

"Oh, Sleep Forever in the Latmian Cave"

John Crowe Ransom, *The World's Body*, 83-86.

"On Hearing a Symphony of Beethoven"

Perrine and Reid, *100 American Poems*, 167-68.

"The Return"

John Crowe Ransom, "The Poet as Woman," *SoR* 2 (Spring 1937): 804-6.
Ransom, *The World's Body*, 107-10.

Sonnets

Debra Fried, "Andromeda Unbound: Gender and Genre in Millay's *Sonnets*," *TCL* 32 (1986): 1-22.

"What's This of Death, from You Who Never Will Die?"

William Elton, *Expl* 7 (Mar. 1949): 37. Reprinted in *The Explicator Cyclopedia* 1:224-25.

Richards, *Practical Criticism*, 62-79 and passim.

MOMADAY, N. SCOTT

[Interview]

Tom King, "Interview: N. Scott Momaday--Literature and the Native Writer," *MELUS* 10 (Winter 1983): 66-72.

"Angle of Geese"

Kenneth Fields, "More Than Language Means," *SoR* 6 (Jan. 1970): 197-200.

Lincoln, *Native American Renaissance*, 99.

"The Bear"

Kenneth Roemer, "Bear and Elk: The Nature(s) of Contemporary American Indian Poetry," in Allen, *Studies in American Indian Literature*, 178-91.

Winters, *Forms of Discovery*, 289-90.

"Before an Old Painting of the Crucifixion"

Winters, *Forms of Discovery*, 291-94.

"Buteo Regalis"

Winters, *Forms of Discovery*, 290-91.

"Crows in a Winter Composition"

Lincoln, *Native American Renaissance*, 100-101.

"Rainy Mountain Cemetery"

Kenneth Lincoln, "Native American Literatures: 'old like hills, like stars,'" in Baker, *Three American Literatures*, 114-24.

The Way to Rainy Mountain (poems in novel)

Kenneth Lincoln, "Native American Literatures: 'old like hills, like stars,'" in Baker, *Three American Literatures*, 114-24.

Lincoln, *Native American Renaissance*, 108-9.

MONTAGUE, JOHN

A Slow Dance

Mariani, *A Useable Past: Essays on Modern and Contemporary Poetry*, 203-13.

MONTOYA, JOSÉ

"Corrido"

José David Saldívar, "Towards a Chicano Poetics: The Making of the Chicano Subject, 1969-1982," *Confluencia* 1 (1986): 10-17.

"El Louie"

Tatum, *Chicano Literature*, 150-51.

"Los Vatos"

José David Saldívar, "Towards a Chicano Poetics: The Making of the Chicano Subject, 1969-1982," *Confluencia* 1 (1986): 10-17.

MOODY

"Ode in Time of Hesitation"

R. P. Blackmur, "Moody in Retrospect," *Poetry* 38 (Sept. 1931): 334-35.

MOORE, JULIA

"Ballad of John Robinson"

Bradley Hayden, "In Memoriam Humor: Julia Moore and the Western Michigan Poets," *EJ* 72 (Sept. 1983): 22-27.

"Hiram Helsel"

Bradley Hayden, "In Memoriam Humor: Julia Moore and the Western Michigan Poets," *EJ* 72 (Sept. 1983): 22-27.

MOORE, MARIANNE

All Que Quiere!

Kenner, *A Homemade World*, 91-118.

"Apparition of Splendor"

Sr. Mary Cecilia, "The Poetry of Marianne Moore," *Thought* 38 (Autumn 1963): 367.

Rebecca Price Parkin, "Certain Difficulties in Reading Marianne Moore: Exemplified in Her 'Apparition of Splendor,'" *PMLA* 81 (June 1966): 167-72.

Rebecca Price Parkin, "Some Characteristics of Marianne Moore's Humor," *CE* 27 (Feb. 1966): 406-7.

"Bird-Witted"

Lloyd Frankenberg, "The Imaginary Garden," *Quarterly Review of Literature* 4, no. 2 (1946): 210-12.

Frankenberg, *Pleasure Dome*, 137-41.

Kenner, *The Pound Era*, 87-89.

Sr. Mary Cecilia, "The Poetry of Marianne Moore," *Thought* 38 (Autumn 1963): 367-69.

"Black Earth"

Blackmur, *The Double Agent*, 150-54.

Charles Tomlinson, "Abundance, Not Too Much: The Poetry of Marianne Moore," *SR* 65 (Autumn 1957): 677-82.

"Camillia Sabina"

Rosenthal, *The Modern Poets*, 141-42.

"The Campertown Elm"

Patricia C. Wilis, " The Campertown Elm," *Marianne Moore Newsletter* 5 (Fall 1981): 8-10.

"A Carriage from Sweden"

Perrine and Reid, *100 American Poems*, 97-98.

Complete Poems

Grace Schulman, "On the Complete Poems of Marianne Moore," *American Poetry Review* 11 (July/Aug. 1982): 35-36.

"Critics and Connoisseurs"

Butterfield, *Modern American Poetry*, 110-25.

Perrine and Reid, *100 American Poets*, 99-100.

"Elephants"

Cleanth Brooks, "Miss Marianne Moore's Zoo," *Quarterly Review of Literature* 4, no. 2 (1946): 179-81.

Wallace Fowlie, "Under the Equanimity of Language," *Quarterly Review of Literature* 4, no. 2 (1946): 175-76.

"A Face"

Bernard F. Engle, *Expl* 34 (Dec. 1975): 29.

"The Fish" (1918 version)

Kenner, *A Homemade World*, 91-118.

"The Fish" (1930 version)

Kenner, *A Homemade World*, 91-118.

Vivienne Koch, "The Peaceable Kingdom of Marianne Moore," *Quarterly Review of Literature* 4, no. 2 (1946): 163-64. Reprinted in Stageberg and Anderson, *Poetry as Experience*, 499.

Sue Renich, *Expl* 21 (Sept. 1962): 7.

Sutton, *American Free Verse*, 111-13.

William A. Sylvester, *Expl* 7 (Feb. 1949): 30. Reprinted in *The Explicator Cyclopedia* 1:225.

Zabel, *Literary Opinion in America*, 433-34; rev. ed., 390-91.

"The Frigate Pelican"

Gray, *American Poetry*, 194-95.

"He 'Digesteth Harde Yron'"

Martin, *Marianne Moore . . . Subversive Modernist*, 76-81.

John Crowe Ransom, "On Being Modern with Distinction," *Quarterly Review of Literature* 4, no. 2 (1946): 140-41.

Wallace Stevens, "About One of Marianne Moore's Poems," *Quarterly Review of Literature* 4, no. 2 (1946): 143-47.

Stevens, *The Necessary Angel*, 93-103.

"The Hero"

Beach, *Obsessive Images*, 213-15.

Mildred E. Hartsock, "Marianne Moore: A Salvo of Barks," *BuR* 11 (Dec. 1962): 17-18.

"The Icosaphere"

Marie Borroff, *Expl* 16 (Jan. 1958): 21. Reprinted in *The Explicator Cyclopedia* 1:225-26.

"In Distrust of Merits"

Marcia Epstein Allentuck, *Expl* 10 (Apr. 1952): 42. Reprinted in *The Explicator Cyclopedia* 1:227-28.

Wallace Fowlie, "Under the Equanimity of Language," *Quarterly Review of Literature* 4, no. 2 (1946): 176-77.

Lloyd Frankenberg, "The Imaginary Garden," *Quarterly Review of Literature* 4, no. 2 (1946): 221-22.

Frankenberg, *Pleasure Dome*, 153-55.

Susan Schweik, "Writing War Poetry Like a Woman," *CritI* 13 (Spring 1987): 532-56.

"The Jerboa"

Cleanth Brooks, "Miss Marianne Moore's Zoo," *Quarterly Review of Literature* 4, no. 2 (1946): 182-83.

Lloyd Frankenberg, "The Imaginary Garden," *Quarterly Review of Literature* 4, no. 2 (1946): 202-3.

Frankenberg, *Pleasure Dome*, 132-33.

Nicholas Joost, "The Pertinence of the Notes to Marianne Moore's 'The Jerboa,'" *Delta Epsilon Sigma Bulletin* 7 (May 1962): 1-30.

Philip Legler, "Marianne Moore and the Idea of Freedom," *Poetry* 83 (Dec. 1953): 158-67.

"Light Is Speech"

Kenner, *A Homemade World*, 91-118.

"Marriage"

Mildred E. Hartsock, "Marianne Moore: A Salvo of Barks," *BuR* 11 (Dec. 1965): 14-37.

Vivienne Koch, "The Peaceable Kingdom of Marianne Moore," *Quarterly Review of Literature* 4, no. 2 (1946): 167.

"The Mind Is an Enchanting Thing"

Frankenberg, *Invitation to Poetry*, 389-90.

"The Monkeys"

Blackmur, *The Double Agent*, 166-67. Reprinted in Blackmur, *Language as Gesture*, 281.

Lisa Steinman, "Moore, Emerson and Kreymborg: The Use of Lists in 'The Monkeys,'" *Marianne Moore Newsletter* 4 (1980): 7-10.

"Nevertheless"

Lloyd Frankenberg, "The Imaginary Garden," *Quarterly Review of Literature* 4, no. 2 (1946): 195-96.

Frankenberg, *Pleasure Dome*, 125.

"No Swan So Fine"

Brooks, Lewis, and Warren, *American Literature*, 2177-78.

Gray, *American Poetry*, 193-94.

"Novices"

Vivienne Koch, "The Peaceable Kingdom of Marianne Moore," *Quarterly Review of Literature* 4, no. 2 (1946): 157.

"An Octopus"

Mildred E. Hartsock, "Marianne Moore: A Salvo of Barks," *BuR* 11 (Dec. 1962): 31-32.

Kenner, *A Homemade World*, 91-118.

"O to Be a Dragon"

Rebecca Price Parkin, "Some Characteristics of Marianne Moore's Humor," *CE* 27 (Feb. 1966): 406.

"The Pangolin"

Martin, *Marianne Moore . . . The Subversive Modernist*, 16-19.

Rebecca Price Parkin, "Some Characteristics of Marianne Moore's Humor," *CE* 27 (Feb. 1966): 403-6.

Sutton, *American Free Verse*, 106-7.

Patricia C. Willis, "Iron Sculpture Similes in 'The Pangolin,'" *Marianne Moore Newsletter* 4 (1980): 2-5.

"The Past Is the Present"

Blackmur, *The Double Agent*, 142-49.

"The Plumet Basilisk"

Bonnie Costello, "Marianne Moore's Debt and Tribute to Wallace Stevens," *CP* 15 (1982): 27-33.

"Poetry"

Lloyd Frankenberg, "The Imaginary Garden," *Quarterly Review of Literature* 4, no. 2 (1946): 207-9.

Frankenberg, *Pleasure Dome*, 137-41.

Gray, *American Poetry*, 195-96.

Kenner, *A Homemade World*, 91-118.

"Roses Only"

Brower, *The Fields of Light*, 48-50.

Kenner, *A Homemade World*, 91-118.

Martin, *Marianne Moore . . . Subversive Modernist*, 72-79.

"See in the Midst of Fair Leaves"

Dan G. Hoffman, *Expl* 10 (Mar. 1952): 34. Reprinted in Locke, Gibson, and Arms, *Readings for Liberal Education*, 3d ed., 203-4; 4th ed., 204-5; 5th ed., 187-88; in *The Explicator Cyclopedia* 1:228-29.

"Silence"

Blackmur, *The Double Agent*, 154-60. Reprinted in Blackmur, *Language as Gesture*, 271-76.

Barbara Charlesworth Gelpi, "From Colonial to Revolutionary: The Modern American Woman Poet," *SJS* 2 (Nov. 1976): 41-42.

"Snakes, Mongooses, Snake-Charmer and the Like"

Rosenthal and Smith, *Exploring Poetry*, 250-51.

"Spenser's Ireland"

Maurice J. O'Sullivan, Jr., "Native Genius for Disunion: Marianne Moore's 'Spenser's Ireland,'" *CP* 7 (Fall 1974): 42-47.

Patricia C. Willis, "The Notes to 'Spenser's Ireland,'" *Marianne Moore Newsletter* 4 (1980): 2-5.

"The Steeple-Jack"

Louise Bogan, "Reading Contemporary Poetry," *CE* 14 (Feb. 1953): 257-60.

Denis Donoghue, "Technique in Hopkins," *Studies* 44 (Winter 1955): 452.

Gray, *American Poetry*, 192-93.

Martin, *Marianne Moore . . . Subversive Modernist*, 14-16.

Sutton, *American Free Verse*, 110-11.

Charles Tomlinson, "Abundance, Not Too Much: The Poetry of Marianne Moore," *SR* 65 (Autumn 1957): 677-82.

"Tell Me, Tell Me"

Rebecca Price Parkin, "Some Characteristics of Marianne Moore's Humor," *CE* 27 (Feb. 1966): 407.

Rebecca Price Parkin, "Some Characteristics of Marianne Moore's Humor," *CE* 27 (Feb. 1966): 407.

"To a Snail"

Francis W. Warlow, *Expl* 26 (Feb. 1968): 51.

"Tom Fool at Jamaica"

Marie Borroff, "'Tom Fool at Jamaica' by Marianne Moore: Meaning and Structure," *CE* 17 (May 1956): 466-69.

Elder Olson, "The Poetry of Marianne Moore," *ChiR* 11 (Spring 1957): 103-4.

"Tract"

Kenner, *A Homemade World*, 91-118.

"What Are Years"

Gray, *American Poetry*, 198-99.

O'Connor, *Sense and Sensibility in Modern Poetry*, 229-30 (quoting Lloyd Frankenberg, *Saturday Review of Literature* 39 [23 Mar. 1946]).

Perrine and Reid, *100 American Poems*, 101-2.

"The Wood-Weasel"

Cleanth Brooks, "Miss Marianne Moore's Zoo," *Quarterly Review of Literature* 4, no. 2 (1946): 182.

MOORE, MERRILL

"Granny Weeks"

Dudley Fitts, "The Sonnets of Merrill Moore," *SR* 47 (Apr./June 1939): 278-79.

"The Gun Barrel Looked at Him with Love in Its Single Eyehole"

Dudley Fitts, "The Sonnets of Merrill Moore," *SR* 47 (Apr./June 1939): 274-75.

"The Sound of Time Hangs Heavy in My Ears"

Dudley Fitts, "The Sonnets of Merrill Moore," *SR* 47 (Apr./June 1939): 291-92.

MOORE, ROSALIE

"The Grasshopper Man"

J. F. Nims and Rosalie Moore, *Poetry: A Critical Supplement*, May 1949, 1-11.

MORGAN, ROBIN

"The Network of the Imaginary Mother"

Cynthia A. Davis, "Weaving Poetry: Robin Morgan's 'The Network of the Imaginary Mother,'" *CP* 11 (Fall 1978): 5-10.

MOSES, W. R.

[Interview]

Jonathan Holden, "An Interview with W. R. Moses," *KanQ* 14 (Spring 1982): 7-18.

Identities

Warren French, "James Purdy, Will Moses: Against the Wilderness," *KanQ* 14 (Spring 1982): 81-92.

Anne Royall Newman, "Extended Vision: The Poetry of W. R. Moses," *KanQ* 14 (Spring 1982): 19-34.

Not Native

Anne Royall Newman, "Extended Vision: The Poetry of W. R. Moses," *KanQ* 14 (Spring 1982): 19-34.

Passage

Anne Royall Newman, "Extended Vision: The Poetry of W. R. Moses," *KanQ* 14 (Spring 1982): 19-34.

MOSS, HOWARD

"The City Lion"

J. F. Nims, *Poetry: A Critical Supplement*, Nov. 1948, 9.

"Notes from the Castle"

Dave Smith, "Castles, Elephants, Buddhas: Some Recent American Poetry," *APR* 10 (May/June 1981): 37-42.

NASH, OGDEN

"The Chipmunk"

Wallace, *God Be with the Clown*, passim.

"Literary Reflection"

Warren Beck, "Boundaries of Poetry," *CE* 4 (Mar. 1943): 347.

"The Turtle"

Perrine, *Sound and Sense*, 135-36. Reprinted 2d ed., 148-49.

NEAL, LAWRENCE P.

[Interview]

Charles H. Rowell, "An Interview with Larry Neal," *Callaloo* 8 (Winter 1985): 11-35.

The Glorious Monster in the Bell of the Horn (verse drama)

Paul Carter Harrison, "Larry Neal: The Genesis of Vision," *Callaloo* 8 (Winter 1985): 170-94.

NEMEROV, HOWARD

"Ars Poetica"

Anita Schaefer, "Nemerov's *Mot Juste* and the Fashionable Poetic," *PAPA* 8 (Fall 1982): 68-76.

"Brainstorm"

Peggy Fitzgibbon, *Expl* 42 (Spring 1984): 58.

Ross Labrie, *Howard Nemerov*, passim.

Ronald J. Palumbo, "Nemerov's 'Brainstorm,'" *Expl* 39 (Spring 1981): 43-44.

"Departure of Ships"

Anita Schaefer, "Nemerov's *Mot Juste* and the Fashionable Poetic," *PAPA* 8 (Fall 1982): 68-76.

"On His Own Terms"

Tom Johnson, "'On His Own Terms,'" *SoR* 23 (Jan. 1987): 25 and passim.

"Painting a Mountain Stream"

Raymond Smith, "Nemerov and Nature: 'The Stillness in Moving Things,'" *SoR* 10 (Jan. 1974): 155-58.

"Runes"

Raymond Smith, "Nemerov and Nature: 'The Stillness in Moving Things,'" *SoR* 10 (Jan. 1974): 163-68.

"The Sanctuary"

Raymond Smith, "Nemerov and Nature: 'The Stillness in Moving Things,'" *SoR* 10 (Jan. 1974): 159-60.

"Santa Claus"

Perrine and Reid, *100 American Poems*, 252-53.

"The View"

Raymond Smith, "Nemerov and Nature: 'The Stillness in Moving Things,'" *SoR* 10 (Jan. 1974): 161-63.

NICHOL, bp

The Martyrology

McCaffery, *North of Intention*, 58-76.

Zyal

McCaffery, *North of Intention*, 30-31.

NIEDECKER, LORINE

"Lake Superior"

Donald Davie, "Lyric Minimum & Epic Scope: Lorine Niedecker," *Sagetrieb* 1 (Fall 1982): 268-76.

Paean to Place

Robert Bertholf, "Lorine Niedecker: A Portrait of a Poet," *Parnassus* 12 (1985): 227-35.

Wintergreen Ridge

Robert Bertholf, "Lorine Niedecker: A Portrait of a Poet," *Parnassus* 12 (1985): 227-35.

NIMS, JOHN FREDERICK

"Love Poem"

Perrine and Reid, *100 American Poems*, 234-35.

"The Magical View of Nature"

William Elton, *Poetry: A Critical Supplement*, Oct. 1949, 10-12.

"Penny Arcade"

Robert Shelley, "A Palmtree of Steel," *Western Review* 15 (Winter 1951): 141-42.

"Winter in the Park"

Robert Shelley, "A Palmtree of Steel," *Western Review* 15 (Winter 1951): 140.

NOLL, BINK

"Quaker Hero, Burning"

Harry Campbell, *Expl* 29 (May 1971): 75.

NORTHRUP, HARRY E.

"Enough the Great Running Chapel"

David E. James, "Poetry/Punk/Production: Some Recent Writing in L.A.," *MinnR*, n.s. 23 (Fall 1984): 127-48.

NORWOOD, ROBERT

Bill Boram

Alex Kizuk, "Religion, Place, & Self in Early Twentieth-Century Canada," *CanL* 115 (Winter 1987): 66-77.

His Lady of the Sonnets

Alex Kizuk, "Religion, Place, & Self in Early Twentieth-Century Canada," *CanL* 115 (Winter 1987): 66-77.

Issa

Alex Kizuk, "Religion, Place, & Self in Early Twentieth-Century Canada," *CanL* 115 (Winter 1987): 66-77.

OANDASAN, WILLIAM

A Branch of California Redwood

Kenneth Lincoln, "Native American Literatures: 'old like hills, like stars,'" in Baker, *Three American Literatures*, 133-37.

Lincoln, *Native American Renaissance*, passim.

"Round Valley Songs"

Kenneth Lincoln, "Native American Literatures: 'old like hills, like stars,'" in Baker, *Three American Literatures*, 133-37.

O'DONNELL, GEORGE MARION

"Return"

John Crowe Ransom, "The Making of a Modern," *SoR* 1, n.s. (Spring 1963): 869-70.

O'HARA, FRANK

"All That Gas"

Marjorie G. Perloff, "The Poetry of John Ashbery and Frank O'Hara," *YES* 8 (1978): 171-96.

"Biotherm"

Blasing, *American Poetry: The Rhetoric of Its Forms*, 158-69.

Mutlu Konuk Blasing, "Frank O'Hara's Poetics of Speech: The Example of 'Biotherm,'" *ConL* 23 (1982): 52-64.

"The Day Lady Died"

Charles Altieri, "The Significance of Frank O'Hara," *IowaR* 4 (Winter 1973): 102-4.

Carroll, *The Poem in Its Skin*, 157-64.

"Digression on *Number 1, 1948*"

Frank O'Hara, *Jackson Pollock* (New York: George Braziller, 1959), 15, 21-22.

Alice C. Parker, *Art and Homosexuality in Frank O'Hara's Poetry* (Ann Arbor: University Microfilms International, 1984, 39-41. [Ph.D. diss., University of Rhode Island, 1983.])

"Early on Sunday"

Marjorie G. Perloff, *Frank O'Hara: A Poet among Painters* (New York: George Braziller, 1977), passim.

Marjorie G. Perloff, "New Thresholds, Old Anatomies: Contemporary Poetry and the Limits of Exegesis," *IowaR* 5 (Winter 1974): 98-99.

"Easter"

Marjorie G. Perloff, "The Poetry of John Ashbery and Frank O'Hara," *YES* 8 (1978): 171-96.

"Essay on Style"

Blasing, *American Poetry: The Rhetoric of Its Forms*, 161.

Marjorie G. Perloff, "New Thresholds, Old Anatomies: Contemporary Poetry and the Limits of Exegesis," *IowaR* 5 (Winter 1974): 91-95.

"Having a Coke with You"

Parker, *Frank O'Hara*, 70-75.

"Homosexuality"

Parker, *Frank O'Hara*, 98-112.

"In Memory of My Feelings"

Mutlu Konuk Blasing, "Frank O'Hara's Poetics of Speech: The Example of 'Biotherm,'" *ConL* 23 (1982): 52-64.

"Mary Desti's Ass"

Parker, *Frank O'Hara*, 119-29.

"Music"

Cook, *Figural Choice in Poetry and Art*, passim.

Marjorie G. Perloff, "Frank O'Hara and the Aesthetics of Attention," *Boundary* 4 (Spring 1976): 780-85.

"Ode to Michael Goldberg"

Marjorie G. Perloff, "'Alterable Noons': The 'poems elastiques' of Blaise Cendrars and Frank O'Hara," *YES* 15 (1985): 160-78.

"Ode to Willem de Kooning"

Parker, *Frank O'Hara*, 55-63.

"On Seeing Larry Rivers' *Washington Crossing the Delaware*

M. Davidson, "Ekphrasis and the Postmodern Painter Poem," *JAAC* 42 (Fall 1983): passim.

"A Pleasant Thought from Whitehead"

Marjorie G. Perloff, "The Poetry of John Ashbery and Frank O'Hara," *YES* 8 (1978): 171-96.

"Song" (*Collected Poems*, 327)

Parker, *Frank O'Hara*, 88-90.

"A Step Away from Them"

Merle Brown, "Poetic Listening," *NLH* 10 (Autumn 1978): 125-39.

Marjorie G. Perloff, "Poetry Chronicle: 1970-71," *ConL* 14 (Winter 1973): 99-103.

"Why I Am Not a Painter"

Ted Berrigan, "The Business of Writing Poetry," in Waldman and Webb, *Talking Poetics from Naropa Institute* 1:47-48.

OLSON, CHARLES

"Blues Skies Motel"

Cook, *Figural Choice in Poetry and Art*, passim.

"In Cold Hell, in Thicket"

Alan Golding, "Charles Olson's Metrical Thicket: Towards a Theory of Freeverse Prosody," *Lang&S* 14 (Winter 1981): 64-78.

Jed Rasula, "The Compost Library," *Sagetrieb* 1 (Fall 1982): 190-219.

"The Death of Europe (A Funeral Poem for Rainer M. Gerhardt)"

Phillip E. Smith II, "Descent into Polis: Charles Olson's Search for Community," *MPS* 8 (Spring 1977): 17-20.

"The K"

Gerald Burns, "In Medias (Olson's)'K,'" *Sagetrieb* 4 (Spring 1985): 110-13.

"The Kingfishers"

Guy Davenport, "Scholia and Conjectures for Olson's 'The Kingfishers,'" *Boundary* 2 (Fall 1973/Winter 1974): 250-62.

G. Hutchinson, "The Pleistocene in the Projective: Some of Olson's Origins," *AL* 54 (Mar. 1982): 81-86.

Thomas F. Merrill, "'The Kingfishers': Charles Olson's 'Marvelous Maneuver,'" *ConL* 17 (Autumn 1976): 506-28.

William V. Spanos, "Charles Olson and Negative Capability: A Phenomenological Interpretation," *ConL* 21 (1980): 38-80.

Letters of Origin

Graham Clarke, "The Poet as Archaelogist: Charles Olson's *Letters of Origin*," in *Modern American Poetry*, ed. R. W. Butterfield (London and Totowa, N.J.: Vision and Barnes & Noble, 1984), 158-72.

"Letter 6"

William V. Spanos, "Charles Olson and Negative Capability: A Phenomenological Interpretation," *ConL* 21 (1980): 38-80.

"Letter 23"

William V. Spanos, "Charles Olson and Negative Capability: A Phenomenological Interpretation," *ConL* 21 (1980): 38-80.

The Maximus Poems

Dikbakar Barua, "One and Many: The Paradox of 'Methodology' in Charles Olson's *Maximus*," *MSE* 9 (1983): 1-21.

Bernstein, *Content's Dream: Essays 1975-1984*, 321-39.

George Butterick, *A Guide to the Maximus Poems of Charles Olson* (Berkeley: University of California Press, 1978), passim.

Don Byrd, *Charles Olson's Maximus* (Urbana: University of Illinois Press, 1980), passim.

Don Byrd, "For Complete Concentration: A Review of Charles Olson, *The Maximus Poems*, vol. III," *Credences* 1 (1977): 101-14.

Paul Christensen, *Charles Olson: Call Him Ishmael* (Austin: University of Texas Press, 1979), passim.

Robert Duncan, "Notes on Poetics Regarding Olson's *Maximus*," in Allen and Tallman, *The Poetics of the New American Poetry*, passim.

David Calvin Heckel, "Literacy, Consciousness, and the Transformation of the Epic into Modernity," *DAI* 45, no. 6 (Dec. 1984): 1741A.

Robert Hogg, "Okeanos Rages," *Sagetrieb* 3 (Spring 1984): 89-104.

Mark Karlins, "The Primacy of Source: The Derivative Poetics of Charles Olson's *The Maximus Poems* (Vol. 1)," *Sagetrieb* 4 (Spring 1985): 33-60.

Kenner, *A Homemade World*, 177-83.

William McPherson, untitled review, *Credences*, n.s. 2 (Summer 1982): 131-139.

Thomas F. Merrill, *The Poetry of Charles Olson: A Primer* (Newark and London: University of Delaware Press and Associated University Presses, 1982), passim.

Sherman Paul, *Olson's Push: Origin, Black Mountain, and Recent American Poetry* (Baton Rouge: Louisiana State University Press, 1978), passim.

Jed Rasula, "The Compost Library," *Sagetrieb* 1 (Fall 1982): 190-219.

Jed Rasula, "Exfoliating Cosmos," *Sagetrieb* 2 (Spring 1983): 35-71.

Rosemarie Waldrop, "Charles Olson: Process and Relationship," *TCL* 23 (December 1977): 467-86.

Barrett Watten, "Olson in Language: Part II," in *Writing/Talks*, ed. Bob Perelman (Carbondale: Southern Illinois University Press, 1985), 157-65.

"Maximus, at the Harbor"

Robert Hogg, "Okeanos Rages," *Sagetrieb* 3 (Spring 1984): 89-104.

"Maximus, To Himself"

Garrett Kaoru Hongo, "Sea and Scholarship: Confessional Narrative in Charles Olson's 'Maximus, to Himself,'" *NER* 8 (Autumn 1985): 118-29.

"The Moon Is the Number 18"

Richard G. Ingher, "Number, Image, Sortilege: A Short Analysis of 'The Moon is the Number 18,'" *Boundary* 2 (Fall 1973-Winter 1974): 323-32.

"On First Looking through Juan de la Cosa's Eyes"

William V. Spanos, "Charles Olson and Negative Capability: A Phenomenological Interpretation," *ConL* 21 (1980): 38-80.

"Place; & Names"

Robert Creeley, "An Image of Man . . . Working Notes on Charles Olson's Concept of Person," *IowaR* 11 (Fall 1980): 29-43.

"The Praises"

Maxine Apsel, "The Praises," *Boundary* (Fall 1973/Winter 1974): 263-68.

"A Round & A Cannon"

Sherman Paul, "Birds, Landscapes, Place, Cosmicity," *IowaR* 11 (Fall 1980): 45-61.

"Songs of Maximus"

William V. Spanos, "Charles Olson and Negative Capability: A Phenomenological Interpretation," *ConL* 21 (1980): 38-80.

"Stevens Song"

Cook, *Figural Choice in Poetry and Art*, passim.

"Tyranian Business"

Michael Davidson, "'From the Latin Speculum': The Modern Poet as Philologist," *ConL* 28 (Summer 1987): 187-205.

"Variations Done for Gerald Van de Wiele"

Charles Altieri, "Olson's Poetics and the Tradition," *Boundary* (Fall 1973/Winter 1974): 183-88.

ONDAATJE, MICHAEL

The Collected Works of Billy the Kid:
Lefthanded Poems

Naomi Jacobs, "Michael Ondaatje and the New Fiction Biographies," *SCL* 11 (1986): 2-18.

D. G. Jones, "Canadian Poetry: Roots & New Directions," *Credences*, n.s. 2 (Fall/Winter 1983): 254-75.

T. D. MacLulich, "Ondaatje's Mechanical Boy: Portait of the Artist as A Photographer," *Mosaic* 14 (Spring 1981): 107-19.

Judith Owen, "I Send You a Picture: Ondaatje's Portrait of Billy the Kid," *SCL* 8 (1983): 117-39.

Coming through Slaughter

B. Maxwell, "Surrealistic Aspects of Michael Ondaatje's *Coming Through Slaughter*," *Mosaic* 18 (Summer 1985): 101-14.

"Henri Rousseau and Friends"

George Johnston, "Diction in Poetry," *CanL* 97 (Summer 1983): 39-44.

"Peter"

Gilliam Harding-Russell, "A Note on Ondaatje's 'Peter': A Creative Myth," *CanPo* 112 (Spring 1987): 205-11.

OPPEN, GEORGE

[Interview]

David McAleavey, "Oppen on Oppen: Extracts from Interviews," *Sagetrieb* 5 (Spring 1986): 59-94.

"Blood from the Stone"

Norman M. Finklestein, "Political Commitment and Poetic Sub- jectification: George Oppen's Test of Truth," *ConL* 22 (Winter 1981): 24-41.

Discrete Series

Alan Golding, "Politics and Style in Oppen's *Discrete Series*," *Ironwood* 13 (Fall 1985): 62-68.

Jeremy Hooker, "Seeing the World: The Poetry of George Oppen," in Freeman, *Not Comforts/But Vision*, 26-41.

Kenner, *A Homemade World*, 158-93.

"Of Being Numerous"

Jeremy Hooker, "The Boundaries of Our Distance: On 'Of Being Numerous,'" *Ironwood* 13 (Fall 1985): 62-68.

"Proletarian Portrait"

Norman M. Finklestein, "Political Commitment and Poetic Sub- jectification: George Oppen's Test of Truth," *ConL* 22 (Winter 1981): 24-41.

"Psalm"

Kenner, *A Homemade World*, 158-93.

"Red Hook"

Cid Corman, "A Poem by George," *Sagetrieb* 5 (Winter 1986): 147-49.

"Return"

Sylvester Pollet, "Oppen's 'Return,'" *Sagetrieb* 2 (Fall 1983): 123-27.

"The sea and a crescent strip of beach"
(from *Seascape: Needle's Eye*)

Kenner, *A Homemade World*, 158-93.

"Song, the Winds of Downhill"

Kenner, *A Homemade World*, 158-93.

ORTIZ, SIMON

[Interview]

Bruchac, "The Story Never Ends: An Interview with Simon Ortiz," *Survival This Way*, 211-29.

Going for the Rain

W. Gingerich, "The Old Voice of Acoma: Simon Ortiz's Mythic Indigenism," *SWR* 64 (Winter 1979): 18-30.

"The Killing of a State Cop"

Lawrence J. Evers, "The Killing of a New Mexican State Trooper: Ways of Telling an Historical Event," in *Critical Essays on American Literature*, ed. Andrew Wiget (Boston: G. K. Hall, 1985), 246-61.

"Woman Singing"

Nicholas O. Warner, "Images of Drinking in 'Woman Singing,' *Ceremony*, and *House Made of Dawn*," *MELUS* 11 (Winter 1984): 15-30.

PADGETT, RON

[Interview]

Ron Padgett, "Stoically Bedazzled," in Waldman and Webb, *Talking Poetics from Naropa Institute* 1:111-40.

PALMER, MICHAEL

Blake's Newton

McCaffery, *North of Intention*, 44-53.

The Circular Gates

McCaffery, *North of Intention*, 44-53.

"Prose 42"

McCaffery, *North of Intention*, 44-53.

"A Reasoned Reply to Gilbert Ryle"

McCaffery, *North of Intention*, 44-53.

"Series"

McCaffery, *North of Intention*, 44-53.

PARKER, DOROTHY

"The Actress"

Daniels, *The Art of Reading Poetry*, 353-54.

PETERS, ROBERT

[Interview]

Don Mark and Robert Peters, "Interview," in Leyland, *Gay Sunshine Interviews* 2:124-41.

PICKTHALL, MARJORIE

"Improvisation on the Flute"

Alex Kizuk, "The Case of the Forgotten Electra: Pickthall's Apostrophes and Feminine Poetics," *SCL* 12 (1987): 15-34.

"Inheritance"

Diana M. A. Relke, "Demeter's Daughter: Marjorie Pickthall and the Quest for Poetic Identity," *CanL* 113 (Winter 1987): 28-43.

"Love Unfound"

Diana M. A. Relke, "Demeter's Daughter: Marjorie Pickthall and the Quest for Poetic Identity," *CanL* 113 (Winter 1987): 28-43.

"Mons Angelorum"

Alex Kizuk, "The Case of the Forgotten Electra: Pickthall's Apostrophes and Feminine Poetics," *SCL* 12 (1987): 15-34.

"Persephone Returning to Hades"

Diana M. A. Relke, "Demeter's Daughter: Marjorie Pickthall and the Quest for Poetic Identity," *CanL* 113 (Winter 1987): 28-43.

"The Sleep-Seekers"

Diana M. A. Relke, "Demeter's Daughter: Marjorie Pickthall and the Quest for Poetic Identity," *CanL* 113 (Winter 1987): 28-43.

PINSKY, ROBERT

[Interview]

Adam J. Sorkin, "An Interview with Robert Pinsky," *ConL* 25 (1984): 1-14.

"An Explanation of America"

Charles Altieri, "Sensibility, Rhetoric, and Will: Some Tensions in Contemporary Poetry," *ConL* 23 (Fall 1982): 451-79.

Jay Parini, "Explaining America: The Poetry of Robert Pinsky," *ChiR* 33 (Summer 1981): 16-26.

Marshall Toman, "Pinsky's 'An Explanation of America,'" *Expl* 42 (Spring 1984): 62-64.

Von Hallberg, *American Poetry and Culture, 1945-1980*, passim.

"Countries and Explanations"

Jay Parini, "Explaining America: The Poetry of Robert Pinksy," *ChiR* 33 (Summer 1981): 16-26.

"First Early Mornings Together"

Jay Parini, "Explaining America: The Poetry of Robert Pinsky," *ChiR* 33 (Summer 1981): 16-26.

"Its Everlasting Possibility"

Jay Parini, "Explaining America: The Poetry of Robert Pinksy," *ChiR* 33 (Summer 1981): 16-26.

"Its Great Emptiness"

Jay Parini, "Explaining America: The Poetry of Robert Pinksy," *ChiR* 33 (Summer 1981): 16-26.

PLATH, SYLVIA

"The Applicant"

Margaret D. Uroff, "Sylvia Plath and Confessional Poetry: A Reconsideration," *IowaR* 8 (Winter 1977): 109-11.

Ariel

S. G. Axelrod, "The Mirror and the Shadow: Plath's Poetics of Self-Doubt," *ConL* 26 (Fall 1985): 286-301.

Barnard, *Sylvia Plath*, passim.

M. L. Broe, *Protean Poetic*, passim.

L. K. Buntzen, *Plath's Incarnations: Woman and the Creative Process* (Ann Arbor: University of Michigan Press, 1983), passim.

Carol Helmstetter Cantrell, "Self and Tradition in Recent Poetry," *MQ* 18 (1977): 343-60.

William V. Davis, "Sylvia Plath's *Ariel*" *MPS* 3 (1972): 176-84.

Greg Johnson, "A Passage to *Ariel*: Sylvia Plath and the Evolution of Self," *SWR* 65 (1980): 1-11.

Suzanne Juhasz, "'The Blood Jet': The Poetry of Sylvia Plath," in Brown and Olson, *Feminist Criticism*, 111-30.

Hugh Kenner, "Sincerity Kills," in Lane, *Sylvia Plath*, passim.

Judith Kroll, *Chapters in a Mythology: The Poetry of Sylvia Plath* (New York: Harper & Row, 1978), passim.

D. F. McKay, "Aspects of Energy in the Poetry of Dylan Thomas and Sylvia Plath," *CritQ* 16 (Spring 1974): 54-56.

Oberg, *Modern American Lyric*, 127-73.

Marjorie Perloff, "Angst and Animism in the Poetry of Sylvia Plath," *JML* 1 (1970): 66-67.

Linda Wagner, *American Modern: Essays in Fiction and Poetry*, 158-64.

Linda Wagner, "Plath's 'Ariel': 'Auspicious Gales,'" *CP* 10 (Fall 1977): 5-7.

"Arrival of the Bee Box"

M. L. Broe, "Recovering the Complex Self: Sylvia Plath's Beeline," *CentR* 24 (Winter 1980): 1-24.

Rose Kamel, "'A Self to Recover': Sylvia Plath's Bee Cycle Poems," *MPS* 4 (Winter 1973): 310-11.

Ries, *Wolf Masks: Violence in Contemporary Poetry*, 42-44.

"The Beekeeper's Daughter"

M. L. Broe, "Recovering the Complex Self: Sylvia Plath's Beeline," *CentR* 24 (Winter 1980): 1-24.

Draper, *Lyric Tragedy*, passim.

Rose Kamel, "'A Self to Recover': Sylvia Plath's Bee Cycle Poems," *MPS* 4 (Winter 1973): 308-10.

"The Bee Meeting"

M. L. Broe, "Recovering the Complex Self: Sylvia Plath's Beeline," *CentR* 24 (Winter 1980): 1-24.

Draper, *Lyric Tragedy*, passim.

Rose Kamel, "'A Self to Recover': Sylvia Plath's Bee Cycle Poems," *MPS* 4 (Winter 1973): 306-8.

"Black Rook in Rainy Weather"

Judith B. Herman, "Reflections on a Kitchen Table: A Note on Sylvia Plath's 'Black Rook in Rainy Weather,'" *NConL* 7 (Dec. 1977): 5.

"The Blood Jet"

Suzanne Juhasz, "'The Blood Jet': The Poetry of Sylvia Plath," in Brown and Olson, *Feminist Criticism*, 111-30.

"Brasilia"

Margaret D. Uroff, "Sylvia Plath on Motherhood," *MQ* 15 (Autumn 1973): 88-89.

"Channel Crossing"

Philip Gardner, "'The Bland Granta': Sylvia Plath at Cambridge," *DR* 60 (Autumn 1980): 496-507.

Collected Poems

Gary Lane, "Influence and Originality in Plath's Poems," in Lane, *Sylvia Plath*, 116-37.

Alan Williamson, "Confession and Tragedy," *Poetry* 142, no. 3 (June 1983): 170-78.

The Colossus

Broe, *Protean Poetic*, passim.

Michael Kirkham, "Sylvia Plath," *QQ* 91 (Spring 1984): 153-66.

Christopher Morris, "Order and Chaos in Plath's 'The Colossus,'" *CP* 15 (Spring 1982): 33-42.

Pamela Smith, "Architectonics: Sylvia Plath's Colossus," in *Sylvia Plath: The Woman and the Work*, ed. Edward Butscher (New York: Dodd, Mead, 1977), passim.

"The Couriers"

Jon Rosenblatt, *Expl* 34 (Dec. 1975): 28.

"Crossing the Water"

Broe, *Protean Poetic*, passim.

"Cut"

Joan Bobbitt, "Lowell and Plath: Objectivity and the Confessional Mode," *ArQ* 33 (Autumn 1977): 315.

Robert Boyers, "Sylvia Plath: The Trepanned Veteran," *CentR* 13 (Spring 1969): 142-46.

Marjorie Perloff, "Angst and Animism in the Poetry of Sylvia Plath," *JML* 1 (1970): 70-72.

R. J. Spendal, "Sylvia Plath's 'Cut,'" *MPS* 6 (Autumn 1975): 128-34.

"Daddy"

Barnard, *Sylvia Plath*, passim.

Sophia B. Blaydes, "Metaphors of Life and Death in the Poetry of Sylvia Plath," *DR* 57 (Autumn 1977): 494-506.

Robert Boyers, "Sylvia Plath: The Trepanned Veteran," *CentR* 13 (Spring 1969): 148-52.

L. K. Bundtzen, *Plath's Incarnations: Woman and the Creative Process* (Ann Arbor: University of Michigan Press, 1983), passim.

Dickinson, *Suggestions for Teachers of "Introduction to Literature"*, 54-55.

Draper, *Lyric Tragedy*, passim.

Judith B. Herman, "Plath's 'Daddy' and the Myth of Tereus and Philomena," *NConL* 7 (1977): 9-10.

Philip Hobsbaum, "The Temptation of Giant Despair," *HudR* 25 (Winter 1972-73): 605-6.

Suzanne Juhasz, "'The Blood Jet': The Poetry of Sylvia Plath," in Brown and Olson, *Feminist Criticism*, 111-30.

Guinevara A. Nance and Judith P. Jones, "Doing Away with Daddy: Exorcism and Sympathetic Magic in Plath's Poetry," *CP* 11 (Spring 1978): 75-81.

Oberg, *Modern American Lyric*, 127-73.

Ostriker, *Stealing the Language*, 122-63.

Margaret D. Uroff, "Sylvia Plath and Confessional Poetry: A Reconsideration," *IowaR* 8 (Winter 1977): 113-15.

"The Disquieting Muses"

Margaret D. Uroff, "Sylvia Plath on Motherhood," *MQ* 15 (Autumn 1973): 72-75.

"Doomsday"

Philip Gardner, "'The Bland Granta': Sylvia Plath at Cambridge," *DR* (Autumn 1980): 496-507.

"Eavesdropper"

Margaret Dickie, "Sylvia Plath's Narrative Strategies," *IowaR* (Spring 1982): 1-14.

"Edge"

Shanta Acharya, "Sylvia Plath's 'Edge': An Analysis," *OJES* 15 (1979): 49-54.

Constance Scheerer, "The Deathly Paradise of Sylvia Plath," *AR* 34 (Summer 1976): 480.

"Electra on Azalea Path"

Draper, *Lyric Tragedy*, passim.

"Event"

Michael Kirkham, "Sylvia Plath," *QQ* 91 (Spring 1984): 153-66.

Margaret D. Uroff, "Sylvia Plath's Women," *CP* 7 (Spring 1974): 50.

"Every Woman Adores a Fascist"

Sophia B. Blaydes, "Metaphors of Life and Death in the Poetry of Denise Levertov and Sylvia Plath," *DR* 57 (Autumn 1977): 494-506.

"Face Lift"

Steven Gould Axelrod, "The Mirror and The Shadow: Plath's Poetics of Self-Doubt," *ConL* 26 (Winter 1985): 286-301.

"Fever 103 Degrees"

Michael Kirkham, "Sylvia Plath," *QQ* 91 (Spring 1984): 153-66.

Thanh-Binh Nguyen, "A Stylistic Analysis of Sylvia Plath's Semantics," *Lang&S* 11 (Spring 1978): 69-81.

Margaret D. Uroff, "Sylvia Plath's Women," *CP* 7 (Spring 1974): 52.

"In Plaster"

Alicia Ostricker, "In Mind: The Divided Self in Women's Poetry," *MQ* 24 (Summer 1983): 351-65.

"Insomniac"

Michael Kirkham, "Sylvia Plath," *QQ* 91 (Spring 1984): 153-66.

"Lady Lazarus"

Barnard, *Sylvia Plath*, passim.

Joan Bobbitt, "Lowell and Plath: Objectivity and the Confessional Mode," *ArQ* 33 (Autumn 1977): 315-16.

L. K. Bundtzen, *Plath's Incarnations: Woman and the Creative Process* (Ann Arbor: University of Michigan Press, 1983), passim.

Carol Helmstetter Cantrell, "Self and Tradition in Recent Poetry," *MQ* 18 (Summer 1977): 354-56.

Draper, *Lyric Tragedy*, passim.

Suzanne Juhasz, "'The Blood Jet': The Poetry of Sylvia Plath," in Brown and Olson, *Feminist Criticism*, 111-30.

Guinevara A. Nance and Judith P. Jones, "Doing Away with Daddy: Exorcism and Sympathetic Magic in Plath's Poetry," *CP* 11 (Spring 1978): 75-81.

Oberg, *Modern American Lyric*, 127-73.

Ostriker, *Stealing the Language*, 122-63.

Ries, *Wolf Masks*, 50-51.

Leonard Sanazaro, "Plath's 'Lady Lazarus,'" *Expl* 41 (Spring 1983): 54-57.

Margaret D. Uroff, "Sylvia Plath and Confessional Poetry: A Reconsideration," *IowaR* 8 (Winter 1977): 111-13.

Susan Van Dyne, "Fueling The Phoenix Fire: The Manuscript of Sylvia Plath's 'Lady Lazarus,'" *MR* 24 (Summer 1983): 395-410.

Linda W. Wagner, *Expl* 41 (Fall 1982): 50-52.

"Leaving Early"

Margaret D. Uroff, "Sylvia Plath's Women," *CP* 7 (Spring 1974): 49-50.

"Lesbos"

Margaret Dickie, "Sylvia Plath's Narrative Strategies," *IowaR* 13 (Spring 1982): 1-14.

Laurin K. Roland, "Sylvia Plath's 'Lesbos': A Self Divided," *CP* 9 (Fall 1976): 61-65.

"Little Fugue"

Marjorie G. Perloff, "On the Road to *Ariel*: The 'Transitional' Poetry of Sylvia Plath," *IowaR* 4 (Spring 1973): 99-102.

"Lorelei"

Draper, *Lyric Tragedy*, passim.

"Love Letter"

Margaret D. Uroff, "Sylvia Plath's Women," *CP* 7 (Spring 1974): 51.

"Magi"

Joyce Carol Oates, "The Death Throes of Romanticism: The Poems of Sylvia Plath," *SoR* 9 (Summer 1973): 506-7.

"Man in Black"

Draper, *Lyric Tragedy*, passim.

"The Manor Garden"

Jerome F. Megna, *Expl* 30 (Mar. 1972): 58.

"Maudlin"

Richard F. Giles, *Expl* 37 (Summer 1979): 24-26.

"Medusa"

Margaret Dickie, "Sylvia Plath's Narrative Strategies," *IowaR* 13 (Spring 1982): 1-14.

"Metaphors"

Penny Stewart, *Expl* 40 (Spring 1982): 59-60.

"Mirror"

Steven Gould Axelrod, "The Mirror and the Shadow: Plath's Poetics of Self-Doubt," *ConL* 26 (Winter 1985): 286-301.

William Freedman, Sylvia Plath's 'Mirror' of Mirrors," *PLL* 23 (Winter 1987): 56-69.

"The Moon and the Yew Tree"

Michael Kirkham, "Sylvia Plath," *QQ* 91 (Spring 1984): 153-66.

"Morning Song"

Marjorie Perloff, "Angst and Animism in the Poetry of Sylvia Plath," *JML* 1 (1970): 68-69.

Margaret D. Uroff, "Sylvia Plath on Motherhood," *MQ* 15 (Autumn 1973): 79-82.

"Nick and the Candlestick"

Deborah Gilbert, "Transformations in 'Nick and the Candlestick,'" *CP* 12 (Spring 1979): 29-32.

"Ouija"

Philip Gardner, "'The Bland Granta': Sylvia Plath at Cambridge," *DR* 60 (Autumn 1980): 496-507.

"Parliament Hill Fields"

Michael Kirkham, "Sylvia Plath," *QQ* 91 (Spring 1984): 153-66.

Marjorie G. Perloff, "On the Road to *Ariel*: The 'Transitional' Poetry of Sylvia Plath," *IowaR* 4 (Spring 1973): 96-99.

"Poppies in July"

Pinsky, *The Situation of Poetry*, 129-31.

"Private Ground"

Robert N. Mollinger, "Sylvia Plath's 'Private Ground,'" *NConL* 5 (Mar. 1975): 14-15.

"Pursuit"

Draper, *Lyric Tragedy*, passim.

"Sheep in Fog"

Jon Rosenblatt, "The Limits of the 'Confessional Mode' in Recent American Poetry," *Genre* 9 (Summer 1976): 157-58.

"Snakecharmer"

Constance Scheerer, "The Deathly Paradise of Sylvia Plath," *AR* 34 (Summer 1976): 471-72.

"Stings"

M. L. Broe, "Recovering the Complex Self: Sylvia Plath's Beeline," *CentR* 24 (Winter 198): 1-24.

Draper, *Lyric Tragedy*, passim.

Rose Kamel, "'A Self to Recover': Sylvia Plath's Bee Cycle Poems," *MPS* 4 (Winter 1973): 313-16.

"The Surgeon at 2 A.M."

Joan Bobbitt, "Lowell and Plath: Objectivity and the Confessional Mode," *ArQ* 33 (Autumn 1977): 316-17.

Constance Scheerer, "The Deathly Paradise of Sylvia Plath," *AR* 34 (Summer 1976): 473-75.

"The Swarm"

M. L. Broe, "Recovering the Complex Self: Sylvia Plath's Beeline," *CentR* 24 (Winter 1980): 1-24.

Draper, *Lyric Tragedy*, passim.

Rose Kamel, "'A Self to Recover': Sylvia Plath's Bee Cycle Poems," *MPS* 4 (Winter 1973): 311-13.

Ellin Sarot, "Becoming More and More Historical: Sylvia Plath's 'The Swarm,'" *CP* 20 (1987): 41-56.

"The Tour"

Margaret D. Uroff, "Sylvia Plath and Confessional Poetry: A Reconsideration," *IowaR* 8 (Winter 1977): 108-9.

"The Town"

Margaret Dickie, "Sylvia Plath's in Narrative Strategies," *IowaR* 13 (Spring 1982): 1-14.

"Tulips"

Marjorie Perloff, "Angst and Animism in the Poetry of Sylvia Plath," *JML* 1 (1970): 69-70.

Constance Scheerer, "The Deathly Paradise of Sylvia Plath," *AR* 34 (Summer 1976): 476.

Margaret D. Uroff, "Sylvia Plath and Confessional Poetry: A Reconsideration," *IowaR* 8 (Winter 1977): 107-8.

Margaret D. Uroff, "Sylvia Plath's Women," *CP* 7 (Spring 1974): 51-52.

"Two Campers in Cloud Country"

Daniel J. Beirne, "Plath's 'Two Campers in Cloud Country,'" *Expl* 42 (Fall 1983): 61-62.

"Wintering"

M. L. Broe, "Recovering the Complex Self: Sylvia Plath's Beeline," *CentR* 24 (Winter 1980): 1-24.

Draper, *Lyric Tragedy*, passim.

Rose Kamel, "'A Self to Recover': Sylvia Plath's Bee Cycle Poems," *MPS* 4 (Winter 1973): 316-17.

"Winter Trees"

Broe, *Protean Poetic*, passim.

"Years"

Y. Renan, "'Angel Faces Clustered like Bright Lice': Comic Elements in Modernist Writing," *CL* (Summer 1983): 247-61.

"You're"

Margaret D. Uroff, "Sylvia Plath on Motherhood," *MQ* 15 (Autumn 1973): 77-78.

"Zoo Keeper's Wife"

Margaret D. Uroff, "Sylvia Plath's Women," *CP* 7 (Spring 1974): 48-49.

PLUMLY, STANLEY

"December 1945"

Charles Altieri, "Sensibility, Rhetoric, and Will: Some Tensions in Contemporary Poetry," *ConL* 23 (Fall 1982): 451-79.

POUND, EZRA

"The Alchemist"

Rosenthal, *The Modern Poets*, 53.

"Ballad of the Goodly Fere"

Abad, *A Formal Approach to Lyric Poetry*, 172-73, 175-76.
Riding and Graves, *A Survey of Modernist Poetry*, 140-42.

"Ballatetta"

Satin, *Reading Poetry*, 1070-71.

Cantos

I. Bell, *Critic as Scientist: The Modernist Poetics of Ezra Pound* (New York: Methuen, 1981), passim.

Christine Brooke-Rose, *A ZBC of Ezra Pound*, passim.

R. Casillo, "Ezra Pound, L. A. Waddell, and the Aryan Tradition of *The Cantos*," *MLS* 15 (Spring 1985): 65-81.

Dickie, *On the Modernist Long Poem*, 106-47.

A. Durant, *Ezra Pound, Identity in Crisis: A Fundamental Reassessment of the Poet and His Work* (New York: Barnes & Noble, 1981), passim.

W. S. Flory, *Ezra Pound and "The Cantos": A Record of Struggle* (New Haven: Yale University Press, 1980), passim.

P. Furia, *Pound's Cantos Declassified* (University Park: Pennsylvania State University Press, 1984), passim.

Laszlo Gefin, *Ideogram* (Austin: University of Texas Press, 1982), passim.

Kenner, *The Pound Era*, 349-81, 414-36, 474-95, 528-34.

Ben D. Kimpel and T. C. Duncan Eaves, "Ezra Pound's Anti-Semitism," *SAQ* 81 (Winter 1982): 56-69.

Ben D. Kimpel and T. C. Duncan Eaves, "Pound's 'Ideogrammatic Method' as Illustrated in Canto 99," *AL* 51 (May 1979): 205-37.

Ben D. Kimpel and T. C. Duncan Eaves, "Two Notes on Ezra Pound's *Cantos*," *MP* (Feb. 1981): 78, 285-88.

Victor P. H. Li, "The Vanity of Length: The Long Poem as Problem in Pound's *Cantos* and Williams' *Paterson*," *Genre* 19 (Spring 1986): 3-20.

C. McDowell and T. Materer, "Gyre and Vortex: W. B. Yeats and Ezra Pound," *TCL* 31 (Winter 1985): 343-67.

W. G. Regier, "Ezra Pound, Adam Smith, Karl Marx," *MinnR* 12 n.s. (Spring 1979): 12, 72-76.

Rosenthal, *Sailing into the Unknown*, 12-25.

Richard Sieburth, "In Pound We Trust: The Economy of Poetry/The Poetry of Economics," *CritI* 14 (Autumn 1987): 142-72.

Wilhelm, *The Later Cantos of Ezra Pound*, passim.

"Canto 1"

Jessica Prinz Pecorino, "Resurgent Icons: Pound's First Canto and the Visual Arts," *JML* 9 (May 1982): 159-74.

"Canto 2"

William Cookson, "Ezra Pound and Myth: A Reader's Guide to Canto II," *Agenda* 15 (1977): 87-92.

"Canto 3"

Kenner, *The Pound Era*, 143.

"Canto 4"

Alan J. Peacock, "Pound, Horace, and Canto 4," *ELN* 17 (Fall 1980): 288-91.

Alan Williamson, "Mythic and Archetypal Methods: A Reading of Canto 4," *SJS* 12 (Fall 1986): 105-10.

"Canto 5"

Kenner, *The Pound Era*, 64-66.

"Canto 6"

Kenner, *The Pound Era*, 339.

"Canto 7"

Brooke-Rose, *A ZBC of Ezra Pound*, 218-19, 263-64.

"Canto 8"

Brooke-Rose, *A ZBC of Ezra Pound*, 172-74.

Michael F. Harper, "Truth and Calliope: Ezra Pound's Malatesta," *PMLA* 96 (Jan. 1981): 86-103.

Fred Moramarco, "The Malatesta Cantos," *Mosaic* 12 (Fall 1978): 107-18.

"Canto 9"

Michael F. Harper, "Truth and Calliope: Ezra Pound's Malatesta," *PMLA* 96 (Jan. 1981): 86-103.

Fred Moramarco, "The Malatesta Cantos," *Mosaic* 12 (Fall 1978): 107-18.

"Canto 10"

Michael F. Harper, "Truth and Calliope: Ezra Pound's Malatesta," *PMLA* 96 (Jan. 1981): 86-103.

Fred Moramarco, "The Malatesta Cantos," *Mosaic* 12 (Fall 1978): 107-18.

"Canto 11"

Brooke-Rose, *A ZBC of Ezra Pound*, 172-74.

Michael F. Harper, "Truth and Calliope: Ezra Pound's Malatesta," *PMLA* 96 (Jan. 1981): 86-103.

Fred Moramarco, "The Malatesta Cantos," *Mosaic* 12 (Fall 1978): 107-18.

"Canto 19"

T. Eaves and B. Kimpel, "The Birth of a Nation: A Note on Pound's Canto 19," *PQ* 62 (Summer 1983): 417-18.

"Canto 20"

Stephen J. Adams, "The Soundscape of the *Cantos*: Some Ideas of Music in the Poetry of Ezra Pound," *Humanities Association Review* 28 (Spring 1977): 177-81.

Kenner, *The Pound Era*, 112-18.

"Canto 23"

Michael Davidson, "'From the Latin Speculum': The Modern Poet as Philologist," *ConL* 28 (Summer 1987): 187-205.

"Canto 25"

Kenner, *The Pound Era*, 307-8.

"Canto 29"

Kenner, *The Pound Era*, 336-67.

"Canto 33"

W. G. Regier, "Ezra Pound, Adam Smith, Karl Marx," *MinnR* 12 (Spring 1979): 72-76.

"Canto 36"

Brooke-Rose, *A ZBC of Ezra Pound*, 236-37 and passim.

"Canto 38"

Kenner, *The Pound Era*, 306-7.

"Canto 45"

Kenner, *The Pound Era*, 315, 326-29.

"Canto 47"

Brooke-Rose, *A ZBC of Ezra Pound*, passim.

Vincent Miller, "Pound's Battle with Time," *YR* 66 (Dec. 1976): 193-208.

Rosenthal, *Sailing into the Unknown*, 12-25.

"Canto 48"

Kenner, *The Pound Era*, 338.

"Canto 72"

Massimo Bacigalupo, "The Poet at War: Ezra Pound's Suppressed Italian Cantos," *SAQ* 83 (Winter 1984): 69-79.

"Canto 73"

Massimo Bacigalupo, "The Poet at War: Ezra Pound's Suppressed Italian Cantos," *SAQ* 83 (Winter 1984): 69-79.

"Canto 74"

Brooke-Rose, *A ZBC of Ezra Pound*, passim.

Kenner, *The Pound Era*, 508-9.

Vincent Miller, "Pound's Battle with Time," *YR* 66 (December 1976): 193-208.

Jessica Prinz Pecorino, "Resurgent Icons: Pound's First Canto and the Visual Arts," *JML* 9 (May 1982): 159-74.

"Canto 75"

Stephen J. Adams, "The Soundscape of the *Cantos*: Some Ideas of Music in the Poetry of Ezra Pound," *Humanities Association Review* 28 (Spring 1977): 181-85.

"Canto 76"

Kenner, *The Pound Era*, 61.

"Canto 80"

Kenner, *The Pound Era*, 13.

Ben D. Kimpel and T. C. Duncan Eaves, *Expl* 41 (Spring 1983): 43.

"Canto 81"

Kenner, *The Pound Era*, 156, 308, 413.

"Canto 83"

Brooke-Rose, *A ZBC of Ezra Pound*, passim.

Kenner, *The Pound Era*, 346.

"Canto 85"

Brooke-Rose, *A ZBC of Ezra Pound*, passim.

Kenner, *The Pound Era*, 16.

Ben D. Kimpel and T. C. Duncan Eaves, "A Note to Ezra Pound's 'Canto 85,'" *ELN* 17 (Winter 1980): 292-93.

James J. Wilhelm, *The Later Cantos of Ezra Pound* (New York: Walker & Co., 1977), passim.

"Canto 86"

Andrew J. Kappel, "What Ezra Pound Says We Owe to Edward VIII, Duke of Windsor," *JML* 9 (May 1982): 313-15.

Daniel D. Pearlman, "The Blue-Eyed Eel Dame Fortune in Pound's Later Cantos," *Agenda* 10 (Autumn/Winter 1971-72): 60-62.

"Canto 87"

Kenner, *The Pound Era*, 526.

"Canto 88"

Brooke-Rose, *A ZBC of Ezra Pound*, passim.

James J. Wilhelm, "The Dragon and the Duel: A Defense of Pound's Canto 88," *TCL* 20 (Apr. 1974): 114-25.

James J. Wilhelm, *The Later Cantos of Ezra Pound* (New York: Walker & Co., 1977), passim.

"Canto 89"

Ben D. Kimpel and T. C. Duncan Eaves, "Pound and Pumpelly," *ELN* 17 (1980): 293-94.

"Canto 91"

Brooke-Rose, *A ZBC of Ezra Pound*, passim.

Kenner, *The Pound Era*, 144.

Daniel D. Pearlman, "The Blue-Eyed Eel Dame Fortune in Pound's Later Cantos," *Agenda* 10 (Autumn/Winter 1971-72): 62-66.

P. L. Surette, "Having His Own Mind to Stand by Him," *HudR* 27 (Winter 1974-75): 500-502, 508.

"Canto 93"

Kenner, *The Pound Era*, 338.

Peter Whigham, "Il suo Paradiso Terrestre," *Agenda* 8 (Spring 1970): 31-34.

"Canto 95"

Brooke-Rose, *A ZBC of Ezra Pound*, 39-40, 141-44.

"Canto 96"

Michael Davidson, "'From the Latin Speculum': The Modern Poet as Philologist," *ConL* 28 (Summer 1987): 187-205.

"Canto 97"

Daniel D. Pearlman, "The Blue-eyed Dame Fortune in Pound's Later Cantos," *Agenda* 10 (Autumn/Winter 1971-72): 71-76.

Richard Sieburth, "In Pound We Trust: The Economy of Poetry/The Poetry of Economics," *CritI* 14 (Autumn 1987): 142-72.

James J. Wilhelm, *The Later Cantos of Ezra Pound* (New York: Walker & Co., 1977), passim.

"Canto 98"

Brooke-Rose, *A ZBC of Ezra Pound*, passim.

"Canto 99"

Ben D. Kimpel and T. C. Duncan Eaves, "Pound's 'Ideogrammatic Method' as Illustrated in Canto 99," *AL* 51 (May 1979): 205-37.

"Canto 101"

John Peck, "Landscape as Ceremony in the Later *Cantos*: From 'The Roads of France' to 'Rock's World,'" *Agenda* 9 (Spring/Summer 1971): 46-51.

"Canto 110"

Donald Davie, "Cypress Versus Rock-Slide: An Appreciation of Canto 110," *Agenda* 8 (Spring 1970): 19-26.

John Peck, "Landscape as Ceremony in the Later *Cantos*: From 'The Roads of France' to 'Rock's World,'" *Agenda* 9 (Spring/Summer 1971): 52-61.

"Canto 112"

John Peck, "Landscape as Ceremony in the Later *Cantos*: From 'The Roads of France' to 'Rock's World,'" *Agenda* 9 (Spring/Summer 1971): 63-66.

"Canto 113"

Ben D. Kimpel and T. C. Duncan Eaves, "Pound and Pumpelly," *ELN* 17 (1980): 293-94.

"Canto 120"

James J. Wilhelm, *The Later Cantos of Ezra Pound* (New York: Walker & Co., 1977), passim.

Cathay

Kenner, *The Pound Era*, 192-222 and passim.

"Dance Figure"

William Skaff, "Pound's Imagism and the Surreal," *JML* 12 (July 1985): 185-210.

"Effects of Music upon a Company of People"

Stephen J. Adams, "The Soundscape of the *Cantos*: Some Ideas of Music in the Poetry of Ezra Pound," *Humanities Association Review* 28 (Spring 1977): 175-77.

"Fan Piece for Her Imperial Lord"

Earl Miner, "Pound, *Haiku* and the Image," *HudR* 9 (Winter 1975): 580-81.

"Four Poems of Departure"

Kenner, *The Pound Era*, 200-202.

"The Game of Chess"

John J. Tucker, "Pound, Vorticism and the New Esthetic," *Mosaic* 16 (Fall 1983): 83-96.

"The Garden"

Van Doren, *Introduction to Poetry*, 46-49.

"Homage to Sextus Propertius"

R. P. Blackmur, "Masks of Ezra Pound," *Hound and Horn* 7 (Jan./Mar. 1934): 184-91. Reprinted in Blackmur, *Language as Gesture*, 130-36.

Thomas Drew-Bear, "Ezra Pound's 'Homage to Sextus Propertius,'" *AL* 37 (May 1965): 204-10.

D. M. Hooley, "Pound's Propertius, Again," *MLN* 100 (1985): 1025-44.

Kenner, *The Pound Era*, 285-86, 302-3 and passim.

J. McCormick, "George Santayana and Ezra Pound," *AL* (October 1982): 413-33.

Vincent E. Miller, "The Serious Wit of Pound's *Homage to Sextus Propertius*," *ConL* 16 (Autumn 1875): 452-62.

Rosenthal, *The Modern Poets*, 55-56.

John Speirs, "Mr. Pound's Propertius," *Scrutiny* 3 (Sept. 1934): 409-18.

J. P. Sullivan, "The Poet as Translator: Ezra Pound and Sextus Propertius," *KR* 23 (Summer 1961): 462-81.

J. P. Sullivan, "Pound's 'Homage to Propertius': The Structure of a Mask," *EIC* 10 (July 1960): 239-49.

"Hugh Selwyn Mauberley"

Amtai F. Avi-ram, "*APO KOINOU* in Audre Lorde and the Moderns: Defining the Differences," *Callaloo* 9 (Winter 1986): 195-96.

I. Bell, "Instruments for Design: Mauberley's Sieve," *ELN* 17 (June 1980): 294-97.

I. Bell, "In the Real Tradition: Edgar Lee Masters and Hugh Selwyn Mauberley," *Criticism* 23 (Spring 1981): 141-54.

R. P. Blackmur, "Masks of Ezra Pound," *Hound and Horn* 7 (Jan./Mar. 1934): 180-84. Reprinted in Blackmur, *Language as Gesture*, 126-30.

Thomas E. Connolly, "Further Notes on *Mauberley*," *Accent* 16 (Winter 1956): 59-67.

Deutsch, *This Modern Poetry*, 115-18.

MacDonald Emslie, *Expl* 14 (Jan. 1956): 26. Reprinted in *The Explicator Cyclopedia* 1:231-32.

Feder, *Ancient Myth in Modern Poetry*, 99-105.

A. L. French, "*Mauberley*: A Rejoinder," *EIC* 16 (July 1966): 356-59.

A. L. French, "'Olympian Apathein': Pound's 'Hugh Selwyn Mauberley' and Modern Poetry," *EIC* 15 (Oct. 1965): 428-45.

Friar and Brinnin, *Modern Poetry*, 527-531.

G. Giovannini, *Expl* 16 (Mar. 1958): 35. Reprinted in *The Explicator Cyclopedia* 1:232-33.

Hoffman, *The Twenties*, 37-46.

David Holbrook, *Lost Bearings in English Poetry* (London: Vision Press 1977), 64-91.

Kenner, *The Pound Era*, 287-88 and passim.

George Knox, "Glaucus in 'Hugh Selwyn Mauberley,'" *ES* 45 (June 1964): 236-37.

Leavis, *New Bearings on English Poetry*, 141-43.

Richard A. Long, *Expl* 10 (June 1952): 56. Reprinted in *The Explicator Cyclopedia* 1:231.

Karl Malkoff, "Allusion as Irony: Pound's Use of Dante in 'Hugh Selywn Mauberley,'" *MinnR* 7 (1967): 81-88.

Christopher Reiss, "In Defence of 'Mauberley,'" *EIC* 16 (July 1966): 351-53.

Rosenthal, *The Modern Poets*, 61-66.

"In a Station of the Metro"

Warren Beck, "Boundaries of Poetry," *CE* 4 (Mar. 1943): 346-47.

Ralph Bevilaqua, "Pound's 'In a Station of the Metro': A Textual Note," *ELN* 8 (June 1971): 293-96.

Brooks and Warren, *Understanding Poetry*, 175-76; rev. ed., 78-80.

John J. Espy, *Expl* 11 (June 1953): 59. Abridged in Gwynn, Condee, and Lewis, *The Case for Poetry*, 287. Reprinted in *The Explicator Cyclopedia* 1:233-34.

Joseph H. Friend, "Teaching the 'Grammar of Poetry,'" *CE* 27 (Feb. 1966): 362-63.

Thomas A. Hanzo, *Expl* 11 (Feb. 1953): 26. Abridged in Gwynn, Condee, and Lewis, *The Case for Poetry*, 287. Reprinted in *The Explicator Cyclopedia* 1:233.

Yoshiyuki Iwamoto, *Expl* 29 (Feb. 1961): 30. Reprinted in *The Explicator Cyclopedia* 1:235.

Kenner, *The Pound Era*, 184-87.

Michael L. Lasser, *Expl* 19 (Feb. 1961): 30. Reprinted in *The Explicator Cyclopedia* 1:234.

W. E. Rogers, *The Three Genres and the Interpretation of Lyric* (Princeton: Princeton University Press, 1983), passim.

Rosenthal and Smith, *Exploring Poetry*, 157-58.

David Simpson, "Pound's Wordsworth; or Growth of a Poet's Mind," *ELH* 45 (1978): 660-86.

John J. Tucker, "Pound, Vorticism, and the New Esthetic," *Mosaic* 16 (Fall 1983): 83-96.

"In Epitaphius Eius"

G. Schmidt, "Pound's 'In Epitaphius Eius,'" *Expl* 40 (Spring 1982): 44-45.

"Langue d'Oc"

J. McCormick, "George Santayana and Ezra Pound," *AL* 54 (October 1983): 413-33.

"Liu Ch'e"

Juhasz, *Metaphor and the Poetry of Williams, Pound and Stevens*, 26.

David Simpson, "Pound's Wordsworth: Or Growth of a Poet's Mind," *ELH* 45 (1978): 660-86.

"Malatesta Cantos"

Michael F. Harper, "Truth and Calliope: Ezra Pound's Malatesta," *PMLA* 96 (Jan. 1981): 86-103.

Fred Moramarco, "The Malatesta Cantos," *Mosaic* 12 (Fall 1987): 107-18.

"Near Perigord"

Thomas E. Connolly, "Ezra Pound's 'Near Perigord': The Background of a Poem," *CL* 8 (Spring 1956): 110-16.

"A Pact"

Mario L. D'Avanzo, *Expl* 24 (Feb. 1966): 51.

"Papyrus"

Daniels, *The Art of Reading Poetry*, 9.

Christopher M. Dawson, *Expl* 9 (Feb. 1951): 30. Reprinted in *The Explicator Cyclopedia* 1:236.

Gilbert Highet, *The Classical Tradition*, (New York: Oxford University Press, 1949), 517.

John Hollander, "The Poem in the Eye," *Shenandoah* 23 (Spring 1972): 24.

Paul C. Ray, "On Fragments and Fragmentation," *WHR* 34 (Summer 1980): 223-32.

"Pisan Cantos"

Brooke-Rose, *A ZBC of Ezra Pound*, passim.

P. Furia, *Pound's Cantos Declassified* (University Park: Pennsylvania State University Press, 1984), passim.

Ben D. Kimpel and T. C. Duncan Eaves, *Expl* 40 (Fall 1981): 43.

Michael North, "Towers and the Visual Map of Pound's *Cantos*," *ConL* 27 (Spring 1986): 17-31.

"Portrait d'une Femme"

Richard J. Giannone, "Eliot's 'Portrait of a Lady' and Pound's 'Portrait d'une Femme,'" *TCL* 5 (Oct. 1959): 131-34.

Perrine and Reid, *100 American Poets*, 82-83.

"The Return"

Deutsch, *Poetry in Our Time*, 124-25.

"Experiment in Verse," special number, *TLS* (Aug. 1956): iii.

Sally M. Gall, "Domestic Monologues: The Problem of 'Voice' in Contemporary American Poetry," *MR* 23 (Autumn 1982): 489-503.

Kenner, *The Pound Era*, 189-91.

Rosenthal, *The Modern Poets*, 51-53.

"The River Song"

Kenner, *The Pound Era*, 203-4.

"Rock-Drill"

Peter Dale Scott, "Anger and Poetic Politics in 'Rock-Drill,'" *SJS* 12 (Fall 1986): 68-82.

"The Seafarer"

Alexander, *The Poetic Achievement of Ezra Pound*, 68-80.

"Separation on the River Kiang"

Kenner, *The Pound Era*, 203-4.

"Siler"

Ian F. A. Bell, *Expl* 38 (Summer 1980): 14-16.

"South Folk in Cold Country"

Kenner, *The Pound Era*, 219-22.

"The Spring"

Kenner, *The Pound Era*, 140-42.

"The Tree"

Alexander, *The Poetic Achievement of Ezra Pound*, 20-43.

PRATT, E. J.

"The Shark"

Bert Case Diltz, *Sense or Nonsense: Contemporary Education at the Crossroads* (Toronto: McClelland and Stewart, 1972), 90-93.

PRINCE, F. T.

"The Old Age Of Michelangelo"

Fred Inglis, "F. T. Prince and the Prospect for Poetry," *University of Denver Quarterly* 1 (Autumn 1966): 34-39.

PUTNAM, PHELPS

"Ballad of a Strange Thing"

F. O. Matthiessen, "Phelps Putnam (1894-1948)," *KR* 11 (Winter 1949): 80-82. Reprinted in Matthiessen, *The Responsibilities of the Critic*, 274-76.

"The Five Seasons"

Morton D. Zabel, "Phelps Putnam and America," *Poetry* 40 (Sept. 1932): 335-44.

"Hasbrouck and the Rose"

F. O. Mattheissen, "Phelps Putnam (1894-1948)," *KR* 11 (Winter 1949): 78-80. Reprinted in Matthiessen, *The Responsibilities of the Critic*, 273-74.

RAKOSI, CARL

"A Journey Far Away"

Philip Wheelwright, "On the Semantics of Poetry," in Chatman and Levin, *Essays on the Language of Literature*, 257-58.

"Punk Rock"

David E. James, "Poetry/Punk/Production: Some Recent Writing in L.A.,"
MinnR, n.s. 23 (Fall 1984): 127-48.

RANSOM, JOHN CROWE

"Amphibious Crocodile"

Richmond C. Beatty, "John Crowe Ransom as Poet," *SR* 52 (Summer 1944):
362-63.

"Antique Harvesters"

Gray, *American Poetry*, 210-11.

Richard Gray, "The 'Compleat Gentleman': An Approach to John Crowe
Ransom," *SoR* 12 (July 1976): 628-31.

Vivienne Koch, "The Achievement of John Crowe Ransom," *SR* 58 (Spring
1950): 252-55.

Vivienne Koch, "The Poetry of John Crowe Ransom," in Rajan, *Modern
American Poetry*, 58-61.

F. O. Matthiessen, "Primarily Language," *SR* 56 (Summer 1948): 394-95.
Reprinted in Matthiessen, *The Responsibilities of the Critic*, 43-44.

Louis D. Rubin, Jr., "The Concept of Nature in Modern Poetry," *AQ* 9
(Spring 1957): 69-70.

Rubin, *The Wary Fugitives*, passim.

"Bells for John Whiteside's Daughter"

Adams, *The Contexts of Poetry*, 12-15.

Brooks, Lewis, and Warren, *American Literature*, 2654.

Gray, *American Poetry* 207-8.

Robert Heilman, "Poetic and Prosaic: Program Notes on Opposite
Numbers," *Pacific Spectator*, 5 (Autumn 1951): 460-85. Abridged in Gwynn,
Condee, and Lewis, *The Case for Poetry*, 293.

Vivienne Koch, "The Poetry of John Crowe Ransom," in Rajan, *Modern American Poetry*, 43-44.

Rubin, *The Wary Fugitives*, passim.

Donald A. Stauffer, "Portrait of the Critic Poet as Equilibrist," *SR* 56 (Summer 1948): 430.

William Vesterman, "The Motives of Meter in 'Bells for John Whiteside's Daughter,'" *SoQ* 22 (Summer 1984): 42-53.

R. P. Warren, "John Crowe Ransom: A Study in Irony," *VQR* 11 (Jan. 1935): 106. Abridged in Gwynn, Condee, and Lewis, *The Case for Poetry*, 293.

R. P. Warren, "Pure and Impure Poetry," *KR* 5 (Spring 1943): 237-40. Reprinted in *Criticism*, 370-72; in Stallman, *Critiques*, 92-94; in Ranson, *The Kenyon Critics*, 26-29; in Engle and Carrier, *Reading Modern Poetry*, 69-71; in West, *Essays in Modern Literary Criticism*, 253-55.

"Blackberry Winter"

G. P. Wasserman, "The Irony of John Crowe Ransom," *University of Kansas City Review* 23 (Winter 1956): 154-55.

"Blue Girls"

Ciardi, *How Does a Poem Mean?* 802-3.

Vivienne Koch, "The Achievement of John Crowe Ransom," *SR* 58 (Spring 1950): 250-52.

Vivienne Koch, "The Poetry of John Crowe Ransom," in Rajan, *Modern American Poetry*, 56-58.

Howard Nemerov, "Summer's Flare and Winter's Flaw," *SR* 56 (Summer 1948): 418.

Scott C. Osborn, *Expl* 21 (Nov. 1962): 22.

William R. Osborne, *Expl* 19 (May 1961): 53. Reprinted in *The Explicator Cyclopedia* 1:237-38.

Perrine and Reid, *100 American Poets*, 138.

Rubin, *The Wary Fugitives*, passim.

Hyatt H. Waggoner, *Expl* 18 (Oct. 1959): 6. Reprinted in *The Explicator Cyclopedia* 1:236-37.

"Captain Carpenter"

Brooks, *Modern Poetry and the Tradition*, 35-37.

Vernon Hall, *Expl* 26 (Nov. 1967): 28.

Richard Kelly, *Expl* 25 (Mar. 1967): 57.

Riding and Graves, *A Survey of Modernist Poetry*, 103-9.

"Conrad in Twilight"

Charles Crupi, *Expl* 29 (Nov. 1970): 20.

Nat Henry, *Expl* 34 (Apr. 1976): 62.

Karl F. Knight, *Expl* 30 (May 1972): 75.

Delmore Schwartz, "Instructed of Much Mortality," *SR* 54 (Summer 1946): 445-46.

"Dead Boy"

Richard Gray, "The 'Compleat Gentleman': An Approach to John Crowe Ransom," *SoR* 12 (July 1976): 626-27.

Vivienne Koch, "The Achievement of John Crowe Ransom," *SR* 58 (Spring 1950): 239.

Vivienne Koch, "The Poetry of John Crowe Ransom," in Rajan, *Modern American Poetry*, 46.

F. O. Matthiessen, "Primarily Language," *SR* 56 (Summer 1948): 398-400. Reprinted in Matthiessen, *The Responsibilities of the Critic*, 47-49.

Rubin, *The Wary Fugitives*, passim.

Stageberg and Anderson, *Poetry as Experience*, 26-27.

G. P. Wasserman, "The Irony of John Crowe Ransom," *University of Kansas City Review* 23 (Winter 1956): 157-58.

"The Equilibrists"

Richmond C. Beatty, "John Crowe Ransom as Poet," *SR* 52 (Summer 1944): 359-60.

Bernard Bergonzi, "A Poem about the History of Love," *CritQ* 4 (Summer 1962): 127-37.

Drew and Sweeney, *Directions in Modern Poetry*, 208-11.

Jane Marston, "Persona and Perspective in John Crowe Ransom's Poetry," *MissQ* 30 (Winter 1976-77): 59-70.

Claire Clements Morton, "Ransom's 'The Equilibrists,'" *Expl* 41 (Summer 1983): 37-38.

Howard Nemerov, "Summer's Flare and Winter's Flaw," *SR* 56 (Summer 1948): 419-20.

Thornton H. Parsons, "Ransom and the Poetics of Monastic Ecstasy," *MLQ* 26 (Dec. 1965): 575-581.

Perrine and Reid, *100 American Poets*, 137.

Rubin, *The Wary Fugitives*, passim.

Henry W. Russell, "John Crowe Ransom: The Measure of Civil Man," *SoR* 23 (Apr. 1987): 256-70.

G. P. Wasserman, "The Irony of John Crowe Ransom," *University of Kansas City Review* 23 (Winter 1956): 158-59.

"The First Travels of Max"

Vivienne Koch, "The Achievement of John Crowe Ransom," *SR* 58 (Spring 1950): 237.

Vivienne Koch, "The Poetry of John Crowe Ransom," in Rajan, *Modern American Poetry*, 44-45.

"Grace"

Richmond C. Beatty, "John Crowe Ransom as Poet," *SR* 52 (Summer 1944): 347-48.

G. P. Wasserman, "The Irony of John Crowe Ransom," *University of Kansas City Review* 23 (Winter 1956): 152-53.

"Here Lies a Lady"

William Bleifuss, *Expl* 11 (May 1953): 51. Reprinted in *The Explicator Cyclopedia* 1: 239-40.

John M. Bradbury, "Ransom as Poet," *Accent* 11 (Winter 1951): 52-54.

Kilby, *Poetry and Life*, 16-17.

F. H. Stocking and Ellsworth Mason, *Expl* 8 (Oct. 1949): 1. Reprinted in *The Explicator Cyclopedia* 1:238-39.

"Janet Waking"

Brooks, *Modern Poetry and the Tradition*, 92-93.

Deutsch, *Poetry in Our Time*, 206-7.

Vivienne Koch, "The Achievement of John Crowe Ransom," *SR* 58 (Spring 1950): 249-50.

Vivienne Koch, "The Poetry of John Crowe Ransom," in Rajan, *Modern American Poetry*, 55-56.

O'Connor, *Sense and Sensibility in Modern Poetry*, 140-41.

Rosenthal and Smith, *Exploring Poetry*, 7-8.

Rubin, *The Wary Fugitives*, passim.

G. P. Wasserman, "The Irony of John Crowe Ransom," *University of Kansas City Review* 23 (Winter 1956): 155-56.

Wheeler, *The Design of Poetry*, 110-20.

"Lady Lost"

Vivienne Koch, "The Achievement of John Crowe Ransom," *SR* 58 (Spring 1950): 247-49.

Vivienne Koch, "The Poetry of John Crowe Ransom," in Rajan, *Modern American Poetry*, 54-55.

"Little Boy Blue"

Charles Mitchell, *Expl* 22 (Sept. 1963): 5.

"Miller's Daughter"

Richmond C. Beatty, "John Crowe Ransom as Poet," *SR* 52 (Summer 1944): 357-58.

"Miriam Tazewell"

Robert Flynn, *Expl* 12 (May 1954): 45. Reprinted in *The Explicator Cyclopedia* 1:240-41.

Vivienne Koch, "The Achievement of John Crowe Ransom," *SR* 58 (Spring 1950): 239-40.

Vivienne Koch, "The Poetry of John Crowe Ransom," in Rajan, *Modern American Poetry*, 46-47.

G. P. Wasserman, "The Irony of John Crowe Ransom," *University of Kansas City Review* 23 (Winter 1956): 156-57.

"Night Voices"

Richmond C. Beatty, "John Crowe Ransom as Poet," *SR* 52 (Summer 1944): 354-55.

"Noonday Grace"

Richmond C. Beatty, "John Crowe Ransom as Poet," *SR* 52 (Summer 1944): 345-46.

"Old Mansion"

Vivienne Koch, "The Achievement of John Crowe Ransom," *SR* 58 (Spring 1950): 245-47.

Vivienne Koch, "The Poetry of John Crowe Ransom," in Rajan, *Modern American Poetry*, 52-53.

"Painted Head"

Richmond C. Beatty, "John Crowe Ransom as Poet," *SR* 52 (Summer 1944): 365-66.

John M. Bradbury, "Ransom as Poet," *Accent* 11 (Winter 1951): 55-56.

Brooks, *Modern Poetry and the Tradition*, 94-95.

Brooks, Lewis, and Warren, *American Literature*, 2657-58.

Vivienne Koch, "The Poetry of John Crowe Ransom," in Rajan, *Modern American Poetry*, 62-64.

Charles Moorman, *Expl* 10 (Dec. 1951): 15. Reprinted in *The Explicator Cyclopedia* 1:241-43.

Rubin, *The Wary Fugitives*, passim.

Virginia Wallach, *Expl* 14 (Apr. 1956): 45. Reprinted in *The Explicator Cyclopedia* 1: 243-44.

"Parting, without a Sequel"

Perrine and Reid, *100 American Poems*, 138-41.

"Philomela"

Edwin Russell, "The Meter-Making Argument," in Ludwig, *Aspects of American Poetry*, 3-4.

Delmore Schwartz, "Instructed of Much Mortality," *SR* 54 (Summer 1946): 443-44.

Samuel H. Woods, Jr., "'Philomela': John Crowe Ransom's *Ars Poetica*," *CE* 27 (Feb. 1966): 408-13.

"Piazza Piece"

Ribner and Morris, *Poetry*, 479-81.

"Prelude to an Evening"

Cleanth Brooks, "The Doric Delicacy," *SR* (Summer 1948): 412-14.

Brooks, *A Shaping Joy*, 279-81.

Vivienne Koch, "The Poetry of John Crowe Ransom," in Rajan, *Modern American Poetry*, 62-64.

Virginia L. Peck, *Expl* 20 (Jan. 1962): 41. Reprinted in *The Explicator Cyclopedia* 1:244.

"The School"

Richmond C. Beatty, "John Crowe Ransom as Poet," *SR* 52 (Summer 1944): 350.

"Spectral Lovers"

Richmond C. Beatty, "John Crowe Ransom as Poet," *SR* 52 (Summer 1944): 353-54.

Cleanth Brooks, "The Doric Delicacy," *SR* 56 (Summer 1948): 410-12.

Brooks, *A Shaping Joy*, 277-79.

Vivienne Koch, "The Achievement of John Crowe Ransom," *SR* 58 (Spring 1950): 240-43.

Vivienne Koch, "The Poetry of John Crowe Ransom," in Rajan, *Modern American Poetry*, 47-50.

Thornton H. Parsons, "Ransom and the Poetics of Monastic Ecstasy," *MLQ* 26 (Dec. 1965): 572-75.

"Spiel of Three Mountebanks"

Howard Nemerov, "Summer's Flare and Winter's Flaw," *SR* 56 (Summer 1948): 422.

"The Swimmer"

Richmond C. Beatty, "John Crowe Ransom as Poet," *SR* 52 (Summer 1944): 345.

"The Tall Girl"

Vivienne Koch, "The Achievement of John Crowe Ransom," *SR* 58 (Spring 1950): 245.

Vivienne Koch, "The Poetry of John Crowe Ransom," in Rajan, *Modern American Poetry*, 51-52.

William Pratt, "Metamorphosis of a Poem," *MissQ* 30 (Winter 1976): 29-58.

"Two in August"

Richmond C. Beatty, "John Crowe Ransom as Poet," *SR* 52 (Summer 1944): 359.

Brooks, Lewis, and Warren, *American Literature*, 2655-56.

Katherine W. Snipes, *Expl* 26 (Oct. 1967): 15.

"Vaunting Oak"

Cleanth Brooks, "The Doric Delicacy," *SR* 56 (Summer 1948): 406-8.

Brooks, *A Shaping Joy*, 273-75.

F. O. Matthiessen, "Primarily Language," *SR* 56 (Summer 1948): 394-95. Reprinted in Matthiessen, *The Responsibilities of the Critic*, 47-49.

"Vision by Sweetwater"

Brooks, Lewis, and Warren, *American Literature*, 2652.

"Winter Remembered"

Bloom, Philbrick, and Blistein, *The Order of Poetry*, 101-4.

Greenfield and Weatherhead, "Introductory Essay: The Experience of a Poem," in *The Poem: An Anthology*, 33-35.

Jane Marston, "Persona and Perspective in John Crowe Ransom's Poetry," *MissQ* 30 (Winter 1976-77): 59-70.

Thornton H. Parsons, "Ransom and the Poetics of Monastic Ecstasy," *MLQ* 26 (Dec. 1965): 582-85.

Riding and Graves, *A Survey of Modernist Poetry*, 229-30.

REED, ISHMAEL

"I Am a Cowboy in the Boat of Ra"

Robert H. Abel, *Expl* 30 (May 1972): 81.*y*

REXROTH, KENNETH R.

[Interview]

Linda Hamalian, "Everson on Rexroth: An Interview," *LitR* 26 (Spring 1983): 423-26.

"Andree Rexroth"

Donald Gutiérrez, "Natural Supernaturalism: The Nature Poetry of Kenneth Rexroth," *LitR* 26 (Spring 1983): 405-22.

"Another Spring"

Donald Gutiérrez, "Natural Supernaturalism: The Nature Poetry of Kenneth Rexroth," *LitR* 26 (Spring 1983): 405-22.

"Autumn in California"

Thurley, *The American Moment: American Poetry in the Mid-century*, 159-67.

"Clear Autumn"

Gutiérrez, *The Maze in the Mind and the World*, passim.

"Confusion"

Donald Gutiérrez, "Love Sacred and Profane: The Erotic Lyrics of Kenneth Rexroth," *Sagetrieb* 2 (Winter 1983): 101-12.

"Growing"

Donald Gutiérrez, "Love Sacred and Profane: The Erotic Lyrics of Kenneth Rexroth," *Sagetrieb* 2 (Winter 1983): 101-12.

"The Homestead Called Damascus"

Lawrence Lipton, "Notes toward an Understanding of Kenneth Rexroth with Special Attention to 'The Homestead Called Damascus,'" *Quarterly Review of Literature* 9 (1957): 37-46.

"Incarnation"

Donald Gutiérrez, "Natural Supernaturalism: The Nature Poetry of Kenneth Rexroth, " *LitR* 26 (Spring 1983): 405-22.

"Inversely, as the Square of their Distance Apart"

Donald Gutiérrez, "Love Sacred and Profane: The Erotic Lyrics of Kenneth Rexroth," *Sagetrieb* 2 (Winter 1983): 101-12.

"Leda Hidden"

Gutiérrez, *The Maze in the Mind and the World*, passim.

Donald Gutiérrez, "Natural Supernaturalism: The Nature Poetry of Kenneth Rexroth, " *LitR* 26 (Spring 1983): 405-22.

"Newhampton, 1922--San Francisco, 1939"

Donald Gutiérrez, "Love Sacred and Profane: The Erotic Lyrics of Kenneth Rexroth," *Sagetrieb* 2 (Winter 1983): 101-12.

"Oaxaca 1925"

Donald Gutiérrez, "Love Sacred and Profane: The Erotic Lyrics of Kenneth Rexroth," *Sagetrieb* 2 (Winter 1983): 101-12.

"She Is Away"

Gutiérrez, *The Maze in the Mind and the World*, passim.

"The Thin Edge of Your Pride"

Donald Gutiérrez, "Love Sacred and Profane: The Erotic Lyrics of Kenneth Rexroth," *Sagetrieb* 2 (Winter 1983): 101-12.

"Time"

Gutiérrez, *The Maze in the Mind and the World*, passim.

REZNIKOFF, CHARLES

"Aphrodite Urania"

Kenner, *A Homemade World*, 165-66.

RICH, ADRIENNE

"Cartographies of Silence"

Charles Altieri, "Sensibility, Rhetoric, and Will: Some Tensions in Contemporary Poetry," *ConL* 23 (Fall 1982): 451-79.

"The Celebration in the Plaza"

Wheeler, *The Design of Poetry*, 145-50.

"Contradictions: Tracking Poems"

Patrick Deane, "A Line of Complicity: Baudelaire--T. S. Eliot--Adrienne Rich," *CRevAS* 18 (Winter 1987): 463-81.

The Dream of a Common Language

Mary J. Carruthers, "The Re-Vision of the Muse: Adrienne Rich, Audre Lorde, Judy Grahn, Olga Broumas," *HudR* 36 (Summer 1983): 293-322.

Catharine Stimpson, "Adrienne Rich and Lesbian/Feminist Poetry," *Parnassus* 12 (Spring/Winter 1985): 249-68.

"From a Survivor"

Karen Alkalay-Gut, "The Lesbian Imperative in Poetry," *ContempR* 242 (1983): 209-11.

"The Mirror in which Two Are Seen as One"

Susan R. Van Dyne, "The Mirrored Vision of Adrienne Rich," *MPS* 8 (Autumn 1977): 161-66.

"Necessities of Life"

Betsy Erkkila, "Dickinson and Rich: Toward a Theory of Female Poetic Influence," *AL* 56 (Dec. 1984): 541-59.

"Newsreel"

Cary Nelson, "Whitman in Vietnam: Poetry and History in Contemporary America," *MR* 16 (Winter 1975): 55-71.

"Phantasia for Elvira Shatayeo"

Pope, *A Separate Vision: Isolation in Contemporary Women's Poetry*, 116-62.

"Reforming the Crystal"

Catharine Stimpson, "Adrienne Rich and Lesbian/Feminist Poetry," *Parnassus* 12 (Spring/Winter 1985): 249-68.

Snapshots of a Daughter-in-Law

Patrick Deane, "A Line of Complicity: Baudelaire--T. S. Eliot--Adrienne Rich," *CRevAS* 18 (Winter 1987): 463-81.

"The Spirit of the Place"

Altieri, *Self and Sensibility in Contemporary American Poetry*, passim.

"The Stranger"

Altieri, *Self and Sensibility in Contemporary American Poetry*, passim.

"Transcendental Etude"

Charles Altieri, "Sensibility, Rhetoric, and Will: Some Tensions in Contemporary Poetry," *ConL* 23 (Fall 1982): 451-79.

"The Trees"

Pope, *A Separate Vision*, passim.

"A Valediction Forbidding Mourning"

Carol Bere, "A Reading of Adrienne Rich's 'A Valediction Forbidding Mourning,'" *CP* 11 (Fall 1978): 33-38.

Edward Proffitt, "Allusion in Adrienne Rich's 'A Valediction Forbidding Mourning,'" *CP* 15 (Fall 1983): 21-24.

RÍOS, ALBERTO

"Corrido"

José David Saldívar, "Towards a Chicano Poetics: The Making of the Chicano Subject, 1969-1982," *Confluencia* 1 (1986): 10-17.

"Los Vatos"

José David Saldívar, "Towards a Chicano Poetics: The Making of the Chicano Subject, 1969-1982," *Confluencia* 1 (1986): 10-17.

"Whispering to Fool the Wind"

Candelaria, *Chicano Poetry: A Critical Introduction*, 179-80, 195-96, 204-5, 218-22.

José David Saldívar, "Towards a Chicano Poetics: The Making of the Chicano Subject, 1969-1982," *Confluencia* 1 (1986): 10-17.

ROCHA, RINA GARCIA

"North Avenue/1600 North"

Norwood and Monk, *The Desert Is No Lady*, passim.

"The Truth in My Eyes"

Norwood and Monk, *The Desert Is No Lady*, passim.

RODRIGUEZ, RICHARD

Hunger of Memory

A. C. Marquez, "Richard Rodriguez's *Hunger of Memory* and the Poetics of Experience," *AQ* 40 (Summer 1984): 130-41.

ROETHKE, THEODORE R.

"The Abyss"

William Heyen, "The Divine Abyss: Theodore Roethke's Mysticism," *TSLL* 11 (Summer 1969): 1052-68.

Malkoff, *Theodore Roethke*, 196-200.

"The Auction"

James McMichael, "The Poetry of Theodore Roethke," *SoR*, n.s. 5 (Winter 1969): 5.

"The Ballad of the Clairvoyant Widow"

Robert Kirsch, "'You're My Toughest Mentor': William Carlos Williams and Theodore Roethke (1940-42)," *JML* 12 (July 1985): 332-44.

"The Big Wind"

John D. Boyd, "Texture and Form in Theodore Roethke's Greenhouse Poems," *MLQ* 32 (Dec. 1971): 415-18.

Kenneth Burke, "The Vegetal Radicalism of Theodore Roethke," *SR* 58 (Winter 1950): 70-71. Reprinted in Burke, *Language as Symbolic Action*, 255-56.

Phillips, *The Confessional Poets*, 114.

"The Boy and the Bush"

Del Ivan Janik, *Expl* 32 (Nov. 1973): 20.

"Bring the Day"

Hilton Kramer, "The Poetry of Theodore Roethke," *Western Review* 18 (Winter 1954): 137.

"Child on Top of a Greenhouse"

H. G. Widdowson, *Stylistics and the Teaching of Literature* (London: Longman Group, 1975), 54-57, 108-14.

"Cuttings"

D. Bogen, "From *Open House* to the Greenhouse: Theodore Roethke's Poetic Breakthrough," *ELH* 47 (Summer 1980): 399-418.

Malkoff, *Theodore Roethke*, 50.

"Cuttings (*later*)"

D. Bogen, "From *Open House* to the Greenhouse: Theodore Roethke's Poetic Breakthrough," *ELH* 47 (Summer 1980): 399-418.

John D. Boyd, "Texture and Form in Theodore Roethke's Greenhouse Poems," *MLQ* 32 (Dec. 1971): 422-24.

Malkoff, *Theodore Roethke*, 49-51.

"The Dance"

Carroll Arnett, "Minimal to Maximal: Theodore Roethke's Dialectic," *CE* 18 (May 1957): 415-16.

David L. Vanderwerken, "Roethke's 'Four for Sir John Davies' and 'The Dying Man," *Research Studies* 41 (June 1973): 125-27.

"The Decision"

Richard A. Blessing, "Theodore Roethke's Sometimes Metaphysical Motion," *TSLL* 14 (Winter 1973): 741-42.

"Dolor"

Jeff Westfall, *Expl* 37 (Spring 1979): 25-26.

"The Donkey"

Penelope Scambly Schoot, "'I Am!' Says Theodore Roethke: A Reading of the Nonsense Poems," *Research Studies* 43 (June 1975): 110.

"The Dying Man" (sequence)

Malkoff, *Theodore Roethke*, 151-59 and passim.

David L. Vanderwerken, "Roethke's 'Four for Sir John Davies' and 'The Dying Man,'" *Research Studies* 41 (June 1973): 130-34.

ROETHKE, THEODORE R.

"Elegy"

Richard A. Blessing, "Theodore Roethke: A Celebration," *TSE* 20 (1972): 176-79.

"Elegy for Jane"

Richard A. Blessing, "Theodore Roethke: A Celebration," *TSE* 20 (1972): 173-74.

Perrine and Reid, *100 American Poems*, 205-6.

Evelyn M. Romig, "An Achievement of H. D. and Theodore Roethke: Psychoanalysis and the Poetics of Teaching," *L&P* 28 (1978): 105-11.

Keith Schlap, "A Syntactic Figure in Two Poems by Theodore Roethke," *Lang&S* 9 (Fall 1978): 238-46.

"The Far Field"

Hugh B. Staples, "The Rose in the Sea-Wind: A Reading of Theodore Roethke's 'North American Sequence,'" *AL* 36 (May 1964): 201-2.

"A Field of Light"

Kenneth Burke, "The Vegetal Radicalism of Theodore Roethke," *SR* 58 (Winter 1950): 94-95. Reprinted in Burke, *Language as Symbolic Action*, 272-73.

Hilton Kramer, "The Poetry of Theodore Roethke," *Western Review* 18 (Winter 1954): 141-42.

Malkoff, *Theodore Roethke*, 93-95.

"Four for Sir John Davies"

James McMichael, "The Poetry of Theodore Roethke," *SoR*, n.s. 5 (Winter 1969): 11-14.

Mills, *Contemporary American Poetry*, 61-62.

Sullivan, *Theodore Roethke: The Garden Master*, 96-100.

David L. Vanderwerken, "Roethke's 'Four for Sir John Davies' and 'The Dying Man,'" *Research Studies* 41 (June 1973): 130-34.

"Fourth Meditation"

Malkoff, *Theodore Roethke*, 165-67.

"Frau Bauman, Frau Schmidt, and Frau Schwartze"

Richard A. Blessing, "Theodore Roethke: A Celebration," *TSE* 20 (1972): 174-76.

"Genesis"

D. Bogen, "From *Open House* to the Greenhouse: Theodore Roethke's Poetic Breakthrough," *ELH* 47 (Summer 1980): 399-418.

"The Gentle"

D. L. Colussi, *Expl* 27 (May 1969): 73.

"Give Way, Ye Gates"

Hilton Kramer, "The Poetry of Theodore Roethke," *Western Review*, 18 (Winter 1954): 138.

Rosenthal, *The Modern Poets*, 241-42.

Sullivan, *Theodore Roethke: The Garden Master*, 65-67.

Vernon, *The Garden and the Map: Schizophrenia in Twentieth Century Literature and Culture*, 179-81.

John Vernon, "Theodore Roethke's *Praise to the End*! Poems," *IowaR* 2 (Fall 1971): 72-74.

"Her Becoming"

Malkoff, *Theodore Roethke*, 164-65 and passim.

"I Am! Says the Lamb"

Jenijoy LaBelle, "William Blake, Theodore Roethke, and Mother Goose: The Unholy Trinity," *Blake Studies* 9 (1980): 74-86.

"I Knew a Woman"

Nicholas Ayo, "Jonson's Greek Ode in Roethke," *AN&Q* 13 (Mar. 1975): 107.

Helen T. Buttell, *Expl* 24 (May 1966): 78.

Nat Henry, *Expl* 27 (Jan. 1969): 31.

Nat Henry, *Expl* 38 (Fall 1979): 16-18.

Jenijoy LaBelle, *Expl* 32 (Oct. 1973): 15.

Dwight L. McCawley, *Expl* 37 (Spring 1979): 10-11.

Virginia L. Peck, *Expl* 22 (Apr. 1964): 66.

"I'm Here"

Malkoff, *Theodore Roethke*, 162-64.

"In a Dark Time"

Richard A. Blessing, "Theodore Roethke's Sometimes Metaphysical Motion," *TSLL* 14 (Winter 1973): 732-35.

John Hobbs, "The Poet as His Own Interpreter: Roethke on 'In a Dark Time,'" *CE* 33 (Oct. 1971): 55-66.

Malkoff, *Theodore Roethke*, 206-11 and passim.

"I Need, I Need"

Vernon, *The Garden and the Map: Schizophrenia in Twentieth Century Literature and Culture*, 175-77.

John Vernon, "Theodore Roethke's *Praise to the End!* Poems," *IowaR* 2 (Fall 1971): 70-71.

"In Evening Air"

Richard A. Blessing, "Theodore Roethke's Sometimes Metaphysical Motion," *TSLL* 14 (Winter 1973): 735-37.

Malkoff, *Theodore Roethke*, 211-12.

Robert D. Newman, "Emily Dickinson's Influence on Roethke's 'In Evening Air,'" *DkS* 57 (1986): 38-40.

"Infirmity"

Richard A. Blessing, "Theodore Roethke's Sometimes Metaphysical Motion," *TSLL* 14 (Winter 1973): 740-41.

"Interlude"

C. E. Nicholson and W. H. Wasilewski, *Expl* 36 (Spring 1978): 26-27.

L. Perrine, "The Theme of Roethke's 'Interlude,'" *Notes on Modern American Literature* 1 (Summer 1977): item 73.

"I Waited"

Richard A. Blessing, "Theodore Roethke's Sometimes Metaphysical Motion," *TSLL* 14 (Winter 1973): 743-44.

"Journey to the Interior"

E. Fred Carlisle, "Metaphoric Reference in Science and Literature: The Example of Watson and Crick and Roethke," *CentR* 29 (Summer 1985): 281-301.

Hugh B. Staples, "The Rose in the Sea-Wind: A Reading of Roethke's 'North American Sequence,'" *AL* 26 (May 1964): 198-200.

"Judge Not"

Robert Kusch, "You're My Toughest Mentor: William Carlos Williams and Theodore Roethke (1940-42)," *JML* 12 (July 1985): 332-44.

ROETHKE, THEODORE R.

"The Kitty-Cat Bird"

Penelope Scambly Schott, "'I Am!' Says Theodore Roethke: A Reading of the Nonsense Poems," *Research Studies* 43 (June 1975): 104-5.

"The Lamb"

Penelope Scambly Schott, "'I Am!' Says Theodore Roethke: A Reading of the Nonsense Poems," *Research Studies* 43 (June 1975): 104.

"A Light Breather"

Wheeler, *The Design of Poetry*, 195-97.

"The Long Alley"

Kenneth Burke, "The Vegetal Radicalism of Theodore Roethke," *SR* 58 (Winter 1950): 85-86, 93-94. Reprinted in *Language as Symbolic Action*, 271-72.

Malkoff, *Theodore Roethke*, 91-93.

Phillips, *The Confessional Poets*, 122-24.

Sullivan, *Theodore Roethke: The Garden Master*, 46-55.

"The Longing"

Hugh B. Staples, "The Rose in the Sea-Wind: A Reading of Theodore Roethke's 'North American Sequence,'" *AL* 36 (May 1964): 193-95.

"The Long Waters"

Thomas Gardner, "Theodore Roethke and the Contemporary American Long Poem," *ELWIU* 11 (Fall 1984): 237-52.

Malkoff, *Theodore Roethke*, 181-84.

Hugh B. Staples, "The Rose in the Sea-Wind: A Reading of Theodore Roethke's 'North American Sequence,'" *AL* 36 (May 1964): 200-201.

"The Lost Son" (sequence)

James Applewhite, "Children in Contemporary Poetry," *SCR* 17 (Spring 1985): 66-72.

Carroll Arnett, "Minimal to Maximal: Theodore Roethke's Dialectic," *CE* 18 (May 1957): 415.

Peter Balakian, "Theodore Roethke, William Carlos Williams and The American Grain," *MLQ* 17 (Winter 1987): 54-66.

Kenneth Burke, "The Vegetal Radicalism of Theodore Roethke," *SR* 58 (Winter 1950): 87-93. Reprinted in Burke, *Language as Symbolic Action*, 266-71.

Deutsch, *Poetry in Our Time*, 184-85.

Brendan Galvin, "Kenneth Burke and Theodore Roethke's 'Lost Son' Poems," *NWR* 2 (Summer 1971): 73-96.

Steven K. Hoffman, "Lowell, Berryman, Roethke, and Ginsberg: The Function of Confessional Poetry," *LitR* 22 (Spring 1979): 329-31.

Hilton Kramer, "The Poetry of Theodore Roethke," *Western Review* 18 (Winter 1954): 138-41.

Malkoff, *Theodore Roethke*, passim.

Mills, *Contemporary American Poetry*, 56-60.

Phillips, *The Confessional Poets*, 119-21.

Theodore Roethke, "Open Letter," in Ciardi, *Mid-Century American Poets*, 68-72.

Fred C. Schutz, "Antecedents of Roethke's 'The Lost Son' in an Unpublished Poem," *NConL* 5 (May 1975): 4-6.

Sullivan, *Theodore Roethke: The Garden Master*, 41-55.

Thurley, *The American Moment: American Poetry in the Mid-Century*, 91-105.

"Love Poems" (sequence in *The Far Field*)

Malkoff, *Theodore Roethke*, 91-95 and passim.

"The Marrow"

Richard A. Blessing, "Theodore Roethke's Sometimes Metaphysical Motion," *TSLL* 14 (Winter 1973): 742-43.

"The Meadow Mouse"

Keith Schlap, "A Syntactic Figure in Two Poems by Theodore Roethke," *Lang&S* 9 (Fall 1978): 238-46.

"Meditation at Oyster River"

Foster, *Theodore Roethke's Meditative Sequences*, passim.

Malkoff, *Theodore Roethke*, 178-80.

Hugh B. Staples, "The Rose in the Sea-Wind: A Reading of Theodore Roethke's 'North American Sequence,'" *AL* 36 (May 1964): 196-98.

"Meditations of an Old Woman"

Ann T. Foster, "Theodore Roethke as Meditative Poet: An Analysis of 'Meditations of an Old Woman,'" *SLitI* 18 (Spring 1985): 49-63.

Foster, *Theodore Roethke's Meditative Sequences*, passim.

Mills, *Contemporary American Poetry*, 63-66.

"The Minimal"

Robert Kusch, "You're My Toughest Mentor: William Carlos Williams and Theodore Roethke (1940-42)," *JML* 12 (July 1985): 332-44.

"The Moment"

Malkoff, *Theodore Roethke*, 205-6.

"The Motion"

Richard A. Blessing, "Theodore Roethke's Sometimes Metaphysical Motion," *TSLL* 14 (Winter 1973): 739.

"My Papa's Waltz"

Ciardi, *How Does a Poem Mean?*, 1003-4.

Ronald R. Janssen, *Expl* 44 (Winter 1986): 43-44.

"North American Sequence"

Susan R. Bowers, "The Explorer's Rose: Theodore Roethke's Mystical Symbol," *CP* 13 (Fall 1980): 41-49.

Foster, *Theodore Roethke's Meditative Sequences*, passim.

Thomas Gardner, "'North American Sequence': Theodore Roethke and the Contemporary American Long Poem, *Essays in Literature* 11 (Fall 1984): 237-52.

James McMichael, "The Poetry of Theodore Roethke," *SoR*, n.s. 5 (Winter 1969): 15-25.

Malkoff, *Theodore Roethke*, 173-90 and passim.

Hugh B. Staples, "The Rose in the Sea-Wind: A Reading of Theodore Roethke's 'North American Sequence,'" *AL* 36 (May 1964): 189-203.

"Old Lady's Winter Words"

Malkoff, *Theodore Roethke*, 112-15.

"O Lull Me, Lull Me"

Vernon, *The Garden and the Map: Schizophrenia in Twentieth Century Literature and Culture*, 183-84.

"Once More, the Round"

Richarde A. Blessing, "Theodore Roethke's Sometimes Metaphysical Motion," *TSLL* 14 (Winter 1973): 748.

"On the Road to Woodlawn"

D. Bogen, "From *Open House* to the Greenhouse: Theodore Roethke's Poetic Breakthrough," *ELH* 47 (Summer 1980): 399-418.

"Open House"

Gerald M. Garmon, *Expl* 28 (Nov. 1969): 28.

"Open Letter"

Malkoff, *Theodore Roethke*, passim.

"Orchids"

John D. Boyd, "Texture and Form in Theodore Roethke's Greenhouse Poems," *MLQ* 32 (Dec. 1971): 419-20.

"The Partner"

David L. Vanderwerken, "Roethke's 'Four for Sir John Davies' and 'The Dying Man,'" *Research Studies* 41 (June 1973): 127.

"Praise"

Jenijoy LaBelle, "Theodore Flopkins--Hopkins Roethke," in *Hopkins Among the Poets: Studies in Modern Responses to Gerard Manley Hopkins* (Hamilton, Ontario: International Hopkins Association, 1985), 80-83.

"The Premonition"

Malkoff, *Theodore Roethke*, 24-25, 27-28, 40-43.

"The Pure Fury"

Malkoff, *Theodore Roethke*, 129-36.

"The Renewal"

Malkoff, *Theodore Roethke*, 136-41.

"The Restored"

Richard A. Blessing, "Theodore Roethke's Sometimes Metaphysical Motion," *TSLL* 14 (Winter 1973): 745-46.

"The Right Thing"

Richard A. Blessing, "Theodore Roethke's Sometimes Metaphysical Motion," *TSLL* 14 (Winter 1973): 746-48.

"Root Cellar"

George Wolff, *Expl* 29 (Feb. 1971): 47.

"The Rose"

Hugh B. Staples, "The Rose in the Sea-Wind: A Reading of Theodore Roethke's 'North American Sequence,'" *AL* 36 (May 1964): 202-3.

"The Sensualists"

Charles Sanders, *Expl* 38 (Summer 1980): 9-10.

"The Sequel"

Richard A. Blessing, "Theodore Roethke's Sometimes Metaphysical Motion," *TSLL* 14 (Winter 1973): 737-39.

"Sequence, Sometimes Metaphysical"

Foster, *Theodore Roethke's Meditative Sequences*, passim.

Malkoff, *Theodore Roethke*, 206-19.

"The Serpent"

Penelope Scambly Schott, "'I Am!' Says Theodore Roethke: A Reading of the Nonsense Poems," *Research Studies* 43 (June 1975): 106-7.

"The Shape of Fire"

Kenneth Burke, "The Vegetal Radicalism of Theodore Roethke," *SR* 58 (Winter 1950): 95-97, 100. Reprinted in Burke, *Language as Symbolic Action*, 272-76.

Phillips, *The Confessional Poets*, 125-27.

Rosenthal, *The Modern Poets*, 242-43.

"Song"

W. R. Slaughter, "Roethke's 'Song,'" *MinnR* 8 (1968): 342-44.

"The Swan"

Charles Sanders, *Expl* 38 (Spring 1980): 26-28.

"The Tree, the Bird"

Richard A. Blessing, "Theodore Roethke's Sometimes Metaphysical Motion," *TSLL* 14 (Winter 1973): 744-45.

"Unfold! Unfold!"

James G. Southworth, "The Poetry of Theodore Roethke," *CE* 21 (Mar. 1960): 337.

"The Vigil"

David L. Vanderwerken, "Roethke's 'Four for Sir John Davies' and 'The Dying Man,'" *Research Studies* 41 (June 1873): 128-30.

"The Visitant"

Kenneth Burke, "The Vegetal Radicalism of Theodore Roethke," *SR* 58 (Winter 1950): 71-72. Reprinted in Burke, *Language as Symbolic Action*, 256-57.

Malkoff, *Theodore Roethke*, 110-12.

"The Waking"

Richard A. Blessing, "The Shaking That Steadies: Theodore Roethke's 'The Waking,'" *BSUF* 12 (Autumn 1971): 17-19.

Neal Bowers, *Expl* 40 (Spring 1982): 51-53.

William V. Davis, "The Escape into Fire: Thoedore Roethke's 'The Waking,'" *NConL* 5 (Mar. 1975): 2-10.

Robert Ely, *Expl* 34 (Mar. 1976): 54.

"A Walk in Late Summer"

James McMichael, "The Poetry of Theodore Roethke," *SoR*, n.s. 5 (Winter 1969): 6-7.

"Where Knock Is Open Wide"

Kenneth Burke, "The Vegetal Radicalism of Theodore Roethke," *SR* 58 (Winter 1954): 135-36.

Ronald Reichertz, *Expl* 26 (Dec. 1967): 34.

Nancy Ann Smith, *Expl* 44 (Spring 1986): 59-60.

Sullivan, *Theodore Roethke: The Garden Master*, 59-63.

Vernon, *The Garden and the Map: Schizophrenia in Twentieth Century Literature and Culture*, 164-75.

John Vernon, "Theodore Roethke's *Praise to the End!* Poems," *IowaR* 2 (Fall 1971): 62-70.

"Words for the Wind"

Malkoff, *Theodore Roethke*, 127-29, 143-45.

ROETHKE, THEODORE R.

"The Wraith"

David L. Vanderwerken, "Roethke's 'Four for Sir John Davies' and 'The Dying Man,'" *Research Studies* 41 (June 1973): 128.

ROSS, ALAN

"Radar"

Perrine and Reid, *100 American Poems*, 281-82.

ROTHENBERG, JEROME

"Abulafia's Circles"

Gitenstein, *Apocalyptic Messianism and Contemporary Jewish-American Poetry*, 47-48, 55, 100-105.

Poems for the Game of Silence

Paul, *In Search of the Primitive*, passim.

Poland, Nineteen Thirty-One

Paul, *In Search of the Primitive*, passim.

RUKEYSER, MURIEL R.

"Boy with His Hair Cut Short"

Walter Gierasch, "Reading Modern Poetry," *CE* 2 (Oct. 1940): 32-33.
Rosenthal and Smith, *Exploring Poetry*, 285-87.

"The Childless Years Alone without a House"

J. F. Nims, *Poetry: A Critical Supplement*, Jan. 1948, 17-18.

"Effort at Speech between Two People"

Perrine and Reid, *100 American Poets*, 217.

"They Came to Me and Said, 'There Is a Child'"

J. F. Nims, *Poetry: A Critical Supplement*, Jan. 1948, 17-18.

SALINAS, LUÍS OMAR

"Darkness under the Trees"

Albert Ríos, "Chicano/Borderlands Literature and Poetry," in *Contemporary Latin American Culture: Unity and Diversity*, ed. C. Gail Guntermann (Tempe: Center for Latin American Studies and Arizona State University Press, 1984), 79-93.

SANCHEZ, SONIA

[Interview]

Herbert Leibowitz, "Exploding Myths: An Interview with Sonia Sanchez," *Parnassus* 12/13 (Spring/Winter 1985): 357-68.

"I've Been a Woman"

David Williams, "The Poetry of Sonia Sanchez," in Evans, *Black Women Writers*, 433-48.

SANDBURG, CARL S.

"Broken-Face Gargoyles"

Bernard S. Oldsey, *Expl* 7 (May 1949): 50. Reprinted in *The Explicator Cyclopedia* 1:262-63.

"Caboose Thoughts"

Richard Crowder, *Expl* 4 (June 1946): 52. Reprinted in *The Explicator Cyclopedia* 1:263-64.

"Chicago"

Charles Allen, "Cadence Free Verse," *CE* 9 (Jan. 1948): 197-98.

Walter Blair, *Literature of the United States* 2:962.

Anne-Marie Brumm, "The Cycle of Life: Motifs in the Chicago Poems of Carl Sandburg," *ZAA* 31 (1983): 237-55.

Perrine and Reid, *100 American Poets*, 53-54.

Robert L. Reid, "The Day Book Poems of Carl Sandburg," *ON* 9 (Fall 1983): 205-18.

"Cool Tombs"

Daniel G. Hoffman, *Expl* 9 (May 1951): 46. Reprinted in *The Explicator Cyclopedia* 1:264.

"Early Lynching"

Ralph P. Boas, *Expl* 1 (June 1943): 67. Reprinted in *The Explicator Cyclopedia* 1:264-65.

"A Fence"

Selma Wagner, *Expl* 27 (Feb. 1969): 42.

"Fog"

Thomas and Brown, *Reading Poems: An Introduction to Critical Study*, 646-47.

"Lost"

Hill, *Constituent and Pattern in Poetry*, 49-50.

"Nocturne in a Deserted Brickyard"

Charles Allen, "Cadence Free Verse," *CE* 9 (Jan. 1948): 195-97.

"Number Man"

J. F. Nims, *Poetry: A Critical Supplement*, Oct. 1947, 1-4.

"On a Flimmering Flume You Shall Ride"

J. F. Nims, *Poetry: A Critical Supplement*, Oct. 1947, 4-5.

The People, Yes

Daniel Hoffman, "'Moonlight dries no mittens': Carl Sandburg Reconsidered," *GaR* 32 (Summer 1978): 390-407.

"Prayers of Steel"

Sigrid Renaux, "The Creative Process in Sandburg's 'Prayers of Steel,'" *RLet* 31 (1982): 151-63.

"To the Ghost of John Milton"

Engle and Carrier, *Reading Modern Poetry*, 32-34.

"Wind Song"

Perrine and Reid, *100 American Poems*, 55.

SANTAYANA, GEORGE

"I Sought on Earth a Garden of Delight"

Philip Blair Rice, "George Santayana," *KR* 2 (Autumn 1940): 469-71.

"O World"

Bert Case Diltz, *Sense or Nonsense: Contemporary Education at the Crossroads* (Toronto: McClelland and Stewart, 1972), 94-96.

SCHWARTZ, DELMORE S.

"A Dog Named Ego"

Stanley Poss, "Low Skies, Some Clearing, Local Frost," *NEQ* 41 (Sept. 1968): 438-42.

"The Heavy Bear Who Goes with Me"

Cohen, *Writing About Literature*, 4, 81-82, 142-43.

Perrine and Reid, *100 American Poems*, 219.

"Tired and Unhappy"

Richard Wilbur, "Poetry's Debt to Poetry," *HudR* 26 (Summer 1973): 290-93.

SCOBIE, STEPHEN

[Interview]

Margery Fee, "Stephen Scobie: Biographical," *CanL* 115 (Winter 1987): 81-102.

"McAlmond's Chinese Opera"

Laurie Ricou, "Prairie Poetry and Metaphors of Plain/s Space," *GPQ* 3 (Spring 1983): 109-19.

Pirates of Pen's Chance

Margery Fee, "Stephen Scobie: Biographical," *CanL* 115 (Winter 1987): 81-102.

SCOTT, DUNCAN CAMPBELL

"At Gull Lake"

D. M. R. Bentley, "Alchemical Transmutation in Duncan Campbell Scott's 'At Gull Lake: August, 1810,' and Some Contingent Speculations," *SCL* 10 (1985): 1-23.

"The Piper of Arll"

D. G. Jones, "The Sleeping Giant," *CanL* 26 (1965). Reprinted in Woodcock, *A Choice of Critics*, 3-24.

Lyle P. Weiss, "Bipolar Paths of Desire: D. C. Scott's Poetic and Narrative Structures," *SCL* 12 (1987): 35-52.

"The Wood by the Sea"

Lyle P. Weiss, "Bipolar Paths of Desire: D. C. Scott's Poetic and Narrative Structures," *SCL* 12 (1987): 35-52.

SCOTT, EVELYN

"The Winter Alone"

Dudley Fitts, "The Verse of Evelyn Scott," *Poetry* 36 (Sept. 1930): 338-43.

SCOTT, F. R.

"Last Rites"

Stephen A. C. Scobie, "The Road Back to Eden: The Poetry of F. R. Scott," *QQ* 79 (Autumn 1972): 319-20.

"Mural"

Stephen A. C. Scobie, "The Road Back to Eden: The Poetry of F. R. Scott," *QQ* 79 (Autumn 1972): 317-19.

SCOTT, F.R.

"Surfaces"

Stephen A. C. Scobie, "The Road Back to Eden: The Poetry of F. R. Scott," *QQ* 79 (Autumn 1972): 315-16.

"Trans Canada"

Stephen A. C. Scobie, "The Road Back to Eden: The Poetry of F. R. Scott," *QQ* 79 (Autumn 1972): 320-23.

SCOTT, WINFIELD TOWNLEY

"Green and Red and Darkness"

Felver and Nurmi, *Poetry: An Introduction and Anthology*, 16-17.

"The U.S. Sailor with the Japanese Skull"

Perrine and Reid, *100 American Poems*, 208-10.

SCULLY, JAMES

"Midsummer"

Perrine and Reid, *100 American Poems*, 272.

SEAY, JAMES

"It All Comes Together outside the Restroom in Hogansville"

David Bottoms, "Note on the Structure of James Seay's 'It All Comes Together outside the Restroom in Hogansville,'" *NConL* 7 (Sept. 1977): 6-7.

SEXTON, ANNE

[Interview]

Barbara Kelves, "The Art of Poetry: Anne Sexton," in McClatchey, *Anne Sexton*, 3-29.

Patricia Marx, "Interview," in McClatchey, *Anne Sexton*, 30-42.

William Packard, "Craft Interview," in McClatchey, *Anne Sexton*, 43-47.

All My Pretty Ones

Richard Howard, "Anne Sexton: 'Some Tribal Female Who Is Known But Forbidden,'" in McClatchey, *Anne Sexton*, 193-203.

"The Boat"

Lauter, *Women as Mythmakers*, 26, 29.

"The Concentrating Mother"

Lauter, *Women as Mythmakers*, 33-34.

"The Death of the Father"

J. D. McClatchey, "Anne Sexton: Somehow to Endure," in McClatchey, *Anne Sexton*, 244-90.

"The Division of Parts"

Lacey, *The Inner War*, 19-21.

J. D. McClatchey, "Anne Sexton: Somehow to Endure," in McClatchey, *Anne Sexton*, 244-90.

"The Double Image"

J. D. McClatchey, "Anne Sexton: Somehow to Endure," in McClatchey, *Anne Sexton*, 244-90.

"Elizabeth Gone"

J. D. McClatchey, "Anne Sexton: Somehow to Endure," in McClatchey, *Anne Sexton*, 244-90.

"For God While Sleeping"

Mills, *Contemporary American Poetry*, 232-33.

"For John, Who Begs Me Not to Enquire Further"

J. D. McClatchey, "Anne Sexton: Somehow to Endure," in McClatchey, *Anne Sexton*, 244-90.

"For My Lover, Returning to His Wife"

Ira Shor, "Anne Sexton's 'For My Lover . . .': Feminism in the Classroom," *CE* 34 (May 1973): 1085-90.

"For the Year of the Insane"

Lacey, *The Inner War*, 26-27.

"The House"

J. D. McClatchey, "Anne Sexton: Somehow to Endure," in McClatchey, *Anne Sexton*, 244-90.

"Housewife"

Ostriker, *Stealing the Language*, 72-73.

"I Dare to Live"

R. B. Axelrod, "'I Dare to Live': The Transforming Art of Anne Sexton," in Brown and Olson, *Feminist Criticism on Theory, Poetry, and Prose*, 131-41.

"In Celebration of My Uterus"

Myra Stark, "Walt Whitman and Anne Sexton: A Note on the Uses of Tradition," *NConL* 8 (Sept. 1978): 7-8.

"The Jesus Papers"

Lauter, *Woman as Mythmakers*, 30-33.

Ostriker, *Stealing the Language*, 158 and passim.

"The Legend of the One-Eyed Man"

William H. Shurr, *Expl* 39 (Spring 1981): 2-3.

"Little Girly, My String Bean, My Lovely Woman"

Lacey, *The Inner War*, 23-24.

Live or Die

Robert Boyers, "*Live or Die*: The Achievment of Anne Sexton," in McClatchey, *Anne Sexton*, 204-15.

"The Lost Ingredient"

Lacey, *The Inner War*, 23.

"The Operation"

J. D. McClatchey, "Anne Sexton: Somehow to Endure," in McClatchey, *Anne Sexton*, 244-90.

Mills, *Contemporary American Poetry*, 228-30.

"Rapunzel"

Mary Carruthers, "Imagining Women: Notes towards a Feminist Poetic," *MR* 20 (Summer 1979): 281-307.

"Ringing the Bells"

Joyce M. Wegs, "Poets in Bedlam: Sexton's Use of Bishop's 'Visits to St. Elizabeth's' in 'Ringing the Bells,'" *CP* 15 (1982): 37-47.

"The Sleeping Beauty"

Thurley, *The American Moment: American Poetry in the Mid-Century*, 71-90.

"Snow White and the Seven Dwarfs"

Mary Carruthers, "Imagining Women: Notes towards a Feminist Poetic," *MR* 20 (Summer 1979): 281-307.

"Some Foreign Letters"

Mills, *Contemporary American Poetry*, 224-27.

"To a Friend Whose Work Has Come to Triumph"

Laurence Perrine, "Theme and Tone in Anne Sexton's 'To a Friend Whose Work Has Come to Triumph,'" *NConL* 7 (May 1977): 2-3.

To Bedlam and Part Way Back

Richard Howard, "Anne Sexton: 'Some Tribal Female Who Is Known But Forbidden,'" in McClatchey, *Anne Sexton*, 193-203.

"The Truth the Dead Know"

Mills, *Contemporary American Poetry*, 227-28.

"You, Dr. Martin"

Lacey, *The Inner War*, 16-17.

SHAPIRO, KARL S.

"Auto Wreck"

Bloom, Philbrick, and Blistein, *The Order of Poetry*, 24-28.

Alice Coleman, "Doors Leap Open," *EJ* 53 (Nov. 1964): 631-33.

Mills, *Contemporary American Poetry*, 110-13.

Perrine and Reid, *100 American Poems*, 35.

"Christmas Eve: Australia"

David Daiches, "The Poetry of Karl Shapiro," *Poetry* 66 (Aug. 1945): 267-69. Reprinted in Engle and Carrier, *Reading Modern Poetry*, 250-51.

"The Dome of Sunday"

Edwin Fussell, "Karl Shapiro: The Paradox of Prose and Poetry," *Western Review* 18 (Spring 1954): 240-42.

"The Leg"

Mills, *Contemporary American Poetry*, 113-15.

"Poet"

Michel Vinavert, *Expl* 4 (Dec. 1945): 23. Reprinted in *The Explicator Cyclopedia* 1:265.

"The Progress of Faust"

Perrine and Reid, *100 American Poems*, 221-23.

SHURIN, AARON

Giving Up the Ghost

Steve Abbott, "New San Francisco Writing and the Poetry of Aaron Shurin," *Credences*, n.s. 1 (Fall/Winter 1981/1982): 185-93.

The Night Sun

Steve Abbott, "New San Francisco Writing and the Poetry of Aaron Shurin," *Credences*, n.s. 1 (Fall/Winter 1981/1982): 185-93.

"Ravings"

Steve Abbott, "New San Francisco Writing and the Poetry of Aaron Shurin," *Credences*, n.s. 1 (Fall/Winter 1981/1982): 185-93.

"A River Then"

Steve Abbott, "New San Francisco Writing and the Poetry of Aaron Shurin," *Credences*, n.s. 1 (Fall/Winter 1981/1982): 185-93.

"A Waist"

Steve Abbott, "New San Francisco Writing and the Poetry of Aaron Shurin," *Credences*, n.s. 1 (Fall/Winter 1981/1982): 185-93.

SILKO, LESLIE MARMON

Ceremony (poems in novel)

Norma Wilson, "Outlook for Survival," *University of Denver Quarterly* 14 (Winter 1980): 22-30.

Laguna Woman

Norma Wilson, "Outlook for Survival," *University of Denver Quarterly* 14 (Winter 1980): 22-30.

"Prayer to the Pacific"

Norma Wilson, "Outlook for Survival," *University of Denver Quarterly* 14 (Winter 1980): 22-80.

"Snow Elk"

Kenneth M. Roemer, "Bear and Elk: The Nature(s) of Contemporary American Indian Poetry," in Allen, *Studies in American Indian Literature*, 178-91.

SILVA, BEVERLY

The Second St. Poems

Norwood and Monk, *The Desert Is No Lady*, passim.

SIMIC, CHARLES

[Interview]

Charles Simic, *The Uncertain Certainty: Interviews, Essays, and Notes on Poetry* (Ann Arbor: University of Michigan Press, 1985), passim.

"The Variant"

David Walker, *"O What Solitude*: The Recent Poetry of Charles Simic," *Ironwood*, 7-8, 66-67.

SIMPSON, LOUIS

"American Poetry"

Bruce Bawer, "Louis Simpson and American Dreams," *AQ* 40 (Summer 1984): 147-62.

Dana Gioia, "Business and Poetry," *HudR* 36 (Spring 1983): 147-71.

"The Art of Storytelling"

John Bensko, "Reflexive Narration in Contemporary American Poetry: Some Examples from Mark Strand, John Ashbery, Norman Dubie, and Louis Simpson," *JNT* 16 (Spring 1986): 81-96.

"Before the Poetry Reading"

Bruce Bawer, "Louis Simpson and American Dreams," *AQ* 40 (Summer 1984): 147-62.

"The Deserted Boy"

Dell Hymes, "Louis Simpson's 'The Deserted Boy,'" *Poetics* 5 (1976): 119-55. Reprinted in Hymes, *In Vain I Tried to Tell You*, 142-83.

"The Green Shepherd"

Perrine and Reid, *100 American Poets*, 266-67.

"In California"

Bruce Bawer, "Louis Simpson and American Dreams," *AQ* 40 (Summer 1984): 147-62.

"Lines Written Near San Francisco"

Bruce Bawer, "Louis Simpson and American Dreams," *AQ* 40 (Summer 1984): 147-62.

"The Previous Tenant"

Stitt, *The World's Hieroglyphicic Beauty: Five American Poets*, 109-39.

"The Rejected"

Bruce Bawer, "Louis Simpson and American Dreams," *AQ* 40 (Summer 1984): 147-62.

"Rubber, coal, uranium, moons, poems"

Bruce Bawer, "Louis Simpson and American Dreams," *AQ* 40 (Summer 1984): 147-62.

"Walt Whitman at Bear Mountain"

Bruce Bawer, "Louis Simpson and American Dreams," *AQ* 40 (Summer 1984): 147-62.

Ronald Moran, "'Walt Whitman at Bear Mountain' and the American Illusion," *CP* 2 (Spring 1969): 5-9.

SKELLEY, JACK

"Monsters"

David E. James, "Poetry/Punk/Production: Some Recent Writing in L.A.," *MinnR*, n.s. 23 (Fall 1984): 127-48.

SMITH, DAVE

"Antelope"

Gary Waller, "I and Ideology: Demystifying the Self of Contemporary Poetry," *Denver Quarterly* 18 (Autumn 1983): 123-38.

Stephen Yenser, "Sea Changes: On Dave Smith," *APR* 11 (Jan./Feb. 1982): 32-35.

Dream Flights

Paul Christensen, "'Malignant Innocence,'" *Parnassus* 12 (Fall/Winter 1984): 154-82.

"Goshawk"

Gary Waller, "I and Ideology: Demystifying the Self of Contemporary Poetry," *Denver Quarterly* 18 (Autumn 1983): 123-38.

Stephen Yenser, "Sea Changes: On Dave Smith," *APR* 11 (Jan./Feb. 1982): 32-35.

"Homage to Edgar Allen Poe"

Paul Christensen, "'Malignant Innocence,'" *Parnassus* 12 (Fall/Winter 1984): 154-82.

Terry Hummer, "Dave Smith's 'Homage to Edgar Allen Poe': 'Pushed' Time and the Obsession of Memory," in *The Giver of Morning: On the Poetry of Dave Smith* (Birmingham, Alabama: Thunder City Press, 1982), passim.

In the House of the Judge

Paul Christensen, "'Malignant Innocence,'" *Parnassus* 12 (Fall/Winter 1984): 154-82.

"The Roundhouse Voice"

Bruce Bawer, "Dave Smith's 'Creative Writing,'" *New Criterion* 4 (Dec. 1985): 27-33.

SMITH, WILLIAM JAY

"American Primitive"

C. F. Burgess, "William Jay Smith's 'American Primitive': Toward a Reading," *ArQ* 26 (Spring 1970): 71-75.

SNODGRASS, W. D.

"April Inventory"

Carroll, *The Poem in Its Skin*, 174-85.

"A Cardinal"

Phillips, *Confessional Poets*, 54-55. First published as "Snodgrass and the Sad Hospital of the World," *UWR* 4 (Spring 1969).

"Heart's Needle"

Phillips, *Confessional Poets*, 57-62. First published as "Snodgrass and the Sad Hospital of the World," *UWR* 4 (Spring 1969).

"The Operation"

Phillips, *Confessional Poets*, 52-53. First published as "Snodgrass and the Sad Hospital of the World," *UWR* 4 (Spring 1969).

"Powwow"

Perrine and Reid, *100 American Poets*, 269-70.

SNYDER, GARY

[Interview]

Uri Hertz, "An Interview With Gary Snyder," *ThirdR* 7 (1985/1986): 51-53, 96.

"After Work"

Anthony Hunt, *Expl* 32 (Apr. 1974): 61.

"August on Sourdough, a Visit from Dick Brewer"

Jody Norton, "The Importance of Nothing: Absence and Its Origins in the Poetry of Gary Snyder," *ConL* 28 (Spring 1987): 41-66.

"Bubbs Creek Haircut"

A. Hunt, "'Bubbs Creek Haircut': Gary Snyder's 'Great Departure' in *Mountains and Rivers Without End*," *WAL* 15 (Fall 1980): 163-75.

"Burning the Small Dead"

Jody Norton, "The Importance of Nothing: Absence and Its Origins in the Poetry of Gary Snyder," *ConL* 28 (Spring 1987): 41-66.

"Cold Mountain Poems"

Jeffrey Miles, "Making It to Cold Mountain: Han-Shan in *The Dharma Bums*," in *Essays on the Literature of Mountaineering*, ed. E. Armand Singer (Morgantown: West Virginia University Press, 1982), 95-105.

Wyatt, *The Fall into Eden*, 188-93.

"Cold Mountain Poem 8"

Jacob Leed, "Gary Snyder, Han Shan, and Jack Kerouac," *JML* (Mar. 1984): 185-93.

"The Dead by the Side of the Road"

Elder, *Imagining the Earth: Poetry and the Vision of Nature*, passim.

"The Egg"

Rebecca A. Pickett, "Snyder's 'The Egg,'" *Expl* 42 (Winter 1984): 18-20.

"For Nothing"

Elder, *Imagining the Earth: Poetry and the Vision of Nature*, passim.

"For the Boy Who Was Dodger Point Lookout Fifteen Years Ago"

Wyatt, *The Fall into Eden*, 186-205.

"Hitch Haiku"

Jody Norton, "The Importance of Nothing: Absence and its Origins in the Poetry of Gary Snyder," *ConL* 28 (Spring 1987): 41-66.

"I Went into the Maverick Bar"

Sherman Paul, "Noble and Simple," *Parnassus* 3 (Spring/Summer 1975): 217-20.

"Marin-An"

Cheng Lok Chua and N. Sasaki, "Zen and the Title of Gary Snyder's 'Marin-An,'" *NConL* 8 (May 1978): 2-3.

"Mid August at Sourdough Mountain Lookout"

Robert Kern, "Toward a New Nature Poetry," *CentR* 19 (Summer 1975): 213-16.

Jody Norton, "The Importance of Nothing: Absence and Its Origins in the Poetry of Gary Snyder," *ConL* 28 (Spring 1987): 41-66.

"Mountains and Rivers without End"

Woon-ping Chin Holaday, "Formlessness and Form in Gary Snyder's 'Mountains and Rivers Without End,'" *Sagetrieb* 5 (1986): 41-52.

"Nooksack Valley"

Sherman Paul, "From Lookout to Ashram: The Way of Gary Snyder," *IowaR* 1 (Fall 1970): 71-72.

Wyatt, *The Fall Into Eden*, 186-205.

"Piute Creek"

Elder, *Imagining the Earth: Poetry and the Vision of Nature*, passim.

"Prayer for the Great Family"

Charles Altieri, "Gary Snyder's *Turtle Island*: The Problem of Reconciling the Roles of Seer and Prophet," *Boundary* 4 (Spring 1976): 766-68.

"Riprap"

Robert Kern, "Clearing the Ground: Gary Snyder and the Modernist Imperative," *Criticism* 19 (Spring 1977): 174-77.

David Robertson, "Gary Snyder Riprapping in Yosemite, 1955," *AmerP* 2 (Fall 1984): 52-59.

Wyatt, *The Fall into Eden*, 186-205.

"River in the Valley"

Patrick D. Murphy, "Gary Snyder's Endless River," *Notes on Modern American Literature* 9 (Spring/Summer 1985): item 4.

"Shark Meat"

Bert Almon, "Buddhism and Energy in the Recent Poetry of Gary Snyder," *Mosaic* 11 (Fall 1977): 117-25.

"Six-Month Song in the Foothills"

Jody Norton, "The Importance of Nothing: Absence and Its Origins in the Poetry of Gary Snyder," *ConL* 28 (Spring 1987): 41-66.

"The Spring"

Jody Norton, "The Importance of Nothing: Absence and Its Origins in the Poetry of Gary Snyder," *ConL* 28 (Spring 1987): 41-66.

"Steak"

Bert Almon, "Buddhism and Energy in the Recent Poetry of Gary Snyder," *Mosaic* 11 (Fall 1977): 117-25.

"Straight-Creek-Great Burn"

Charles Altieri, "Gary Snyder's *Turtle Island*: The Problem of Reconciling the Roles of Seer and Prophet," *Boundary* 4 (Spring 1976): 764-65.

"this poem is for bear"

Elder, *Imagining the Earth: Poetry and the Vision of Nature*, passim.

"True Night"

Wyatt, *The Fall into Eden*, 186-205.

"Water"

Jody Norton, "The Importance of Nothing: Absence and Its Origins in the Poetry of Gary Snyder," *ConL* 28 (Spring 1987): 41-66.

"Wave"

Bert Almon, "Buddhism and Energy in the Recent Poetry of Gary Snyder," *Mosaic* 11 (Fall 1977): 117-25.

Michael Davidson, "'From the Latin Speculum': The Modern Poet as Philologist," *ConL* 28 (Summer 1987): 187-205.

SOMMER, RICHARD

"The First Planet After Her Death"

Alberta T. Turner, "Implied Metaphor: A Problem in Evaluating Contemporary Poetry," *IowaR* 5 (Winter 1974): 114-15.

SOTO, GARY

The Elements of San Joaquin

Raymund Paredes, "The Evolution of Chicano Literature," in Baker, *Three American Literatures*, 68-72.

Alberto Ríos, "Chicano/Borderlands Literature and Poetry," in *Contemporary Latin American Culture: Unity and Diversity*, ed. C. Gail Guntermann (Tempe: Center for Latin American Studies and Arizona State University Press, 1984), 79-93.

The Tale of Sunlight

Raymund Paredes, "The Evolution of Chicano Literature," in Baker, *Three American Literatures*, 68-72.

"Where Sparrows Work Hard"

Candelaria, *Chicano Poetry: A Critical Introduction*, 176, 194-95, 209-11, 222-24, 235-37.

SOUSTER, RAYMOND

"The Cat at Currie's"

Louis Dudek, "Groundhog among the Stars," *CanL* 22 (1964). Reprinted in Woodcock, *A Choice of Critics*, 169-84.

The Colour of the Times

Louis Dudek, "Groundhog among the Stars," *CanL* 22 (1964). Reprinted in Woodcock, *A Choice of Critics*, 169-84.

"Coureurs-de-Bois"

Louis Dudek, "Groundhog among the Stars," *CanL* 22 (1964). Reprinted in Woodcock, *A Choice of Critics*, 169-84.

"The Hunter"

Louis Dudek, "Groundhog among the Stars," *CanL* 22 (1964). Reprinted in Woodcock, *A Choice of Critics*, 169-84.

"Night Watch"

Louis Dudek, "Groundhog among the Stars," *CanL* 22 (1964). Reprinted in Woodcock, *A Choice of Critics*, 169-84.

"A Shadow"

George Johnson, "Diction in Poetry," *CanL* 97 (Summer 1983): 39-44.

SOUTHWELL, ROBERT

"The Burning Babe"

Thomas Parkinson, "Robert Duncan's *Ground Work*," *SoR* 21 (Winter 1985): 52-62.

SPENCER, THEODORE

"The Circus: Or One View of It"

Perrine and Reid, *100 American Poems*, 189-90.

SPICER, JACK

"After Lorca"

Lori Chamberlain, "Ghostwriting the Text: Translation and the Poetics of Jack Spicer," *ConL* 26 (1985): 426-42.

Burton Hatlen, "Crawling into Bed with Sorrow: Jack Spicer's 'After Lorca,'" *Ironwood* 28 (1986): 118-35.

Billy the Kid

Frank Sadler, "The Frontier in Jack Spicer's 'Billy the Kid,'" *CP* 9 (Fall 1976): 15-21.

SQUIRES, RADCLIFFE

"The Garden of Ariadne"

Brewster Ghiselin, "Temenos and Transcendence: Poetry of Radcliffe Squires," *WHR* 38 (Autumn 1984): 274-78.

"The Garden of Hecate"

Brewster Ghiselin, "Temenos and Transcendence: Poetry of Radcliffe Squires," *WHR* 38 (Autumn 1984): 274-78.

"The Garden of Medusa"

Brewster Ghiselin, "Temenos and Transcendence: Poetry of Radcliffe Squires," *WHR* 38 (Autumn 1984): 274-78.

"The Garden of Niobe"

Brewster Ghiselin, "Temenos and Transcendence: Poetry of Radcliffe Squires," *WHR* 38 (Autumn 1984): 274-78.

"The Garden of the World"

Brewster Ghiselin, "Temenos and Transcendence: Poetry of Radcliffe Squires," *WHR* 38 (Autumn 1984): 274-78.

STAFFORD, WILLIAM S.

"Connections"

George S. Lensing, "William Stafford, Mythmaker," *MPS* 6 (Spring 1975): 7-9.

Lensing and Moran, *Four Poets and the Emotive Imagination: Robert Bly, James Wright, Louis Simpson, and William Stafford*, 205-7.

"At Cove on the Crooked River"

John Lauber, "World's Guest--William Stafford," *IowaR* 5 (Spring 1974): 91-92.

"The Farm on the Great Plains"

Richard Hugo, "Problems with Landscapes in Early Stafford Poems," *KanQ* 2 (Spring 1970): 35.

"Fifteen"

Dennis Daley Lunch, "Journeys in Search of Oneself: The Metaphor of the Road in William Stafford's *Traveling Through the Dark* and *The Rescued Year*," *MPS* 7 (Autumn 1976): 129-30.

"The Gift"

Stitt, *The World's Hieroglyphic Beauty*, 57-87.

"In California"

John Lauber, "World's Guest--William Stafford," *IowaR* 5 (Spring 1974): 94.

"One Home"

John Lauber, "World's Guest--William Stafford," *IowaR* 5 (Spring 1974): 90-91.

"Our People"

John Lauber, "World's Guest--William Stafford," *IowaR* 5 (Spring 1974: 88-89.

"A Ritual to Read to Each Other"

Dana Gioia, "Business and Poetry," *HudR* 36 (Spring 1983): 147-71.

"Shadows"

George S. Lensing, "William Stafford, Mythmaker," *MPS* 6 (Spring 1975): 9-13.

"Summer Will Rise"

John Lauber, "World's Guest--William Stafford," *IowaR* 5 (Spring 1974): 96.

STAFFORD, WILLIAM S.

"Traveling through the Dark"

Ronald K. Giles, *Expl* 43 (Spring 1985): 44-45.

Lensing and Moran, *Four Poets and the Emotive Imagination: Robert Bly, James Wright, Louis Simpson, and William Stafford*, 198-200.

Dennis Daley Lynch, "Journeys in Search of Oneself: The Metaphor of the Road in William Stafford's *Traveling through the Dark* and *The Rescued Year*," *MPS* 7 (Autumn 1976): 127-29.

"Writing the Australian Crawl"

Tom Hansen, "On Writing Poetry: Four Contemporary Poets," *CE* 44 (Mar. 1982): 265-73.

STANTON

"Dandelion"

Perrine and Reid, *100 American Poems*, 283-84.

STAUFFER, DONALD

"The Lemmings"

Adams, *The Contexts of Poetry*, 109-11.

STEIN, GERTRUDE S.

"A Box"

Jonathan C. George, *Expl* 31 (Feb. 1973): 42.

"Composition as Explanation"

B. Bassoff, "Gertrude Stein's 'Composition as Explanation,'" *TCL* 24 (Spring 1978): 76-80.

"Lipschitz"

Harry R. Garvin, *Expl* 14 (Dec. 1955): 18. Reprinted in *The Explicator Cyclopedia* 1:267-68.

"A Long Dress"

Ruth H. Brady, *Expl* 34 (Feb. 1976): 47.

STEPHENS, ALAN

"The Dragon of Things"

Donald W. Markos, "Alan Stephens: The Lineaments of the Real," *SoR* 11 (Apr. 1975): 346-47.

"First Twenty-Four Hours"

Donald W. Markos, "Alan Stephens: The Lineaments of the Real," *SoR* 11 (Apr. 1975): 351-53.

"The Green Cape"

Donald W. Markos, "Alan Stephens: The Lineaments of the Real," *SoR* 11 (Apr. 1975): 349-51.

"Homily"

Donald W. Markos, "Alan Stephens: The Lineaments of the Real," *SoR* 11 (Apr. 1975): 335-36.

"Little Things"

Nat Henry, *Expl* 11 (Dec. 1950): 20. Reprinted in *The Explicator Cyclopedia* 2:325-26.

Lysander Kemp, *Expl* 8 (May 1950): 50. Reprinted in *The Explicator Cyclopedia* 2:325.

"The Main Deep"

Brooks and Warren, *Understanding Poetry*, 170-73; rev. ed., 74-77.

"The Open World"

Donald W. Markos, "Alan Stephens: The Lineaments of the Real," *SoR* 11 (Apr. 1975): 338-40.

"Prologue: Moments in a Glade"

Winters, *Forms of Discovery*, 339-41.

"The Rivals"

Frankenberg, *Invitation to Poetry*, 58.

"The Three Sisters"

Donald W. Markos, "Alan Stephens: The Lineaments of the Real," *SoR* 11 (Apr. 1975): 347-48.

"Tree Meditation"

Donald W. Markos, "Alan Stephens: The Lineaments of the Real," *SoR* 11 (Apr. 1975): 353-55.

"A Walk in the Void"

Donald W. Markos, "Alan Stephens: The Lineaments of the Real," *SoR* 11 (Apr. 1975): 333-35.

STEVENS, WALLACE

"Academic Discourse at Havana"

Friar and Brinnin, *Modern Poetry*, 537.

"Anecdote of Men by the Thousand"

Quinn, *The Metamorphic Tradition*, 77.

"Anecdote of the Jar"

Abad, *A Formal Approach to Lyric Poetry*, 145-47.

Howard Baker, "Wallace Stevens and Other Poetry," *SoR* 1 (Autumn 1935): 376-77.

Bornstein, *Transformations of Romanticism*, 171-72.

Brooks, Lewis, and Warren, *American Literature*, 2156-57.

Sr. Madeline DeFrees, "Pegasus and Six Blind Indians," *EJ* 59 (Oct. 1970): 935.

Don Geiger, "Wallace Stevens' Wealth," *Perspective*, 7 (Autumn 1954): 160.

Gray, *American Poetry*, 167-68.

Donald Gutiérrez, "Circular Art: Round Poems of Wallace Stevens and William Carlos Williams, *CP* 14 (1981): 53-56.

Gutiérrez, *The Maze in the Mind and the World*, passim.

Robert Hass, "Wendell Berry: Finding the Land," *MPS* 2 (1971): 32-34.

Samuel Jay Keyser, "Wallace Stevens: Form and Meaning in Four Poems," *CE* 37 (Feb. 1976): 585-89.

J. P. Kirby, *Expl* 3 (Nov. 1944): 16. Reprinted in *The Explicator Cyclopedia* 1:268-69.

Murray Krieger, "*Ekphrasis* and the Still Movement of Poetry; or, *Laokoon* Revisited," in McDowell, *The Poet as Critic*, 24-25.

Frank Lentricchia, "Anatomy of a Jar," *SAQ* 86 (Fall 1987): 379-402.

Patricia Merivale, "Wallace Stevens' 'Jar': The Absurd Detritus of Romantic Myth," *CE* 26 (Apr. 1965): 527-32.

C. D. Narasimhaiah, "Wallace Stevens," in *Studies in American Literature: Essays in Honor of William Mulder*, ed. Jagdish Cander and Narindar S. Pradhan (Delhi: Oxford University Press, 1976), 227-28.

Rosenthal, *The Modern Poets*, 125-26.

M. Strom, "Wallace Stevens' Earthly Anecdotes," *NEQ* 58 (Sept. 1985): 421-41.

Charles C. Walcutt, "Interpreting the Symbol," *CE* 14 (May 1953): 449-51.

T. Weiss, "The Nonsense of Winters' *Anatomy*," *Quarterly Review of Literature* 1 (Spring 1944): 228.

Winters, *Anatomy of Nonsense*, 93-95. Reprinted in Winters, *In Defense of Reason*, 435-37.

"Anecdote of the Prince of Peacocks"

Vendler, *Wallace Stevens: Words Chosen out of Desire*, passim.

"The Apostrophe in Vicentine"

Frank Doggett, "Wallace Stevens and the World We Know," *EJ* 48 (Oct. 1959): 369-70.

Quinn, *The Metamorphic Tradition*, 75-76.

Sr. M. Bernetta Quinn, O.S.F., "Metamorphosis in Wallace Stevens," *SR* 60 (Spring 1952): 243-44.

"Arcades of Philadelphia the Past"

R. D. Ackerman, *Expl* 24 (May 1966): 80.

Paul Sanders, *Expl* 25 (May 1967): 72.

"Arrival at the Waldorf"

Robert Mollinger, *Expl* 31 (Jan. 1973): 40.

"Asides on the Oboe"

Beach, *Obsessive Images*, 132-33.

Hi Simons, "The Genre of Wallace Stevens," *SR* 53 (Autumn 1945): 579.

"The Auroras of Autumn"

Beach, *Obsessive Images*, 338-40.

Robert J. Bertholf, "Renewing the Set: Wallace Stevens' 'The Auroras of Autumn,'" *BSUF* 17 (Spring 1976): 37-45.

Bloom, *A Map of Misreading*, 186-92.

Donald David, "'The Auroras of Autumn,'" *Perspective* 7 (Autumn 1954): 125-36.

Richard F. Patteson, "The Failure of Consolation in *The Auroras of Autumn*," *CP* 8 (Fall 1975): 37-46.

Lucy Pollard-Gott, "Fractal Repetition Structure in Stevens' Poetry," *Lang&S* 19 (1986): 233-49.

John Reiss, *Expl* 39 (Fall 1980): 22.

Joseph N. Riddel, "Wallace Stevens' 'Visibility of Thought,'" *PMLA* 77 (Sept. 1962): 486-88.

Stephen Shapiro, "'That Which Is Always Beginning': Stevens's Poetry of Affirmation," *PMLA* 100 (Mar. 1985): 220-33.

C. Roland Wagner, "The Idea of Nothingness in Wallace Stevens," *Accent* 12 (Spring 1952): 116-17.

"The Auroras of Autumn" I

Ralph J. Mills, Jr., "Wallace Stevens: The Image of the Rock," *Accent* 18 (Spring 1958): 84.

"The Auroras of Autumn" II

Joseph Bennett, "Five Books, Four Poets," *HudR* 4 (Spring 1951): 134-36.

Frank Doggett, "The Poet of Earth: Wallace Stevens," *CE* 22 (Mar. 1961): 378-80.

"The Auroras of Autumn" III

Frank A. Doggett, "Why Read Wallace Stevens?" *Emory University Quarterly* 18 (Summer 1962): 84-85.

"The Auroras of Autumn" VIII

Frank Doggett, "The Poet of Earth: Wallace Stevens," *CE* 22 (Mar. 1961): 380.

"Autumn Refrain"

Terrance King, *Expl* 36 (Summer 1978): 19-20.

Robert Pack, "Wallace Stevens' Sufficient Muse, " *SoR* 11 (Oct. 1975): 771-73.

"Banal Sojourn"

William W. Bevis, "The Arrangement of *Harmonium*," *ELH* 37 (Sept. 1970): 457, 467.

"Bantams in Pine-Woods"

Marius Bewley, "The Poetry of Wallace Stevens," *PR* 16 (Sept. 1949): 898-905.

R. P. Blackmur, "Wallace Stevens," *Hound and Horn*, 5 (Jan./Mar. 1932): 247-48. Reprinted in Blackmur, *Language as Gesture*, 242-43.

Brooks, Lewis, and Warren, *American Literature*, 2157.

Mario L. D'Avanzo, "Emerson and Shakespeare in Stevens's 'Bantams in Pine-Woods,'" *AL* 49 (Mar. 1977): 103-7.

Gray, *American Poetry*, 166-67.

Mildred E. Hartsock, *Expl* 18 (Mar. 1960): 33. Reprinted in *The Explicator Cyclopedia* 1:270-71.

William Van O'Connor, "Wallace Stevens on 'The Poems of Our Climate,'" *University of Kansas City Review* 15 (Winter 1948): 106-7.

Fred H. Stocking, *Expl* 3 (Apr. 1945): 45. Reprinted in *The Explicator Cyclopedia* 1:269.

"The Bed of Old John Zeller"

J. M. Kertzer, "The Argument of Wallace Stevens: 'a logic of transformation certitudes,'" *Mosaic* 18 (Winter 1985): 27-43.

"The Bird with the Coppery, Keen Claws"

Louis H. Leiter, "Sense in Nonsense: Wallace Stevens' 'The Bird with the Coppery, Keen Claws,'" *CE* 26 (Apr. 1965): 551-54.

"Blanche McCarthy"

Harold Bloom, "Poetic Crossing II: American Stances," *GaR* 30 (Winter 1976): 790-92.

"The Bouquet"

George McFadden, "Poet, Nature, and Society in Wallace Stevens," *MLQ* 23 (Sept. 1962): 269-70.

"Bouquet of Roses in Moonlight"

J. F. Nims, *Poetry: A Critical Supplement*, Oct. 1947, 9.

"Certain Phenomena of Sound"

William W. Heath, *Expl* 12 (Dec. 1953): 16. Reprinted in *The Explicator Cyclopedia* 1:271-72.

Lise Rodgers, *Expl* 39 (Summer 1981): 39-41.

"Chaos in Motion and Not in Motion"

Vendler, *Wallace Stevens: Words Chosen Out of Desire*, passim.

"Chocorua to Its Neighbor"

Robert Pact, "The Abstracting Imagination of Wallace Stevens: Nothingness and the Hero," *ArQ* 11 (Autumn 1955): 206-8.

Roy Harvey Pearce, "The Cry and the Occasion: 'Chocorua to Its Neighbor,'" *SR* 15 (Oct. 1979): 777-91.

"A Clear Day and No Memories"

William Bevis, "Stevens' Toneless Poetry," *ELH* 41 (Summer 1974): 269-72.

Richard Blessing, "Wallace Stevens and the Necessary Reader: A Technique of Dynamism," *TCL* 18 (Oct. 1972): 255-56.

Stephen Shapiro, "'That Which Is Always Beginning': Stevens's Poetry of Affirmation," *PMLA* 100 (Mar. 1985): 220-33.

"The Comedian as the Letter C"

Richard P. Adams, "'The Comedian as the Letter C': A Somewhat Literal Reading," *TSE* 18 (1970): 95-114.

Howard Baker, "Wallace Stevens," *SoR* 1 (Autumn 1935): 377-81.

R. P. Blackmur, "Wallace Stevens," *Hound and Horn* 5 (Jan./Mar. 1932): 248-55. Reprinted in Blackmur, *The Double Agent*, 94-102; in Blackmur, *Language as Gesture*, 243-49.

Bloom, *Wallace Stevens: The Poems of Our Climate*, 68-87.

M. J. Collie, "The Rhetoric of Accurate Speech: A Note on the Poetry of Wallace Stevens," *EIC* 12 (Jan. 1962): 59-60.

Eleanor Cook, "Wallace Stevens: 'The Comedian as the Letter C,'" *AL* 49 (May 1977): 192-205.

Bonnie Costello, "Marianne Moore's Debt and Tribute to Wallace Stevens," *CP* 15 (1982): 27-33.

James V. Cunningham, "The Poetry of Wallace Stevens," *Poetry* 75 (Dec. 1949): 151-59. Reprinted in Howe, *Modern Literary Criticism*, 356-60; in Cunningham, *Tradition and Poetic Structure*, 111-16.

Guy Davenport, "Spinoza's Tulips: A Commentary on 'The Comedian as the Letter C,'" *Perspective* 7 (Autumn 1954): 147-54.

Frank Doggett, "Our Nature Is Her Nature," in Langford and Taylor, *The Twenties*, 39-40.

Carol Flake, *Expl* 30 (Nov. 1971): 26.

Frankenberg, *Pleasure Dome*, 210-15.

P. Furia and M. Roth, "Stevens' Fusky Alphabet," *PMLA* 93 (Jan. 1978): 66-77.

Don Geiger, "Wallace Stevens' Wealth," *Perspective* 7 (Autumn 1954): 165.

David L. Green, "'The Comedian as the Letter C,' Carlos, and Contact," *TCL* 27 (Fall 1981): 262-71.

Edward Guereschi, "'The Comedian as the Letter C': Wallace Stevens' Anti-Mythological Poem," *CentR* 8 (Fall 1964): 465-77.

Hoffman, *The Twenties*, 183-85.

George McFadden, "Poet, Nature, and Society in Wallace Stevens," *MLQ* 23 (Sept. 1962): 263-64.

K. E. Marre, "Narrative Comedy in Wallace Stevens' 'The Comedian as the Letter C,'" *UDR* 12 (Summer 1976): 133-49.

Miller, *Poets of Reality*, 220-21.

Samuel French Morse, "Wallace Stevens, Bergson, Pater," *ELH* 31 (Mar. 1964): 17-34.

James E. Mulqueen, "A Reading of Wallace Stevens' 'The Comedian as the Letter C,'" *CimR* 13 (Oct. 1970): 35-42.

James E. Mulqueen, "Wallace Stevens: Radical Transcendentalist," *MQ* 11 (Spring 1970): 336-39.

Francis Murphy, "'The Comedian as the Letter C,'" *Wisconsin Studies in Contemporary Literature* 2 (Spring/Summer 1962): 80-99.

O'Connor, *Sense and Sensibility in Modern Poetry*, 141-42.

William Van O'Connor, "Wallace Stevens on 'The Poems of Our Climate,'" *University of Kansas City Review* 15 (Winter 1948): 109.

Pearce, *The Continuity of American Poetry*, 387-89.

Lucy Pollard-Gott, "Fractal Repetition Structure in Steven's Poetry," *Lang&S* 19 (1986): 233-49.

A. Poulin, Jr., "Crispin as Everyman, as Adam: 'The Comedian as the Letter C,'" *CP* 5 (Spring 1972): 5-23.

John N. Serio, "'The Comedian' as the Idea of Order in *Harmonium*," *PLL* 12 (Winter 1976): 81-101.

Hi Simons, "'The Comedian as the Letter C': Its Sense and Its Significance," *SoR* 5 (Winter 1940): 453-68.

Fred H. Stocking, *Expl* 3 (Mar. 1945): 43. Reprinted in *The Explicator Cyclopedia* 1:272-73.

Janis P. Stout, "Stevens' 'Comedian' as Journey Narrative," *CP* 14 (1981): 31-48.

T. Weiss, "The Nonsense of Winters' *Anatomy*," *Quarterly Review of Literature* 1 (Spring 1944): 229.

Winters, *Anatomy of Nonsense*, 98-103. Reprinted in Winters, *In Defense of Reason*, 439-44.

"Connoisseur of Chaos"

Abad, *A Formal Approach to Lyric Poetry*, 148-51.

Bornstein, *Transformation of Romanticism*, 202-3.

Beverly Cole, "An Anchorage of Thought: Defining the Role of Aphorism in Wallace Stevens' Poetry," *PMLA* 91 (Mar. 1976): 213-15.

P. Furia and M. Roth, "Stevens' Fusky Alphabet," *PMLA* 93 (Jan. 1978): 66-77.

"Cortege for Rosenbloom"

Richard Ellmann, "Wallace Stevens' Ice Cream," *KR* 19 (Winter 1957): 90-92.

"The Course of a Particular"

William Bevis, "Stevens' Toneless Poetry," *ELH* 41 (Summer 1974): 273-75.

Richard Blessing, "Wallace Stevens and the Necessary Reader: A Technique of Dynamism," *TCL* 18 (Oct. 1972): 256.

D. Bromwich, "Wordsworth, Frost, Stevens, and the Poetic Vocation," *SIR* 21 (Spring 1982): 87-100.

J. Bump, "Stevens and Lawrence: The Poetry of Nature and the Spirit of the Age," *SoR* 18 (Jan. 1982): 44-61.

Sigurd Burckhardt and Roy Harvey Pearce, "Poetry, Language, and the Condition of Modern Man," *CentR* 4 (Winter 1960): 9-13.

Gerald Graff, *Poetic Statement and Critical Dogma* (Evanston: Northwestern University Press, 1970), 27-30, 144-45.

Robert Pack, "The Abstracting Imagination of Wallace Stevens: Nothingness and the Hero," *ArQ* 11 (Autumn 1955): 198-99.

Stephen Shapiro, "'That Which Is Always Beginning': Stevens's Poetry of Affirmation," *PMLA* 100 (Mar. 1985): 220-33.

"Credences of Summer"

Sandy Cohen, "A Calculus of the Cycle: Wallace Stevens' 'Credences of Summer,' An Alternative View," *BSUF* 17 (Spring 1976): 31-36.

Bernard Heringman, "The Poetry of Synthesis," *Perspective* 7 (Autumn 1954): 171-74.

J. Dennis Huston, "'Credences of Summer': An Analysis," *MP* 67 (Feb. 1970): 263-72.

Isabel G. MacCaffrey, "The Other Side of Silence: 'Credences of Summer' as an Example," *MLQ* 30 (Sept. 1969): 417-38.

Ralph J. Mills, Jr., "Wallace Stevens: The Image of the Rock," *Accent* 17 (Spring 1958): 77-78, 81.

Harold H. Watts, "Wallace Stevens and the Rock of Summer," *KR* 14 (Winter 1952): 122-24.

"The Cuban Doctor"

Jon Rosenblatt, "Stevens' 'The Cuban Doctor,'" *Expl* 37 (Summer 1979): 14-15.

"Cy Est Pourtraicte, Madame Ste. Ursule, et Les Unze Mille Vierges"

Ashby Bland Crowder, "'Cy Est Pourtraicte, Madame Ste. Ursule, Et Les Unze Mille Vierges': Stevens' Parable of Reconciliation," *ELN* 19 (1981): 50-52.

"The Death of a Soldier"

R. P. Blackmur, "Wallace Stevens," *Hound and Horn* 5 (Jan./Mar. 1932): 229-30. Reprinted in Blackmur, *The Double Agent*, 74-75.

Samuel Joy Keyser, "Wallace Stevens: Form and Meaning in Four Poems," *CE* 37 (Feb. 1976): 578-84.

"Depression Before Spring"

William W. Bevis, "The Arrangement of *Harmonium*," *ELH* 37 (Sept. 1970): 457-67.

Frank Doggett, "Our Nature Is Her Nature," in Langford and Taylor, *The Twenties*, 37-38.

"Description without Place"

Michael T. Beehler, "Meteoric Poetry: Wallace Stevens' 'Description Without Place,'" *Criticism* 19 (Summer 1977): 241-59.

Robert Pack, "The Abstracting Imagination of Wallace Stevens: Nothingness and the Hero," *ArQ* 11 (Autumn 1955): 199-200.

"Disillusionment of Ten O'Clock"

R. P. Blackmur, "Examples of Wallace Stevens," *Hound and Horn* 5 (Jan./Mar. 1932): 228-29. Reprinted in Blackmur, *The Double Agent*, 73-74; in Blackmur, *Language as Gesture*, 226-27.

Randall Jarrell, "Reflections on Wallace Stevens," *PR* 18 (May/June 1951): 337-38.

"Domination of Black"

Harold Bloom, "Poetic Crossing: Rhetoric and Psychology," *GaR* 30 (Fall 1976): 495-524.

Bornstein, *Transformations of Criticism*, 195-97.

Frank Doggett, "Our Nature Is Her Nature," in Langford and Taylor, *The Twenties*, 36-37.

Dorothy Pettit, "'Domination of Black': A Study in Involvement," *EJ* 51 (May 1962): 347-48.

William J. Rooney, "'Spelt from Sibyl's Leaves'--A Study in Contrasting Methods of Evaluation," *JAAC* 13 (June 1955): 512-14.

Bruce Ross, "Stevens' 'Domination of Black,'" *Expl* 40 (Spring 1982): 41-42.

"The Dove in Spring"

Vendler, *Wallace Stevens: Words Chosen out of Desire*, passim.

"Dutch Graves in Bucks County"

Jefferson Humphries, "Shards from the Wreckage: Antimaxims in Modern Poetry," *SAQ* 86 (Winter 1987): 30-31.

"The Dwarf"

Robert Pack, "The Abstracting Imagination of Wallace Stevens: Nothingness and the Hero," *ArQ* 11 (Autumn 1955): 197-98.

"Earthly Anecdote"

George Betar, *Expl* 22 (Feb. 1964): 43.

Frankenberg, *Pleasure Dome*, 198-99.

Miller, *Poets of Reality*, 234-35.

Rosenthal, *The Modern Poets*, 122-23.

Hugh L. Smith, *Expl* 24 (Dec. 1965): 37.

"The Emperor of Ice-Cream"

R. P. Blackmur, "Wallace Stevens," *Hound and Horn* 5 (Jan./Mar. 1932): 230-32. Reprinted in Blackmur, *The Double Agent*, 75-77; in Blackmur, *Language as Gesture*, 227-29.

Warren Carrier, "Commonplace Costumes and Essential Gaudiness: Wallace Stevens' 'Emperor of Ice-Cream,'" *CollL* 1 (Fall 1974): 230-35.

Beverly Coyle, "An Anchorage of Thought: Defining the Role of Aphorism in Wallace Stevens' Poetry," *PMLA* 91 (Mar. 1976): 212-13.

Taylor Culbert and John M. Violette, "Wallace Stevens' Emperor," *Criticism* 2 (Winter 1960): 38-47.

Sr. Madeline DeFrees, "Pegasus and Six Blind Indians," *EJ* 59 (Oct. 1970): 933-34.

Dickinson, *Suggestions for Teachers of "Introduction to Literature*," 42-43.

Drew and Sweeney, *Directions in Modern Poetry*, 227-31. Abridged in Gwynn, Condee, and Lewis, *The Case for Poetry*, 341.

Richard Ellman, "Wallace Stevens' Ice Cream," *KR* 19 (Winter 1957): 92-95. Reprinted in Ludwig, *Aspects of American Poetry*, 203-22.

Robert F. Fleissner, "Stevens in Wittenberg: 'The Emperor of Ice-Cream,'" *Research Studies* 42 (Dec. 1974): 256-60.

Friar and Brinnin, *Modern Poetry*, 538.

Max Herzberg and Wallace Stevens, *Expl* 7 (Nov. 1948): 18. Reprinted in *The Explicator Cyclopedia* 1:275.

Kenneth Lash and Robert Thackaberry, *Expl* 6 (Apr. 1948): 36. Abridged in Gwynn, Condee, and Lewis, *The Case for Poetry*, 342. Reprinted in *The Explicator Cyclopedia* 1:273-74.

James E. Mulqueen, "Wallace Stevens: Radical Transcendentalism," *MQ* 11 (Spring 1970): 330-31.

C. D. Narasimhaiah, "Wallace Stevens," in *Studies in American Literature: Essays in Honor of William Mulder*, ed. Jagdish Chander and Narinder S. Pradhan (Delhi: Oxford University Press, 1976), 221-25.

Ralph Nash, "About 'The Emperor of Ice-Cream,'" *Perspective* 7 (Autumn 1954): 122-24.

Edward Neill, "The Melting Moment: Stevens' Rehabilitation of Ice Cream," *ArielE* 4 (Jan. 1973): 88-96.

Elder Olson, "The Poetry of Wallace Stevens," *CE* 16 (Apr. 1955): 397-98.

Rosenthal, *The Modern Poets*, 129-30.

Stuart Silverman, "The Emperor of Ice-Cream," *WHR* 26 (Spring 1972): 165-68.

Shirley H. Strobel, *Expl* 41 (Summer 1983): 33-35.

Kermit Vanderbilt, "More Stevens and Shakespeare," *CollL* 2 (Spring 1975): 143-45.

T. Weiss, "The Nonsense of Winters' *Anatomy*," *Quarterly Review of Literature* 1 (Spring 1944): 226.

C. T. Wright, "Stevens and the Black Emperor of Key West," *ArQ* 35 (Spring 1979): 65-76.

Michael Zimmerman, "Wallace Stevens' Emperor," *ELN* 4 (Dec. 1966): 119-23.

"Esthétique du Mal"

Robert J. Bertholf, "Parables and Wallace Stevens' 'Esthétique du Mal,'" *ELH* 42 (Winter 1975): 669-89.

Frank Doggett, "The Poet of Earth: Wallace Stevens," *CE* 22 (Mar. 1961): 376.

Richard Ellmann, "Wallace Stevens' Ice Cream," *KR* 19 (Winter 1957): 100-101.

Frankenberg, *Pleasure Dome*, 249-51.

Ellwood Johnson, "Title and Substance of Wallace Stevens' 'Esthétique du Mal,'" *NConL* 8 (Nov. 1978): 2-3.

Janet McCann, "Wallace Stevens' 'Esthétique du Mal,' Section X," *AN&Q* 15 (Apr. 1977): 111-13.

Martz, *The Poem of the Mind*, 196-97.

Louis L. Martz, "The World of Wallace Stevens," in Rajan, *Modern American Poetry*, 106.

Pearce, *The Continuity of American Poetry*, 400-404, 425-26.

Wylie Sypher, "Connoiseur of Chaos: Wallace Stevens," *PR* 13 (Winter 1946): 84-86.

"Esthétique du Mal" VII

Ralph J. Mills, Jr., "Wallace Stevens: The Image of the Rock," *Accent* 18 (Spring 1958): 82-83.

"Evening without Angels"

Friar and Brinnin, *Modern Poetry*, 537.

"The Examination of the Hero in Time of War"

James E. Mulqueen, "Wallace Stevens: Radical Transcendentalism," *MQ* 11 (Spring 1970): 333-34.

"Extracts from Addresses to the Academy of Fine Ideas"

J. M. Kertzer, "The Argument of Wallace Stevens: 'a logic of transforming certitudes,'" *Mosaic* 18 (Winter 1985): 27-43.

"Farewell to Florida"

Adelyn Dougherty, "Structures of Sound in Wallace Stevens' 'Farewell to Florida,'" *TSLL* 16 (Winter 1975): 755-64.

Dwight Eddins, "Wallace Stevens: America the Primordial," *MLQ* 32 (Mar. 1971): 85-86.

"Final Soliloquy of the Interior Paramour"

Charles Altieri, "The Poem as Act: A Way to Reconcile Presentational and Mimetic Theories," *IowaR* 6 (Summer/Fall 1975): 116-22.

Sharon Cameron, "'The Sense against Calamity': Ideas of a Self in Three Poems by Wallace Stevens," *ELH* 43 (Winter 1976): 593-603.

Gray, *American Poetry*, 180-81.

Judith McDaniel, "Wallace Stevens and the Scientific Imagination," *ConL* 15 (Spring 1974): 230.

Robert Pack, "Wallace Stevens' Sufficient Muse," *SoR* 11 (Oct. 1975): 767-70.

"Flyer's Fall"

Harold H. Watts, "Wallace Stevens and the Rock of Summer," *KR* 14 (Winter 1952): 133-34.

"Forces, the Will & the Weather"

Bruce Babington, "Wallace Stevens's 'Forces, the Will & the Weather,'" *YES* 10 (1980): 210-23.

"Frogs Eat Butterflies"

Don Geiger, "Wallace Stevens' Wealth," *Perspective* 7 (Autumn 1954): 158-60.

Robert McIlvaine, *Expl* 33 (Oct. 1974): 14.

John N. Serio, "'The Comedian' as the Idea of Order in *Harmonium*," *PLL* 12 (Winter 1976): 102-3.

"From the Packet of Anacharsis"

Michael D. Channing, "'From the Packet of Anacharsis': A Tentative Identification," *ELN* 16 (1978): 51-54.

"The Glass of Water"

Warren G. French, *Expl* 19 (Jan. 1961): 23. Reprinted in *The Explicator Cyclopedia* 1:276-77.

David H. Owen, "'The Glass of Water,'" *Perspective* 7 (Autumn 1954): 181-83.

Eric Sellin, *Expl* 17 (Jan. 1959): 28. Reprinted in *The Explicator Cyclopedia* 1:276.

Sr. Therese, S.N.D., *Expl* 21 (Mar. 1963): 56.

"God Is Good. It Is a Beautiful Night"

Frank A. Doggett, "Why Read Stevens?" *Emory University Quarterly* 18 (Summer 1962): 89-91.

"The Good Man Has No Shape"

Richard Gustafson, "The Practick of the Maker in Wallace Stevens," *TCL* 9 (July 1963): 88.

Janet McCann, "Wallace Stevens' 'The Good Man Has No Shape,'" *NConL* 6 (Mar. 1976): 9-10.

"The Green Plant"

Marjorie Perloff, "Irony in Wallace Stevens's *The Rock*," *AL* 36 (Nov. 1964): 335-36.

"The Hermitage at the Center"

Marjorie Perloff, "Irony in Wallace Stevens's *The Rock*," *AL* 36 (Nov. 1964): 338-39.

"A High-Toned Old Christian Woman"

Gray, *American Poetry*, 159-60.

William Van O'Connor, "Wallace Stevens on 'The Poems of Our Climate,'" *University of Kansas City Review* 15 (Winter 1948): 110.

Perrine and Reid, *100 American Poems*, 72-73.

Wallace, *God Be with the Clown: Humor in American Poetry*, passim.

A. E. Waterman, "Poetry as Play: 'A High-Toned Old Christian Woman,'" *CEA* 26 (Jan. 1964): 7.

"Holiday in Reality"

Bernard Heringman, "The Poetry of Synthesis," *Perspective* 7 (Autumn 1954): 169-71.

"Homunculus et La Belle Étoile"

Norman Silverstein, *Expl* 13 (May 1955): 40. Reprinted in *The Explicator Cyclopedia* 1:277-78.

"The House That Jack Built"

Miller, *The Linguistic Moment: From Wordsworth to Stevens*, passim.

"The House Was Quiet and the World Was Calm"

J. V. Cunningham, "The Poetry of Wallace Stevens," *Poetry* 75 (Dec. 1949): 164-65. Reprinted in Howe, *Modern Literary Criticism*, 365-66.

Quinn, *The Metamorphic Tradition*, 76.

"How to Live. What to Do"

Ralph J. Mills, Jr., "Wallace Stevens: The Image of the Rock," *Accent* 18 (Spring 1958): 76-77.

"The Idea of Order at Key West"

Bloom, *Wallace Stevens: The Poems of Our Climate*, 88-114.

Bornstein, *Transformations of Romanticism*, 197-202.

Brooks, Lewis, and Warren, *American Literature*, 2158-61.

William Burney, *Expl* 38 (Spring 1980): 15-17.

A. Chavkin, "Wallace Stevens' Transformation of the Romantic Landscape Meditation: 'The Idea of Order at Key West,'" *CEA* 44 (Mar. 1982): 2-4.

Deutsch, *Poetry in Our Time*, 248-50.

Frank Doggett, "Wallace Stevens and the World We Know," *EJ* 48 (Oct. 1959): 370-71.

Drew, *Discovering Poetry*, 261-62.

Friar and Brinnin, *Modern Poetry*, 537-38.

Gray, *American Poetry*, 169-70.

Richard Gustafson, "The Practick of the Maker in Wallace Stevens," *TCL* 9 (July 1963): 84-85.

J. M. Kertzer, "The Argument of Wallace Stevens: 'a logic of transforming certitudes,'" *Mosaic* 18 (Winter 1985): 27-43.

Todd M. Lieber, "Robert Frost and Wallace Stevens: 'What to Make of a Diminished Thing,'" *AL* 47 (Mar. 1975): 71-73.

Louis L. Martz, "Wallace Stevens: The World as Meditation," *YR* 47 (Summer 1958): 521-22.

Louis L. Martz, "The World of Wallace Stevens," in Rajan, *Modern American Poetry*, 101-3. Reprinted in Martz, *The Poem of the Mind*, 191-93, 205-6.

James E. Porter, *Expl* 39 (Fall 1980): 47-48.

D. Walker, *The Transparent Lyric*, passim.

Kenneth Walker, *Expl* 32 (Apr. 1974): 59.

"In a Bad Time"

C. Roland Wagner, "The Idea of Nothingness in Wallace Stevens," *Accent* 12 (Spring 1952): 119.

"The Indigo Glass in the Grass"

Gerald Kinneavy, *Expl* 42 (Fall 1983): 41-42.

"Infanta Marina"

Marius Bewley, "The Poetry of Wallace Stevens," *PR* 16 (Sept. 1949): 906.

S. J. Keyer and A. Prince, "Folk Etymology in Sigmund Freud, Christian Morgenstern, and Wallace Stevens," *CritI* 6 (Autumn 1979): 65-78.

"The Irish Cliffs of Moher"

Judith McDaniel, "Wallace Stevens and the Scientific Imagination," *ConL* 15 (Spring 1974): 227-28.

"July Mountain"

Beverly Coyle, "An Anchorage of Thought: Defining the Role of Aphorism in Wallace Stevens' Poetry," *PMLA* 91 (Mar. 1976): 215-16.

"Landscape with Boat"

Watts, *Hound and Quarry*, 48-49.

Harold H. Watts, "Wallace Stevens and the Rock of Summer," *KR* 14 (Winter 1952): 128-30.

"Large Red Man Reading"

Frank Doggett, "Wallace Stevens and the World We Know," *EJ* 48 (Oct. 1959): 371-73.

Laurette Veza, "Wallace Stevens: 'Poesis, Poesis, the Literal Characters, the Vatic Lines,'" *EA* 33 (Jan./Mar. 1980): 1-11.

"Last Looks at the Lilacs"

Frank Doggett, "Our Nature Is Her Nature," in Langford and Taylor, *The Twenties*, 38.

James Rother, "Modernism and the Nonsense Style," *ConL* 15 (Spring 1974): 192-95.

"The Latest Freed Man"

Lynette Carpenter, "The Evolution of 'The Latest Freed Man,'" *SoR* 15 (Oct. 1979): 968-84.

"Lebensweisheitspielerei"

Marjorie Perloff, "Irony in Wallace Stevens's *The Rock*," *AL* 36 (Nov. 1964): 341.

"Less and Less Human, O Savage Spirit"

C. Roland Wagner, "The Idea of Nothingness in Wallace Stevens," *Accent* 12 (Spring 1952): 113-14.

"Life Is Motion"

Elder Olson, "The Poetry of Wallace Stevens," *CE* 16 (Apr. 1955): 396-97.

Hugh L. Smith, Jr., *Expl* 19 (Apr. 1961): 48. Reprinted in *The Explicator Cyclopedia* 1:282-83.

"Life on a Battleship"

Frankenberg, *Pleasure Dome*, 240-42.

William Van O'Connor, "The Politics of a Poet," *Perspective* 1 (Summer 1948): 206-7.

"Like Decorations in a Nigger Cemetery"

Ardyth Bradley, "Wallace Stevens' Decorations," *TCL* (Oct. 1961): 114-17.

Paul McBrearty, "Wallace Stevens's 'Like Decorations in a Nigger Cemetery': Notes toward an Explication," *TSLL* 15 (Summer 1973): 341-56.

Helen Hennessy Vendler, "Stevens' 'Like Decorations in a Nigger Cemetery,'" *MR* 7 (Winter 1966): 136-46.

"Lions in Sweden"

Ramon Guthrie, *Expl* 20 (Dec. 1961): 32. Reprinted in *The Explicator Cyclopedia* 1:283.

"The Lord of Sugar-Cane"

Don Geiger, "Wallace Stevens' Wealth," *Perspective* 7 (Autumn 1954): 157-58.

"Loneliness in Jersey City"

Dwight Eddins, "Wallace Stevens: America the Primordial," *MLQ* 32 (Mar. 1971): 78-79.

"Long and Sluggish Lines"

Marjorie Perloff, "Irony in Wallace Stevens's *The Rock*," *AL* 36 (Nov. 1964): 337-38.

"Looking across the Fields and Watching the Birds Fly"

Marius Bewley, "The Poetry of Wallace Stevens," *Commonweal* 62 (Sept. 23, 1955): 620-21.

Marjorie Perloff, "Irony in Wallace Stevens's *The Rock*," *AL* 36 (Nov. 1964): 334-35.

"Madame La Fleurie"

Judith McDaniel, "Wallace Stevens and the Scientific Imagination," *ConL* 15 (Spring 1974): 233-34.

Marjorie Perloff, "Irony in Wallace Stevens's *The Rock*," *AL* 36 (Nov. 1964): 336.

"Man and Bottle"

Bornstein, *Transformations of Romanticism*, 6-7.

"The Man on the Dump"

Lynette Carpenter, "The Evolution of 'The Latest Freed Man,'" *SoR* 15 (Oct. 1979): 968-84.

Harold E. Toliver, *Pastoral: Forms and Attitudes* (Berkeley and London: University of California Press, 1971), 310-12.

"The Man Whose Pharynx Was Bad"

Marius Bewley, "The Poetry of Wallace Stevens," *PR* 16 (Sept. 1949): 908-10.

Bloom, *Wallace Stevens: The Poems of Our Climate*, 48-67.

T. Weiss, "The Nonsense of Winters' *Anatomy*," *Quarterly Review of Literature* 1 (Spring 1944): 230.

"The Man with the Blue Guitar"

Richard P. Adams, "Wallace Stevens and Schopenhauer's *The World as Will and Idea*," *TSE* 20 (1972): 143-51.

Baker, *Syntax in English Poetry, 1870-1930*, 160-61.

Bloom, *Wallace Stevens: The Poems of Our Climate*, 115-35.

Merle E. Brown, "Concordia Discors in the Poetry of Wallace Stevens," *AL* 34 (May 1962): 249-54.

David Cavitch, *Expl* 27 (Dec. 1968): 30.

J. V. Cunningham, "The Styles and Procedures of Wallace Stevens," *University of Denver Quarterly* 1 (Spring 1966): 19-21.

Frankenberg, *Pleasure Dome*, 222-27.

Edward Guereschi, "Wallace Stevens' Testimonial Poem: 'The Man with the Blue Guitar,'" *UDR* 14 (Spring 1980): 55-64.

Miller, *The Linguistic Moment: From Wordsworth to Stevens*, 4-13.

Miller, *Poets of Reality*, 252-53, 260-62.

Joseph N. Riddel, "Wallace Stevens--'It Must Be Human,'" *EJ* 56 (Apr. 1967): 526-27.

J. R. Sheridan, "The Picasso Connection: Wallace Stevens's 'The Man With the Blue Guitar,'" *ArQ* 35 (Spring 1979): 77-89.

Hi Simons, "The Genre of Wallace Stevens," *SR* 53 (Oct./Dec. 1945): 571-74.

"The Man with the Blue Guitar, XVI"

J. M. Kertzer, "The Argument of Wallace Stevens: 'a logic of transforming certitudes,'" *Mosaic* 18 (Winter 1985): 27-43.

"Memorandum"

Dwight Eddins, "Wallace Stevens: America the Primordial," *MLQ* 32 (Mar. 1971): 77-78.

"The Men That Are Falling"

John C. McCloskey, *Expl* 23 (Jan. 1965): 41.

Ralph J. Mills, Jr., "Wallace Stevens: The Image of the Rock," *Accent* 18 (Spring 1958): 78-79.

"Metamorphosis"

Quinn, *The Metaphoric Tradition*, 57-58.

Sr. M. Bernetta Quinn, O.S.F., "Metamorphosis in Wallace Stevens," *SR* 60 (Spring 1952): 235-36.

James G. Turner, *Expl* 38 (Spring 1980): 6-7.

"Metaphors of a Magnifico"

Marius Bewley, "The Poetry of Wallace Stevens," *PR* 16 (Sept. 1949): 903-04.

Bornstein, *Transformations of Romanticism*, 213-14.

Joseph Carrol, *Expl* 41 (Fall 1982): 45-47.

Don Geiger, "Wallace Stevens' Wealth," *Perspective* 7 (Autumn 1954): 156.

Bruce King, "Wallace Stevens' 'Metaphors of a Magnifico,'" *ES* 49 (Oct. 1969): 450-52.

Alexander S. Liddie, *Expl* 21 (Oct. 1962): 15.

Tapscott, *American Beauty: William Carlos Williams and the Modernist Whitman*, passim.

"Le Monocle de Mon Oncle"

R. P. Blackmur, "Wallace Stevens," *Hound and Horn* 5 (Jan./Mar. 1932): 232-33, 245-46. Reprinted in Blackmur, *The Double Agent*, 77-78, 91-93; in Blackmur, *Language as Gesture*, 229-30.

Bloom, *Wallace Stevens: The Poems of Our Climate*, 37-44.

Beverly Coyle, "An Anchorage of Thought: Defining the Role of Aphorism in Wallace Stevens' Poetry," *PMLA* 91 (Mar. 1976): 211-12.

Donald Davie, "'Essential Gaudiness': The Poems of Wallace Stevens," *TC* 153 (June 1953): 455-62.

Frank Doggett, "Our Nature Is Her Nature," in Langford and Taylor, *The Twenties*, 38-39.

Richard Ellmann, "Wallace Stevens' Ice Cream," *KR* 19 (Winter 1957): 97-99.

William A. Fahey, *Expl* 15 (Dec. 1956): 16. Reprinted in *The Explicator Cyclopedia* 1:280-81.

Frankenberg, *Pleasure Dome*, 205-7.

R. M. Gay, *Expl* 6 (Feb. 1948): 27. Reprinted in *The Explicator Cyclopedia* 1:279-80.

Leila Goldman, *Expl* 37 (Fall 1978): 26-28.

Frank Lentricchia, Jr., "Wallace Stevens: The Ironic Eyes," *YR* 56 (Spring 1967): 344-45.

Isabel G. MacCaffrey, "The Ways of Truth in 'Le Monocle de Mon Oncle,'" in *Wallace Stevens: A Celebration*, ed. Frank Doggett and Robert Buttel (Princeton: Princeton University Press, 1980), 201-14.

Earl Roy Miner, *Expl* 13 (Mar. 1955): 28. Reprinted in *The Explicator Cyclopedia* 1:281-82.

Robert Pack, "Wallace Stevens: The Secular Mystery and the Comic Spirit," *Western Review* 20 (Autumn 1955): 57-59.

Delmore Schwartz, "In the Orchards of Imagination," *New Republic* 131 (Nov. 1954): 17.

T. Weiss, "The Nonsense of Winters' *Anatomy*," *Quarterly Review of Literature* 1 (Spring 1944): 225-26.

"The Motive for Metaphor"

J. M. Kertzer, "The Argument of Wallace Stevens: 'a logic of transforming certitudes,'" *Mosaic* 18 (Winter 1985): 27-43.

John Crowe Ransom, "The Concrete Universal: Observations on the Understanding of Poetry, II," *KR* 17 (Summer 1955): 400-402.

Vendler, *Wallace Stevens: Words Chosen out of Desire*, passim.

"Mrs. Alfred Uruguay"

Friar and Brinnin, *Modern Poetry*, 536.

"New England Verses"

Beverly Coyle, "An Anchorage of Thought: Defining the Role of Aphorism in Wallace Stevens' Poetry," *PMLA* 91 (Mar. 1976): 209-11.

"No Possum, No Sop, No Taters"

Merle E. Brown, "Concordia Discors in the Poetry of Wallace Stevens," *AL* 34 (May 1962): 247-49.

"Note on Moonlight"

Robert Pack, "Wallace Stevens' Sufficient Muse," *SoR* 11 (Oct. 1975): 778.

Walker, *The Transparent Lyric*, passim.

"Notes toward a Supreme Fiction"

Richard P. Adams, "Wallace Stevens and Schopenhauer's *The World as Will and Idea*," *TSE* 20 (1972): 153-67.

Bloom, *Poetry and Regression*, 279-93.

Bloom, *The Ringers in the Tower: Studies in Romantic Tradition*, 235-55.

Bornstein, *Transformations of Romanticism*, 218-30.

Merle E. Brown, "Concordia Discors in the Poetry of Wallace Stevens," *AL* 34 (May 1962): 254-62.

Wilson O. Clough, *Expl* 28 (Nov. 1969): 24.

Frank Doggett, *Expl* 15 (Feb. 1957): 30. Reprinted in *The Explicator Cyclopedia* 1:278-79.

Frank Doggett, "This Invented World: Stevens' 'Notes Toward a Supreme Fiction,'" *ELH* 28 (Sept. 1961): 284-99.

Frankenberg, *Pleasure Dome*, 257-67.

Friar and Brinnin, *Modern Poetry*, 535-36.

Gray, *American Poetry*, 174-80.

Bernard Heringman, "The Poetry of Synthesis," *Perspective* 7 (Autumn 1954): 167-68.

Juhasz, *Metaphor and the Poetry of Williams, Pound, and Stevens*, 140-61.

Frank Lentricchia, Jr., "Wallace Stevens: The Ironic Eye," *YR* 56 (Spring 1967): 348-50.

Louis L. Martz, "The World of Wallace Stevens," in Rajan, *Modern American Poetry*, 98-101.

Miller, *Poets of Reality*, 248-49.

James E. Mulqueen, "Wallace Stevens: Radical Transcendentalist," *MQ* 11 (Spring 1970): 335-36.

Pearce, *The Continuity of American Poetry*, 395-400.

Joseph N. Riddel, "Wallace Stevens--'It Must Be Human,'" *EJ* 56 (Apr. 1967): 527-30.

Joseph N. Riddel, "Wallace Stevens' 'Notes toward a Supreme Fiction,'" *Wisconsin Studies in Contemporary Literature* 2 (Spring/Summer 1961): 23-42.

Steven Shapiro, "'That Which Is Always Beginning': Stevens's Poetry of Affirmation,' *PMLA* 100 (Mar. 1985): 220-33.

Andrew Taylor, "Stevens' *Notes Toward a Supreme Fiction*: A Reading," *SoRA* 4 (1971): 284-99.

411

Toliver, *Pastoral: Forms and Attitudes*, 313-15.

"Not Ideas about the Thing but the Thing Itself"

William Bevis, "Stevens' Toneless Poetry," *ELH* 41 (Summer 1974): 280-82.

Peckham and Chatman, *Word, Meaning, Poem*, 312-19.

Marjorie Perloff, "Irony in Wallace Stevens's *The Rock*," *AL* 36 (Nov. 1964): 339-40.

Toliver, *Pastoral: Forms and Attitudes*, 320-22.

"Nuances of a Theme by Williams"

Rosenthal, *The Modern Poets*, 121-22.

"Oak Leaves Are Hands"

Quinn, *The Metamorphic Tradition*, 85.

Sr. M. Bernetta Quinn, O.S.F., "Metamorphosis in Wallace Stevens," *SR* 60 (Spring 1952): 250-51.

"Of Hartford in a Purple Light"

Norman Silverstein, *Expl* 18 (Dec. 1959): 20. Reprinted in *The Explicator Cyclopedia* 1:283-84.

"Of Ideal Time and Choice"

Kenneth John Atchity, "Wallace Stevens: 'Of Ideal Time and Choice,'" *Research Studies* 41 (Sept. 1973): 141-53.

"O Florida, Veneral Soil"

Frank Doggett, "Our Nature Is Her Nature," in Langford and Taylor, *The Twenties*, 38.

"Of Mere Being"

William Bevis, "Stevens' Toneless Poetry," *ELH* 41 (Summer 1974): 279-80.

Frank Doggett, "The Poet of Earth: Wallace Stevens," *CE* 22 (Mar. 1961): 374-75.

"Of Modern Poetry"

Bornstein, *Transformations of Romanticism*, 2-5.

William Van O'Connor, "Wallace Stevens on 'The Poems of Our Climate,'" *University of Kansas City Review* 15 (Winter 1948): 108-9.

D. Walker, *The Transparent Lyric*, passim.

"Of the Manner of Addressing Clouds"

R. P. Blackmur, "Examples of Wallace Stevens," *Hound and Horn* 5 (Jan./Mar. 1932): 225-27. Reprinted in Blackmur, *The Double Agent*, 70-72; in Blackmur, *Language as Gesture*, 223-24.

"One of the Inhabitants of the West"

Marjorie Perloff, "Irony in Wallace Stevens's *The Rock*," *AL* 36 (Nov. 1964): 331-32.

"On the Edge of Space"

N. Prothro, "'On the Edge of Space': Wallace Stevens's Last Poems," *NEQ* 57 (Sept. 1984): 347-58.

"On the Road Home"

Lynette Carpenter, "The Evolution of 'The Latest Freed Man,'" *SoR* 15 (Oct. 1979): 968-84.

"An Ordinary Evening in New Haven"

Bloom, *Poetry and Repression*, 273-79.

Bloom, *Wallace Stevens: Poems of Our Climate*, 305-37.

Merle E. Brown, "Concordia Discors in the Poetry of Wallace Stevens," *AL* 34 (May 1962): 262-69.

Beverly Coyle, "An Anchorage of Thought: Defining the Role of Aphorism in Wallace Stevens' Poetry," *PMLA* 91 (Mar. 1976): 216-17.

P. Furia and M. Roth, "Stevens' Fusky Alphabet," *PMLA* 93 (Jan. 1978): 66-77.

Frank Lentricchia, Jr., "Wallace Stevens: The Ironic Eye," *YR* 56 (Spring 1967): 339, 346-48.

Joseph N. Riddel, "Wallace Stevens' 'Visibility of Thought,'" *PMLA* 77 (Sept. 1962): 493-98.

Steven Shapiro, "'That Which is Always Beginning': Stevens's Poetry of Affirmation," *PMLA* 100 (Mar. 1985): 220-33.

Lewis Turco, "The Agonism and the Existentiality: Stevens," CP 6 (Spring 1973): 32-44.

C. Roland Wagner, "The Idea of Nothingness in Wallace Stevens," *Accent* 12 (Spring 1952): 120-21.

"The Ordinary Women"

R. P. Blackmur, "Examples of Wallace Stevens, " *Hound and Horn* 5 (Jan./Mar. 1932): 227-28. Reprinted in Backmur, *The Double Agent*, 72-73; in Blackmur, *Language as Gesture*, 225-26.

Don Geiger, "Wallace Stevens' Wealth," *Perspective* 7 (Autumn 1954): 160-63.

Fred H. Stocking, *Expl* 4 (Oct. 1945): 4. Reprinted in *The Explicator Cyclopedia* 1:284-85.

"The Owl in the Sarcophagus"

Frank Doggett, "The Poet of Earth: Wallace Stevens," *CE* 22 (Mar. 1961): 378.

Miller, *Poets of Reality*, 268-70.

J. Hillis Miller, "Wallace Stevens' Poetry of Being," *ELH* 31 (Mar. 1964): 86-105.

Ralph J. Mills, Jr., "Wallace Stevens: The Image of the Rock," *Accent* 18 (Spring 1958): 83.

Joseph N. Riddel, "Wallace Stevens' 'Visibility of Thought,'" *PMLA* 77 (Sept. 1962): 488.

C. Roland Wagner, "The Idea of Nothingness in Wallace Stevens," *Accent* 12 (Spring 1952): 115-16.

"Owl's Clover"

Frankenberg, *Pleasure Dome*, 227-31.

Louis L. Martz, "Wallace Stevens: The World as Meditation," *YR* 47 (Summer 1958): 523-26. Reprinted in Martz, *The Poem of the Mind*, 209-11.

Leonora Woodman, "'A Giant on the Horizon': Wallace Stevens and the 'Idea of Man,'" *TSLL* 15 (Winter 1974): 771-85.

"Page from a Tale"

Richard Lee Drace, *Expl* 38 (Fall 1979): 46-47.

"The Paltry Nude Starts on a Spring Voyage"

Frank Doggett, "Our Nature Is Her Nature," in Langford and Taylor, *The Twenties*, 37.

"Peter Quince at the Clavier"

Cooper and Holmes, *Preface to Poetry*, 63.

R. W. Desai, "Stevens' 'Peter Quince at the Clavier' and *Pericles*," *ELN* 23 (1986): 57-59.

Carol Flake, "Wallace Stevens' 'Peter Quince at the Clavier': Sources and Structure,'" *ELN* 12 (Dec. 1974): 116-20.

Newell F. Ford, "Peter Quince's Orchestra," *MLN* 75 (May 1960): 405-11.

Robert G. Goulet and Jean Watson Rosenbaum, "The Perception of Immortal Beauty: 'Peter Quince at the Clavier,'" *CollL* 2 (Winter 1975): 66-72.

Neil D. Isaacs, "The Autoerotic Metaphor," *L&P* 15 (Spring 1965): 103-4.

Wendall S. Johnson, "Some Functions of Poetic Form," *JAAC* 13 (June 1955): 501-3.

Eugene Paul Nassar, "Reply," *CE* 27 (Feb. 1966): 431.

Eugene Paul Nassar, "Wallace Stevens: 'Peter Quince at the Clavier,'" CE 26 (Apr. 1965): 549-51.

Phyllis E. Nelson, *Expl* 24 (Feb. 1966): 52.

O'Connor, *Sense and Sensibility in Modern Poetry*, 149-50.

William Van O'Connor, "Tension and Structure of Poetry," *SR* 51 (Autumn 1943): 559.

Laurence N. Perrine, "'Peter Quince at the Clavier': A Protest," *CE* 27 (Mar. 1966): 430.

Laurence Perrine, "Rebuttal: 'Peter Quince at the Clavier': A Protest," *CE* 27 (Feb. 1966): 430.

Perrine and Reid, *100 American Poems*, 68-70.

Joseph N. Riddel, "Stevens' 'Peter Quince at the Clavier': Immortality as Form," *CE* 23 (Jan. 1962): 307-9.

Rosenthal, *The Modern Poets*, 126-28.

Sanders, *The Discovery of Poetry*, 336-41.

John N. Serio, "'The Comedian' as the Idea of Order in *Harmonium*," *PLL* 12 (Winter 1976): 97-98.

Fred H. Stocking, *Expl* 5 (May 1947): 47. Reprinted in *The Explicator Cyclopedia* 1:285-86.

Mary Jane Storm, *Expl* 14 (Nov. 1955): 9. Reprinted in *The Explicator Cyclopedia* 1:286-87.

Walsh, *Doors into Poetry*, 146-49.

Charles Wolfe, *Expl* 33 (Feb. 1975): 43.

"The Plain Sense of Things"

William Bevis, "Stevens' Toneless Poetry," *ELH* 41 (Summer 1974): 282-83.

Judith McDaniel, "Wallace Stevens and the Scientific Imagination," *ConL* 15 (Spring 1974): 228-29.

Robert Pack, "Wallace Stevens' Sufficient Muse," *SoR* 11 (Oct. 1975): 773-76.

Marjorie Perloff, "Irony in Wallace Stevens's *The Rock*," *AL* 36 (Nov. 1964): 340-41.

"The Planet on the Table"

Dana Gioia, "Business and Poetry," *HudR* 36 (Spring 1983): 147-71.

Vendler, *Wallace Stevens: Words Chosen out of Desire*, passim.

"The Pleasures of Merely Circulating"

M. Brown, "'Errours Endlesse Traine': Our Turning Points and the Dialectical Imagination," *PMLA* 99 (Jan. 1984): 9-25.

"The Plot against the Giant"

Frankenberg, *Pleasure Dome*, 201.

Albert W. Levi, "A Note on Wallace Stevens and the Poem of Perspective," *Perspective* 7 (Autumn 1954): 138-39.

Rosenthal, *The Modern Poets*, 123.

Wheeler, *The Design of Poetry*, 68.

"The Poem as Icon"

Miller, *The Linguistic Moment: From Wordsworth to Stevens*, passim.

Leonora Woodman, "'A Giant on the Horizon': Wallace Stevens and the 'Idea of Man,'" TSLL 15 (Winter 1974): 783-84.

"The Poems of Our Climate"

Friar and Brinnin, *Modern Poetry*, 537.

"Poem Written at Morning"

Juhasz, *Metaphor and the Poetry of Williams, Pound, and Stevens*, 138-39.

"Poetry Is a Destructive Force"

Samuel Joy Keyser, "Wallace Stevens: Form and Meaning in Four Poems," CE 37 (Feb. 1976): 584-85.

"A Postcard from the Volcano"

Beaty and Matchett, *Poetry: From Statement to Meaning*, 204-5.

"A Primitive Like an Orb"

Marius Bewley, "The Poetry of Wallace Stevens," *PR* 16 (Sept. 1949): 913-14.

Alfred Corn, "Wallace Stevens: Pilgrim in Metaphor," YR 71 (Jan. 1982): 225-35.

Watts, *Hound and Quarry*, 54-55.

"Prologues to What Is Possible"

Janet McCann, "'Prologues to What Is Possible,'" BSUF 17 (Spring 1976): 46-50.

Judith McDaniel, "Wallace Stevens and the Scientific Imagination," *ConL* 15 (Spring 1974): 231-32.

Marjorie Perloff, "Irony in Wallace Stevens's *The Rock*," *AL* 36 (Nov. 1964): 332-34.

Joseph N. Riddel, "Wallace Stevens--'It Must Be Human,'" *EJ* 56 (Apr. 1967): 532-33.

"Reality"

Richard Blessing, "Wallace Stevens and the Necessary Reader: A Technique of Dynamism," *TCL* 18 (Oct. 1972): 257.

"The Red Fern"

Louis L. Martz, "The World of Wallace Stevens," in Rajan, *Modern American Poetry*, 97-98.

C. D. Narasimhaiah, "Wallace Stevens," in *Studies in American Literature: Essays in Honor of William Mulder*, ed. Jagdish Chander and Narindar S. Pradhan (Delhi: Oxford University Press, 1976), 228-31.

"Repetition of a Young Captain"

Bernard Heringman, "The Poetry of Synthesis," *Perspective* 7 (Autumn 1954): 168-69.

"Restatement of Romance"

Watts, *Hound and Quarry*, 52-53.

"The River of Rivers in Connecticut"

Stephen Shapiro, "'That Which Is Always Beginning': Stevens's Poetry of Affirmation," *PMLA* 100 (Mar. 1985): 220-33.

"The Rock"

Bloom, *Wallace Stevens: The Poems of Our Climate*, 338-74.

Isabel G. MacCaffrey, "A Point of Central Arrival: Stevens' 'The Rock,'" *ELH* 40 (Winter 1973): 606-33.

Janet McCann, "Wallace Stevens' 'The Rock,'" *CP* 16 (1983): 45-56.

Judith McDaniel, "Wallace Stevens and the Scientific Imagination," *ConL* 15 (Spring 1974): 234-36.

Miller, *The Linguistic Moment: From Wordsworth to Stevens*, 390-422.

J. Hillis Miller, "Stevens' Rock and Criticism as Cure," *GaR* 30 (Spring 1976): 5-31.

Ralph J. Mills, Jr., "Wallace Stevens: The Image of the Rock," *Accent* 18 (Spring 1958): 85-89.

Marjorie Perloff, "Irony in Wallace Stevens's *The Rock*," *AL* 36 (Nov. 1964): 327-42.

"Sad Strains of a Gay Waltz"

Matthiessen, *The Responsibilities of the Critic*, 15-16.

"Sailing after Lunch"

Bornstein, *Transformations of Romanticism*, 176-78.

"The Sail of Ulysses"

Nancy W. Prothro, "The Wealth of Poverty, the Jewel of Need: Wallace Stevens' 'The Sail of Ulysses,'" *CP* 15 (1982): 1-10.

"Sea Surface Full of Clouds"

Harold C. Ackerman, Jr., "Notes Towards an Explication of Stevens' 'Sea Surface Full of Clouds,'" *CP* 2 (Spring 1969): 73-77.

Richard P. Adams, "Pure Poetry: Wallace Stevens' 'Sea Surface Full of Clouds,'" *TSE* 21 (1974): 91-122.

R. P. Blackmur, "Wallace Stevens," *Hound and Horn* 5 (Jan./Mar. 1932): 233-35. Reprinted in Blackmur, *The Double Agent*, 79-80; in Blackmur, *Language as Gesture*, 230-32.

David R. Ferry, *Expl* 6 (June 1948), 56. Reprinted in *The Explicator Cyclopedia* 1:287-88.

L. Kramer, "Ocean and Vision: Imaginative Dilemma in Wordsworth, Whitman, and Stevens," *JEGP* 79 (Apr. 1980): 210-30.

Albert W. Levi, "A Note on Wallace Stevens and the Poem of Perspective," *Perspective* 7 (Autumn 1954): 141-42.

Miller, *Poets of Reality*, 239-41.

Ransom, *The World's Body*, 58-60.

Joseph N. Riddel, "'Disguised Pronunciamento': Wallace Stevens, 'Sea Surface Full of Clouds,'" *University of Texas Studies in English* 37 (1958): 177-86.

M. L. Rosenthal, *Expl* 19 (Mar. 1961): 38. Reprinted in *The Explicator Cyclopedia* 1:288-89.

Rosenthal, *The Modern Poets*, 130-31.

"The Sense of the Sleight-of-Hand Man"

Perrine and Reid, *100 American Poems*, 70-71.

"Seventy Years Later"

Miller, *The Linguistic Moment: From Wordworth to Stevens*, passim.

"Six Significant Landscapes"

Albert W. Levi, "A Note on Wallace Stevens and the Poem of Perspective," *Perspective* 7 (Autumn 1954): 142-44.

Charles Moorman, *Expl* 17 (Oct. 1958): 1. Reprinted in *The Explicator Cyclopedia* 1:289-90.

"The Snow Man"

Abad, *A Formal Approach to Lyric Poetry*, 144-45.

Richard P. Adams, "Wallace Stevens and Schopenhauer's *The World as Will and Idea*," *TSE* 20 (1972): 137-39.

William Bevis, "Stevens' Toneless Poetry," *ELH* 41 (Summer 1974): 257-69.

R. P. Blackmur, "Wallace Stevens," *Hound and Horn* 5 (Jan./Mar. 1932): 242-43. Reprinted in Blackmur, *The Double Agent*, 87-89; in Blackmur, *Language as Gesture*, 237-38.

Richard Blessing, "Wallace Stevens and the Necessary Reader: A Technique of Dynamism," *TCL* 18 (Oct. 1972): 252-53.

Bloom, *Poetry and Repression*, 269-71.

Bloom, *Wallace Stevens: The Poems of Our Climate*, 48-67.

Merle Brown, "Poetic Listening," *NLH* 10 (Autumn 1978): 125-39.

Sharon Cameron, "'The Sense Against Calamity': Ideas of Self in Three Poems by Wallace Stevens," *ELH* 43 (Winter 1976): 584-87.

Frank A. Doggett, "Why Read Wallace Stevens?" *Emory University Quarterly* 18 (Summer 1962): 88.

Gray, *American Poetry*, 158-59.

D. H. Hesla, "Singing in Chaos: Wallace Stevens and Three or Four Ideas," *AL* 57 (May 1985): 240-62.

Robert Kern, "Toward a New Nature Poetry," *CentR* 19 (Summer 1975): 210-12.

Samuel Jay Keyser, "Wallace Stevens: Form and Meaning in Four Poems," *CE* 37 (Feb. 1976): 589-97.

Frank Lentricchia, Jr., "Wallace Stevens: The Ironic Eye," *YR* 56 (Spring 1967): 342-43.

Pinsky, *The Situation of Poetry*, 71-74.

C. Roland Wagner, "The Idea of Nothingness in Wallace Stevens," *Accent* 12 (Spring 1952): 118.

D. Walker, *The Transparent Lyric*, passim.

"So-and-So Reclining on Her Couch"

Robert M. Farnsworth, *Expl* 10 (June 1952): 60. Reprinted in *The Explicator Cyclopedia* 1:290-91.

P. Furia and M. Roth, "Stevens' Fusky Alphabet," *PMLA* 93 (Jan. 1978): 66-77.

Richard Gustafson, "The Practick of the Maker in Wallace Stevens," *TCL* 9 (July 1963): 83-85.

"Some Friends from Pascagoula"

Kenner, *A Homemade World*, 52-53.

J. M. Linebarger, *Expl* 35 (Winter 1976): 12-13.

"Someone Puts a Pineapple Together"

Miller, *Poets of Reality*, 242-44.

"Somnambulisma"

Janet McCann, *Expl* 35 (Winter 1976): 6-8.

"Sonatina to Hans Christian"

Frank Doggett, "Wallace Stevens and the World We Know," *EJ* 48 (Oct. 1959): 367.

"Study of Images"

Warren Carrier, "Wallace Stevens' Pagan Vantage," *Accent* 13 (Summer 1953): 165-68. Reprinted in Engle and Carrier, *Reading Modern Poetry*, 361-64.

"Study of Images I"

Richard Lee Drace, *Expl* 38 (Winter 1980): 47-48.

"Study of Two Pears"

Richard Blessing, "Wallace Stevens and the Necessary Reader: A Technique of Dynamism," *TCL* 18 (Oct. 1972): 253-54.

Juhasz, *Metaphor and the Poetry of Williams, Pound, and Stevens*, 35-37.

Miller, *Poets of Reality*, 250-51.

"Sunday Morning"

R. P. Blackmur, "Wallace Stevens," *Hound and Horn* 5 (Jan./Mar. 1932): 240-41, 244. Reprinted in Blackmur, *The Double Agent*, 85-87, 90; in Blackmur, *Language as Gesture*, 236-37.

Bloom, *Wallace Stevens: The Poems of Our Climate*, 27-35.

Brooks, Lewis, and Warren, *American Literature*, 2155-56.

Price Caldwell, "'Sunday Morning': Stevens' Makeshift Romantic Lyric," *SoR* 15 (Oct. 1979): 933-52.

J. V. Cunningham, "The Poetry of Wallace Stevens," *Poetry* 75 (Dec. 1949): 159-64. Reprinted in Howe, *Modern Literary Criticism*, 360-65; in Cunningham, *Tradition and Poetic Structure*, 117-22.

Frank Doggett, "Our Nature Is Her Nature," in Langford and Taylor, *The Twenties*, 40-41.

Drew, *Poetry: A Modern Guide*, 217-21.

Dwight Eddins, "Wallace Stevens: America the Primordial," *MLQ* 32 (Mar. 1971): 75-77.

Richard Ellmann, "Wallace Stevens' Ice Cream," *KR* 19 (Winter 1957): 95-97.

Frankenberg, *Pleasure Dome*, 215-17.

Philip Furia, "Nuances of a Theme by Milton: Wallace Stevens's 'Sunday Morning,'" *AL* 46 (Mar. 1974): 83-87.

Don Geiger, "Wallace Stevens' Wealth," *Perspective* 7 (Autumn 1954): 164-65.

Gray, *American Poetry*, 160-66.

Richard Gustafson, "The Practick of the Maker in Wallace Stevens," *TCL* 9 (July 1963): 85-86.

James L. Hill, "The Frame for the Mind: Landscape in 'Lines Composed a Few Miles Above Tintern Abbey,' 'Dover Beach,' and 'Sunday Morning,'" *CentR* 18 (Winter 1974): 43-48.

Kenner, *A Homemade World*, 75-78.

Frank Lentricchia, Jr., "Patriarchy Against Itself: The Young Manhood of Wallace Stevens," *CritI* 13 (Summer 1987): 742-86.

Frank Lentricchia, Jr., "Wallace Stevens: The Ironic Eye," *YR* 56 (Spring 1967): 339-42.

Martz, *The Poem of the Mind*, 197-99.

Louis L. Martz, "The World of Wallace Stevens," in Rajan, *Modern American Poetry*, 107-8.

Masse, *American Literature in Context IV: 1900-1930*, passim.

Miller, *Poets of Reality*, 222-23.

Robert Pack, "Wallace Stevens: The Secular Mystery and the Comic Spirit," *Western Review* 20 (Autumn 1955): 53-55.

Joseph N. Riddel, "Walt Whitman and Wallace Stevens: Functions of a 'Literatus,'" *SAQ* 61 (Autumn 1962): 512-13.

Schneider, *Poems and Poetry*, 488.

Carol Kyros Walker, "The Subject as Speaker in 'Sunday Morning,'" *CP* 10 (Spring 1977): 25-31.

T. Weiss, "The Nonsense of Winters' *Anatomy*," *Quarterly Review of Literature* 1 (Spring 1944): 232-33.

Winters, *The Anatomy of Nonsense*, 88-91, 105-8. Reprinted in Winters, *In Defense of Reason*, 431-34, 447-56; in Locke, Gibson, and Arms, *Readings for Liberal Education*, 530-33; 3d ed., 193-96; 4th ed., 194-97; 5th ed., 174-77; in Locke, Gibson, and Arms, *Forms of Discovery*, 274-77.

A. Yvor Winters, "Poetic Styles, Old and New," in Allen, *Four Poets on Poetry*, 72-75.

Michael Zimmerman, "The Pursuit of Pleasure and the Uses of Death: Wallace Stevens' 'Sunday Morning,'" *University of Kansas City Review* 33 (Winter 1966): 113-23.

"Tattoo"

R. P. Blackmur, "Wallace Stevens," *Hound and Horn* 5 (Jan./Mar. 1932): 235-36. Reprinted in Blackmur, *The Double Agent*, 81-82; in Blackmur, *Language as Gesture*, 232-33.

"Tea at the Palaz of Hoon"

Bloom, *Wallace Stevens: The Poems of Our Climate*, 48-67.

Dana Gioia, "Business and Poetry," *HudR* 36 (Spring 1983): 147-71.

Samuel French Morse, "Wallace Stevens, Bergson, Pater," *ELH* 31 (Mar. 1964): 13-14.

"That Which Cannot Be Fixed"

Marius Bewley, "The Poetry of Wallace Stevens," *PR* 16 (Sept. 1949): 910-11.

"Things of August"

John Berryman, *Poetry: A Critical Supplement*, Dec. 1949, 1-9.

"Thirteen Ways of Looking at a Blackbird"

Price Caldwell, "Metaphoric Structures in Wallace Stevens' 'Thirteen Ways of Looking at a Blackbird,'" *JEGP* 71 (July 1972): 321-35.

Beverly Coyle, "An Anchorage of Thought: Defining the Role of Aphorism in Wallace Stevens' Poetry," *PMLA* 91 (Mar. 1976): 207-9.

Frank Doggett, "Wallace Stevens and the World We Know," *EJ* 48 (Oct. 1959): 368.

John J. Hafner, "One Way of Looking at 'Thirteen Ways of Looking at a Blackbird,'" *CP* 3 (Spring 1970): 61-65.

John V. Hagopian, "Thirteen Ways of Looking at a Blackbird," *AN&Q* 1 (Feb. 1963): 84-85.

Kenner, *A Homemade World*, 78-81.

Albert W. Levi, "A Note on Wallace Stevens and the Poem of Perspective," *Perspective* 7 (Autumn 1954): 144-46.

Elizabeth McBride, "Circularity and Completion in 'Thirteen Ways of Looking at a Blackbird,'" *CP* 16 (1983): 11-21.

Peter L. McNamara, "The Multi-Faceted Blackbird and Wallace Stevens' Poetic Vision," *CE* 25 (Mar. 1964): 446-48.

Willis Monie, *Expl* 34 (Sept. 1975): 2.

Rosenthal, *The Modern Poets*, 125-29.

Robert S. Ryf, "X Ways of Looking at Y: Stevens' Elusive Blackbirds," *Mosaic* 11 (Fall 1977): 93-101.

Unger and O'Connor, *Poems for Study*, 608-16.

"A Thought Revolved"

Robert Mollinger, *Expl* 33 (Sept. 1974): 1.

"To the One of Fictive Music"

Richard E. Amacher, *Expl* 11 (Apr. 1953): 43. Reprinted in *The Explicator Cyclopedia* 1:291-92.

Bloom, *Wallace Stevens: The Poems of Our Climate*, 44-47.

Louis L. Martz, "The World of Wallace Stevens," in Rajan, *Modern American Poetry*, 95.

Pam Pugsley, *Expl* 42 (Fall 1983): 42-45.

John N. Serio, "'The Comedian' as the Idea of Order in *Harmonium*," *PLL* 12 (Winter 1976): 98-99.

"To the Roaring Wind"

Abad, *A Formal Approach to Lyric Poetry*, 40-41, 180.

"Two Figures in Dense Violet Light"

Robert W. Buttel, *Expl* 9 (May 1951): 45. Reprinted in *The Explicator Cyclopedia* 1:293.

"Two Illustrations that the World Is What You Make of It"

Marjorie Perloff, "Irony in Wallace Stevens's 'The Rock,'" *AL* 36 (Nov. 1964): 337, 341.

"Two Tales of Liadof"

Frankenberg, *Pleasure Dome*, 254-56.

"The Ultimate Poem Is Abstract"

J. F. Nims, *Poetry: A Critical Supplement*, Oct. 1947, 7-9.

"Variations on a Summer Day"

Edward Butscher, "Wallace Stevens' Neglected Fugue: 'Variations on a Summer Day,'" *TCL* 19 (July 1973): 153-64.

"The Virgin Carrying a Lantern"

Howard Baker, "Wallace Stevens and Other Poets," *SoR* 1 (Autumn 1935): 374-76.

"The Well Dressed Man with a Beard"

Frank Doggett, "The Poet of Earth: Wallace Stevens," *CE* 22 (Mar. 1961): 377-78.

"The Weeping Burgher"

Samuel French Morse, "Wallace Stevens, Bergson, Pater," *ELH* 31 (Mar. 1964): 4-5.

"What We See Is What We Think"

Baker, *Syntax in English Poetry, 1870-1930*, 162-65.

Walker, *The Transparent Lyric*, passim.

"The Woman in Sunshine"

Richard Blessing, "Wallace Stevens and the Necessary Reader: A Technique of Dynamism," *TCL* 18 (Oct. 1972): 254-55.

Bornstein, *Transformations of Romanticism*, 215-16.

Robert Pack, "Wallace Stevens' Sufficient Muse," *SoR* 11 (Oct. 1975): 776-77.

"Woman Looking at a Vase of Flowers"

Frank Doggett, *Expl* 19 (Nov. 1960): 7. Reprinted in *The Explicator Cyclopedia* 1:293-94.

Ralph Freedman, "Wallace Stevens and Rainer Maria Rilke," in McDowell, *The Poet as Critic*, 63.

J. M. Kertzer, "The Argument of Wallace Stevens: 'a logic of transforming certitudes,'" *Mosaic* 18 (Winter 1985): 27-43.

"The World as Meditation"

Sharon Cameron, "'The Sense against Calamity': Ideas of a Self in Three Poems by Wallace Stevens," *ELH* 43 (Winter 1976): 587-92.

Louis L. Martz, "Wallace Stevens: The World as Meditation," *YR* 47 (Summer 1958): 517-18, 534. Reprinted in Martz, *The Poem of the Mind*, 200-202, 218-20.

Marjorie Perloff, "Irony in Wallace Stevens's 'The Rock,'" *AL* 36 (Nov. 1964): 330-31.

STICKNEY, TRUMBALL

"In Ampezzo"

Ross C. Murfin, "The Poetry of Trumball Stickney," *NEQ* 48 (Dec. 1975): 543-46, 553.

"Lakeward"

Ross C. Murfin, "The Poetry of Trumball Stickney," *NEQ* 48 (Dec. 1975): 547-49.

STONE, RUTH

"Cocks and Mares"

Susan Gubar, "On Ruth Stone," *IowaR* 12 (Spring/Summer 1981): 323-30.

STRAND, MARK

"Keeping Things Whole"

Mark Irwin, "The Architecture of Absence through Metaphor," *SubStance* 23/24 (1979): 193-96.

"The Man in the Mirror"

Harold Bloom, "Dark and Radiant Peripheries: Mark Strand and A. R. Ammons," *SoR* 8 (Winter 1972): 136-38.

"The Story of Our Lives"

John Bensko, "Reflexive Narration in Contemporary American Poetry: Some Examples from Mark Strand, John Ashbery, Norman Dubie, and Louis Simpson," *JNT* 16 (Spring 1986): 81-96.

"The Untelling"

R. Miklitsch, "Beginnings and Endings: Mark Strand's 'The Untelling,'" *LitR* 21 (Spring 1978): 357-73.

SWAN, JON

"The Magpie"

Perrine and Reid, *100 American Poems*, 286-87.

SWENSON, MAY

Half Sun Half Sleep

Lauter, *Women as Mythmkers*, chap. 8, passim.

"Lion"

Perrine and Reid, *100 American Poems*, 250-51.

"Snow in New York"

Charles Sanders, *Expl* 38 (Fall 1979): 41-42.

To Mix with Time

Lauter, *Women as Mythmakers*, chap. 8, passim.

TAFT, ROBERT W.

"Attack on Barbados at Sandy Point"

Rolfe Humphries, *Expl* 18 (Apr. 1960): 44.

TAGGARD, GENEVIEVE

"The Four Songs"

Donald A. Stauffer, "Genesis, or the Poet as Maker," in Abbot, *Poets at Work*, 63-70.

TATE, ALLEN

[Interview]

Irv Broughton, "An Interview with Allen Tate," *WHR* 32 (Autumn 1978): 317-86.

"Again the Native Hour"

August H. Mason, *Expl* 7 (Dec. 1948): 23. Reprinted in *The Explicator Cyclopedia* 1:295-96.

Samuel H. Monk, *Expl* 6 (June 1948): 58. Reprinted in *The Explicator Cyclopedia* 1:294-95.

"The Buried Lake"

Alan Williamson, "Allen Tate and the Personal Epic," *SoR* 12 (Oct. 1976): 727-32.

"Causerie"

Vivienne Koch, "The Poetry of Allen Tate," *KR* 11 (Summer 1949): 366-67. Reprinted in Ransom, *The Kenyon Critics*, 174-75; in Rajan, *Modern American Poetry*, 20-21.

"The Cross"

Robert Dupree, "The Mirrors of Analogy: Three Poems of Allen Tate," *SoR* 8 (Oct. 1972): 778-85.

Sr. Mary Bernetta, O.S.F., "Allen Tate's Inferno," *Renascence* 3 (Spring 1951): 118.

Frederick Morgan, "Recent Verse," *HudR* 1 (Summer 1948): 263-64.

Richard J. O'Dea, "Allen Tate's 'The Cross,'" *Renascence* 18 (Spring 1966): 156-60.

Charles C. Walcutt, *Expl* 6 (Apr. 1948): 41. Reprinted in *The Explicator Cyclopedia* 1:296-97.

Winters, *Forms of Discovery*, 322-23.

"Death of Little Boys"

David V. Harrington and Carole Schneider, *Expl* 26 (Oct. 1967): 16.

Vivienne Koch, "The Poetry of Allen Tate," *KR* 11 (Summer 1949), 357-60. Reprinted in Ransom, *The Kenyon Critics*, 172-74; in Rajan, *Modern American Poetry*, 12-14.

Roy Harvey Pearce, "A Small Crux in Allen Tate's 'Death of Little Boys': Postscript," *MLN* 75 (Mar. 1960): 213-14.

Southworth, *More Modern American Poets*, 97.

Radcliffe Squires, "Mr. Tate: Whose Wreath Should Be a Moral," in Ludwig, *Aspects of American Poetry*, 265-66, 268.

Thompson Uhlman, *Expl* 28 (Mar. 1970): 58.

Winters, *The Anatomy of Nonsense*, 198-202. Reprinted in Winters, *In Defense of Reason*, 529-33.

"Fragment of a Meditation"

Vivienne Koch, "The Poetry of Allen Tate," *KR* 11 (Summer 1949): 363-64. Reprinted in Rajan, *Modern American Poetry*, 17-18.

"If It Would All Please Hurry"

Donald Revell, "Tate's Urgent Candor and Urgent Calm," *APR* 16 (Jan./Feb. 1987): 43-47.

"Last Days of Alice"

Brooks, *Modern Poetry and the Tradition*, 104.

Robert Dupree, "The Mirrors of Analogy: Three Poems of Allen Tate," *SoR* 8 (Oct. 1972): 774-78.

Sr. Mary Bernetta, O.S.F., "Allen Tate's Inferno," *Renascence* 3 (Spring 1951): 117.

Delmore Schwartz, "The Poetry of Allen Tate, *SoR* 5 (Winter 1940): 427-30.

"The Maimed Man"

Alan Williamson, "Allen Tate and the Personal Epic," *SoR* 12 (Oct. 1976): 726-27.

"The Meaning of Death"

Brooks, *Modern Poetry and the Tradition*, 106-8.

Brooks, Lewis, and Warren, *American Literature*, 2666-67.

Howard Nemerov, "The Current of the Frozen Stream," *Furioso* 3 (Fall 1948): 55-56.

Howard Nemerov, "The Current of the Frozen Stream," *SR* 67 (Autumn 1959): 590-92.

"The Meaning of Life"

Brooks, *Modern Poetry and the Tradition*, 105-6.

Brooks, Lewis, and Warren, *American Literature*, 2665-66.

R. K. Meiners, *Expl* 19 (June 1961): 63. Reprinted in *The Explicator Cyclopedia* 1:297-99.

Howard Nemerov, "The Current of the Frozen Stream," *Furioso* 3 (Fall 1948): 54-55.

Howard Nemerov, "The Current of the Frozen Stream," *SR* 67 (Autumn 1959): 589-92.

"The Mediterranean"

Robert Dupree, "The Mirrors of Analogy: Three Poems of Allen Tate," *SoR* 8 (Oct. 1972): 785-90.

R. K. Meiners, "The Art of Allen Tate: A Reading of 'The Mediterranean,'" *University of Kansas City Review* 27 (Winter 1960): 155-59.

Louis D. Rubin, Jr., "The Concept of Nature in Modern Southern Poetry," *AQ* 9 (Spring 1957): 64-65.

"Message from Abroad"

Vivienne Koch, "The Poetry of Allen Tate," *KR* 11 (Summer 1949): 364-65. Reprinted in Ransom, *The Kenyon Critics*, 174; in Rajan, *Modern American Poetry*, 18-20.

"More Sonnets at Christmas, I"
("Again the native hour lets down the locks")

Radcliffe Squires, "Allen Tate: A Season at Monteagle," *MQR* 10 (Winter 1971): 58.

"More Sonnets at Christmas, IV"
("Gay citizen, myself, and thoughtful friend")

Radcliffe Squires, "Allen Tate: A Season at Monteagle," *MQR* 10 (Winter 1971): 58-59.

"Mother and Son"

Denis Donoghue, "Nuances of a Theme by Allen Tate," *SoR* 12 (Oct. 1976): 711-13.

Sr. Mary Bernetta, O.S.F., "Allen Tate's Inferno," *Renascence* 3 (Spring 1951): 114-15.

Southworth, *More Modern American Poets*, 99.

"Mr. Pope"

Margaret Morton Blum, "Allen Tate's 'Mr. Pope': A Reading," *MLN* 74 (Dec. 1959): 706-9.

Daniels, *The Art of Reading Poetry*, 312-14.

Felver and Nurmi, *Poetry: An Introduction and Anthology*, 123-24, 128.

Rubin, *The Wary Fugitives: Four Poets of the South*, 64-135.

James Edward Tobin, *Expl* 15 (Mar. 1957): 35. Reprinted in *The Explicator Cyclopedia* 1:299-300.

"The Oath"

Brooks, *Modern Poetry and the Tradition*, 108-9.

"Ode to Our Young Pro-Consuls of the Air"

Hoffman, *The Twenties*, 385-88.

"Ode to the Confederate Dead"

Brooks, Lewis, and Warren, *American Literature*, 2663-64.

Denis Donoghue, "Technique in Hopkins," *Studies* 44 (Winter 1955): 449-50.

Lilian Feder, "Allen Tate's Use of Classical Literature," *CentR* 4 (Winter 1960): 98-103.

Friar and Brinnin, *Modern Poetry*, 538-39.

Hoffman, *The Twenties*, 151-53.

Vivienne Koch, "The Poetry of Allen Tate," *KR* 11 (Summer 1949): 370-72. Reprinted in Rajan, *Modern American Poetry*, 24-26.

Louis D. Rubin, Jr., "The Concept of Nature in Modern Poetry," *AQ* 9 (Spring 1957): 70-71.

Louis D. Rubin, Jr., "The Serpent in the Mulberry Bush Again," *SoR* 12 (Oct. 1976): 744-57.

Rubin, *The Wary Fugitives: Four Poets and the South*, passim.

Schlauch, *Modern English and American Poetry*, 97-98.

Southworth, *More Modern American Poets*, 100-101.

Allen Tate, "Narcissus as Narcissus," *VQR* 14 (Jan. 1938): 108-22.

Tate, *Reason in Madness*, 136-51. Reprinted in Tate, *On the Limits of Poetry*, 248-62; in Engle and Carrier, *Reading Modern Poetry*, 207-19.

Alan Williamson, "Allen Tate and the Personal Epic," *SoR* 12 (Oct. 1976): 717-20.

"Retroduction to American History"

Southworth, *More Modern American Poets*, 99-100.

"Seasons of the Soul"

Richmond C. Beatty, "Allen Tate as a Man of Letters," *SAQ* 47 (Apr. 1948): 233-34.

Alwyn Berland, "Violence in the Poetry of Allen Tate," *Accent* 11 (Summer 1951): 165-71.

Brooks, Lewis, and Warren, *American Literature*, 2670-74.

Deutsch, *Poetry in Our Time*, 199-202.

Vivienne Koch, "The Poetry of Allen Tate," *KR* 11 (Summer 1949): 374-78. Reprinted in Ransom, *The Kenyon Critics*, 177-81; in Rajan, *Modern American Poetry*, 28-30.

Radcliffe Squires, "Allen Tate: A Season at Monteagle," *MQR* 10 (Winter 1971): 62-65.

Alan Williams, "Allen Tate and the Personal Epic," *SoR* 12 (Oct. 1976): 721-25.

"Shadow and Shade"

Southworth, *More Modern American Poets*, 97-98.

"Sonnet at Christmas"

Delmore Schwartz, "The Poetry of Allen Tate," *SoR* 5 (Winter 1940): 425-27.

"The Subway"

Deutsch, *Poetry in Our Time*, 198-99.

Joe Horrell, "Some Notes on Conversion in Poetry," *SoR* 7 (Summer 1941): 119-22.

Ransom, *The New Criticism*, 222-25. Reprinted in part in Stallman, *The Critic's Notebook*, 252-53.

Louis D. Rubin, Jr., "The Concept of Nature in Modern Poetry," *AQ* 9 (Spring 1957): 66-67.

Winters, *Primitivism and Decadence*, 4-5. Reprinted in Winters, *In Defense of Reason*, 19-20; in part in Stallman, *The Critic's Notebook*, 250-52.

"The Swimmers"

Perrine and Reid, *100 American Poems*, 183-84.

Alan Williamson, "Allen Tate and the Personal Epic," *SoR* 12 (Oct. 1976): 727.

"Winter Mask"

Radcliffe Squires, "Allen Tate: A Season at Monteagle," *MQR* 10 (Winter 1971): 61-62.

"The Wolves"

Richmond C. Beatty, "Allen Tate as a Man of Letters," *SAQ* 47 (Apr. 1948): 232.

Richard J. O'Dea, "Allen Tate's Vestigial Morality," *Personalist* 49 (Spring 1968): 256-62.

TATE, JAMES

"Breathing"

Robert Hass, "A Review of James Tate's *Absences*," *OhR* 14 (Winter 1973), 90-92.

"The Life of Poetry"

Donald Revell, "The Desperate Buck and Wing: James Tate and the Failure of Ritual," *WHR* 38 (Winter 1984): 372-79.

"The Lost Pilot"

Donald Revell, "The Desperate Buck and Wing: James Tate and the Failure of Ritual," *WHR* 38 (Winter 1984): 372-79.

"Men get down on their knees"

Robert Hass, "A Review of James Tate's *Absences*," *OhR* 14 (Winter 1973): 88-89.

"Poem to Some of My Recent Poems"

Donald Revell, "The Desperate Buck and Wing: James Tate and the Failure of Ritual," *WHR* 38 (Winter 1984): 372-79.

TEASDALE, SARA

"The Net"

Laurence Perrine, "The Untranslatable Language," *EJ* 60 (Jan. 1971): 61. Reprinted in Perrine, *The Art of Total Relevance*, 46.

THESEN, SHARON

[Interview]

Constance Rooke, "Getting into Heaven: An Interview with Diana Hartog, Paulette Jiles, and Sharon Thesen," *Malahat Review* 83 (Summer 1988): 5-52.

The Beginning of the Long Dash

Stephen Scobie, "The Barren Reach of Modern Desire: Intertextuality in Sharon Thesen's *The Beginning of the Long Dash*," *Malahat Review* 83 (Summer 1988): 89-97.

Holding the Pose

Phyllis Webb, "Imaginations [*sic*] Companion," *Malahat Review* 83 (Summer 1988): 83-88.

"The Occasions"

Stephen Scobie, "The Barren Reach of Modern Desire: Intertextuality in Sharon Thesen's *The Beginning of the Long Dash*," *Malahat Review* 83 (Summer 1988): 89-97.

THOMAS, ROSEMARY

"The Big Nosed Adolescent Boys"

Warren Carrier, "A Facade of Modernity, and a Personal Poet," *Western Review* 16 (Spring 1952): 251.

"St. Francis of Assisi"

Warren Carrier, "A Facade of Modernity, and a Personal Poet," *Western Review* 16 (Spring 1952): 252.

THOMPSON, FRANCIS

"Grace of the Way"

Terence L. Connolly, S.J., *Expl* 9 (June 1951): 56. Reprinted in *The Explicator Cyclopedia* 1:332-33.

George C. Williams, *Expl* 9 (Nov. 1950): 16. Reprinted in *The Explicator Cyclopedia* 1:332.

"The Hound of Heaven"

Brooks and Warren, *Understanding Poetry*, rev. ed., 283-85.

"The New Year's Chimes"

W. G. Wilson, "Francis Thompson's Outlook on Science," *ContempR* 192 (Nov. 1957): 266.

"The Nineteenth Century"

W. G. Wilson, "Francis Thompson's Outlook on Science," *ContempR* 192 (Nov. 1957): 264.

"Sad Semele"

Myrtle Pihlman Pope, *Expl* 17 (Feb. 1959): 35. Reprinted in *The Explicator Cyclopedia* 2:342-43.

THOMSON, JAMES (B. V.)

"The City of Dreadful Night"

David DeCamp, *Expl* 7 (Feb. 1949): 29. Reprinted in *The Explicator Cyclopedia* 2:342-43.

"The Vine"

Tate, *Reason in Madness*, 66-71. Reprinted in Tate, *On the Limits of Poetry*, 78-82; in Stallman, *Critiques*, 57-60.

Allen Tate, "Tension in Poetry," *SoR* 4 (Summer 1938): 104-8.

TODD, RUTHVEN

"Rivers: On Living in Brooklyn"

J. F. Nims, *Poetry: A Critical Supplement*, May 1948, 18-20.

TOLSON, MELVIN B.

"Harlem Gallery"

Joy Flasch, *Melvin B. Tolson* (Boston: Twayne, 1972), passim.

Mariann Russell, *Melvin B. Tolson's "Harlem Gallery": A Literary Analysis* (Columbia: University of Missouri Press, 1980), passim.

Patricia R. Schroeder, "Point and Counterpoint in 'Harlem Gallery,'" *CLAJ* 27 (Dec. 1983): 152-68.

Gordon E. Thompson, "Ambiguity in Tolson's 'Harlem Gallery,'" *Callaloo* 9 (Winter 1986): 159-70.

TOOMER, JEAN

Balo

McKay, *Jean Toomer, Artist*, passim.

"Beehive"

Robert Jones, "Jean Toomer as Poet: A Phenomenology of the Spirit," *BALF* 21 (Fall 1987): 253-87.

"Blue Meridian"

Bernard Bell, "Jean Toomer's 'Blue Meridian': The Poet as Prophet of New Order of Man," *BALF* 14 (1980): 77-80.

Robert Jones, "Jean Toomer as Poet: A Phenomenology of the Spirit," *BALF* 21 (Fall 1987): 253-87.

McKay, *Jean Toomer, Artist*, passim.

Wagner, *Black Poets of the United States*, 272-81.

"Bona and Paul"

Jack M. Christ, "Jean Toomer's 'Bona and Paul': The Innocence and Artifice of Words," *Negro American Literature Forum* 9 (1975): 44-46.

Cane

Donald G. Ackley, "Theme and Vision in Jean Toomer's *Cane*," *Studies in Black Literature* 1 (Spring 1970): 45-65.

John Armstrong, "The Real Negro," *New York Tribune* (14 Oct. 1923): 26. Reprinted in Durham, *Studies in Cane*, 27-28.

Houston A. Baker, Jr., ed., "Journey Toward Black Art: Jean Toomer's *Cane*," in *Singers of Daybreak: Studies in Black American Literature* (Washington: Howard University Press, 1976), 53-80.

Bernard Bell, "A Key to the Poems in *Cane*," *CLAJ* 14 (1971): 251-58.

Bernard W. Bell, "Portrait of the Artist as High Priest of Soul: Jean Toomer's *Cane*," *Black World* 23 (Sept. 1974): 4-19, 92-97.

Louise Blackwell, "Jean Toomer's *Cane* and Biblical Myth," *CLAJ* 17 (1974): 535-42.

Susan Blake, "The Spectatorial Artist and the Structure of *Cane*," *CLAJ* 17 (1974): 516-34.

Bontemps, *The Harlem Renaissance Remembered*, 51-62 and passim.

Arna Bontemps, "The Negro Renaissance: Jean Toomer and the Harlem Writers of the 1920's," in Hill, *Anger and Beyond*, 20-36. Reprinted in Durham, *Studies in Cane*, 75-78.

Ann Marie Bush and Louisa D. Mitchell, "Jean Toomer: A Cubist Poet," *BALF* 5 (1971): 106-8.

Patricia Chase, "The Women in *Cane*," *CLAJ* 14 (1971): 259-73.

Cooke, *Afro-American Literature in the Twentieth Century*, 177-99 and passim.

Frank Durham, "The Poetry of South Carolina's Turbulent Year: Self-Interest, Atheism, and Jean Toomer," *SHR* 5 (Winter 1971): 76-80. Reprinted in Durham, *Studies in Cane*, 11-14.

Emanuel and Gross, *Dark Symphony*, 95-98.

Alice P. Fischer, "The Influence of Ouspensky's *Tertium Organum* upon Jean Toomer's *Cane*," *CLAJ* 17 (1974): 504-15.

William C. Fischer, "The Aggregate Man in Jean Toomer's *Cane*," *Studies in the Novel* 3 (1971): 190-215.

Nick Aaron Ford, "Jean Toomer and His *Cane*," *LHRev* 2 (Spring 1983): 16-27.

Gross, *Heroic Ideal in American Literature*, 142-46 and passim.

Joe Blyden Jackson, "Jean Toomer's *Cane*: An Issue of Genre," in French, *The Twenties*, 317-33. Reprinted in Jackson, *The Waiting Years*, 189-97.

Robert Jones, "Jean Toomer as Poet: A Phenomenology of the Spirit," *BALF* 21 (Fall 1987): 253-87.

Michael Krasny, "The Aesthetic Structure of Jean Toomer's *Cane*," *Negro American Literature Forum* 4 (1970): 42-43.

McKay, *Jean Toomer, Artist*, passim.

Benjamin McKeever, "*Cane* as Blues," *Negro American Literature Forum* 4 (1970): 61-63.

Nathaniel Mackey, "Sound and Sentiment, Sound and Symbol," *Callaloo* 10 (Winter 1987): 29-54.

Odette C. Martin, "*Cane*: Method and Myth," *Obsidian II* 2 (Spring 1976): 5-20.

James M. Mellard, "Solipsism, Symbolism, and Demonism: The Lyrical Mode in Fiction," *SHR* 7 (Winter 1973): 37-54.

J. Saunders Redding, *To Make a Poet Black* (Chapel Hill: University of North Carolina Press, 1939), 104-6. Reprinted in Durham, *Studies in Cane*, 51-53.

Herbert W. Rice, "An Incomplete Circle: Repeated Images in Part Two of *Cane*," *CLAJ* 29 (1986): 442-61.

Herbert W. Rice, "Repeated Images in Part One of *Cane*," *BALF* 17 (1983): 100-105.

Charles W. Scruggs, "The Mark of Cain and the Redemption of Art: A Study in Theme and Structure of Jean Toomer's *Cane*," *AL* 44 (1972): 276-91.

Marian L. Stein, "The Poet-Observer and Fern in Jean Toomer's *Cane*," *Markham Review* 2 (1970): 64-65.

Darwin Turner, "Jean Toomer's *Cane*: A Critical Analysis," *Negro Digest* 18 (Jan. 1969): 54-61.

Wagner, *Black Poets of the United States*, 259-81 and passim.

"Cotton Song"

Udo Jung, "'Spirit Torsos of Exquisite Strength': The Theme of Individual Weakness vs. Collective Strength in Two of Toomer's Poems," *CLAJ* 19 (Dec. 1975): 261-64.

"Easter"

McKay, *Jean Toomer, Artist*, passim.

"Five Vignettes"

Robert Jones, "Jean Toomer as Poet: A Phenomenology of the Spirit," *BALF* 21 (Fall 1987): 253-87.

"Georgia Dusk"

Robert Jones, "Jean Toomer as Poet: A Phenomenology of the Spirit," *BALF* 21 (Fall 1987): 253-87.

"Her Lips Are Copper Wire"

Robert Jones, "Jean Toomer as Poet: A Phenomenology of the Spirit," *BALF* 21 (Fall 1987): 253-87.

"The Lost Dancer"

Robert Jones, "Jean Toomer as Poet: A Phenomenology of the Spirit," *BALF* 21 (Fall 1987): 253-87.

"Mill House"

Franklin Davenport, "'Mill House,'" *Banc* 2 (May/June 1972): 6-7.

Susan Taylor, "'Blend Us with Thy Being': Jean Toomer's Mill House Poems," Ph.D. dissertation, Boston College, 1977, passim.

"Mr. Costyve Duditch"

McKay, *Jean Toomer, Artist*, passim.

Natalie Mann

McKay, *Jean Toomer, Artist*, passim

"November Cotton Flower"

Robert Jones, "Jean Toomer as Poet: A Phenomenology of the Spirit," *BALF* 21 (Fall 1987): 253-87.

"Prayer"

Udo Jung, "'Spirit-Torsos of Exquisite Strength': The Theme of Individual Strength in Two of Toomer's Poems," *CLAJ* 19 (Dec. 1975): 264-67.

"The Promise"

Robert Jones, "Jean Toomer as Poet: A Phenomenology of the Spirit," *BALF* 21 (Fall 1987): 253-87.

"Reapers"

Dolly Withrow, "Cutting through Shade," *CLAJ* 21 (Sept. 1977): 98-99.

"Song of the Son"

Bernard Bell, "A Key to the Poems in *Cane*," *CLAJ* 14 (Mar. 1971): 254-55.

"Sound Poem (I)"

Robert Jones, "Jean Toomer as Poet: A Phenomenology of the Spirit," *BALF* 21 (Fall 1987): 253-87.

"They Are Not Missed"

Robert Jones, "Jean Toomer as Poet: A Phenomenology of the Spirit," *BALF* 21 (Fall 1987): 253-87.

"To Gurdjieff Dying"

Robert Jones, "Jean Toomer as Poet: A Phenomenology of the Spirit," *BALF* 21 (Fall 1987): 253-87.

TOSTEVIN, LEMIRE

Color of Her Speech

McCaffery, *North of Intention*, 88-92.

TRINIDAD, DAVID

Pavane

David E. James, "Poetry/Punk/Production: Some Recent Writing in L.A.," *MinnR*, n.s. 23 (Fall 1984): 127-48.

TUCKERMAN, FREDERICK GODDARD

"As Eponina Brought, to Move the King"

Edwin H. Cady, "Frederick Goddard Tuckerman," in Gohdes, *Essays on American Literature*, 147-48.

"The Cricket"

Winters, *Forms of Discovery*, 259-62.

"An Upper Chamber in a Darkened House"

Edwin H. Cady, "Frederick Goddard Tuckerman," in Gohdes, *Essays on American Literature*, 149-51.

Eugene England, "Tuckerman's Sonnet I:10: The First Post-Symbolist Poem," *SoR* 12 (Apr. 1976): 323-47.

TWICHELL, CHASE

Northern Spy

Kathy Callaway, "Apple Genii," *Parnassus* 10 (Spring/Summer 1982): 185-208.

"Physics"

Kathy Callaway, "Apple Genii," *Parnassus* 10 (Spring/Summer 1982): 185-208.

"Webster's Second"

Kathy Callaway, "Apple Genii," *Parnassus* 10 (Spring/Summer 1982): 185-208.

TYLER

"The Granite Butterfly"

William Carlos Williams, untitled review, *Accent* 6 (Winter 1946): 203-6.

UPDIKE, JOHN

"Ex-Basketball Player"

Virginia Busha, "Poetry in the Classroom: 'Ex-Basketball Player,'" *EJ* 59 (May 1970): 643-45.

"Leaves"

G. W. Hunt, "Reality, Imagination, and Art: The Significance of Updike's 'Best' Story," *SSF* 16 (Summer 1979): 219-29.

"Pigeon Feathers"

W. Shurr, "The Lutheran Experience in John Updike's 'Pigeon Feathers,'" *SSF* 14 (Fall 1977): 329-35.

"Shillington"

Edward R. Ducharme, "Close Reading and Teaching," *EJ* 59 (Oct. 1970): 938-42.

VAN DOREN, MARK

"January Chance"

Deutsch, *Poetry in Our Time*, 68-69.

VERY, JONES

"The Baker's Island Lights"

Carl Dennis, "Correspondence in Very's Nature Poetry," *NEQ* 43 (June 1970): 265-66.

"The Columbina"

Carl Dennis, "Correspondence in Very's Nature Poetry," *NEQ* 43 (June 1970): 263-65.

"The Hand and the Foot"

Yvor Winters, "Jones Very: A New England Mystic," *American Review* 7 (May 1936): 161-63.

Winters, *Maule's Curse*, 127-29. Reprinted in Winters, *In Defense of Reason*, 264-66.

"The Lost"

Carl Dennis, "Correspondence in Very's Nature Poetry," *NEQ* 43 (June 1970): 268-70.

Yvor Winters, "Jones Very: A New England Mystic," *American Review* 7 (May 1936): 171-72.

Winters, *Maule's Curse*, 138-39. Reprinted in Winters, *In Defense of Reason*, 274-76.

"Man in Harmony with Nature"

Carl Dennis, "Correspondence in Very's Nature Poetry," *NEQ* 43 (June 1970): 257-58.

"The New Birth"

Carl Dennis, "Correspondence in Very's Nature Poetry," *NEQ* 43 (June 1970): 259.

"The Revelation of the Spirit through the Material World"

Carl Dennis, "Correspondence in Very's Nature Poetry," *NEQ* 43 (June 1970): 259-60.

"To the Canary Bird"

Carl Dennis, "Correspondence in Very's Nature Poetry," *NEQ* 43 (June 1970): 261-62.

"The Tree" (p. 70 of *Poems and Essays*, 1886)

Carl Dennis, "Correspondence in Very's Nature Poetry," *NEQ* 43 (June 1970): 262-63.

"The Tree" (p. 121 of *Poems and Essays* 1886)

Carl Dennis, "Correspondence in Very's Nature Poetry," *NEQ* 43 (June 1970): 267-68.

"The True Light"

Carl Dennis, "Correspondences in Very's Nature Poetry," *NEQ* 43 (June 1970): 258-59.

VIERECK, PETER V.

"Better Come Quietly"

J. F. Nims, *Poetry: A Critical Supplement*, Dec. 1947, 1-4.

"Blindman's Buff"

J. F. Nims, *Poetry: A Critical Supplement*, Dec. 1947, 6-8.

"Crass Times Redeemed by Dignity of Souls"

Ciardi, *How Does a Poem Mean?*, 952-53.

"Don't Look But Mary Is Everybody"

Richard P. Benton, *Expl* 20 (Dec. 1961): 30. Reprinted in *The Explicator Cyclopedia*, 1:334-36.

"Game Called on Account of Darkness"

J. F. Nims, *Poetry: A Critical Supplement* Dec. 1947, 9-10.

"Like a Sitting Breeze"

Peter Viereck, "Correspondence Relating to 'Like a Sitting Breeze,'" *ASch* 20 (Spring 1951): 216-17.

"Six Theological Cradle Songs"

Peter Viereck, "My Kind of Poetry," in Ciardi, *Mid-Century American Poets*, 26-27.

"Some Lines in Three Parts"

Peter Viereck, "My Kind of Poetry," in Ciardi, *Mid-Century American Poets*, 26-27.

"Vale from Carthage (Spring 1944)"

Kreuzer, *Elements of Poetry*, 93-96.

Perrine and Reid, *100 American Poems*, 241.

VILLANUEVA, ALMA

"Dreaming"

Sánchez, *Contemporary Chicano Poetry: A Critical Approach to an Emerging Literature*, 52-53, 308-9.

"Her Myth (of Creation)"

Sánchez, *Contemporary Chicano Poetry: A Critical Approach to an Emerging Literature*, 55-56, 328-29.

VIZENOR, GERALD

Earthdivers

Franchot Ballinger, "Sacred Reversals: Tricksters in Gerald Vizenor's *Earthdivers: Tribal Narratives in Mixed Descent*," *AIQ* 9 (Winter 1985): 31-47.

Patricia Haseltine, "The Voices of Gerald Vizenor: Survival through Transformation," *AIQ* 9 (Winter 1985): 31-47.

VOBORTH, J. IVALOO

"Animal Thirst"

Kenneth Lincoln, "Native American Literatures: 'old like hills, like stars,'" in Baker, *Three American Literatures*, 129-33.

VOBORTH, J. IVALOO

Lincoln, *Native American Renaissance*, passim.

Thunder-Root

Kenneth Lincoln, "Native American Literatures: 'old like hills, like stars,'" in Baker, *Three American Literatures*, 129-33.

Lincoln, *Native American Renaissance*, passim.

WAGONER, DAVID

"Cuckoo"

Robert Peters, "Thirteen Ways of Looking at David Wagoner's New Poems," *WHR* 35 (Autumn 1981): 267-72.

"The Sand Behind the Wind"

Sara McAulay, "'Getting There' and Going Beyond: David Wagoner's Journey Without Regret," *LitR* 28 (Fall 1984): 93-98.

"A Sea Change"

Sara McAulay, "'Getting There' and Going Beyond: David Wagoner's Journey without Regret," *LitR* 28 (Fall 1984): 93-98.

WAH, FRED

"Earth"

George Bowering, "The Poems of Fred Wah," *CP* 12 (Fall 1979): 3-13.

"Here"

George Bowering, "The Poems of Fred Wah," *CP* 12 (Fall 1979): 3-13.

Pictograms from the Interior of B.C.

McCaffery, *North of Intention*, 30-38.

"plan for a tree"

George Bowering, "The Poems of Fred Wah," *CP* 12 (Fall 1979): 3-13.

"Song"

George Bowering, "The Poems of Fred Wah," *CP* 12 (Fall 1979): 3-13.

WAKOWSKI, DIANE

[Interview]

Larry Smith, "A Conversation with Diane Wakowski," *ChiR* 29 (Summer 1977): 115-25.

"Beauty"

Alice Ostriker, "In Mind: The Divided Self in Women's Poetry," *MQ* 24 (Summer 1983): 351-65.

Dancing on the Grave of a Son of a Bitch

Lauter, *Women as Mythmakers*, passim.

"George Washington and the Loss of His Teeth"

Ostriker, *Stealing the Language*, 154-58.

Inside the Blood Factory

Lauter, *Women as Mythmakers*, passim.

The Magellanic Clouds

Lauter, *Women as Mythmakers*, passim.

Motorcycle Betrayal Poems

Lauter, *Women as Mythmakers*, passim.

Smudging

Lauter, *Woman as Mythmakers*, passim.

Virtuoso Literature for Two and Four Hands

Lauter, *Women as Mythmakers*, passim.

Waiting for the King of Spain

Lauter, *Women as Mythmakers*, passim.

"3 of swords--for dark men under the white moon"

Lauter, *Women as Mythmakers*, 99-100.

WALKER, MARGARET

For My People

Richard Barksdale, "Margaret Walker: Folk Orature and Historical Prophecy," in Miller, *Black American Poets Between Worlds, 1940-1960*, passim.

Ron Baxter Miller, "The Intricate Design of Margaret Walker," in Miller, *Black American Poets Between Worlds, 1940-1960*, passim.

Eleanor W. Traylor, "'Bolder Measures Crashing Through': Margaret Walker's Poem of the Century," *Callaloo* 10 (Fall 1987): 570-95.

WARREN, ROBERT PENN

[Interview]

Edwin Thomas Wood, "On Native Soil: A Talk with Robert Penn Warren," *MissQ* 37 (Spring 1984): 179-86.

"Acquaintance with Time in Early Autumn"

Bedient, *In the Heart's Last Kingdom*, passim.

"Aged Man Surveys the Past Time"

Brooks, *Modern Poetry and the Tradition*, 78-79.

W. P. Southard, "Speculation," *KR* 7 (Autumn 1945): 666-67.

Audubon: A Vision

Bedient, *In the Heart's Last Kingdom*, passim.

"Ballad: Between the Boxcars"

Cleanth Brooks, "Episode and Anecdote in the Poetry of Robert Penn Warren," *YR* 70 (October 1980): 551-67.

"The Ballad of Billie Potts"

Deutsch, *Poetry in Our Time*, 202-3.

Ruth Herschberger, "Poised Between the Two Alarms . . . ," *Accent* 4 (Summer 1944): 245.

Sam Hynes, "Robert Penn Warren: The Symbolic Journey," *University of Kansas City Review* 17 (Summer 1951): 280-81.

M. L. Rosenthal, "Robert Penn Warren's Poetry," *SAQ* 62 (Autumn 1963): 501-3.

W. P. Southard, "Speculation," *KR* 7 (Autumn 1945): 670-73.

John L. Stuart, "The Achievement of Robert Penn Warren," *SAQ* 47 (Oct. 1948): 570-74.

John L. Stewart, "Robert Penn Warren and the Knot of History," *ELH* 26 (Mar. 1959): 117, 120-22.

"Bearded Oaks"

Beach, *Obssessive Images*, 324-25.

Brooks, *Modern Poetry and the Tradition*, 81-82. Reprinted in Engle and Carrier, *Reading Modern Poetry*, 106-8.

O'Connor, *Sense and Sensibility in Modern Poetry*, 154-55.

"Blow West Wind, Blow"

Sr. M. Bernetta Quinn, O.S.F., "Robert Penn Warren's Promised Land," *SoQ* 8 (Apr. 1972): 337-39.

Brothers to Dragons

R. Law, "*Brothers to Dragons*: The Fact of Violence vs. the Possibility of Love," *AL* 49 (Jan. 1978): 560-79.

"Caribou Near Arctic"

Bedient, *In the Heart's Last Kingdom*, passim.

"The Child Next Door"

James Wright, "The Stiff Smile of Mr. Warren," *KR* 20 (Autumn 1958): 648-55.

"Composition in Red and Gold"

Sr. M. Bernetta Quinn, O.S.F., "Robert Penn Warren's Promised Land," *SoQ* 8 (Apr. 1972): 335-36.

"Crime"

W. P. Southard, "Speculation," *KR* 7 (Autumn 1945): 661-62.

"Dead Horse in Field"

Bedient, *In the Heart's Last Kingdom*, passim.

"Dragon Country: To Jacob Boehme"

Brooks, *A Shaping Joy*, 223-24.

Cleanth Brooks, "Episode and Anecdote in the Poetry of Robert Penn Warren," *YR* 70 (Oct. 1980): 551-67.

Perrine and Reid, *100 American Poems*, 203-4.

"The Dream He Never Knew the End of"

William Bedford Clark: "Warren's Audubon: The Artist as Hero," *SAQ* 81 (Autumn 1982): 387-98.

"Folly on Royal Street before the Raw Face of God"

Bedient, *In the Heart's Last Kingdom*, passim.

"The Garden"

W. P. Southard, "Speculation," *KR* 7 (Autumn 1945): 668.

"Gold Glade"

Sr. M. Bernetta Quinn, O.S.F., "Robert Penn Warren's Promised Land," *SoQ* 8 (Apr. 1972): 354-55.

"History"

Brooks, *Modern Poetry and the Tradition*, 85-87.

Jefferson Humphries, "Shards from the Wreckage: Antimaxims in Modern Poetry," *SAQ* 86 (Winter 1987): 30-31.

"History among the Rocks"

Brooks, *Modern Poetry and the Tradition*, 77-78.

Incarnations

G. Rotella, "'One Flesh': Robert Penn Warren's *Incarnations*," *Renascence* 31 (Autumn 1978): 25-42.

"Letter from a Coward to a Hero"

Brooks, *Modern Poetry and the Tradition*, 82-85.

W. P. Southard, "Speculation," *KR* 7 (Autumn 1945): 659-60.

"Love's Parable"

Howard Nemerov, "The Phoenix in the World," *Furioso* 3 (Spring 1948): 36-46.

"Man Coming of Age"

W. P. Southard, "Speculation," *KR* 7 (Autumn 1945): 657-58.

"The Mango on the Mango Tree"

Frederick Brantley, "The Achievement of Robert Penn Warren," in Rajan, *Modern American Poetry*, 78-79.

"Mexico Is a Foreign Country"

W. P. Southard, "Speculation," *KR* 7 (Autumn 1945): 668-70.

"Monologue at Midnight"

Beach, *Obssessive Images*, 315-16.

Frederick Brantley, "The Achievement of Robert Penn Warren," in Rajan, *Modern American Poetry*, 76-77.

"Now and Then"

Joseph Parisi, "Homing In," *Shenandoah* 30 (1979): 99-107

"October Picnic Long Ago"

Peter Stitt, "Robert Penn Warren: Life's Instancy and the Astrolabe of Joy," *GaR* 34 (Winter 1980): 711-31.

"Old Nigger on One-Mule Cart Encountered Late at Night When Driving Home from Party in the Back Country"

Cleanth Brooks, "Episode and Anecdote in the Poetry of Robert Penn Warren," *YR* 70 (Oct. 1980): 551-67.

"Original Sin: A Short Story"

Richard E. Amacher, *Expl* 8 (May 1950): 52. Reprinted in *The Explicator Cyclopedia* 1:336-37.

Frederick Brantley, "The Achievement of Robert Penn Warren," in Rajan, *Modern American Poetry*, 77-78.

Clifford M. Gordon, *Expl* 9 (Dec. 1950): 21. Reprinted in *The Explicator Cyclopedia* 1:337-38.

"Pondy Woods"

M. L. Rosenthal, "Robert Penn Warren's Poetry," *SAQ* 62 (Autumn 1963): 500-501.

"Pursuit"

William Frost, *Expl* 11 (Feb. 1953): 22. Reprinted in *The Explicator Cyclopedia* 1:338-39.

W. P. Southard, "Speculation," *KR* 7 (Autumn 1945): 662-65.

Robert Penn Warren, in Friar and Brinnin, *Modern Poetry*, 542.

"Red-Tail Hawk and Pyre of Youth"

Bedient, *In the Heart's Last Kingdom*, passim.

"The Return: An Elegy"

Frederick Brantley, "The Achievement of Robert Penn Warren," in Rajan, *Modern American Poetry*, 75-76.

Brooks, *Modern Poetry and the Tradition*, 79-80.

"Revelation"

Robert Penn Warren, in Friar and Brinnin, *Modern Poetry*, 541-542.

"South of San Francisco"

Stitt, *The World's Hieroglyphic Beauty--Five American Poets*, 215-40.

"Speleology"

Cleanth Brooks, "Episode and Anecdote in the Poetry of Robert Penn Warren," *YR* 70 (Oct. 1980): 551-67.

Peter Stitt, "Robert Penn Warren: Life's Instancy and the Astrolabe of Joy," *GaR* 34 (Winter 1980): 711-31.

"Sunset Walk in Thaw-Time in Vermont"

Bloom, *A Map of Misreading*, 193-98.

"Swimming in the Pacific"

Peter Stitt, "Robert Penn Warren: Life's Instancy and the Astrolabe of Joy," *GaR* 34 (Winter 1980): 711-31.

"Tell Me a Story"

William Bedford Clark, "Warren's Audubon: The Artist as Hero," *SAQ* 81 (Autumn 1982): 387-98.

"Terror"

Rubin, *The Wary Fugitives: Four Aspects and the South*, 345.

Robert Penn Warren, in Friar and Brinnin, *Modern Poetry*, 542-43.

"Tires on Wet Asphalt at Night"

Peter Stitt, "Robert Penn Warren: Life's Instancy and the Astrolabe of Joy," *GaR* 34 (Winter 1980): 711-31.

"Variation: Ode to Fear"

Beach, *Obsessive Images*, 216-18.

"Was Not the Lost Dolphin"

William Bedford Clark, "Warren's Audubon: The Artist as Hero," *SAQ* 81 (Autumn 1982): 387-98.

"We Are Only Ourselves"

William Bedford Clark, "Warren's Audubon: The Artist as Hero," *SAQ* 81 (Autumn 1982): 387-98.

"Why Have I Wandered the Asphalt of Midnight"

Peter Stitt, "Robert Penn Warren: Life's Instancy and the Astrolabe of Joy," *GaR* 34 (Winter 1980): 711-31.

WATKINS, VERNON

"Arakhova and the Daemon"

J. F. Nims, *Poetry: A Critical Supplement*, Mar. 1947, 1-3.

"Ballad of the Mari Lwyd"

Robert Gorham Davis, "Eucharist and Roasting Pheasant," *Poetry* 73 (Dec. 1948): 171.

"Music of Colours: The Blossom Scattered"

John Berryman, *Poetry: A Critical Supplement*, Dec. 1949, 14-16.

WEBB, PHYLLIS

"Sunday Water, Ghazal 1"

Susan Glickman, "'Proceeding Before the Amorous Invisible': Phyllis Webb and the Ghazal," *CanL* 115 (Winter 1987): 48-61.

Water and Light

Susan Glickman, "'Proceeding Before the Amorous Invisible': Phyllis Webb and the Ghazal," *CanL* 115 (Winter 1987): 48-61.

WEINER, HANNAH

"The Clairvoyant Journal"

Bernstein, *Content's Dream: Essays 1975-1984*, 266-70.

Sixteen

Joan Retallack, "The Meta-Physick of Play: $L=A=N=G=U=A=G=E$ USA," *Parnassus* 12 (Fall/Winter 1984): 213-44.

WEISS, THEODORE

Recoveries

Willard Spiegelman, "Reaching Surprises: Theodore Weiss's Talkies," *Parnassus* 12 (Fall/Winter 1984): 315-29.

WELCH, DON

"Gifts and Myths:2"

Mark Sanders, "Measurements of Compatibility in Contemporary Nebraska Poetry: The Verse of William Kloefkorn, Ted Kooser, and Don Welch," *CP* 13 (Fall 1980): 65-72.

WELCH, JAMES

"Magic Fox"

Kenneth Lincoln, "Native American Literatures: 'old like hills, like stars,'" in Baker, *Three American Literatures*, 152-53.

Riding the Earthboy 40

Kenneth Lincoln, "Native American Literatures: 'old like hills, like stars,'" in Baker, *Three American Literatures*, 152-61.

Alan Velie, "James Welch's Poetry," *American Indian Culture and Research Journal* 3, no. 1 (1979): 19-38.

Winter in the Blood (poems in novel)

Kenneth Lincoln, "Native American Literatures: 'old like hills, like stars,'" in Baker, *Three American Literatures*, 143-51.

Lincoln, *Native American Renaissance*, passim.

Alan Velie, "James Welch's Poetry," *American Indian Culture and Research Journal* 3, no. 1 (1979): 19-38.

WHEELWRIGHT, JOHN BROOKS

"Father"

Austin Warren, *New England Saints* (Ann Arbor: University of Michigan Press, 1956), 174-75.

WIENERS, JOHN

[Interview]

Charley Shively, "John Wieners," in Leyland, *Gay Sunshine Interviews* 2:259-77.

WILBUR, RICHARD

"Advice to a Prophet"

John P. Farrell, "The Beautiful Changes in Richard Wilbur's Poetry," *ConL* 12 (Winter 1971): 78-79.

Mills, *Contemporary American Poetry*, 174-75.

"The Aspen and the Stream"

John P. Farrell, "The Beautiful Changes in Richard Wilbur's Poetry," *ConL* 12 (Winter 1971): 83-84.

"Ballade for the Duke of Orleans"

Paul Cummins, "Richard Wilbur's 'Ballade for the Duke of Orleans,'" *CP* 1 (Fall 1968): 42-45.

"A Baroque Wall Fountain in the Villa Sciarra"

Perrine and Reid, *100 American Poems*, 255-57.

"Beasts"

Anne Williams, *Expl* 37 (Summer 1979): 27-28.

Charles R. Woodward, *Expl* 36 (Spring 1978): 6-7.

"Boy at the Window"

John P. Farrell, "The Beautiful Changes in Richard Wilbur's Poetry," *ConL* 12 (Winter 1971): 86-87.

"Castles and Distances"

Thomas Cole, "Wilbur's Second Volume," *Poetry* 82 (Apr. 1953): 38-39.

"Ceremony"

J. F. Nims, *Poetry: A Critical Supplement*, Feb. 1948, 1-6.

"The Death of a Toad"

Abbe, *You and Contemporary Poetry*, 73-76.

Sanders, *The Discovery of Poetry*, 182-86.

"Driftwood"

John P. Farrell, "The Beautiful Changes in Richard Wilbur's Poetry," *ConL* 12 (Winter 1971): 84-85.

J. F. Nims and Richard Wilbur, *Poetry: A Critical Supplement*, Dec. 1948, 1-7.

"Epistemology"

R. H. Miller, *Expl* 34 (Jan. 1976): 37.

"Exeunt"

Philip C. Kolin, "The Subtle Drama of Richard Wilbur's 'Exeunt,'" *NConL* 5 (Jan. 1975): 11-13.

"For the New Railway Station in Rome"

Perrine and Reid, *100 American Poems*, 258-59.

"Grasse: The Olive Trees"

Thomas Cole, "Wilbur's Second Volume," *Poetry* 82 (Apr. 1953): 37-38.

"Junk"

Mills, *Contemporary American Poetry*, 163-66.

"Looking into History"

John P. Farrell, "The Beautiful Changes in Richard Wilbur's Poetry," *ConL* (Winter 1971): 79-83.

"Love Calls Us to the Things of This World"

Jerome, *Poetry: Premeditated Art*, 180-83.
Frank Littler, *Expl* 40 (Spring 1982): 53-55.
Stitt, *The World's Hieroglyphic: Five American Poets*, 9-38.

"The Mill"

Perrine and Reid, *100 American Poems*, 260-61.

"October Maples, Portland"

Helen Day, *Expl* 40 (Fall 1981): 60-62.

"A Plain Song for Comadre"

William Heyen, "On Richard Wilbur," *SoR* 9 (Summer 1973): 629-30.

"Poplar, Sycamore"

Mills, *Contemporary American Poetry*, 161-62.

"Praise in Summer"

Craig S. Abbott, *Expl* 39 (Spring 1981): 13-14.

"The Puritans"

Mary S. Mattfield, *Expl* 28 (Feb. 1970): 53.

"A Simile for Her Smile"

J. F. Nims, *Poetry: A Critical Supplement*, Feb. 1948, 6-9.

"Statues"

John P. Farrell, "The Beautiful Changes in Richard Wilbur's Poetry," *ConL* 12 (Winter 1971): 85-86.

"Still, Citizen Sparrow"

Dickinson, *Suggestions for Teachers of "Introduction to Literature,"* 51-52.
Charles R. Woodard, *Expl* 34 (Feb. 1976): 46.

"To an American Poet Just Dead"

J. F. Nims and Richard Wilbur, *Poetry: A Critical Supplement*, Dec. 1948: 7-9.

"A Wood"

William Heyen, "On Richard Wilbur," *SoR* 9 (Summer 1973): 618-25.

"Year's-End"

Wheeler, *The Design of Poetry*, 197-201.

WILKINSON, ANNE

"Climate of the Brain"

William Walsh, "The Shape of Canadian Poetry," *SR* 87 (Jan./Mar. 1979): 73-95.

"In June and Gentle Oven"

A. J. M. Smith, "A Reading of Anne Wilkinson," *CanL* 10 (1961). Reprinted in Woodcock, *Choice of Critics*, 123-30.

"The Red and the Green"

A. J. M. Smith, "A Reading of Anne Wilkinson," *CanL* 10 (1961). Reprinted in Woodcock, *Choice of Critics*, 123-30.

"Summer Acres"

William Walsh, "The Shape of Canadian Poetry," *SR* 87 (Jan./Mar. 1979): 73-95.

"Variations on a Theme"

A. J. M. Smith, "A Reading of Anne Wilkinson," *CanL* 10 (1961). Reprinted in Woodcock, *Choice of Critics*, 123-30.

WILLIAMS, CLARENCE

"Ugly Chile"

Adams, *The Contexts of Poetry*, 44-46.

WILLIAMS, JONATHAN

[Interview]

John Browning, "Jonathan Williams & Thomas Meyer," in Leyland, *Gay Sunshine Interviews* 2:279-88.

Blues & Roots/Rue and Bluets

X. J. Kennedy, "Piping Down the Valleys Wild," *Parnassus* 12 (Fall/Winter 1984): 183-89.

"Credo"

Kenner, *A Homemade World*, 184-85.

Get Hot or Get Out

X. J. Kennedy, "Piping Down the Valleys Wild," *Parnassus* 12 (Fall/Winter 1984): 183-89.

"Uncle Iv Surveys His Domain from His Rocker of a Sunday Afternoon as Aunt Dory Starts to Chop the Kindlin"

X. J. Kennedy, "Piping Down the Valleys Wild," *Parnassus* 12 (Fall/Winter 1984): 183-89.

WILLIAMS, OSCAR

"The Leg in the Subway"

Robert Russell, *Expl* 19 (Dec. 1960): 18. Reprinted in *The Explicator Cyclopedia* 1:339-40.

"The Praying Mantis Visits a Penthouse"

Cooper and Holmes, *Preface to Poetry*, 163-65.

WILLIAMS, WILLIAM CARLOS

"Address"

Paul Mariani, "Tomlinson's Use of the Williams Triad," *ConL* 18 (Summer 1977): 409-11.

"The Agonized Spires"

Neil Myers, "William Carlos Williams' *Spring and All*," *MLQ* 26 (June 1965): 295-96.

"Another Year"

Mary Ellen Solt, "William Carlos Williams: Poems in the American Idiom," *Folio* 25 (Winter 1960): 12-14.

"Asphodel, That Greeny Flower"

Duffey, *A Poetry of Presence*, 107-14.

Marc Hofstadter, "A Different Speech: William Carlos Williams' Later Poetry," *TCL* 23 (Dec. 1977): 451-66.

Juhasz, *Metaphor and the Poetry of Williams, Pound, and Stevens*, 49-74.

Paul L. Mariani, "The Satyr's Defense: Williams' 'Asphodel,'" *ConL* 14 (Winter 1973): 1-18.

Miller, *Poets of Reality*, 356-58.

Helge N. Nilsen, "Notes on the Theme of Love in the Later Poetry of William Carlos Williams," *ES* 50 (June 1969): 273-83.

Linda Welshimer Wagner, "The Last Poems of William Carlos Williams," *Criticism* 6 (Fall 1964): 362-65.

"The Attic Which Is Desire"

Willis D. Jacobs, *Expl* 25 (Mar. 1967): 61.

"The Avenue of Poplars"

Neil Baldwin, "Varities of Influence: The Literary Relationship of William Carlos Williams and Louis Zukofsky," *Credences*, n.s. 2 (Summer 1982): 93-103.

"Between Walls"

M. Alan Babcock, *Expl* 45 (Winter 1987): 48-49.

Willis D. Jacobs, *Expl* 28 (Apr. 1970): 68.

Miller, *Poets of Reality*, 345-47.

Alfred F. Rosa, *Expl* 30 (Nov. 1971): 21.

John L. Simons, "The Lying Cinders: Patterns of Linguistic Unity in William Carlos Williams' 'Between Walls,'" *CP* 10 (Spring 1977): 63-70.

"The Birth of Venus"

Mariani, *A Usable Past*, passim.

"Blizzard"

Juhasz, *Metaphor and the Poetry of Willams, Pound, and Stevens*, 45-46.

"The Botticellian Trees"

Linda Funkhouser and Daniel C. O'Connell, "'Measure' in William Carlos Williams' Poetry: Evidence from His Readings," *JML* 12 (Mar. 1985): 34-60.

Sutton, *American Free Verse*, 126-28.

"Bruegel" [sic]

Christopher S. Braider, "The Art of the Ambidextrous: The Fall of Icarus, the Death of Allegory, and the Meaning of Spatial Realism in the Light of William Carlos Williams's *Pictures from Bruegel*," *SLRev* 4 (Fall 1987): 143-74.

"Burning the Christmas Greens"

James K. Guimond, "William Carlos Williams and the Past: Some Clarifications," *JML* 1 (May 1971): 496-98.

William Carlos Williams, in Friar and Brinnin, *Modern Poetry*, 546.

"By the Road to the Contagious Hospital"

Charles V. Hartung, "A Poetry of Experience," *University of Kansas City Review* 25 (Autumn 1958): 67-68.

John Hollander, "The Poem in the Eye," *Shenandoah* 23 (Spring 1972): 30-32.

Winters, *Primitivism and Decadence*, 67-70. Reprinted in Winters, *In Defense of Reason*, 78-82.

"Catastrophic Birth"

Miller, *Poets of Reality*, 354-55.

"The Catholic Bells"

Linda Funkhouser and Daniel C. O'Connell, "'Measure' in William Carlos Williams' Poetry: Evidence from His Readings," *JML* 12 (Mar. 1985): 34-60.

"Children's Games"

Christopher S. Braider, "The Art of the Ambidextrous: The Fall of Icarus, the Death of Allegory, and the Meaning of Spatial Realism in the Light of William Carlos Williams's *Pictures from Bruegel*," *SLRev* 4 (Fall 1987): 143-74.

"Classic Scene"

Abad, *A Formal Approach to Lyric Poetry*, 271-72.

"The Clouds"

Burke, *Language as Symbolic Action*, 288-90.

William Carlos Williams, in Friar and Brinnin, *Modern Poetry*, 545.

"The Cold Night"

Charles V. Hartung, "A Poetry of Experience," *University of Kansas City Review* 25 (Autumn 1958): 66-67.

"A Coronal"

Willis D. Jacobs, *Expl* 29 (Apr. 1971): 64.

"Daisy"

Lois Bar-Yaacev, *Expl* 41 (Summer 1983): 35-37.

"The Dance"

Duffey, *A Poetry of Presence*, 216-17.

Donald Gutiérrez, "Circular Art: Round Poems of Wallace Stevens and William Carlos Williams," *CP* 14 (1981): 53-56.

Gutiérrez, *The Maze in the Mind and the World*, passim.

"Death"

Duffey, *A Poetry of Presence*, 157-59.

"Death the Barber"

Neil Myers, "William Carlos Williams' *Spring and All*, *MLQ* 26 (June 1965): 291.

"Dedication for a Plot of Ground"

Duffey, *A Poetry of Presence*, 162-63.

"The Descent" (from *Paterson*)

Neil Myers, "Decreation in Williams' 'The Descent,'" *Criticism* 14 (Fall 1972): 315-27.

Rapp, *William Carlos Williams and Romantic Idealism*, 123-32.

Maria Anita Stefanelli, "A Stylistic Analysis of Williams' 'The Descent,'" *Lang&S* 16 (Spring 1983): 187-210.

"The Descent of Winter"

Duffey, *A Poetry of Presence*, 141-45 and passim.

"The Desert Music"

Lois Bar-Yaacev, "'The Desert Music': An American Form," *CP* 18 (1985): 85-102.

Duffey, *A Poetry of Presence*, 102-5 and passim.

Neil Myers, "Williams' Imitation of Nature in 'The Desert Music,'" *Criticism* 12 (Winter 1970): 38-50.

Mary Ellen Solt, "William Carlos Williams: Poems in the American Idiom," *Folio* 25 (Winter 1960): 9-11.

"A Dream of Love"

Duffey, *A Poetry of Presence*, 196-214.

David A. Fedo, "The Meaning of Love in William Carlos Williams's 'A Dream of Love,'" *ConL* 23 (1982): 169-90.

"Elaine"

Linda Welshimer Wagner, "The Last Poems of William Carlos Williams," *Criticism* 6 (Fall 1964): 368-70.

"An Elegy for D. H. Lawrence"

Mary Ellen Solt, "William Carlos Williams: Poems in the American Idiom," *Folio* 25 (Winter 1960): 14-16.

"Fish"

Ronald McFarland, "The Variable Voice in William Carlos Williams's 'Fish,'" *Sagetrieb* 2 (Fall 1983): 129-34.

"Flowers by the Sea"

Rosenthal and Smith, *Exploring Poetry*, 51-53.

A. J. M. Smith, "Refining Fire: The Meaning and Use of Poetry," *QQ* 61 (Autumn 1954): 355-56.

"A Flowing River"

Marshall W. Stearns, "Syntax, Sense, Sound, and Dr. Williams," *Poetry* 66 (Apr. 1945): 36-37.

"Full Moon"

Emerson Brown, Jr., "William Carlos Williams' 'Full Moon' and the Medieval Dawn Song," *SHR* 11 (Winter 1977): 175-83.

"The Gift"

Duffey, *A Poetry of Presence*, 220-21.

Perrine and Reid, *100 American Poems*, 78-79.

"Good Night"

Duffey, *A Poetry of Presence*, 132.

"The Great Figure"

James E. Breslin, "William Carlos Williams and Charles Demuth: Cross-Fertilization in the Arts," *JML* 6 (Apr. 1977): 258-61.

Cook, *Figural Choice in Poetry and Art*, passim.

Peter Halter, "Dialogue of the Sister Arts: Number-Poems and Number-Paintings in America, 1920-1970," *ES* (1982): 207-19.

"Great Mullen"

Lois Bar-Yaacev, *Expl* 41 (Summer 1983): 35-37.

Willis D. Jacobs, *Expl* 28 (Mar. 1970): 63.

"The Hard Core of Beauty"

Mariani, *A Usable Past*, passim.

"El Hombre"

Cook, *Figural Choice in Poetry and Art*, passim.

Duffey, *A Poetry of Presence*, 128-29.

Rosenthal, *The Modern Poets*, 121.

"The Horse Show"

Perrine and Reid, *100 American Poems*, 80-81.

"The Hunter"

Willis D. Jacobs, *Expl* 29 (Mar. 1971): 60.

"The Hunters in the Snow"

Sayre, *The Visual Text of William Carlos Williams*, 128-31.

David M. Wyatt, "Completing the Picture: Williams, Berryman, and 'Spatial Form,'" *CLQ* 13 (Dec. 1977): 251-57.

Vincent Yang, *Expl* 40 (Fall 1981): 44-46.

Kora in Hell

Duffey, *A Poetry of Presence*, 49-60 and passim.

Harvey Feinberg, "The American Kora: Myth in the Art of William Carlos Williams," *Sagetrieb* 5 (Fall 1986): 73-92.

Stephen Fredman, *Poet's Prose: The Crisis in American Verse* (Cambridge: Cambridge University Press, 1983), passim.

Patrick Moore, "Cubist Prosody: William Carlos Williams and the Conventions of Verse Lineation," *PQ* 65 (1986): 513-36.

"Landscape with the Fall of Icarus"

Christopher S. Braider, "The Art of the Ambidextrous: The Fall of Icarus, the Death of Allegory, and the Meaning of Spatial Realism in the Light of William Carlos Williams's *Pictures from Bruegel*," *SLRev* 4 (Fall 1987): 143-74.

Duffey, *A Poetry of Presence*, 217-19.

Peter Quartermain, "'Actual Word Stuff, Not Thoughts for Thoughts,'" *Credences*, n.s. 2 (Summer 1982): 104-22.

"Lear"

J. F. Nims, *Poetry: A Critical Supplement*, May, 1948, 1-7.

"Lines: Leaves Are Grey-green"

Frederick Morgan, "William Carlos Williams: Imagery, Rhythm, Form," *SR* 55 (Autumn 1947): 676 and passim.

"The Locust Tree in Flower"

Duffey, *A Poetry of Presence*, 148-50.

Miller, *Poets of Reality*, 304-5.

Linus L. Phillips and Mrs. William W. Deaton, *Expl* 26 (Nov. 1967): 26.

"Love Song"

Kurt Heinzelman, "Staging the Poem: William Carlos Williams' *A Dream of Love*," *ConL* 18 (Autumn 1977): 491-508.

Miller, *Poets of Reality*, 321.

"Many Loves" (verse play)

Duffey, *A Poetry of Presence*, 196-214.

"The Monstrous Marriage"

William Carlos Williams, in Friar and Brinnin, *Modern Poetry*, 545-46.

"Nantucket"

Charles V. Hartung, "A Poetry of Experience," *University of Kansas City Review* 25 (Autumn 1958): 67.

"Ol' Bunk's Band"

Nathaniel Mackey, "Sound and Sentiment, Sound and Symbol," *Callaloo* 10 (Winter 1987): 29-54.

"The Orchestra"

Gray, *American Poetry*, 190-91.

Linda Welshimer Wagner, "The Last Poems of William Carlos Williams," *Criticism* 6 (Fall 1964): 365-67.

Paterson

J. Burbick, "Grimaces of a New Age: The Postwar Poetry and Painting of William Carlos Williams and Jackson Pollock," *Boundary* 10 (Spring 1982): 109-23.

Dickie, *On the Modernist Long Poem*, 77-105.

Duffey, *A Poetry of Presence*, 69-98, 215-23.

Chris Hall, "Two Poems of Place: Williams' *Paterson* and Marlatt's *Steveston*," *CRevAS* 15 (Summer 1984): 141-57.

J. Hans, "Presence and Absence in Modern Poetry," *Criticism* 22 (Fall 1981): 320-40.

David Hurry, "Shakespeare, Heroes and Fools in William Carlos Williams' *Paterson*," *Literary Review* 25 (Spring 1982): 317-30.

David Hurry, "The Use of Freudian Dream Symbolism in William Carlos Williams' *Paterson*," *L&P* 31 (1981): 16-20.

David Hurry, "William Carlos Williams' *Paterson* and Freud's *Interpretation of Dreams*," *L&P* 28 (1978): 170-77.

Kenner, *The Pound Era*, 509-16.

Robert Kusch, "'You're My Toughest Mentor': William Carlos Williams and Theodore Roethke (1940-42)," *JML* 12 (July 1985): 332-44.

James Laughlin, "William Carlos Williams and the Making of *Paterson*: A Memoir," *YR* 71 (Jan. 1982): 185-98.

Victor P. H. Li, "The Vanity of Length: The Long Poem as Problem in Pound's Cantos and Williams' *Paterson*," *Genre* 19 (Spring 1986): 3-20.

Mariani, *A Usable Past*, 17-106.

Paul Mariani, "The Whore/Virgin and the Wounded One-Horned Beast," *University of Denver Quarterly* 13 (Summer 1978): 102-30.

Mariani, *William Carlos Williams: A New World Naked*, passim.

K. D. Matthews, "Competitive Giants: Satiric Bedrock in Book One of William Carlos Williams' *Paterson*," *JML* 12 (July 1985): 237-60.

Joseph N. Riddel, "'Keep Your Pecker Up'--*Paterson* Five and the Question of Metapoetry," *Glyph* 8 (Fall 1980): 203-31.

M. L. Rosenthal and Sally M. Gall, "William Carlos Williams's *Paterson*," *Sagetrieb* 1 (Spring 1982): 13-47.

Stephen J. Tapscott, "Williams's *Paterson*: Doctor and Democrat," *YES* 8 (1978): 77-94.

Woodward, *At Last, the Real Distinguished Thing*, passim.

"Peasant Wedding"

Christopher S. Braider, "The Art of the Ambidextrous: The Fall of Icarus, the Death of Allegory, and the Meaning of Spatial Realism in the Light of William Carlos Williams's *Pictures from Bruegel*," *SLRev* 4 (Fall 1987): 143-74.

"Perpetuum Mobile"

David A. Fedo, "The Meaning of Love in William Carlos Williams's 'A Dream of Love,'" *ConL* 23 (1982): 169-90.

Kurt Heinzelman, "Staging the Poem: William Carlos Williams' 'A Dream of Love,'" *ConL* 18 (Autumn 1977): 491-508.

"Philomena Andronico"

Karl Schapiro, "The Meaning of the Discarded Poem," in Abbott, *Poets at Work*, 105-11.

Pictures from Bruegel

Christopher S. Braider, "The Art of the Ambidextrous: The Fall of Icarus, the Death of Allegory, and the Meaning of Spatial Realism in the Light of William Carlos Williams's *Pictures from Bruegel*," *SLRev* 4 (Fall 1987): 143-74.

Duffey, *A Poetry of Presence*, 98-114, 215-23.

Donald W. Markos, "Memory as a New 'Present' in Williams's Later Poems," *SoR* 24 (Spring 1988): 303-13.

"The Pink Church"

Duffey, *A Poetry of Presence*, 170-81.

Sutton, *American Free Verse*, 147-49.

"Poem"

Kenner, *A Homemade World*, 85-86.

Kenner, *The Pound Era*, 397-99.

"Portrait of a Lady"

Mordecai Marcus, "Dialogue and Allusion in William Carlos Williams' 'Portrait of a Lady,'" *CP* 10 (Fall 1977): 71-72.

Peter Quartermain, "'Actual Word Stuff, not Thoughts for Thoughts,'" *Credences*, n.s. 2 (Summer 1982): 104-22.

"Portrait of a Woman at Her Bath"

Wagner, "The Last Poems of William Carlos Williams," 372-73.

"The Pot of Flowers"

James E. Breslin, "William Carlos Williams and Charles Demuth: Cross-Fertilization in the Arts," *JML* 6 (Apr. 1977): 250-58.

"Queen-Ann's Lace"

Arthur W. Glowka, *Expl* 39 (Summer 1981): 25-26.

O'Connor, *Sense and Sensibility in Modern Poetry*, 119-20.

William Van O'Connor, "Symbolism and the Study of Poetry," *CE* 6 (Apr. 1946): 378-79.

Sayre, *The Visual Text of William Carlos Williams*, 21-25.

Douglas L. Verdier, *Expl* 40 (Fall 1981): 46-47.

"The Red Wheelbarrow"

Charles Altieri, "Objective Image and Act of Mind in Modern Poetry," *PMLA* 91 (Jan. 1976): 111-12.

Stanley Archer, "*Glazed* in Williams's 'The Red Wheelbarrow,'" *CP* 9 (Fall 1976): 27.

Beaty and Matchett, *Poetry: From Statement to Meaning*, 181-82.

Thomas Dilworth, *Expl* 40 (Summer 1982): 40-41.

J. P. Gee, "The Structure of Perception in the Poetry of William Carlos Williams," *PoT* 6 (1985): 375-97.

Hall, *The Pleasures of Poetry*, 41-44.

Homer Hogan, *Poetry of Relevance 2* (Toronto: Methuen, 1970), 7-10.

John Hollander, "The Poem in the Eye," *Shenandoah* 23 (Spring 1972): 25.

John Hollander, "'Sense Variously Drawn Out': Some Observations on English Enjambment," in *Literary Theory and Structure: Essays in Honor of William K. Wimsatt* (New Haven: Yale University Press, 1973), 217-18.

Kenner, *A Homemade World*, 57-61.

Peter Quartermain, "'Actual Word Stuff, not Thoughts for Thoughts,'" *Credences*, n.s. 2 (Summer 1982): 104-22.

Rosenthal, *The Modern Poets*, 113-14.

Sutton, *American Free Verse*, 120-21.

"The Revelation"

Gray, *American Poetry*, 181-82.

"The Right of Way"

Neil Myers, "William Carlos Williams' *Spring and All*," *MLQ* 26 (June 1965): 293-94.

"The Rose"

Duffey, *A Poetry of Presence*, 137-38.

Neil Myers, "William Carlos Williams' *Spring and All*," *MLQ* 26 (June 1965): 297-99.

"Russia"

Duffey, *A Poetry of Presence*, 170-81.

"St. Francis Einstein of the Daffodils"

William Carlos Williams, in Friar and Brinnin, *Modern Poetry*, 546.

"Saxifrage Is My Flower"

Kenner, *A Homemade World*, 87-88.

"Sea-Trout and Butterfish"

Gray, *American Poetry*, 182-83.

Selected Poems

Duffey, *A Poetry of Presence*, 151-67.

Patrick Moore, "Cubist Prosody: William Carlos Williams and the Conventions of Verse Lineation," *PQ* 65 (1986): 513-36.

"The Semblables"

Duffey, *A Poetry of Presence*, 155-57.

"Shadows"

Donald W. Markos, "Memory as a New 'Present' in Williams's Later Poems," *SoR* 24 (Spring 1988): 303-13.

"Song"

Brooks, Lewis, and Warren, *American Literature*, 2146.

Juhasz, *Metaphor and the Poetry of Williams, Pound, and Stevens*, 46.

"A Sort of Song"

Brooks, Lewis, and Warren, *American Literature*, 2145-46.

Cook, *Figural Choice in Poetry and Art*, passim.

"Spring and All"

J. P. Gee, "The Structure of Perception in the Poetry of William Carlos Williams: A Stylistic Analysis," *PoT* 6 (1985): 375-97.

Kenner, *A Homemade World*, 60-62.

Miller, *The Linguistic Moment: From Wordsworth to Stevens*, passim.

"Spring Strains"

Duffey, *A Poetry of Presence*, 129-30.

"Struggle of Wings"

Riding and Graves, *A Survey of Modernist Poetry*, 201-4.

"The Term"

Willis D. Jacobs, *Expl* 25 (May 1967): 73.

Pinsky, *The Situation of Poetry: Contemporary Poetry and Its Traditions*, 62-65.

"This Is Just to Say"

Wheeler, *The Design of Poetry*, 63-68, 70-72, 79-80, 82-87, 282-83.

"The Three Graces"

Frank Jones, *Poetry: A Critical Supplement*, Nov. 1949, 16-17.

"To a Dog Injured in the Street"

Abbe, *You and Contemporary Poetry*, 35-38.

"To a Poor Old Woman"

Willis D. Jacobs, "Williams' 'To a Poor Old Woman,'" *CP* 1 (Fall 1968): 16.

Juhasz, *Metaphor and the Poetry of Williams, Pound, and Stevens*, 42-43.

"To a Solitary Disciple"

Richard J. Calhoun, "'No Ideas but in Things': William Carlos Williams in the Twenties," in Langford and Taylor, *The Twenties*, 31-32.

Miller, *Poets of Reality*, 320-21.

"To Be Recited to Flossie on Her Birthday"

Seamus Cooney, *Expl* 32 (Nov. 1973): 24.

"To Daphne and Virginia"

Rapp, *William Carlos Williams and Romantic Idealism*, 132-36.

"To Mark Anthony in Heaven"

John G. Hammond, *Expl* 36 (Summer 1978): 26-29.

"To Waken an Old Lady"

Deutsch, *Poetry in Our Time*, 101.

Nat Henry, *Expl* 30 (May 1972): 80.

Willis D. Jacobs, *Expl* 29 (Sept. 1970): 6.

Neil Myers, "Sentimentalism in the Early Poetry of William Carlos Williams," *AL* 37 (Jan. 1966): 462-63.

"Tract"

Walter Gierasch, *Expl* 3 (Mar. 1945): 35. Reprinted in *The Explicator Cyclopedia* 1:340-41.

"The Trees"

Bernard Duffey, *A Poetry of Presence*, 165-66.

"A Unison"

Duffey, *A Poetry of Presence*, 166-67.

Kenner, *The Pound Era*, 510-12.

"The Wanderer"

Duffey, *A Poetry of Presence*, 13-16 and passim.

Rapp, *William Carlos Williams and Romantic Idealism*, 3-29.

"The Well-Disciplined Bargeman"

Jack Hardie, *Expl* 33 (Nov. 1974): 20.

"When chivalry like summer's crimson fruit"

Ann W. Fisher, "William Carlos Williams' *Endymion* Poem: 'Philip and Oradie,'" *IowaR* 11 (Spring/Summer 1980): 48-67.

Sutton, *American Free Verse*, 122-23.

"The Widow's Lament in Springtime"

Gray, *American Poetry*, 184.

Steve Harvey, *Expl* 45 (Winter 1987): 49-50.

"Without Invention Nothing Is Well Spaced"

Joel A. Conarroe, *Expl* 27 (Dec. 1968): 26.

"The World Contracted to a Recognizable Image"

William V. Davis, *Expl* 32 (Oct. 1973): 13.

Myrtle P. Pope, *Expl* 33 (Feb. 1975): 50.

Edmond Schraepen, *Expl* 35 (Fall 1976): 6-7.

"The Yachts"

Emily K. Dalgarno, "De Quincey and Williams' 'The Yachts,'" *AN&Q* 14 (Apr. 1976): 119-21.

Deutsch, *Poetry in Our Time*, 102-4.

Richard S. Donnell, *Expl* 17 (May 1959): 52. Reprinted in *The Explicator Cyclopedia* 1:341-42.

Perrine and Reid, *100 American Poems*, 74-76.

Elisabeth Schneider, *Expl* 25 (Jan. 1967): 40.

Sutton, *American Free Verse*, 123-24.

Unger and O'Connor, *Poems for Study*, 9-10.

"The Yellow Chimney"

Miller, *Poets of Reality*, 300-301.

Marshall W. Stearns, "Syntax, Sense, Sound, and Dr. Williams," *Poetry* 66 (Apr. 1945): 38-39.

"The Young Housewife"

Willis D. Jacobs," *Expl* 28 (May 1970): 81.

"Young Sycamore"

Kenner, *The Pound Era*, 402-3.

Robert G. Lint, "The Structural Image in Williams' 'Young Sycamore,'" *Lang&S* 7 (Summer 1974): 205-8.

Miller, *The Linguistic Moment: From Wordsworth to Stevens*, 349-89.

WINTERS, YVOR

"Before Disaster"

Ciardi, *How Does a Poem Mean?* 1005-7.

"The Brink"

Terry Comito, "Winters' 'Brink,'" *SoR* 17 (Oct. 1981): 851-872.

"By the Road to the Air-Base"

Douglas L. Peterson, "Yvor Winters' 'By the Road to the Air-Base,'" *SoR* 15 (July 1979): 567-74.

"The Invaders"

Donald F. Drummond, "Yvor Winters: Reason and Moral Judgment," *ArQ* 5 (Spring 1949): 15-16.

"Midas"

Howard Kaye, "The Post-Symbolist Poetry of Yvor Winters," *SoR* 7 (Jan. 1971): 191-93.

"The Old Age of Theseus"

Donald F. Drummond, "Yvor Winters: Reason and Moral Judgment," *ArQ* 5 (Spring 1949): 11-14.

"Orpheus"

Howard Kaye, "The Post-Symbolist Poetry of Yvor Winters," *SoR* 7 (Jan. 1971): 188-89.

"The Slow Pacific Swell"

Howard Kaye, "The Post-Symbolist Poetry of Yvor Winters," *SoR* 7 (Jan. 1971): 185-87.

"A Spring Serpent"

Howard Kaye, "The Post-Symbolist Poetry of Yvor Winters," *SoR* 7 (Jan. 1971): 183-85.

"A Summer Commentary"

Allan Swallow, *Expl* 9 (Mar. 1951): 35. Reprinted in *The Explicator Cyclopedia* 1:342-43; in Swallow, *An Editor's Essays of Two Decades*, 215-19.

"To the Holy Spirit"

John Finlay, "The Unfleshed Eye: A Reading of Yvor Winter's 'To the Holy Spirit,'" *SoR* 17 (Oct. 1977): 873-86.

WOODS, JOHN

"Best in the Orchard"

Dave Smith, "Fifty Years, Mrs. Carter: The Poetry of John Woods," *MQ* 17 (Summer 1976): 413-17.

WRIGHT, CHARLES

"Bar Giamaica, 1959-60"

Calvin Bedient, "Tracing Charles Wright," *Parnassus* 10 (Spring/Summer 1982): 55-74.

"Death"

Calvin Bedient, "Tracing Charles Wright," *Parnassus* 10 (Spring/Summer 1982): 55-74.

The Southern Cross

Calvin Bedient, "Tracing Charles Wright," *Parnassus* 10 (Spring/Summer 1982): 55-74.

WRIGHT, JAMES

"At Peace with the Ocean off Misquamicut"

Kathy Callaway, "The Very Rich Hours of the Duke of Fano," *Parnassus* 10 (Spring/Summer 1982): 58-72.

"Blue Teal Mother"

Victoria Frenkel Harris, "Relationship and Change: Text and Content of James Wright's 'Blue Mother' and Robert Bly's 'With Pale Women in Maryland,'" *AmerP* 3 (Fall 1985): 43-55.

"A Fit against the Country"

Kevin Stein, "The Rhetoric of Containment, Vulnerability, and Integration in the Work of James Wright," *CP* 20 (1987): 117-27.

"In Fear of Harvests"

Kevin Stein, "The Rhetoric of Containment, Vulnerability, and Integration in the Work of James Wright," *CP* 20 (1987): 117-27.

"The Journey"

Kathy Callaway, "The Very Rich Hours of the Duke of Fano," *Parnassus* 10 (Spring/Summer 1982): 58-72.

"Redwings"

Kevin Stein, "The Rhetoric of Containment, Vulnerability, and Integration in the work of James Wright," *CP* 20 (1987): 117-27.

"Wherever Home Is"

Stitt, *The World's Hieroglyphic Beauty: Five American Poets*, 161-93.

WRIGHT, RICHARD

"Between the World and Me"

Kenneth Kinnamon, "Richard Wright: Proletarian Poet," *CP* 2 (Spring 1969): 44-45.

"Fb-Eye Blues"

John McCluskey, Jr., "'Two-Stepping': Richard Wright's Encounter with Blue-Jazz," *AL* 55 (Oct. 1983): 340-41.

"Lying in a Hammock at William Duffy's Farm in Pine Island, Minnesota"

David James, *Expl* 44 (Fall 1982): 54-55.

Laurence Perrine, "Comment on 'Babble and Doodle,'" *CE* 44 (Apr. 1982): 431-33.

WYLIE, ELINOR

"Castilian"

Richard E. Amacher, *Expl* 7 (Nov. 1948): 16. Reprinted in *The Explicator Cyclopedia* 1:344.

"Cold-Blooded Creatures"

C. C. Walcutt, "Critic's Taste or Artist's Intention," *University of Kansas City Review* 12 (Summer 1946): 279-82.

"Hymn to Earth"

W. Nelson Francis, *Expl* 17 (Mar. 1959): 40. Reprinted in *The Explicator Cyclopedia* 1:344-45.

"Puritan Sonnet"

Perrine and Reid, *100 American Poems*, 86-87.

"Sanctuary"

Kreuzer, *Elements of Poetry*, 165-66.

"This Corruptible"

Deutsch, *Poetry in Our Time*, 231.

"The Tortoise in Eternity"

Richard E. Amacher, *Expl* 6 (Mar. 1948): 33. Reprinted in *The Explicator Cyclopedia* 1:345.

"Velvet Shoes"

Laurence Perrine, *Expl* 13 (Dec. 1954): 17. Reprinted in *The Explicator Cyclopedia* 1:345-46.

Macklin Thomas, "Analysis of the Experience in Lyric Poetry," *CE* 9 (Mar. 1948): 318-19.

Thomas J. Wertenbaker, "Into the Poet's Shoes," *EJ* 53 (May 1964): 370-72.

YERBY, FRANK

"Wisdom"

Alan C. Lupack, "Frank Yerby's 'Wisdom,'" *NConL* 7 (Sept. 1977): 8.

ZAMORA, BERNICE

"Andando"

Sánchez, *Contemporary Chicano Poetry: A Critical Approach to an Emerging Literature*, 245, 250-52.

"Bearded Lady"

Sánchez, *Contemporary Chicano Poetry: A Critical Approach to an Emerging Literature*, 245-46, 258-60.

"Gata Poem"

Sánchez, *Contemporary Chicano Poetry: A Critical Approach to an Emerging Literature*, 218-30.

"Restless Serpents"

José David Saldívar, "Towards a Chicano Poetics: The Making of the Chicano Subject, 1969-1982," *Confluencia* 1 (1986): 10-17.

ZUKOFSKY, LOUIS

"A"

B. Ahearn, "Origins of '*A*': Zukofsky's Materials for Collage," *ELH* 45 (Spring 1978): 152-76.

Burton Hatlen, "Art and/as Labor: Some Dialectical Patterns in '*A*'-1 through '*A*'-10," *ConL* 25 (Summer 1984): 205-34.

Kenner, *A Homemade World*, 171-73, 189-93.

Reno Odlin, "Brief Notes on '*A*,'" *Sagetrieb* 1 (Spring 1982): 100-102.

Peter Quartermain, "'Actual Word Stuff, not Thoughts for Thoughts," *Credences*, n.s. 2 (Summer 1982): 104-22.

William Sylvester, "Creeley, Duncan, Zukofsky 1968: Melody Moves the Light," *Sagetrieb* 2 (Spring 1983): 97-104.

"*A*'-12"

John Taggart, "Louis Zukofsky: Songs of Degrees," *Credences*, n.s. 1 (Fall/Winter 1981/1982): 122-49.

"*A*'-13"

Peter Quartermain, "Actual Word Stuff, not Thoughts for Thoughts," *Credences*, n.s. 2 (Summer 1982): 104-22.

"*A*'-22"

D. Byrd, "Getting Ready to Read '*A*,'" *Boundary* 10 (Winter 1982): 291-308.

"*A*'-23"

D. Byrd, "Getting Ready to Read '*A*,'" *Boundary* 10 (Winter 1982): 291-308.

John Taggart, "Louis Zukofsky: Songs of Degrees," *Credences*, n.s. 1 (Fall/Winter 1981/1982): 122-49.

"*A*'-24"

John Taggart, "Louis Zukofsky: Songs of Degrees," *Credences*, n.s. 1 (Fall/Winter 1981/1982): 122-49.

"*All*"

Burton Hatlen, "Zukofsky, Wittgenstein, and the Poetics of Absence," *Sagetrieb* 1 (Spring 1982): 63-93.

"All" (MS. 138 at University of Texas)

Peter Quartermain, "Actual Word Stuff, not Thoughts for Thoughts," *Credences*, n.s. 2 (Summer 1982): 104-22.

"Anew"

L. S. Dembo, "Louis Zukofsky: Objectivist Poetics and the Quest for Form," *AL* 44 (Mar. 1972): 85-86.

"'An' Song" (beginning "*A*'-22")

Bruce Comens, "Soundings: The 'An' Song Beginning '*A*'-22," *Sagetrieb* 5 (Spring 1986): 95-106.

"For You I Have Emptied the Meaning"

L. S. Dembo, "Louis Zukofsky: Objectivist Poetics and the Quest for Form," *AL* 44 (Mar. 1972): 86-87.

"Glad They Were There"

L. S. Dembo, "Louis Zukofsky: Objectivist Poetics and the Quest for Form," *AL* 44 (Mar. 1972): 84-85.

"Has the Sum"

L. S. Dembo, "Louis Zukofsky: Objectivist Poetics and the Quest for Form," *AL* 44 (Mar. 1972): 86.

"It's a Gay Li - ife"

Bernstein, *Content's Dream: Essays 1975-1984*, 70-71.

"A Last Cigarette"

L. S. Dembo, "Louis Zukofsky: Objectivist Poetics and the Quest for Form," *AL* 44 (Mar. 1972): 82-83.

"Mantis" and "'Mantis': an Interpretation"

L. S. Dembo, "Louis Zukofsky: Objectivist Poetics and the Quest for Form," *AL* 44 (Mar. 1972): 87-91.

Heller, *Conviction's Net of Branches: Essays on the Objectivist Poets and Poetry*, passim.

"Poem Beginning 'The'"

L. S. Dembo, "Louis Zukofsky: Objectivist Poetics and the Quest for Form," *AL* 44 (Mar. 1972): 91-94.

Linda Simon, "A Preface to Zukofsky," *Sagetrieb* 2 (Spring 1983): 89-96.

"Preface - 1927"

Linda Simon, "A Preface to Zukofsky," *Sagetrieb* 2 (Spring 1983): 89-96.

"Songs of Degrees"

John Taggart, "Louis Zukofsky: Songs of Degrees," *Credences*, n.s. 1 (Fall/Winter 1981/1982): 122-49.

"10/22"

Burton Hatlen, "Zukofsky, Wittgenstein, and the Poetics of Absence," *Sagetrieb* 1 (Spring 1982): 63-93.

"To My Wash-Stand"

Burton Hatlen, "Zukofsky, Wittgenstein, and the Poetics of Absence," *Sagetrieb* 1 (Spring 1982): 63-93.

"A Wish"

John Taggart, "Louis Zukofsky: Songs of Degrees," *Credences*, n.s. 1 (Fall/Winter 1981/1982): 122-49.

Main Sources Consulted

All shortened titles for explications found under individual poets in this volume of *Guide to American Poetry Explication* are given full citations here, as is the range of volumes and issues for most journals and periodicals examined. Included as well are the full titles of all journals and periodicals consulted. Like earlier editions of the checklist, not all entries below offer explications, but we have included them because they otherwise have direct bearing on poetics, on the critical principles guiding much explication, or on the sociocultural background and conditions of poetic production. Some have piecemeal explications on a poem or poems that, when read as an ensemble, constitute a noteworthy commentary. Titles added to the Main Sources since the third (1980) edition of the *Checklist* are not identified with the comment "no explication," although this descriptor is kept where it appeared previously.

Also new to the *Guide* are specific bio-bibliographic materials on both individual poets and ethnic, regional, or aesthetic groups, especially annotated ones, with the anticipation that they may lead users of this volume to other explications or related materials.

Finally, all journals and periodicals cited in the *Checklist* are entered here, although for a number of these we have not been able to survey every volume and issue since approximately 1977. For example, some journals suspended publication or published irregularly; volumes were occasionally incomplete; or only a few issues could be located. On occasion computer searches yielded stray articles with pertinent explications in journals not particularly specialized in either literary criticism (*Journal of Aesthetics and*

497

Art Criticism) or modern poetry (*Early American Literature, Studies in Romanticism*); further searches in these journals were not warranted. In incorporating all modern American citations from the earlier editions of *Poetry Explication*, we were of course bound to come across some references to periodicals we simply could not track down, even with the resources of the University of Rhode Island and Brown University libraries. Accordingly, some of the following periodicals appear by title only, with no reference to the range of issues checked for explications.

ABAD, GEMINO H. *A Formal Approach to Lyric Poetry*. Quezon City, Philippines: University of the Philippines Press, 1978.

ABBE, GEORGE. *You and Contemporary Poetry*. North Guilford, Conn.: Author-Audience Publication, 1957.

ABBOTT, CHARLES D., ed. *Poets at Work*. New York: Harcourt, Brace & Co., 1948.

Accent: A Quarterly of New Literature, 1 (Autumn 1940)-20, no. 4 (Autumn 1960).

ACKROYD, PETER. *T. S. Eliot: A Life*. New York: Simon & Schuster, 1984.

ACOSTA-BELEN, EDNA, ed. *The Puerto Rican Woman*. New York: Praeger, 1978.

Acts, no. 1 (1982)-no. 7 (1987).

ADAMS, HAZARD. *The Contexts of Poetry*. Boston: Little, Brown & Co., 1963.

ADAMS, ROBERT M. *Strains of Discord: Studies in Literary Openness*. Ithaca, N.Y.: Cornell University Press, 1958.

Adelphi

Agenda 1 (1959)-10 (1972).

ALEXANDER, MICHAEL. *The Poetic Achievement of Ezra Pound*. Berkeley and Los Angeles: University of California Press, 1979.

ALLEN, DONALD, and WARREN TALLMAN, eds. *The Poetics of the New American Poetry*. New York: Grove Press, 1973.

ALLEN, DON CAMERON, ed. *Contexts of Poetry: Interviews, 1961-1971*. Bolinas, Calif.: Four Seasons, 1973.

_____, ed. *Four Poets on Poetry*. Baltimore: Johns Hopkins Press, 1959.

_____, ed. *The Moment of Poetry*. Baltimore: Johns Hopkins Press, 1962.

ALLEN, HAROLD B., ed. *Readings in Applied English Linguistics*. New York: Appleton-Century-Crofts, 1958.

ALLEN, PAULA GUNN, ed. *Studies in American Indian Literature: Critical Essays and Course Designs*. New York: Modern Language Association of America, 1983.

ALTIERI, CHARLES. "From Experience to Discourse: American Poetry and Poetics in the Seventies." *Contemporary Literature* 21, no. 2 (1980): 191-224.

_____. *Self and Sensibility in Modern Poetry*. Cambridge: Cambridge University Press, 1984.

_____. "Sensibility, Rhetoric, and Will: Some Tensions in Contemporary Poetry." *Contemporary Literature* 23, no. 4 (1982): 451-479.

_____, ed. *Modern Poetry*. Arlington Heights, Ill.: AHM Publishing Corp., 1979.

American Imago: A Psychoanalytic Journal for Culture, Science, and the Arts 25 (1968)-44, no. 4 (1987).

American Indian Culture and Research Journal

American Indian Quarterly: A Journal of Anthropology, History, and Literature 1 (1974)-11 (Fall 1987).

American Indian Quarterly 9 (Winter 1985). Special issue on Gerald Vizenor.

American Literary Realism, 1870-1910 18, no. 1 (1985)-20, no. 2 (1988).

American Literature: A Journal of Literary History, Criticism, and Bibliography 1 (1929)-60, no. 3 (1988).

American Notes and Queries 1 (1962)-24 (1986).

American Poetry

The American Poetry Review 1 (Apr./Oct. 1933)-16 (Apr. 1987).

American Quarterly 1 (1949)-40, no. 2 (June 1988).

The American Review 1 (Apr./Oct. 1933)-9 (Oct. 1937).

The American Scholar 52, no. 1 (Winter 1982/1983)-57, no. 3 (Summer 1988).

American Studies 12 (1971)-28, no. 2 (Fall 1987).

The Americas Review: A Review of Hispanic Literature and Art of the USA

Another Chicago Mag 1 (1977)-15 (1986).

The Antioch Review

Ariel: A Review of International English Literature 1, no. 1 (Jan. 1970)-19, no. 1 (1988).

Arizona Quarterly 1 (1945)-44, no. 2 (1988).

ARNOLD, IVOR A. "Diachronie des styles de la poésie québécoise, 1960-1980." *Studies in Canadian Literature* 12 (1987): 3-14.

ARNSTEIN, FLORA S. *Adventure into Poetry*. Stanford: Stanford University Press, 1951. (No explication)

Atlantic Monthly 251, no. 1 (Jan. 1983)-262, no. 2 (Aug. 1988).

BAKER, HOUSTON A., Jr. *Blues, Ideology, and Afro-American Literature: A Vernacular Theory*. Chicago: University of Chicago Press, 1984.

_____. *Modernism and the Harlem Renaissance*. Chicago: University of Chicago Press, 1987.

_____, ed. *Three American Literatures: Essays in Chicano, Native American, and Asian-American Literature for Teachers of American Literature*. New York: Modern Language Association of America, 1982.

BAKER, WILLIAM E. *Syntax in English Poetry, 1970-1930*. Berkeley and Los Angeles: University of California Press, 1967.

Ball State University Forum

Banc

BARNARD, C. K. *Sylvia Plath*. Boston: Twayne, 1978.

BARTHES, ROLAND. *Image/Music/Text*. Translated by Stephen Heath. New York: Hill & Wang, 1974.

_____. *The Pleasure of the Text*. Translated by Richard Miller. New York: Hill & Wang, 1975.

BARTLETT, LEE. "What is 'Language Poetry'?" *Critical Inquiry* 12 (Summer 1986): 741-52.

_____, ed. *The Beats: Essays in Criticism*. Jefferson, N. C. and London: McFarland & Co., 1981.

_____, ed. *The Emergence of William Everson*. Metuchen and London: Scarecrow Press, 1979.

_____, ed. *Selected Essays and Interviews of William Everson*. Berkeley: Oyez, 1980.

BARTLETT, PHYLLIS. *Poems in Process*. New York: Oxford University Press, 1951.

BASLER, ROY P. *Sex, Symbolism, and Psychology in Literature*. New Brunswick, N.J.: Rutgers University Press, 1948.

BEACH, JOSEPH WARREN. *Obsessive Images: Symbolism in Poetry of the 1930's and 1940's*. Edited by William Van O'Connor. Minneapolis: University of Minnesota Press, 1960.

_____. *A Romantic View of Poetry*. Minneapolis: University of Minnesota Press, 1944.

BEATTIE, ALEXANDER MUNRO. *The Advent of Modernism in Canadian Poetry in English, 1912-1940.* Ann Arbor: University Microfilms, 1957.

BEATY, JEROME, and WILLIAM H. MATCHETT. *Poetry: From Statement to Meaning.* New York: Oxford University Press, 1965.

BEDIENT, CALVIN. *In the Heart's Last Kingdom: Robert Penn Warren's Major Poetry.* Cambridge: Harvard University Press, 1984.

BEEHLER, MICHAEL. *T. S. Eliot, Wallace Stevens, and the Discourses of Difference.* Baton Rouge and London: Louisiana State University Press, 1987.

BELGION, MONTGOMERY. *Reading for Profit.* Chicago: Henry Regnery Co., 1950.

BELL, IAN F. A. *Critic as Scientist: The Modern Poetics of Ezra Pound.* London: Methuen, 1981.

BELLAMY, JOE DAVID, ed. *American Poetry Observed: Poets on Their Own Work.* Champaign: University of Illinois Press, 1988.

Bennington Review

BERNSTEIN, CHARLES. *Content's Dream: Essays 1975-1984.* Los Angeles: Sun & Moon Press, 1986.

BIGSBY, C. W. E., ed. *The Black American Writer.* 2 vols. Deland, Fla.: Everett/Edwards, 1969.

Black American Literature Forum 10 (1976)-22, no. 1 (1988).

BLACKMUR, R. P. *The Double Agent: Essays in Craft and Elucidation.* New York: Arrow Editions, 1935.

_____. *The Expense of Greatness.* New York: Arrow Editions, 1940.

_____. *Language as Gesture: Essays in Poetry.* New York: Harcourt, Brace & Co., 1952.

Black Studies

Black World

BLAIR, WALTER, and W. K. CHANDLER. *Approaches to Poetry*. New York: D. Appleton-Century Co., 1935.

BLAIR, WALTER, and JOHN C. GERBER. *Better Reading 2: Literature*. Chicago: Scott, Foresman & Co., 1948.

BLAIR, WALTER, THEODORE HORNBERGER, and RANDALL STEWART, eds. *Literature of the United States*. Chicago: Scott, Foresman & Co., 1947. Reprint. 2 vols., 1953. Rev. ed., 1 vol., 1957.

BLASING, MUTLU KONUK. *American Poetry: The Rhetoric of Its Forms*. New Haven: Yale University Press, 1987.

BLICKSBERG, CHARLES I., ed. *American Literary Criticism, 1900-1950*. New York: Hendricks House, 1951.

BLOOM, EDWARD A., CHARLES H. PHILBRICK, and ELMER M. BLISTEIN. *The Order of Poetry: An Introduction*. New York: Odyssey Press, 1961.

BLOOM, HAROLD. *Figures of Capable Imagination*. New York: Seabury Press, 1976.

_____. *A Map of Misreading*. New York: Oxford University Press, 1975.

_____. *Poetry and Repression: Revisionism from Blake to Stevens*. New Haven and London: Yale University Press, 1976.

_____. *The Ringers in the Tower: Studies in Romantic Tradition*. Chicago: University of Chicago Press, 1971.

_____. *Wallace Stevens: The Poems of Our Climate*. Ithaca, N.Y.: Cornell University Press, 1977.

_____, ed. *James Merrill*. New York: Chelsea, 1985.

BLOOM, JAMES D. *The Stock of Available Reality: R. P. Blackmur and John Berryman*. Lewisburg, Pa.: Bucknell University Press, 1984.

BONTEMPS, ARNA, ed. *The Harlem Rensaissance Remembered*. New York: Dodd, 1972.

Book Forum

BORNSTEIN, GEORGE. *Transformations of Romanticism in Yeats, Eliot, and Stevens.* Chicago and London: University of Chicago Press, 1976.

BORROFF, MARIE. *Language and the Poet: Verbal Artistry in Frost, Stevens, and Moore.* Chicago and London: University of Chicago Press, 1979.

Boston University Studies in English 1 (1955)-5 (1961).

BOULTON, MARJORIE. *The Anatomy of Poetry.* London: Routledge & Kegan Paul, 1953.

Boundary 2: A Journal of Postmodern Literature and Culture 1 (Fall 1972)-14, no. 3 (1986).

Boundary 2 12 (Winter 1984). Special issue: "On Feminine Writing."

Boundary 2 14, nos. 1-2 (Fall 1985/Winter 1986). Supplement: "The L=A=N=G=U=A=G=E Poets," edited by Charles Bernstein.

BOWERS, FREDSON, ed. *English Studies in Honor of James Southall Wilson.* University of Virginia Studies, vol. 4. Charlottesville: University of Virginia Press, 1951.

BOWRA, C. M. *The Creative Experiment.* London: Macmillan & Co., 1949.

_____. *The Heritage of Symbolism.* London: Macmillan & Co., 1947.

BRADY, FRANK, JOHN PALMER, and MARTIN PRICE, eds. *Literary Theory and Structure: Essays in Honor of William K. Wimsatt.* New Haven: Yale University Press, 1973.

Breadloaf Quarterly. [See *New England Quarterly.*]

BROE, MARY L. *Protean Poetic: The Poetry of Sylvia Plath.* Columbia: University of Missouri Press, 1980.

BROOKE-ROSE, CHRISTINE. *A ZBC of Ezra Pound.* Berkeley and Los Angeles: University of California Press, 1971.

BROOKS, CLEANTH, Jr. *Modern Poetry and the Tradition*. Chapel Hill: University of North Carolina Press, 1939.

_____. *A Shaping Joy: Studies in the Writer's Craft*. London: Methuen & Co., 1971.

_____. *The Well Wrought Urn*. New York: Reynal and Hitchcock, 1947.

BROOKS, CLEANTH, Jr., R. W. B. LEWIS, and ROBERT PENN WARREN. *American Literature: The Makers and the Making*. New York: St. Martin's Press, 1973.

BROOKS, CLEANTH, Jr., JOHN THIBAUT PURSER, and ROBERT PENN WARREN. *An Approach to Literature*. Rev. ed. New York: F. S. Crofts & Co., 1942. 3d ed., 1952. 4th ed., 1964.

BROOKS, CLEANTH, Jr., and ROBERT PENN WARREN, eds. *Understanding Poetry: An Anthology for College Students*. New York: Henry Holt & Co., 1938. Rev. ed., 1950. 4th ed., 1964.

BROWER, REUBEN ARTHUR. *The Fields of Light: An Experiement in Critical Reading*. New York: Oxford University Press, 1951.

_____. *Forms of Lyric: Selected Papers from the English Institute*. New York: Columbia University Press, 1970.

BROWN, C. L., and K. OLSON, eds. *Feminist Criticism: Essays on Theory, Poetry, and Prose*. Metuchen, N.J.: Scarecrow Press, 1978.

BROWN, HARRY, and JOHN MILSTEAD. *Patterns in Poetry: An Introductory Anthology*. Glenview, Ill.: Scott, Foresman & Co., 1968.

BROWN, L. *Amiri Baraka*. Boston: Twayne, 1980.

BROWN, WENTWORK K., and STERLING P. OLMSTEAD. *Language and Literature*. New York: Harcourt, Brace & World, 1962.

BRUCE-NOVOA. *Chicano Poetry: A Response to Chaos*. Austin: University of Texas Press, 1982.

BRUCHAC, JOSEPH III, ed. *Songs from This Earth from Turtle's Back: Contemporary American Indian Poetry*. Greenfield Center, N.Y.: Greenfield Review Press, 1983.

505

_____, ed. *Survival This Way: Interviews with American Indian Poets*. Tucson: University of Arizona Press, 1987.

BRUNNER, EDWARD. *Splendid Failure: Hart Crane and the Making of The Bridge*. Urbana: University of Illinois Press, 1985.

Bucknell Review: A Scholarly Journal of Letters, Arts, and Sciences 1 (1941)-31, no. 2 (1988).

Bulletin of the New York Public Library 80 (1977)-. [Now *Bulletin of Research in the Humanities*.]

BURKE, KENNETH. *Counter-Statement*. New York: Harcourt, Brace & Co., 1931.

_____. *A Grammar of Motives*. Berkeley and Los Angeles: University of California Press, 1968.

_____. *Language as Symbolic Action: Essays on Life, Literature, and Method*. Berkeley and Los Angeles: University of California Press, 1968.

_____. *Permanance and Change*. New York: New Republic, 1935. (No explication)

_____. *The Philosophy of Literary Form*. Baton Rouge: Lousiana State University Press, 1941.

_____. *A Rhetoric of Motives*. New York: Prentice-Hall, 1950. (No explication)

BUSH, R. *T. S. Eliot: A Study in Character and Style*. New York: Oxford University Press, 1983.

BUTTERFIELD, R. W. (HERBIE). *Modern American Poetry*. London: Barnes & Noble, 1984.

California English Journal

Callaloo: A Black South Journal of Arts and Letters 1 (1977)-11, no. 2 (1988).

Callaloo: A Black South Journal of Arts and Letters 8 (Winter 1985). "Larry Neal: A Special Issue."

Calyx: A Journal of Art and Literature by Women 8, no. 2 (Spring 1984). Special issue: "Bearing Witness/Sobreviviendo: An Anthology of Native American/Latina Art and Literature."

The Cambridge Quarterly 1 (1965/1966)-17, no. 2 (1988).

CAMPBELL, JANE, and JAMES DOYLE, eds. *The Practical Vision: Essays in English Literature in Honour of Flora Roy.* Waterloo, Ontario: Wilfrid Laurier University Press, 1978.

Canadian Literature 1 (1959)-117 (Summer 1988).

Canadian Poetry: Studies, Documents, Reviews 1 (1936)-31 (1968).

Canadian Review of American Studies 1 (1970)-18 (Winter 1987).

CANDELARIA, CORDELIA. *Chicano Poetry: A Critical Introduction.* Westport, Conn.: Greenwood Press, 1986.

Carleton Miscellany 1 (1960)-18 (1980).

CARROLL, PAUL. *The Poem in Its Skin.* Chicago: Follett Publishing Co., 1968.

CASTRO, MICHAEL. *Interpreting the Indian: Twentieth-Century Poets and the Native American.* Albuquerque: University of New Mexico Press, 1983.

Catholic World

CEA Critic: An Official Journal of the College English Association 1, no. 1 (Oct. 1939)-40, no. 1 (Nov. 1977).

The Centennial Review (Michigan State University) 1 (1957)-32 (1988). [Formerly *Centennial Review of Arts and Sciences*.]

Chariton Review

CHATMAN, SEYMOUR. *An Introduction to the Language of Poetry.* Boston: Houghton Mifflin Co., 1968.

Chicago Review 1 (1946)-35 (Spring 1986).

Chimera 1 (1976)-1, no. 2 (1976).

MAIN SOURCES CONSULTED

CIARDI, JOHN. *How Does a Poem Mean?* Boston: Houghton Mifflin Co., 1959.

_____, ed. *Mid-Century American Poets*. New York: Twayne Publishers, 1950.

Cimarron Review 1 (1985-1986)-3 (Spring 1988).

CLARK, DAVID R. *Lyric Resonance: Glosses on Some Poems of Yeats, Frost, Crane, Cummings, and Others*. Amherst: University of Massachusetts Press, 1972.

CLAUSEN, CHRISTOPHER. "Grecian Thought in the Home Fields: Reflections on Southern Poetry." *Georgia Review* 32 (Summer 1978): 283-305.

_____. "Poetry in a Discouraging Time." *Georgia Review* 35 (Winter 1981): 703-15.

COFFMAN, STANLEY K. *Imagism: A Chapter for the History of Modern Poetry*. Norman: University of Oklahoma Press, 1951. (No explication)

COHAN, B. BERNARD. *Writing about Literature*. Chicago: Scott, Foresman & Co., 1963.

Colby Library Quarterly

College English 1 (Oct. 1939)-49, no. 4 (Apr. 1987).

College Language Association Journal (Morgan State College, Baltimore) 19 (1975)-30, no. 3 (1987).

College Literature

COLLINS, MARTHA, ed. *Critical Essays on Louise Bogan*. Boston: G. K. Hall, 1984.

COLLINS, MICHAEL J. "Formal Allusion in Modern Poetry." *Concerning Poetry* 9 (Spring 1976): 5-12.

Colorado Quarterly 24, no. 4 (Spring 1976)-28, no. 4 (Winter 1980).

Commonweal

Comparative Drama 1 (1967)-22 (Summer 1988).

Comparative Literature 30, no. 1 (1978)-40, no. 1 (1988).

Comparative Literature Studies (University of Illinois) 13, no. 1 (1976)-24, no. 4 (1988).

Concerning Poetry 1, no. 1 (Fall 1968)-19, no. 1 (Spring 1986).

Confluencia: Revista Hispánica de Cultura y Literatura

Connecticut Review

Contemporary Literature 1 (1960)-28, no. 1 (Spring 1987). [Supersedes *Wisconsin Studies in Contemporary Literature*.]

Contemporary Review (London) 228, no. 1320 (Jan. 1976)-249, no. 1451 (Dec. 1986).

COOK, A. *Figural Choice in Poetry and Art*. Hanover, N.H. and London: University Press of New England, 1985.

COOKE, MICHAEL G. *Afro-American Literature in the Twentieth Century: Achievement of Intimacy*. New Haven: Yale University Press, 1984.

COOKSON, WILLIAM, ed. *Ezra Pound: Selected Prose, 1909-1965*. New York: New Directions, 1975.

COOPER, CHARLES W., and JOHN HOLMES. *Preface to Poetry*. New York: Harcourt, Brace & Co., 1946.

COOPER, EMMANUEL. *The Sexual Perspective: Homosexuality and Art in the Last 100 Years in the West*. London: Routledge & Kegan Paul, 1986.

Cornell Studies in English

CORNWELL, ETHEL F. *The "Still Point": Theme and Variations in the Writings of T. S. Eliot, Coleridge, Yeats, Henry James, Virginia Woolf, and D. H. Lawrence*. New Brunswick, N.J.: Rutgers University Press, 1962.

COWAN, LOUISE. *The Fugitive Group: A Literary History*. Baton Rouge: Louisiana State University Press, 1959.

COWLEY, MALCOLM, MAXINE KUMIN, ROBERT LANGBAUM, DONALD HALL, et al. "The Place of Poetry: Symposium Responses." *Georgia Review* 35 (Winter 1981): 716-56.

CRANE, R. S., ed. *Critics and Criticism: Ancient and Modern*. Chicago: University of Chicago Press, 1952. (No explication)

Credences 1 (1975)-n.s. 3 (1985)

Credences 3, no. 7 (Feb. 1979). Special issue: "In Celebration of Kenneth Irby."

Credences n.s. 2 (Fall/Winter 1983). Special issue: "Canadian Poetry Festival."

The Critic 1 (Spring 1947)-1, no. 2 (Autumn 1947).

Critical Inquiry 1 (1974)-13, no. 4 (Summer 1987).

Critical Quarterly 1, no. 1 (Spring 1959)-27, no. 4 (Winter 1985).

The Critical Review (Canberra, Australia)

A Critical Supplement to 'Poetry,'" Oct. 1948-Dec. 1949. (The listing in this checklist is incomplete and limited to poems by widely recognized contemporaries. The poems explicated appear in the corresponding issues of *Poetry: A Magazine of Verse*.)

Criticism: A Quarterly for Literature and the Arts 1, no. 1 (Winter 1959)-30, no. 2 (Spring 1988).

CUNNINGHAM, CORNELIUS CARMAN. *Literature as a Fine Art: Analysis and Interpretation*. New York: Thomas Nelson & Sons, 1941.

CUNNINGHAM, J. V. *Tradition and Poetic Structure*. Denver: Alan Swallow, 1960.

Daedalus 106, no. 1 (1977)-117, no. 2 (1988).

DAICHES, DAVID. *The Place of Meaning in Poetry*. Edinburgh and London: Oliver & Boyd, 1935.

_____. *A Study of Literature for Readers and Critics*. Ithaca, N.Y.: Cornell University Press, 1948.

DAICHES, DAVID, and WILLIAM CHARVAT. *Poems in English, 1530-1940*. New York: Ronald Press, 1950.

Dalhousie Review 55, no. 4 (Winter 1975/1976)-64, no. 4 (Winter 1984/1985).

DANIELS, EARL. *The Art of Reading Poetry*. New York: Farrar & Rinehart, 1941.

Delta Epsilon Sigma Bulletin

DE MAN, PAUL. *Allegories of Reading*. New Haven: Yale University Press, 1979.

Denver Quarterly 1 (1966)-12 (1978); 13 (1978)-22, no. 4 (1988). [Formerly *University of Denver Quarterly*.]

DERRIDA, JACQUES. *Dissemination*. Translated by Barbara Johnson. Chicago: University of Chicago Press, 1981.

_____. *Positions*. Translated by Alan Bass. Chicago: University of Chicago Press, 1981.

DEUTSCH, BABETTE. *Poetry in Our Time*. New York: Henry Holt & Co., 1952.

_____. *This Modern Poetry*. New York: W. W. Norton & Co., 1935.

Diacritics 8, no. 1 (1978)-17, no. 3 (1987).

The Dial 78 (Jan. 1925)-86 (July 1929).

DICKIE, MARGARET. *On the Modernist Long Poem*. Iowa City: University of Iowa Press, 1986.

DICKINSON, LEON T. *Suggestions for Teachers of "Introduction to Literature,"* 5th ed. Teacher's Manual. See Locke, Gibson, and Arms, *Readings for Liberal Education*.

Dickinson Studies: Emily Dickinson (1830-86), U.S. Poet

Dictionary of Literary Biography. Vol. 5, *American Poets since World War II*, edited by Donald Greiner. Detroit: Gale, 1980. Vol. 41, *Afro-American Poets Since 1955*, edited by Trudier Harris. Detroit: Gale, 1985.

Dissertation Abstracts International

DOUGLAS, WALLACE, ROY LAMSON, and HALLETT SMITH. *The Critical Reader*. New York: W. W. Norton & Co., 1949. Rev. ed., edited by Roy Lamson, Hallett Smith, Hugh N. MacLean, Wallace Douglas, 1962.

DOYLE, CHARLES, ed. *Wallace Stevens*. Critical Heritage Series. London: Routledge & Kegan Paul, 1986.

The Drama Review 28, no. 1 (1984)-32, no. 1 (1988).

DRAPER, RONALD P. *Lyric Tragedy*. New York: St. Martin's, 1985.

DREW, ELIZABETH. *Discovering Poetry*. New York: W. W. Norton & Co., 1933.

_____. *The Enjoyment of Literature*. New York: W. W. Norton & Co., 1935. (No explication)

_____. *Poetry: A Modern Guide to Its Understanding and Enjoyment*. New York: W. W. Norton & Co., 1959.

DREW, ELIZABETH, and JOHN L. SWEENEY. *Directions in Modern Poetry*. W. W. Norton & Co., 1940.

DUDEK, LOUIS, and MICHAEL GNAROWSKI, eds. *The Making of Modern Poetry in Canada*. Toronto: Ryerson, 1967.

DUFFEY, BERNARD. *A Poetry of Presence: The Writing of William Carlos Williams*. Madison: University of Wisconsin Press, 1986.

DURAND, REGIS, ed. *Myth and Ideology in American Culture*. Villeneuve d'Ascq: Université de Lille III, 1976.

DURHAM, FRANK, ed. *Studies in "Cane."* Columbus, Ohio: Merrill, 1970.

Early American Literature 1 (1966)-23, no. 2 (1988).

EASTMAN, MAX. *Enjoyment of Poetry*. Rev. ed. New York: Charles Scribner's Sons, 1930. (No explication)

_____. *The Literary Mind*. New York: Charles Scribner's Sons, 1931.

EDWARDS, THOMAS R. *Imagination and Power: A Study of Poetry on Public Themes*. New York: Oxford University Press, 1971.

ELDER, J. *Imagining the Earth: Poetry and the Vision of Nature*. Urbana and Chicago: University of Illinois Press, 1985.

ELH: A Journal of English Literary History 1, no. 1 (Apr. 1934)-55, no. 2 (Summer 1988).

ELIOT, T. S. *Essays, Ancient and Modern*. New York: Harcourt, Brace & Co., 1936. (No explication)

_____. *The Sacred Wood: Essays on Poetry and Criticism*. London: Methuen & Co., 1920. (No explication)

_____. *Selected Essays*. New York: Harcourt, Brace & Co., 1932. (No explication)

_____. *The Use of Poetry and the Use of Criticism*. New York: Harcourt, Brace & Co., 1933. (No explication)

EMANUEL, JAMES, and THEODORE L. GROSS, eds. *Dark Symphony: Negro Literature in America*. New York: Free Press, 1968.

EMPSON, WILLIAM. *Seven Types of Ambiguity*. London: Chatto & Windus, 1947.

Emory University Quarterly 1 (1945)-23 (1967).

Encounter 1 (1953)-70 (1988).

ENGLE, PAUL, and WARREN CARRIER. *Reading Modern Poetry*. Chicago: Scott, Foresman & Co., 1955.

English 1 (1936)-37, no. 157 (Spring 1988).

English "A" Analyst (Northwestern University), no. 1 (1947)-17 (1949).

English Institute Annual 1939-1942: English Institute Essays. New York: Columbia University Press, 1940-43, 1946-48, 1947-49, 1950-52.

English in Texas

The English Journal (High School and College Edition), 14 (Jan. 1925)-77, no. 4 (1988).

English Language Notes 1, no. 1 (Sept. 1963)-23, no. 4 (June 1986).

English Literature in Transition (1880-1920) 26, no. 1 (1983)-31, no. 2 (1988).

English Record

English Studies: A Journal of English Language and Literature 57, nos. 1-6 (1976)-67, no. 6 (Dec. 1986).

English Studies in Canada

ERISMAN, FRED, and RICHARD W. ETULAIN, eds. *Fifty Western Writers: A Bio-Bibliographical Sourcebook*. Westport, N.Y.: Greenwood Press, 1982.

ESQ: A Journal of the American Renaissance 1 (1955)-33, no. 1 (1987).

Essays and Studies by Members of the English Association. Oxford: Clarendon Press, 11 (1925)-33 (1947). New series 3 (1950)-20 (1969).

Essays in Criticism: A Quarterly Journal of Literary Criticism 1, no. 1 (Jan. 1951)-38, no. 1 (Jan. 1988).

Essays in Literature (Western Illinois University) 1, no. 1 (Spring 1974)-12, no. 2 (Fall 1985).

Essays on Canadian Writing

Études Anglaises: Grande-Bretagne, États-Unis 29, no. 1 (Jan./Mar. 1976)-38, no. 4 (Oct./Dec. 1985).

Études Littéraires 1 (1968)-21. no. 1 (Spring 1988).

EVANS, MARI, ed. *Black Women Writers, 1950-1980: A Critical Evaluation*. Garden City, N.J.: Doubleday, Anchor, 1984.

Explicator 1 (Oct. 1942)-46, no. 4 (Summer 1988).

The Explicator Cyclopedia. Edited by Charles Child Walcutt and J. Edwin Whitesell. Vol. 1, *Modern Poetry*. Chicago: Quadrangle Books, 1966.

FABB, NIGEL, DEREK ATTRIDGE, ALAN DURANT, and COLIN McCABE, eds. *The Linguistics of Writing*. New York: Methuen, 1988.

FASS, EKBERT. *Young Robert Duncan: Portrait of the Poet as Homosexual in Society*. Santa Barbara, Calif: Black Sparrow Press, 1983.

FEDER, LILLIAN. *Ancient Myth in Modern Poetry*. Princeton: Princeton University Press, 1971.

FEIDELSON, CHARLES, and PAUL BRODTKORB, Jr., eds. *Interpretations of American Literature*. New York: Oxford University Press, 1959.

FELVER, CHARLES S., and MARTIN K. NURMI. *Poetry: An Introduction and Anthology*. Columbus, Ohio: Charles E. Marrill Books, 1967.

Feminist Studies 7, no. 1 (1981)-14, no. 1 (1988).

Field 1 (1969)-38 (1988).

Field 35 (Fall 1986). "Randall Jarrell: A Symposium."

Folio

Fortnightly 1 (1865)-182 (1954).

Forum for Modern Language Studies (University of St. Andrews, Scotland) 1 (1965)-24, no. 2 (Apr. 1988).

Four Quartets 21 (May 1972). Special issue on Robert Penn Warren.

FRAISTAT, NEIL, ed. *Poems in Their Place: The Intertextuality and Order of Poetic Collections*. Chapel Hill: University of North Carolina Press, 1986.

FRANKENBERG, LLOYD. *Invitation to Poetry*. New York: Doubleday & Co., 1956.

_____. *Pleasure Dome: On Reading Modern Poetry*. Boston: Houghton Mifflin Co., 1949.

FREEMAN, JOHN, ed. *Not Comforts/But Vision: Essays on the Poetry of George Oppen*. Devon, England: Interim, 1985.

FRENCH, WARREN. *The Twenties: Fiction, Poetry, Drama*. Deland, Fla.: Everett/Edwards, 1974.

FRIAR, KIMON, and JOHN MALCOLM BRINNIN, eds. *Modern Poetry, American and British*. New York: Appleton-Century Crofts, 1951.

FRIEDMAN, NORMAN, and CHARLES A. McLAUGHLIN. *Poetry: An Introduction to Its Form and Art*. New York: Harper & Brothers, 1961.

FROST, WILLIAM, ed. *Modern Poetry*. Vol. 7 of Maynard Mack, Leonard Dean, and William Frost, eds., *English Masterpieces: An Anthology of English Literature from Chaucer to T. S. Eliot*. New York: Prentice-Hall, 1950.

FROULA, CHRISTINE. *A Guide to Ezra Pound's Selected Poems*. New York: New Directions, 1983.

FRYE, NORTHROP. *Spiritus Mundi: Essays on Literature, Myth, and Society*. Bloomington: Indiana University Press, 1977.

Furioso

FUSSELL, EDWIN. *Lucifer in Harness: American Meter, Metaphor, and Diction*. Princeton: Princeton Unversity Press, 1973.

Gamut

GARDNER, THOMAS. "American Poetry of the 1970s: A Preface." *Contemporary Literature* 23 (1982): 407-10.

GASTON, P. L. *W. D. Snodgrass*. Boston: Twayne, 1978.

GELFANT, BLANCHE H. *Women Writing in American: Voices in Collage*. Hanover, N.H. and London: University Press of New England, 1984.

GELPHI, ALBERT. *The Tenth Muse: The Psyche of the American Poet*. Cambridge: Harvard University Press, 1973.

Genre 1 (1978)-19, no. 3 (Fall 1986).

The Georgia Review 31, no. 1 (Spring 1977)-39, no. 4 (Winter 1985).

GISH, N. *Time in the Poetry of T. S. Eliot: A Study in Structure and Theme*. New York: Barnes & Noble, 1981.

GITENSTEIN, R. BARBARA. *Apocalyptic Messianism and Contemporary Jewish-American Poetry*. Albany: State University of New York Press, 1986.

Glyph 1 (1977)-8 (1981).

GOHDES, CLARENCE, ed. *Essays on American Literature in Honor of Jay B. Hubbell*. Durham: Duke University Press, 1967.

GOODMAN, PAUL. *The Structure of Literature*. Chicago: University of Chicago Press, 1954.

GORDON, EDWARD J., and EDWARD S. NOYES, eds. *Essays on the Teaching of English: Reports of the Yale Conference on the Teaching of English*. New York: Appleton-Century-Crofts, 1960.

GRAY, RICHARD, ed. *American Poetry of the Twentieth Century*. London: Cambridge University Press, 1976.

Great Plains Quarterly

GREEN, RAYNA, ed. *That's What She Said: Contemporary Poetry and Fiction by Native American Women*. Bloomington: Indiana University Press, 1984.

GREENE, THEODORE M. *The Arts and the Art of Criticism*. Princeton: Princeton University Press, 1940.

GREENFIELD, STANLEY B., and A. KINGSLEY WEATHERHEAD. *The Poem: An Anthology*. New York: Appleton-Century-Crofts, 1968.

GROSS, THEODORE L. *The Heroic Ideal in American Literature*. New York: Free Press, 1971.

GUTIÉRREZ, DONALD. *The Maze in the Mind and the World: Labyrinths in Modern Literature*. Troy, N.Y.: Whitson, 1986.

GWYNN, FREDERICK L., RALPH W. CONDEE, and ARTHUR O. LEWIS, eds. *The Case for Poetry*. Englewood Cliffs, N.J.: Prentice-Hall, 1954.

HADAS, R. *Form, Cycle, Infinity: Landscape Imagery in the Poetry of Robert Frost and George Seferis*. Lewisburg, Pa.: Bucknell University Press, 1985.

HALL, DONALD. *The Pleasures of Poetry*. New York: Harper & Row, 1971.

HAMILTON, G. ROSTREVOR. *The Tell-Tale Article: A Critical Approach to Modern Poetry*. New York: Oxford University Press, 1950. (No explication)

HARDY, JOHN EDWARD. *The Curious Frame: Seven Poems in Text and Context*. Notre Dame: University of Notre Dame Press, 1962.

The Harlem Renaissance: An Annotated Bibliography and Commentary. New York: Garland, 1982.

The Harvard Wake 5 (Spring 1946); *Wake* 7 (Autumn 1948)-12 (1953).

HATCHER, ANNA, ed. *Essays on English and American Literature by Leo Spitzer*. Princeton: Princeton University Press, 1962.

HATCHER, JOHN. *From the Auroral Darkness: The Life and Poetry of Robert Hayden*. Oxford: George Ronald, 1984.

HAYDEN, J. O. *Inside Poetry Out: An Introduction to Poetry*. Chicago: Nelson-Hall, 1982.

HELLER, M. *Conviction's Net of Branches: Essays on the Objectivist Poets and Poetry*. Carbondale and Edwardsville: Southern Illinois University Press, 1985.

HERRERA-SOBEK, MARÍA, ed. *Beyond Stereotypes: The Critical Analysis of Chicana Literature*. New York: Bilingual Press/Editorial Bilingue, 1985.

HILL, ARCHIBALD A. *Constituent and Pattern in Poetry*. Austin: University of Texas Press, 1976.

HILL, HERBERT, ed. *Anger and Beyond: The Negro Writer in the United States*. New York: Harper & Row, 1966.

HOFFMAN, DANIEL G. *Barbarous Knowledge: Myth in the Poetry of Yeats, Graves, and Muir*. New York: Oxford University Press, 1967.

HOFFMAN, FREDERICK J. *The Twenties: American Writing in the Postwar Decade*. New York: Viking Press, 1955.

The Hollins Critic 1 (1964)-25, no. 3 (June 1988).

Hound and Horn 1 (Sept. 1927)-7 (July/Sept. 1934).

HOWARD, H. A. *American Indian Poetry*. Boston: Twayne, 1979.

HOWARD, RICHARD. *Alone with America*. New York: Atheneum, 1980.

HOWE, IRVING, ed. *Modern Literary Criticism*. Boston: Beacon Press, 1958.

The Hudson Review 1 (Spring 1948)-41, no. 2 (Summer 1988).

Humanities Association Review/La Revue de l'Association des Humanités 16 (1965)-31 (1980). [Formerly *Humanities Association Bulletin*.]

Huntington Library Quarterly: A Journal for the History and Interpretation of English and American Civilization 1 (1937)-51, no. 3 (1988).

HUTCHEON, LINDA. *A Poetics of Postmodernism*. London: Methuen, 1988.

HYMAN, STANLEY EDGAR. *The Armed Vision*. New York: Vintage Books, 1955.

HYMES, DELL. *"In Vain I Tried to Tell You": Essays in Native American Ethnopoetics*. Philadelphia: University of Pennsylvania Press, 1981.

Illinois Quarterly

Indian Literature (Calcutta)

INGE, M. THOMAS, et al., eds. *Black American Writers: Bibliographical Essays*. 2 vols. New York: St. Martin's, 1978.

Iowa English Bulletin

MAIN SOURCES CONSULTED

The Iowa Review 1, no. 1 (Winter 1970)-15, no. 3 (Fall 1985).

Ironwood

ISAACS, E. *An Introduction to the Poetry of Yvor Winters*. Athens, Ohio: Swallow, 1981.

JACKSON, BLYDEN. *The Waiting Years: Essays on American Negro Literature*. Baton Rouge: Louisiana State University Press, 1976.

JACKSON, RICHARD. "The Deconstructed Moment in Modern Poetry." *Contemporary Literature* 23, no. 3 (1982): 306-22.

JACOBSON, ROMAN, and LINDA WAUGH. *The Sound Shape of Language*. Bloomington: Indiana University Press, 1979.

JARRELL, RANDALL. *Poetry and the Age*. New York: Vintage Books, 1953.

JAY, G. *T. S. Eliot and the Poetics of Literary History*. Baton Rouge: Louisiana State University Press, 1983.

JEROME, JUDSON. *Poetry: Premeditated Art*. Boston: Houghton Mifflin Co., 1968.

JONES, DAVID, and KATE DANIELS, eds. *Of Solitude and Silence: Writings on Robert Bly*. Boston: Beacon Press, 1981.

Journal of Aesthetics and Art Criticism

Journal of American Culture 1 (1978)-11, no. 2 (Summer 1988).

Journal of English and Germanic Philology 24 (1925)-80, no. 4 (1982).

Journal of English Literary History 43, no. 1 (Spring 1976)-52, no. 4 (Winter 1985).

The Journal of Ethnic Studies 9 (1981)-16, no. 3 (1988).

Journal of Modern Literature 1 (1970)-14, no. 1 (Summer 1987).

Journal of Narrative Technique 7, no. 1 (Winter 1977)-16, no. 2 (Spring 1986).

Journal of Popular Culture 12, no. 2 (1978)-21, no. 4 (1988).

Journal of the History of Ideas

JUHASZ, SUZANNE. *Metaphor and the Poetry of Williams, Pound, and Stevens*. Lewisburg, Pa.: Bucknell University Press, 1974.

_____. *Naked and Fiery Forms: Modern American Poetry by Women, A New Tradition*. New York: Octagon Books, 1976.

Kansas Quarterly 8, no. 1 (1976)-17, no. 4 (1985). [Formerly *KM*.]

KEITH, W. J. *Canadian Literature in English*. London and New York: Longman, 1985.

KELLNER, BRUCE. *The Harlem Renaissance: A Historical Dictionary for the Era*. New York: Methuen, 1987.

KENNER, HUGH. *A Homemade World: The American Modernist Writers*. New York: William Morrow, 1975.

_____. *The Mechanic Muse*. New York: Oxford University Press, 1987.

_____. *The Pound Era*. Berkeley and Los Angeles: University of California Press, 1971.

The Kenyon Review 1 (Winter 1939)-32, no. 1 (1970).

KILBY, CLYDE S. *Poetry and Life: An Introduction to Poetry*. New York: Odyssey Press, 1953.

KIRBY, THOMAS AUSTIN, and WILLIAM JOHN OLIVE, eds. *Essays in Honor of Esmond Linworth Marilla*. Baton Rouge: Louisiana State University Press, 1970.

KIRK, RICHARD RAY, and ROGER PHILIP McCUTCHEON. *An Introduction to the Study of Poetry*. New York: American Book Co., 1934.

KLINKOWITZ, JEROME. *Literary Disruptions: The Making of a Post-Contemporary American Fiction*. Urbana, Chicago, and London: University of Illinois Press, 1975.

KNIGHT, G. WILSON. *The Burning Oracle: Studies in the Poetry of Action*. London, New York, and Toronto: Oxford University Press, 1939.

KNIGHTS, L. C. *Explorations: Essays in Criticism*. New York: George M. Stewart, 1947.

KREUZER, JAMES R. *Elements of Poetry*. New York: Macmillan Co., 1955.

KRIEGER, MURRAY. *The New Apologists for Poetry*. Minneapolis: University of Minnesota Press, 1956.

_____. *The Play and the Place of Criticism*. Baltimore: Johns Hopkins University Press, 1967.

KRISTEVA, JULIA. *Desire in Language*. Translated by Thomas Gora, Alice Jardine, and Leon S. Roudiez. New York: Columbia University Press, 1980.

KROEBER, KARL, ed. *Traditional Literatures of the American Indians*. Lincoln: University of Nebraska Press, 1981.

LABRIE, ROSS. *Howard Nemerov*. Boston: Twayne, 1980.

LACEY, H. *To Raise, Destroy, and Create: The Poetry, Drama, and Fiction of Imamu Amiri Baraka*. Troy, N.Y.: Whitson, 1981.

LACEY, PAUL A. *The Inner War: Forms and Themes in Recent American Poetry*. Philadelphia: Fortress Press, 1972.

LANE, GARY, ed. *Sylvia Plath: New Views on the Poetry*. Baltimore: Johns Hopkins University Press, 1979.

LANGBAUM, ROBERT. *The Mysteries of Identity: A Theme in Modern Literature*. New York: Oxford University Press, 1977.

_____. *The Poetry of Experience: The Dramatic Monologue in Modern Literary Experience*. New York: Random House, 1957.

LANGFORD, RICHARD E., and WILLIAM E. TAYLOR. *The Twenties: Poetry and Prose*. Deland, Fla.: Everett/Edwards, 1966.

The Langston Hughes Review

Language and Style: An International Journal 9, no. 1 (Winter 1976)-18, no. 1 (Winter 1986).

LAUTER, ESTELLA. *Women as Mythmakers: Poetry & Visual Art by Twentieth-Century Women*. Bloomington: Indiana University Press/Midlands, 1984.

LEAVIS, F.R. *Education and the University: A Sketch for an English School*. London: Chatto & Windus, 1965.

_____. *New Bearings in English Poetry: A Study of the Contemporary Situation*. Ann Arbor: University of Michigan Press, 1960.

LEHMAN, DAVID, ed. *New Essays on John Ashbery*. Ithaca, N.Y.: Cornell University Press, 1980.

LEHMAN, DAVID, and CHARLES BERGER, eds. *James Merrill: Essays in Criticism*. Ithaca, N.Y.: Cornell University Press, 1982.

LENSING, GEORGE S., and RONALD MORGAN. *Four Poets and the Emotive Imagination: Robert Bly, James Wright, Louis Simpson, and William Stafford*. Baton Rouge: Louisiana State University Press, 1976.

LENSINK, JUDY NOLTE. *Old Southwest/New Southwest: Essays on a Region and Its Literature*. Tucson: University of Arizona Press, 1987.

LENTRICCHIA, FRANK, Jr. *After the New Criticism*. Chicago: University of Chicago Press, 1980.

_____. *Criticism and Social Change*. Chicago: University of Chicago Press, 1985.

LEYLAND, WINSTON, ed. *Angels of the Lyre*. San Francisco: Gay Sunshine Press, 1975.

_____. *Gay Sunshine Interviews*. 2 vols. San Francisco: Gay Sunshine Press, 1982.

_____. *Orgasms of Light*. San Francisco: Gay Sunshine Press, 1977.

Life and Letters

MAIN SOURCES CONSULTED

LINCOLN, KENNETH. *Native American Renaissance*. Berkeley and Los Angeles: University of California Press, 1983.

Literary Criterion

Literary Criticism

Literary Review: An International Journal of Contemporary Writing 19, no. 3 (Spring 1976)-29, no. 4 (Summer 1986).

Literature and Psychology (Fairleigh Dickinson University) 27, no. 1 (1977)-33, no. 1 (1987).

LOCKE, LOUIS G., WILLIAM M. GIBSON, and GEORGE ARMS, eds. *Readings for Liberal Education*. Vol. 2, *Introduction to Literature*. New York: Rinehart & Co., 1948. 3d ed., 1957. 4th ed., New York: Holt, Rinehart & Winston, 1962. 5th ed., 1967.

London Quarterly and Holborn Review

LOURIE, DICK, ed. *Come to Power: Eleven Contemporary American Indian Poets*. Trumansburg, N.Y.: Crossing Press, 1974.

LUDWIG, RICHARD M., ed. *Aspects of American Poetry: Essays Presented to Howard Mumford Jones*. Columbus: Ohio State University Press, 1962.

McCAFFERY, STEVE. *North of Intention: Critical Writings, 1973-1986*. New York and Toronto: Roof Books; Nightwood Editions, 1986.

McCLATCHY, J. D., ed. *Anne Sexton: The Artist and Her Critics*. Bloomington and London: Indiana University Press, 1978.

McDOWELL, FREDERICK P. W., ed. *The Poet as Critic*. Evanston: Northwestern University Press, 1967.

MACK, MAYNARD, LEONARD DEAN, and WILLIAM FROST, eds. *English Masterpieces: An Anthology of Imaginative Literature from Chaucer to T. S. Eliot*. 7 Vols. New York: Prentice-Hall, 1950.

McKAY, N. *Jean Toomer, Artist*. Chapel Hill and London: University of North Carolina Press, 1984.

McNeese Review (McNeese State College, La.)

McPHERSON, JAMES M., LAURENCE B. HOLLAND, JAMES M. BANNER, Jr., NANCY J. WEISS, and MICHAEL D. BELL, eds. *Blacks in America: Bibliographical Essays*. New York: Doubleday, 1971.

The Malahat Review 75 (1986)-83 (1988).

The Malahat Review 78 (1987). Special issue on George Johnston.

MALKOFF, KARL. *Theodore Roethke: An Introduction to the Poetry*. New York and London: Columbia University Press, 1966.

MANDEL, ELI. *Another Time*. Toronto: Hunter Rose Co., 1977.

Marianne Moore Newsletter

MARIANI, PAUL. *A Usable Past: Essays on Modern and Contemporary Poetry*. Amherst: University of Massachusetts Press, 1984.

_____. *William Carlos Williams: A New World Naked*. New York: McGraw-Hill, 1971. Rev. ed. 1982.

The Markham Review

MARTIN, ROBERT K. *The Homosexual Tradition in American Poetry*. Austin and London: University of Texas Press, 1979.

MARTIN, TAFFY. *Marianne Moore ... Subversive Modernist*. Austin: University of Texas Press, 1986.

MARTING, DIANE E., ed. *Women Writers of Spanish America: An Annotated Bio-Bibliographical Guide*. New York: Greenwood Press, 1987.

MARTZ, LOUIS L. *The Poetry of Meditation: A Study in English Religious Literature*. New Haven: Yale University Press, 1966.

Massachusetts Review: A Quarterly of Literature, the Arts, and Public Affairs (University of Massachusetts) 17, no. 1 (Spring 1976)-28, no. 1 (Spring 1987).

Massachusetts Studies in English

MASSE, A. *American Literature in Context*. Vol. 4, *1900-1930*. New York: Methuen, 1982.

MATTHIESSEN, F. O. *The Responsibilities of the Critic*. Edited by John Rackliffe. New York: Oxford University Press, 1952.

MELHEM, D. H. *Gwendolyn Brooks: Poetry and the Heroic Voice*. Lexington: University Press of Kentucky, 1987.

MELUS: The Journal of the Society for the Study of the Multi-Ethnic Literature of the United States

MERRILL, THOMAS F. *The Poetry of Charles Olson--A Primer*. Newark: University of Delaware Press, 1982.

MERSMANN, JAMES F. *Out of the Vietnam Vortex: A Study of Poets and Poetry against the War*. Wichita: University Press of Kansas, 1974.

Michigan Quarterly Review

Mid-Hudson Language Studies

Midwest Quarterly: A Journal of Contemporary Thought (Pittsburgh, Kans.) 24, no. 2 (Winter 1983)-28, no. 4 (Summer 1987).

MILLER, J. HILLIS. *The Linguistic Moment: From Wordsworth to Stevens*. Princeton: Princeton University Press, 1985.

_____. *Poets of Reality: Six Twentieth-Century Writers*. Cambridge: Harvard Univesity Press, 1965.

_____, ed. *William Carlos Williams*. Englewood Cliffs, N.J.: Prentice-Hall, 1966.

MILLER, JAMES E., Jr., KARL SHAPIRO, and BERNICE SLOTE. *Start with the Sun: Studies in Cosmic Poetry*. Lincoln: University of Nebraska Press, 1960.

MILLER, R. BAXTER, ed. *Black American Poets between Worlds, 1940-1960*. Tennessee Studies in Literature, 30. Knoxville: University of Tennessee Press, 1986.

_____, ed. "Does Man Love Art?' The Humanistic Aesthetics of Gwendolyn Brooks." In *Black American Literature and Humanism*. Lexington: University Press of Kentucky, 1981, 95-112.

MILLET, FRED B. *Reading Poetry: A Method of Analysis with Selections for Study*. New York: Harper & Brothers, 1950.

MILLS, RALPH J., Jr. *Contemporary American Poetry*. New York: Random House, 1965.

MINER, EARL, ed. *Literary Uses of Typology from the Late Middle Ages to the Present*. Princeton: Princeton University Press, 1977.

The Minnesota Review 6 (Spring 1976)-25 (Fall 1985).

MIRANDE, ALFREDO, and EVANGELINA ENRÍQUEZ. *La Chicana: The Mexican-American Woman*. Chicago and London: University of Chicago Press, 1979.

Mississippi Quarterly: The Journal of Southern Culture 29, no. 1 (Winter 1975-1976)-38, no. 4 (Fall 1985).

The Missouri Review

Modern Age: A Quarterly Review (Chicago) 19, no. 1 (Winter 1975)-30, no. 2 (Spring 1986).

Modern Drama

Modern Language Notes 40 (Jan. 1925)-103, 3 (Apr. 1988).

Modern Language Quarterly 1, no. 1 (Mar. 1940)-46, 2 (June 1985).

The Modern Language Review 77, no. 1 (1982)-83, no. 2 (Apr. 1988).

Modern Language Studies 10, no. 1 (1980)-18, no. 1 (Winter 1988).

Modern Philology: A Journal Devoted to Research in Medieval and Modern Literature 22 (Aug. 1924)-84, no. 4 (May 1987).

Modern Poetry Studies

MOFFETT, JUDITH. *James Merrill: An Introduction to the Poetry*. New York: Columbia University Press, 1984.

MOLESWORTH, CHARLES. "Contemporary Poetry and the Metaphors for the Poem," *Georgia Review* 32 (Summer 1978): 319-31.

MAIN SOURCES CONSULTED

Mosaic: A Journal for the Interdisciplinary Study of Literature 9, no. 2 (Winter 1976)-21, no. 1 (Winter 1988).

MUNRO, C. LYNN. "Jean Toomer: A Bibliography of Secondary Sources." *Black American Literature Forum* 21 (Fall 1987): 275-87.

NASSAR, EUGENE PAUL. *The Cantos of Ezra Pound: The Lyric Mode*. Baltimore: Johns Hopkins University Press, 1975.

The Nation

Negro American Literature Forum

Negro Digest

NEILSON, KENNETH P. *The World of Langston Hughes' Music*. Hollis, N.Y.: All Seasons Art, 1982.

NELSON, H. *Robert Bly: An Introduction to the Poetry*. New York: Columbia University Press, 1984.

New Criterion

The New England Quarterly: A Historical Review of New England Life and Letters 57, no. 1 (1984)-61, no. 2 (June 1988).

New England Review and Breadloaf Quarterly

New Letters: A Magazine of Fine Writing

New Literary History: A Journal of Theory and Interpretation (University of Virginia) 8, no. 1 (1977)-19, no. 3 (1988).

New Mexico Quarterly Review

New Republic

NICOLSON, MARJORIE HOPE. *The Breaking of the Circle*. Evanston: Northwestern University Press, 1950.

The Nineteenth Century and After

NORRIS, CHRISTOPHER. *Paul De Man: Deconstruction and the Critique of Aesthetic Ideology*. New York: Methuen, 1988.

Northwest Review

NORWOOD, VERA, and JANICE MONK, eds. *The Desert Is No Lady*. New Haven: Yale University Press, 1987.

Notes & Queries 31 (1981)-35 (1988).

Notes on Contemporary Literature

Notes on Modern American Literature

OBERG, ARTHUR. *Modern American Lyric: Lowell, Berryman, Creeley, and Plath*. New Brunswick, N.J.: Rutgers University Press, 1978.

Obsidian II: Black Literature in Review

O'CONNOR, WILLIAM VAN. *Sense and Sensibility in Modern Poetry*. Chicago: University of Chicago Press, 1948.

The Ohio Review

The Old Northwest: A Journal of Regional Life and Letters

Osmania Journal of English Studies

OSTRIKER, ALICIA. *Stealing the Language: The Emergence of Women's Poetry in America*. Boston: Beacon Press, 1986.

_____. *Writing Like a Woman*. Ann Arbor: University of Michigan Press, 1983.

Pacific Spectator

PALMER, HERBERT. *Post-Victorian Poetry*. London: J. M. Dent & Sons, 1938.

Papers on Language & Literature: A Journal for Scholars and Critics of Language and Literature 1, no. 1 (Winter 1965)-23, no. 2 (Spring 1987).

PARKER, ALICE C. *Homosexuality in Frank O'Hara's Poetry*. Ann Arbor: UMI, 1984.

Parnassus: Poetry in Review 1 (1972/1973)-14 (1988).

PARRATE, HENRI-DOMINIQUE. "Fragments d'une réalité éclatée: Prolegomenes à une socio-esthétique vécue de la littérature acadienne à la fin de 1986." *Studies in Canadian Literature* 11 (1986): 140-60.

Partisan Review

PAUL, SHERMAN. *In Search of the Primitive: Rereading David Antin, Jerome Rothenberg, and Gary Snyder*. Baton Rouge: Louisisana State University Press, 1986.

_____. *The Lost America of Love: Rereading Robert Creeley, Edward Dorn, and Robert Duncan*. Baton Rouge: Louisiana State University Press, 1981.

_____. *Olson's Push: Origin, Black Mountain, and Recent American Poetry*. Baton Rouge: Louisiana State University Press, 1978.

PEARCE, ROY HARVEY. *The Continuity of American Poetry*. Princeton: Princeton University Press, 1961.

PECKHAM, MORSE, and SEYMOUR CHATMAN. *Word, Meaning, Poem*. New York: Thomas Crowell Co., 1961.

PERLOFF, MARJORIE. *Frank O'Hara: Poet Among Painters*. Austin: University of Texas Press, 1977.

_____. "Pound/Stevens: Whose Era?" *New Literary History: A Journal of Theory and Interpretation* 13 (1982): 485-514.

PERRINE, LAURENCE. *The Art of Total Relevance*. Rowley, Mass.: Newbury House Publishers, 1976.

_____. *Sound and Sense: An Introduction to Poetry*. New York: Harcourt, Brace & Co., 1956. 2d. ed., 1963.

PERRINE, LAURENCE, and JAMES M. REID. *100 American Poems of the Twentieth Century*. New York: Harcourt Brace & World, 1966.

The Personalist

Perspective

PESEROFF, JOYCE, ed. *Robert Bly: When Sleepers Awake*. Ann Arbor: University of Michigan Press, 1984.

PHILLIPS, ROBERT. *The Confessional Poets*. Carbondale: Southern Illinois University Press, 1973.

Philological Quarterly (Iowa City, Iowa)

PIERCY, MARGE, ed. *Early Ripening: American Women's Poetry Now*. Gainesville, Fla.: Pandora Press, 1988.

PINSKY, ROBERT. *The Situation of Poetry: Contemporary Poetry and Its Traditions*. Princeton: Princeton University Press, 1976.

PINTO, VIVIAN DE SOLA. *Crisis in English Poetry, 1880-1940*. London: Hutchinson's University Library, 1951.

Ploughshares 12 (1986)-14 (1988).

Poet and Critic

PMLA: Publications of the Modern Language Association of America 40 (Mar. 1925)-101, no. 6 (Nov. 1986).

Poetics Today 1 (1979)-8 (1988).

Poetry: A Magazine of Verse. Mar. 1947-May 1948. [See the note under *A Critical Supplement to "Poetry."*]

Politics and Letters (incorporating *The Critic*), 1 (Summer 1947)-1, no. 4 (Summer 1948).

POPE, DEBORAH. *A Separate Vision: Isolation in Contemporary Women's Poetry*. Baton Rouge: Louisiana State University Press, 1984.

PORTUGUÉS, PAUL. *The Visionary Poetics of Allen Ginsberg*. Santa Barbara, Calif.: Ross-Erikson, 1978.

POTTLE, FREDERICK A. *The Idiom of Poetry*. Ithaca, N.Y.: Cornell University Press, 1941.

POWERS, WILLIAM K. *Sacred Language: The Nature of Supernatural Discourse in Lakota*. Norman: University of Oklahoma Press, 1986.

Prairie Schooner 61 (1987)-62 (1988).

Princeton Encyclopedia of Poetry and Poetics. Edited by Alex Preminger. Princeton: Princeton University Press, 1965.

PRYSE, MARJORIE, and HORTENSE J. SPILLERS, eds. *Conjuring: Black Women, Fiction, and Literary Tradition*. Bloomington: Indiana University Press, 1985.

Publications of the Arkansas Philological Association

The Quarterly Journal of Speech 56 (1970)-72 (1986).

Quarterly Review of Literature 1, no. 1 (Autumn 1943); 2 (Fall 1944)-4, no.4 (1946).

QUASHA, GEORGE, and JEROME ROTHENBERG, eds. *America A Prophecy: A New Reading of American Poetry Since Pre-Columbian Times to the Present*. New York: Random House, Vintage, 1973 [1974].

Queen's Quarterly 82, no. 1 (Spring 1975)-92, no. 4 (Winter 1985).

QUINN, Sr. M. BERNETTA. *The Metamorphic Tradition in Modern Poetry*. New Brunswick, N.J.: Rutgers University Press, 1955.

RABATE, JEAN-MICHEL. *Language, Sexuality and Ideology in Ezra Pound's Cantos*. Albany: State University of New York Press, 1986.

RAJAN, B., ed. *Modern American Poetry*. New York: Roy Publishers, 1950.

RAMPERSAD, ARNOLD. *The Life of Langston Hughes*: Vol. 1, *1902-1941*. New York: Oxford University Press, 1986.

RANSOM, JOHN CROWE. *God without Thunder*. New York: Harcourt Brace & Co., 1930. (No explication)

_____. *The New Criticism*. Norfolk, Conn.: New Directions, 1941.

_____. *The World's Body*. New York: Charles Scribner's Sons, 1938.

_____, ed. *The Kenyon Critics: Studies in Modern Literature from the "Kenyon Review."* Cleveland and New York: World Publishing Co., 1951.

RAPP, CARL. *William Carlos Williams and Romantic Idealism*. Hanover and London: University Press of New England, 1984.

RECK, RIMA DELL, ed. *Exploration of Literature*. Baton Rouge: Louisiana State University Press, 1966

REILLY, JOHN M. "Jean Toomer: An Annotated Checklist of Criticism." *Resources for American Literary Study* 4 (1975): 27-56.

Renascence 38 (1986)-40 (1988).

Research Studies 1, no. 1 (June 1929)-45 (Dec. 1977). [Formerly *Research Studies of the State College of Washington*.]

Resources for American Literary Study

Review of English Studies: A Quarterly Journal of English Literature and the English Language

Revista Letras (Parná, Brazil)

Revue d'Histoire Littéraire du Québec et du Canada Française

RIBNER, IRVING, and HARRY MORRIS. *Poetry: A Critical and Historical Introduction*. Chicago: Scott, Foresman & Co., 1962.

RICHARDS, I. A. *How to Read a Page*. New York: W. W. Norton, 1942.

_____. *The Philosophy of Rhetoric*. New York: Oxford University Press, 1936.

_____. *Practical Criticism*. New York: Harcourt, Brace, & Co., 1929.

_____. *Principles of Literary Criticism*. 2d ed.. London: Kegan Paul, Trench, Trubner & Co., 1926.

_____. *Science and Poetry*. 2d ed.. Kegan Paul, Trench, Trubner & Co., 1935.

RICHARDS, I. A., G. K. OGDEN, and JAMES WOOD. *The Foundations of Aesthetics*. 2d ed.. New York: Lear Publishers, 1948.

RICKS, CHRISTOPHER. *The Force of Poetry*. New York: Clarendon, 1984.

RIDING, LAURA, and ROBERT GRAVES. *A Survey of Modernist Poetry*. New York: Doubleday, Doran & Co., 1928.

RIES, LAWRENCE R. *Wolf Masks: Violence in Contemporary Poetry*. Port Washington, N.Y.: Kennikat Press, 1977.

Robinson Jeffers Newsletter

ROBINSON, J. S. *H. D.: The Life and Work of an American Poet*. Boston: Houghton Mifflin Co., 1982.

Rocky Mountain Review of Language and Literature

ROSENBERG, JEROME H. *Margaret Atwood*. Boston: Twayne, 1984.

ROSENHEIM, EDWARD W. *What Happens in Literature: A Student's Guide to Poetry, Drama, and Fiction*. Chicago: University of Chicago Press, 1960.

_____. *Sailing into the Unknown: Yeats, Pound, and Eliot*. New York: Oxford University Press, 1978.

ROSENTHAL, M. L. *The Modern Poets: A Critical Introduction*. New York: Oxford University Press, 1960.

ROSENTHAL, M. L., and A. J. M. SMITH. *Exploring Poetry*. New York: Macmillan, 1955.

ROSS, ANDREW. *The Failure of Modernism: Symptoms of American Poetry*. New York: Columbia University Press, 1987.

ROTELLA, GUY. *Three Contemporary Poets of New England: William Meredith, Philip Booth, and Peter Davison*. Boston: Twayne, 1983.

ROTHENBERG, JEROME, ed. *Shaking the Pumpkin: Traditional Poetry of the Indian North Americas*. Rev. ed. New York: Van Der Marck, 1986.

ROTHENBERG, JEROME, and DIANE ROTHENBERG. *Symposium of the Whole: A Range of Discourse toward an Ethnopoetics*. Berkeley and Los Angeles: University of California Press, 1983.

RUBIN, LOUIS D., Jr. *The Wary Fugitives—Four Poets and the South*. Baton Rouge: Louisiana State University Press, 1978.

Sagetrieb 1, no. 1 (1982)-6, no. 2 (1987).

Sagetrieb 1 (Winter 1982). Special issue on Robert Creeley.

Sagetrieb 2 (Winter 1983). Special issue on Kenneth Rexroth.

Sagetrieb 3 (Fall 1984). Special issue on William Carlos Williams.

Sagetrieb 4, 2/3 (Fall/Winter 1985). Special issue: "Robert Duncan Issue."

Salmagundi nos. 9-12 (1969/1970)-n.s. 80 (1988).

SALUSINSZKY, IMRE, ed. *Criticism in Society*. New York: Methuen, 1987.

SÁNCHEZ, MARTA ESTER. *Contemporary Chicano Poetry: A Critical Approach to an Emerging Literature*. Berkeley, Los Angeles, and London: University of California Press, 1985.

SANDERS, THOMAS E. *The Discovery of Poetry*. Glenview, Ill.: Scott, Foresman & Co., 1967.

San Jose Studies 3, no. 1 (Feb. 1977)-12, no. 1 (Winter 1986).

San Jose Studies 12 (Fall 1986). "Ezra Pound Centenary Issue."

SATIN, JOSEPH. *Reading Poetry* (Part Four of *Reading Literature*). Boston: Houghton Mifflin, 1964.

Saturday Review

SAVAGE, D. S. *The Personal Principle: Studies in Modern Poetry*. London: George Routledge & Sons, 1944.

SAYRE, HENRY M. *The Visual Text of William Carlos Williams*. Urbana and Chicago: University of Illinois Press, 1983.

SCHLAUCH, MARGARET. *Modern English and American Poetry: Techniques and Ideologies*. London: C. A. Watts & Co., 1956.

SCHNEIDER, ELISABETH. *Aesthetic Motive*. New York: Macmillan, 1939.

SCHNEIDER, ELISABETH W. *Poems and Poetry*. New York: American Book Co., 1964.

SCHOR, NAOMI. *Reading in Detail: Aesthetics and the Feminine*. New York: Methuen, 1987.

SCHORER, MARK, JOSEPHINE MILES, and GORDON McKENZIE, eds. *Criticism: The Foundations of Modern Literary Judgment*. New York: Harcourt,
Brace & Co., 1948.

SCHULTZ, ROBERT. "Dispersions and Freedom: The Situation of Contemporary Poetry." *Virginia Quarterly Review* 60 (Winter 1984): 645-60.

SCHWARTZ, NARDA LACEY, ed. *Articles on Women Writers: A Bilbliography*. Vol. 2, *1976-1984*. Santa Barbara: ABC-Clio, 1986.

SCOTT, A. F. *The Poet's Craft*. Cambridge: Cambridge University Press, 1957.

SCOTT, NATHAN A., Jr. *Rehearsals of Discomposure*. New York: King's Crown Press, 1952.

Scrutiny

Sewanee Review 33 (Jan. 1925)-95, no. 3 (Summer 1987).

Sewanee Review 74 (Jan./Mar. 1966). Special issue.

SEWELL, ELIZABETH. *The Orphic Voice: Poetry and Natural History*. New Haven: Yale University Press, 1962.

_____. *The Structure of Poetry*. London: Routledge & Kegan Paul, 1951.

SHAW, H. *Gwendolyn Brooks*. Boston: Twayne, 1980.

Shenandoah

SIMON, SHERRY. "The Language of Difference: Minority Writers in Quebec." *Canadian Literature*, Supplement no. 1: *A/Part*, edited by J. M. Bumsted (May 1987). Papers from the 1984 Ottawa Conference on Language, Culture and Literary Identity in Canada.

SKELTON, ROBIN. *The Poetic Pattern*. Berkeley and Los Angeles: University of California Press, 1956.

SMITH, DAVE. *Local Assays: On Contemporary American Poetry*. Champaign: University of Illinois Press, 1985.

SMITH, LARRY. *Lawrence Ferlinghetti: Poet-At-Large*. Carbondale and Edwardsville: Southern Illinois University Press, 1979.

South Atlantic Quarterly 74, no. 1 (Winter 1975)-87, no. 3 (Summer 1988).

South Atlantic Quarterly 83 (Winter 1984): Special issue: "Essays on Ezra Pound."

South Carolina Review

Southern Humanities Review 9, no. 1 (Winter 1975)-20, no. 4 (Fall 1986).

The Southern Quarterly: A Journal of the Arts in the South 15, no. 2 (Jan. 1977)-24, no. 4 (Summer 1986).

The Southern Quarterly 21 (Fall 1983). "Special Aiken Issue."

The Southern Review (Baton Rouge, La.) 1 (July 1935)-7 (Spring 1942).

The Southern Review (Baton Rouge, La.) n.s. 1, no. 1 (Jan. 1965)-24, no. 1 (Jan. 1988).

Southern Review: Literary and Interdisciplinary Essays (Adelaide, Australia)

Southwest Review 62 (1977)-72 (1987).

SOUTHWORTH, HAMES G. *More Modern American Poets*. New York: Macmillan, 1954.

_____. *Some Modern American Poets*. Oxford: Basil Blackwell, 1950.

SPITZER, LEO. *A Method of Interpreting Literature*. Northampton: Smith College, 1949.

SPIVAK, GAYATRI CHAKRAVORTY. *In Other Worlds: Essays in Cultural Politics*. New York: Methuen, 1987.

STAGEBERG, NORMAN C., and WALLACE ANDERSON. *Poetry as Experience*. New York: American Book Co., 1952.

STALLMAN, ROBERT WOOSTER, ed. *The Critic's Notebook*. Minneapolis: University of Minnesota Press, 1950.

_____, ed. *Critiques and Essays in Criticism, 1920-1948*. New York: Ronald Press, 1949.

STALLMAN, R. W., and R. E. WATTERS. *The Creative Reader: An Anthology of Fiction, Drama, and Poetry*. New York: Ronald Press, 1954.

Stanford Literture Review

STAUFFER, DONALD A. *The Nature of Poetry*. New York: W. W. Norton, 1946.

STEVENS, WALLACE. *The Necessary Angel*. New York: Alfred A. Knopf, 1951.

STEVENSON, LIONEL. *Appraisals of Canadian Literature*. Toronto: Macmillan, 1926.

STITT, PETER. *The World's Hieroglyphic Beauty: Five American Poets*. Athens: University of Georgia Press, 1985.

STONE, EDWARD. *A Certain Morbidness: A View of American Literature*. Carbondale: Southern Illinois University Press, 1969.

STOUCK, DAVID. *Major Canadian Authors*. Lincoln and London: University of Nebraska Press, 1984.

Studies: An Irish Quarterly Review

Studies in American Indian Literature

Studies in Black American Literature 1 (1984)-3 (1988).

Studies in Black Literature 1, no. 1 (1970)-8, no. 3 (1977); irregular since 1977.

Studies in Canadian Literature 1 (1975)-13, no. 1 (1988).

Studies in Latin American Popular Culture

Studies in Philology 22 (Jan. 1925)-85, no. 1 (Winter 1988).

Studies in Romanticism

Studies in Short Fiction

Studies in the Literary Imagination 13, no. 2 (Fall 1980)-17, no. 2 (Fall 1984).

Studies in the Novel 16, no. 1 (1984)-20, no. 1 (1988).

Style 19 (1985)-22, no. 2 (Summer 1988).

SubStance: A Review of Theory and Literary Criticism 10 (1974)-17, no. 1 (1988).

SULLIVAN, ROSEMARY. *Theodore Roethke: The Garden Master*. Seattle and London: University of Washington Press, 1975.

Susquehanna University Studies

SUTTON, WALTER. *American Free Verse: The Modern Revolution in Poetry*. New York: New Directions, 1973.

SWALLOW, ALAN. *An Editor's Essays of Two Decades*. Seattle and Denver: Experiement Press, 1962.

SWANN, BRIAN, ed. *Smoothing the Ground: Essays on Native American Oral Literature*. Berkeley and Los Angeles: University of California Press, 1983.

SWANN, BRIAN, and ARNOLD KRUPAT, eds. *Recovering the Word: Essays on Native American Literature*. Berkeley and Los Angeles: University of California Press, 1987.

TAPSCOTT, STEPHEN. *American Beauty: William Carlos Williams and the Tradition of the Modernist Whitman*. New York: Columbia University Press, 1984.

TATE, ALLEN. *On the Limits of Poetry*. New York: Swallow Press and William Morrow & Co., 1948.

_____. *Reactionary Essays on Poetry and Ideas*. New York: Charles Scribner's Sons, 1936.

_____. *Reason in Madness*. New York: G. P. Putnam's Sons, 1941.

_____, ed. *The Language of Poetry*. Princeton: Princeton University Press, 1942.

TATUM, CHARLES M. *Chicano Literature*. Boston: Twayne, 1982.

Tennessee Studies in Literature

Texas Quarterly

Texas Studies in Literature and Language: A Journal of the Humanities 1, no. 1 (Spring 1959)-30, no. 2 (Summer 1988).

Thalia: Studies in Literary Humor

Third Rail: A Review of International Arts & Literature

THOMAS, WRIGHT, and STUART GERRY BROWN. *Reading Poems: An Introduction to Critical Study*. New York: Oxford University Press, 1941.

Thought: A Review of Culture and Idea

THURLEY, GEOFFREY. *The American Moment: American Poetry in the Mid-Century*. New York: St. Martin's, 1977.

Times Literary Supplement (London)

TOLIVER, HAROLD E. *Pastoral: Forms and Attitudes*. Berkeley and Los Angeles: University of California Press, 1971.

Topic

TriQuarterly 56 (Winter 1983)-73 (Fall 1988).

TSCHUMI, RAYMOND. *Thought in Twentieth-Century English Poetry*. London: Routledge & Kegan Paul, 1951.

Tulane Studies in English

TURCO, LEWIS PUTNAM. *Visions and Revisions of American Poetry*. Fayetteville: University of Arkansas Press, 1986.

Twentieth Century

Twentieth Century Literature: A Scholarly and Critical Journal 1, no. 1 (Jan. 1956)-34, no. 2 (Spring 1988)

Twentieth Century Literature 24 (Spring 1978). Special issue on Gertrude Stein.

Twentieth Century Literature 30 (Summer/Fall 1984). Special issue on Marianne Moore.

UNGER, LEONARD. *The Man in the Name: Essays on the Experience of Poetry*. Minneapolis: University of Minnesota Press, 1956.

UNGER, LEONARD, and WILLIAM VAN O'CONNOR. *Poems for Study*. New York: Rinehart & Co., 1953.

University of Colorado Studies in Language and Literature

University of Dayton Review 12, no. 2 (Spring 1976)-16, no. 3 (Winter 1983-1984).

University of Denver Quarterly. [Absorbed by *Denver Quarterly*.]

University of Kansas City Review. [Formerly *University Review*.]

University of Mississippi Studies in English

University of Toronto Quarterly: A Canadian Journal of the Humanities 47 (1977/1978)-56 (Summer 1987).

University of Windsor Review (Windsor, Ontario) 11, no. 1 (Fall/Winter 1975)-19, no. 2 (Spring/Summer 1985).

University Review. [See *University of Kansas City Review*.]

VAN DOREN, MARK. *Introduction to Poetry*. New York: William Sloane Associates, 1951.

VELIE, ALAN R. *Four American Indian Literary Masters: N. Scott Momaday, James Welch, Leslie Marmon Silko, and Gerald Vizenor*. Norman: University of Oklahoma Press, 1982.

VENDLER, HELEN. *Wallace Stevens: Words Chosen out of Desire*. Knoxville: University of Tennessee Press, 1984.

VENUTI, LAWRENCE. "The Ideology of the Individual in Anglo-American Criticism: The Example of Coleridge and Eliot." *Boundary*, (Fall 1985/Winter 1986): 161-93.

VERNON, JOHN. *The Garden and the Map: Schizophrenia in Twentieth Century Literature and Culture*. Urbana: University of Illinois Press, 1973.

Victorian Poetry

Virginia Quarterly Review: A National Journal of Literature and Discussion 52, no. 1 (Winter 1976)-52, no. 4 (Autumn 1986).

The Visionary Company: A Magazine of the Twenties

VOGLER, THOMAS. *Preludes to Vision: The Epic Venture in Blake, Wordsworth, Keats, and Hart Crane*. Berkeley and Los Angeles: University of California Press, 1971.

VON HALLBERG, ROBERT. *American Poetry and Culture, 1945-1980*. Cambridge: Harvard University Press, 1985.

Vort [irregular publication since 1973]

Vort 1 (Summer 1973): Special issue on David Bromige and Ken Irby.

Vort 3 (1975): Special issue on Jackson Mac Low and Armand Schwerner.

WAGGONER, HYATT HOWE. *The Heel of Elohim: Science and Values in Modern American Poetry*. Norman: University of Oklahoma Press, 1950.

WAGNER, JEAN. *Black Poets of the United States: From Paul Laurence Dunbar to Langston Hughes*. Translated by Kenneth Douglas. Urbana: University of Illinois Press, 1973.

WAGNER, LINDA W. *American Modern: Essays in Fiction and Poetry*. Port Washington: Kennikat, 1980.

WAIN, JOHN, ED. *Interpretations: Essays on Twelve English Poems*. London: Routledge & Kegan Paul, 1955.

Wake. See *The Harvard Wake*

WALDMAN, ANNE, and MARILYN WEBB, eds. *Talking Poetics From Naropa Institute*. 2 vols. Boulder and London: Shambala, 1978-79.

WALKER, D. *The Transparent Lyric: Reading and Meaning in the Poetry of Stevens and Williams*. Princeton: Princeton University Press, 1984.

WALLACE, A. DOYLE, and WOODBURN O. ROSS, eds. *Studies in Honor of John Wilcox*. Detroit: Wayne State University Press, 1958.

WALLACE, R. *God Be with the Clown: Humor in American Poetry*. Columbia: University of Missouri Press, 1984.

WALSH, CHAD. *Doors into Poetry*. Englewood Cliffs, N.J.: Prentice-Hall, 1962.

WALSH, J. *American War Literature, 1914 to Vietnam*. New York: St. Martin's, 1982.

WALSH, WILLIAM. *The Use of Imagination: Educational Thought and the Literary Mind*. London: Chatto & Windus, 1959.

Walt Whitman Quarterly Review

WARREN, AUSTIN. *Rage for Order: Essays in Criticism*. Chicago: University of Chicago Press, 1948.

WATKINS, EVAN. *The Critical Act: Criticism and Community*. New Haven: Yale University Press, 1978.

WATTERS, REGINALD EYRE. *A Check List of Canadian Literature and Background Materials, 1628-1950*. Toronto: Humanities Research Council of Canada; University of Toronto Press, 1960.

WATTS, HAROLD H. *Hound and Quarry*. London: Routledge & Kegan Paul, 1953.

WEITZ, MORRIS. *Philosophy of the Arts*. Cambridge: Harvard University Press, 1950.

MAIN SOURCES CONSULTED

WELLS, E. K. *The Ballad Tree*. New York: Ronald Press, 1950.

WELLS, HENRY W. *New Poets from Old: A Study in Literary Genetics*. New York: Columbia University Press, 1940.

WESLING, DONALD, ed. *Internal Resistance: The Poetry of Ed Dorn*. Berkeley and Los Angeles: University of California Press, 1985.

WEST, RAY B., Jr., ed. *Essays in Modern Literary Criticism*. New York: Rinehart & Comapny, 1952.

Western American Literature 18, no. 1 (1984)-23, no. 1 (1988).

Western Folklore

Western Humanities Review 30, no. 1 (Winter 1976)-39, no. 4 (Winter 1985).

The Western Review 11 (Autumn 1946)-23 (Spring 1959).

WESTON, S. B. Wallace Stevens: An Introduction to the Poetry. New York: Columbia University Press, 1977.

West Virginia University Philosophical Papers

WHEELER, CHARLES B. *The Design of Poetry*. New York: W. W. Norton, 1966.

WHEELER, KENNETH, VIRGINIA LEE LUSSIER, and CATHARINE R. STIMPSON, eds. *Women, the Arts, and the 1920s in Paris and New York*. New Brunswick, N.J.: Transaction Books, 1982.

WHEELWRIGHT, PHILIP. *The Burning Fountain: A Study in the Language of Symbolism*. Bloomington: Indiana University Press, 1954.

WHITEMAN, BRUCE. "Leonard Cohen: An Annotated Bibliography." In *The Annotated Bibliography of Canada's Major Authors*. Vol. 2. Edited by Bruce Whiteman and Robert Lecker. Downsview, Ontario: ECW, 1980.

WIDDOWSON, H. G. *Stylistics and the Teaching of Literature*. London: Longman Group, 1975.

WIGET, ANDREW. "Sending A Voice: The Emergence of Contemporary Native American Poetry." *College English* 46, no. 6 (Oct. 1984): 598-609.

William & Mary Quarterly 42, no. 1 (1985)-45, no. 1 (1988).

WILLIAMSON, ALAN. *Introspection and Contemporary Poetry.* Cambridge: Harvard University Press, 1984.

WILLIAMSON, GEORGE. *The Proper Wit of Poetry.* Chicago: University of Chicago Press, 1961.

WILSON, EDMUND. *Axel's Castle.* New York: Charles Scribner's Sons, 1931.

WIMSATT, WILLIAM K., Jr. *The Verbal Icon: Studies in the Meaning of Poetry.* Lexington: University of Kentucky Press, 1954.

WINTERS, YVOR. *The Anatomy of Nonsense.* Norfolk, Conn.: New Directions, 1943.

_____. *Forms of Discovery: Critical and Historical Essays on the Forms of the Short Poem in English.* Chicago: Alan Swallow, 1967.

_____. *The Function of Criticism: Problems and Exercises.* Denver: Alan Swallow, 1957.

_____. *In Defense of Reason.* New York: Swallow Press; William Morrow & Co., 1947. 3d ed., Denver: Alan Swallow, 1960.

_____. *Maule's Curse.* Norfolk, Conn.: New Directions, 1938.

_____. *Primitivism and Decadence.* New York: Arrow Editions, 1933.

Wisconsin Studies in Contemporary Literature. [Superseded by *Contemporary Literature.*]

Women and Literature 1 (1980)-3 (1983).

Women's Studies: An Interdisciplinary Journal 1 (1973)-13 (1986).

WOODCOCK, GEORGE. *The World of Canadian Writing.* Seattle: University of Washington Press, 1980.

_____, ed. *A Choice of Critics: Selections from "Canadian Literature."* Toronto: Oxford University Press, 1966.

WOODWARD, K. *At Last, The Real Distinguished Thing: The Late Poetry of Eliot, Pound, Stevens, and Williams*. Columbus: Ohio State University Press, 1980.

World Literature Today: A Literary Quarterly of the University of Oklahoma 52 (1978)-61, no. 4 (Autumn 1987).

WORMHOUDT, ARTHUR. *The Demon Lover: A Psychoanalytical Approach to Literature*. New York: Exposition Press, 1949.

WRIGHT, GEORGE T. *The Poet in the Poem: The Personae of Eliot, Yeats, Donne*. Berkeley and Los Angeles: University of California Press, 1960.

WYATT, DAVID. *The Fall into Eden: Landscape and Imagination in California*. Cambridge: Cambridge University Press, 1986.

WYLIE, DIANA E., ed. *Elizabeth Bishop and Howard Nemerov: A Reference Guide*. Boston: G. K. Hall, 1983.

The Yale Review 66, no. 1 (Oct. 1976)-77, no. 2 (Winter 1988).

Yearbook of English Studies 1 (1971)-17 (1986).

YODER, R. A. *Emerson and the Orphic Poet in America*. Berkeley and Los Angeles: University of California Press, 1978.

YOUNG, IAN, ed. *The Male Muse: A Gay Anthology*. Trumansburg, NY: Crossing Press, 1973.

_____, ed. *Son of the Male Muse: New Gay Poetry*. Trumansburg, N.Y.: Crossing Press, 1983.

ZABEL, M. D., ed. *Literary Opinion in America*. New York: Harper & Brothers, 1937. Rev. ed. 1951.

Zeitschrift für Anglistik und Amerikanistik

ZITNER, SHELDON P., JAMES D. KISSANE, and MYRON M. LIBERMAN. *A Preface to Literary Analysis*. Chicago: Scott, Foresman & Co., 1964.